From Eden to Interstellar Space

From Eden *to* Interstellar Space

*Thomas Nagel, Biblical Hermeneutics,
and the Search for "the True Extent of Reality"*

Sarah Anne Beattie

☙PICKWICK *Publications* · Eugene, Oregon

FROM EDEN TO INTERSTELLAR SPACE
Thomas Nagel, Biblical Hermeneutics, and the Search for "the True Extent of Reality"

Copyright © 2025 Sarah Anne Beattie. All rights reserved. Except for brief quotations in critical publications or reviews, no part of this book may be reproduced in any manner without prior written permission from the publisher. Write: Permissions, Wipf and Stock Publishers, 199 W. 8th Ave., Suite 3, Eugene, OR 97401.

Pickwick Publications
An Imprint of Wipf and Stock Publishers
199 W. 8th Ave., Suite 3
Eugene, OR 97401

www.wipfandstock.com

PAPERBACK ISBN: 979-8-3852-0539-4
HARDCOVER ISBN: 979-8-3852-0540-0
EBOOK ISBN: 979-8-3852-0541-7

Cataloguing-in-Publication data:

Names: Beattie, Sarah Anne, author.
Title: From Eden to interstellar space : Thomas Nagel, biblical hermeneutics, and the search for "the true extent of reality" / Sarah Anne Beattie.
Description: Eugene, OR: Pickwick Publications, 2025. | Includes bibliographical references.
Identifiers: ISBN 979-8-3852-0539-4 (paperback). | ISBN 979-8-3852-0540-0 (hardcover). | ISBN 979-8-3852-0541-7 (ebook).
Subjects: LCSH: Nagel, Thomas, 1937–. | Bible—Hermeneutics. | Cosmology. | Epistemology.
Classification: BS476 B43 2025 (paperback). | BS476 (ebook).

VERSION NUMBER 01/09/25

Biblical quotations throughout will appear in italics. Quotations from the book of Genesis (also in italics) are, unless stated, from Robert Alter's *The Five Books of Moses*, copyright © 2004 Robert Alter. All rights reserved.

All other biblical quotations are from the New Revised Standard Version Bible, copyright © 1989 National Council of the Churches of Christ in the United States of America. Used by permission. All rights reserved worldwide.

Cover image: "Cosmic Cliffs" in the Carina Nebula. NASA's James Webb Space Telescope, 2022 (Image Credits: NASA, ESA, CSA, STScI).

For Wallace Mata

Contents

List of Illustrations | ix
Preface | xi
Acknowledgments | xv
List of Abbreviations | xix

Introduction: Beyond the Bitter River:
  Extending the Boundaries of the Thinkable | 1

Part I: Thomas Nagel and Biblical Hermeneutics? | 19
1 Belief and the Pursuit of Truth: An Epistemological Dance | 21
2 The Dragons Take Flight in the Realm of the Unbelievable | 45
3 Guardians of the Thinkable | 57
4 An Astonishing World | 72
5 A Spider's Story | 84
6 From the Known into the Unknown:
   Reflection on the Impossible | 98
7 No Way Back: A Hermeneutic of Radical
   Departure from the Familiar | 112

**Part II: Into the Light: Extending the Boundaries
  of the Thinkable** | 131
8 Ancient Light: Into the Remote Mists of
   the Ancient Imagination | 133
9 Getting Our Bearings: From Eden to Interstellar Space | 157

10 Virgin Territory: Beyond the Shady Groves of Reason | 172
11 Into the Realm of the Dragon: A Cosmic Battle | 191
12 An Indeterminate In/conclusion | 218

Epilogue | 241
Bibliography | 243

List of Illustrations

1. *Bat and Apple* (Dr. Nachum Ulanovsky and Dr. Yossi Yovel, Weizmann Institute of Science) | 19

2. *Compact Muon Solenoid Tracker Outer Barrel (Large Hadron Collider)* (Maximilien Brice/CERN © CERN) | 131

3. *The Standard Model Set in Stone* (© CERN) | 151

4. Arthur Boyd, *The Expulsion*, 1948, oil on hardboard, 102 x 122 cm, Art Gallery NSW, Sydney, Australia | 157

5. *Pioneer 10 Golden Plaque* (NASA Ames) | 159

6. Fra Angelico, *The Annunciation*, ca. 1426, tempera on panel, 162 x 192 cm, Museo Nacional del Prado, Madrid, Spain (© Photographic Archive Museo Nacional del Prado) | 172

7. Giusto di Menabuoi, *The Woman Clothed with the Sun and the Seven-Headed Dragon*, ca. 1350, Baptistery of Padua | 191

8. *"Pillars of Creation" in the Eagle Nebula, Hubble Telescope, 2014* (NASA/ESA/Hubble Heritage Team [STScI/AURA]/J. Hester, P. Scowen [Arizona State U]) | 193

9. *Monkey Head Nebula, Hubble Telescope, 2015* (NASA, ESA, and the Hubble Heritage Team [STScI/AURA]) | 193

10. *Composite Image of Cassiopeia A Supernova Remnant* (NASA/DOE/Fermi LAT Collaboration, CXC/SAO/JPL-Caltech/Steward/O. Krause, et al., and NRAO/AUI) | 213

Preface

I realize that it is dangerous to enter into discussion of a topic on which one is not an expert.[1]

—Thomas Nagel

Philosopher Thomas Nagel's acknowledgment of this danger was substantiated by the outraged response to his latest book, *Mind and Cosmos: Why the Materialist Neo-Darwinian Conception of Nature Is Almost Certainly False*, in which he questions the "materialist account of how we and our fellow organisms came to exist." This appeared to be outrage that either ignored, or was perhaps fueled by, his admission that this was "just the opinion of a layman who reads widely in the literature that explains contemporary science to the nonspecialist," and his acknowledgment that such literature might present a situation, "with a simplicity and confidence that does not reflect the most sophisticated thought in those areas."[2]

Theologian and biblical scholar G. B. Caird also acknowledged the dangers facing the layperson or "amateur" who ventures into academic territory without sufficient expertise. He makes, however, the thought-provoking comment that in writing about the language of the Bible:

> Only an amateur could undertake to write on such a subject, since one life-time is too short for anyone to become expert on more than one of the qualifying disciplines . . . A prudent expert cultivates his own garden, not wasting time in looking over

1. Nagel, *View From Nowhere*, 78.
2. Nagel, *Mind and Cosmos*, 5.

> the fence at what his neighbors are doing. The amateur accepts cuttings from everyone, hoping that they will take in his own soil. I have tried to find out what writers in all these fields have been saying and I have made use of their ideas when they have caught my fancy. But it is not my intention to trespass on the grounds of any of them. I am content to leave the Semitic philologist to grapple with the origins and affinities of Hebrew, the psychologist to discourse on the relations of words and mind ... the philosopher to investigate the truth of propositions and the mystical bond between words and the objects they denote [and the physicists to grapple with the mysteries of quantum reality]. I am, if I may be allowed to readjust my metaphor, a walker on the common out of which they have carved their allotments. I offer to other wayfarers on the same paths this guide to the things that may catch their eye or their ear.[3]

In this respect, it could be said that an undertaking to write about a contemporary approach to biblical hermeneutics may also have to be taken by an "amateur." This is in the sense of a person who is not an expert in many of the fields that now appear to be relevant to biblical interpretation but who recognizes the impact of, and need to interact with, perspectives of reality that are emerging within different disciplines.

This is a book that is, consequently, a potentially imprudent but hopefully not an impudent attempt to navigate with integrity across the now crowded and often complex twenty-first-century "common." It is a navigation in search of "cuttings" that is undertaken in the belief that it is of considerable significance for biblical hermeneutics that the gates between important but once fenced off and fiercely guarded territories have now been at least unlatched if not yet left open. It is, however, a navigation that does not anticipate a smooth passage as it cannot always proceed with circumspection but must at times throw caution to the wind and rush headlong into the cross-currents of contemporary epistemology. While there are considerable risks involved in such an approach, it is made in the belief that, in the early nineteenth-century words of philosopher Thomas Carlyle:

> The present is an important time: as all present time necessarily is. The poorest Day that passes over us is the conflux of two Eternities; it is made up of currents that issue from the remotest Past, and flow onwards to the remotest Future. We were wise

---

3. This is an appropriation and slight adaptation of Caird's opening words in his preface to Caird, *Language and Imagery*, vii.

indeed, could we discern truly the signs of our own time; and by that knowledge of its wants and advantages, wisely adjust our own position to it. Let us, instead of gazing idly into the obscure distance, look calmly around us, for a little, on the perplexed scene where we stand. Perhaps, on a more serious inspection, something of its perplexity will disappear, some of its distinctive characters and deeper tendencies more clearly reveal themselves: whereby our own relations to it, our own true aims and endeavors in it, may also become clearer.[4]

4. Carlyle, "Signs of the Times," 63–64.

Acknowledgments

THEORETICAL PHYSICIST AND NOBEL prize winner Murray Gell-Mann once wrote that unlike the experimental particle physicist, his work did not require a laboratory, elaborate equipment, or a large staff, but simply a pencil, some paper, and a wastepaper basket, and even those were not always essential. In order to work, he needed only "a good night's sleep, freedom from distractions, and time unburdened by worries and obligations."[1]

In the process of writing this book, and as a daughter, sister, wife, mother, and aunt, I have often reflected on his words, with varying degrees of envy when his essential requirements have seemed elusive if not impossible. I have, however, continued to believe that biblical interpretation and biblical theology must be done amidst life, with all its distractions, worries, obligations and subsequent lack of sleep. This is because the Bible is about life and the relationships that are integral to it; relationships with and between God, humankind, the world we live in and the other species that exist within it. The challenges of remaining immersed in life while writing this book have also been outweighed by the benefits that these relationships can bring and not least in the support of family and longsuffering friends who have lent a sympathetic ear when it has all seemed too hard. My beloved sister Vicky, husband Matthew, and father Michael were not able to finish this journey with me, but I cherish their unconditional love and support over so many years. My mother Jill is a continual source of encouragement as are my children Emilie and Alex, his partner Hannah, and my nieces Maddy and Marianne. They are an inspiration in what they have all been able to achieve amidst significant challenges. In many respects, this book is

1. Gell-Mann, *Quark and the Jaguar*, 6.

for them as they navigate through the complexity of the twenty-first-century world. It is also for the Wednesday night group that over the last sixteen years has provided fellowship and stimulating discussion about biblical interpretation and theology. It has been a privilege to learn with and from them and their voices are evident on many pages. A particular voice that resonates throughout the book belongs to Winsome who, as a ninety-year-old scientist and lifelong Anglican, struggled to reconcile her commitment to both, particularly in relation to the opening chapters of the book of Genesis. When asked to sum up the most important issue in one sentence, her response was, however, immediate: "How can we be better human beings?" It is this question that has driven this book in an attempt to consider whether a secular humanism supported by science and technology can provide an answer or if there is still a potentially vital role for religion and specifically Christian faith.

I would not have had the confidence to embark on this venture without the support and encouragement of Professor John Davidson whose wisdom, personal faith, extensive knowledge of and interest in the Classics, poetry, art, and the Bible have been invaluable. His suggestion about the position of "the Christian in the middle" in relation to "liberal" and "conservative" theologies as well as the science and religion debate has played a significant role in my thinking. The friendship, support and encouragement from Dr. Nicola Hoggard Creegan have also been invaluable and I am very grateful for the opportunities that she has provided for me to explore my ideas at conferences and seminars. I am also very grateful for the scholarship from the University of Divinity in Melbourne, Australia, the support from the faculty at Stirling College, and particularly the contribution of Dr. Brian Macallan. His knowledge, enthusiasm, encouragement, and support have been invaluable in enabling me to traverse a wide range of disciplines and take risks in undertaking an ambitious but hopefully worthwhile project.

I have been very fortunate to have the help of my goddaughter Caroline when attempting to master the intricacies of Word document formatting and any remaining errors are my own. I am also grateful for her comments on the final draft from the perspective of a different generation to my own. I would like to thank the team at Wipf and Stock for their encouragement and support in getting this draft ready for publication. Lastly, my thanks go to Deryck Sheriffs who supervised my MA thesis. His wonderful course on the Old Testament in the context of the ancient Near East, Israel, and present day was the source of my interest in the role of both the arts and sciences in biblical interpretation. I hope that he will be glad that the Large Hadron Collider still features in my writing and also that I am now spelling the Higgs boson correctly.

List of Abbreviations

ANE	Ancient Near East
BCE	Before Common Era
CERN	European Organization for Nuclear Research
CWS	Closed World Structures
EHT	Event Horizon Telescope
HARMONI	High Angular Resolution Monolithic Optical and Near-infrared Integral field
ICT	Information and Communication Technology
IONS	Institute of Noetic Sciences
LHC	Large Hadron Collider
LIGO	Laser Interferometer Gravitational-Wave Observatory
NASA	National Aeronautics and Space Administration
STEAM	Science, Technology, Engineering, Arts, and Mathematics
STEM	Science, Technology, Engineering, and Mathematics
TDE	Tidal Disruption Event
TED	Technology Entertainment Design
VLBI	Very Long Baseline Interferometry

Introduction
Beyond the Bitter River
Extending the Boundaries of the Thinkable

The central problem of epistemology is the first-person problem of what to believe and how to justify one's beliefs.[1]

Any conception of the world must include some acknowledgment of its incompleteness: at a minimum it will admit the existence of things or events we don't know about. The issue is only how far beyond our actual conception of the world we should admit that the world may extend. I claim that it may contain not only what we don't know and can't yet conceive, but also what we never could conceive—and that this acknowledgment of the likelihood of its own limits should be built into our conception of reality.[2]

CONTEXT

THE QUEST TO DISCOVER and record knowledge about what Nagel calls "the true extent of reality"[3] concerning the world and how far it might

---

1. Nagel, *View from Nowhere*, 69.

2. Nagel, *View from Nowhere*, 108. In an earlier work, Nagel refers to philosopher Colin McGinn's suggestion that we may be "constitutionally incapable" of forming a conception of how consciousness arises in matter, as a possibility but also as a "premature pessimism" (Nagel, *Other Minds*, 106n7).

3. Nagel, *Mind and Cosmos*, 14. For Nagel this is a reality "that extends vastly beyond initial appearances," and also beyond physical facts. See Nagel, *Mind and Cosmos*, 74, 13.

extend, has been ongoing in varying forms throughout recorded human history. One of the oldest extant "world" maps is carved, with an accompanying explanatory cuneiform inscription, on a clay tablet dated between the seventh and fifth centuries BCE.[4] Babylonian in origin and cosmographical in style, it depicts the known world surrounded by the cosmic "Bitter River" or Earthly Ocean, beyond which are unknown and potentially threatening faraway places inhabited by legendary beasts.[5] To cross the Bitter River was, therefore, a potentially radical departure from the familiar and "thinkable"[6] to a world of which there was awareness but little knowledge or understanding beyond the myths of the ancient imagination.[7]

Over 2,500 years later, in early 2013, a rival claimant to the title of the "oldest" world map emerged from "archaeological excavation" that occurred not within the Earth but from a Lagrangian point in space 1.5 million kilometers away from it.[8] Instruments in the Planck satellite, which is orbiting the point, have now mapped the tiny anisotropies or temperature fluctuations in the ancient light of the Cosmic Microwave Background[9] to show the distribution of matter in the early stages of the universe, approximately 380,000 years after the Big Bang.[10] In another once unthinkable endeavor, the Voyager space-crafts are passing through the heliopause, the hypothesized boundary of our solar system, and

---

4. According to Jerry Brotton, the "urge to map is a basic, enduring human instinct," and the ancient map is "an early example of one of the most basic objectives of human understanding: to impose some kind of order and structure onto the vast, apparently limitless space of the known world" (Brotton, *History of the World*, 4, 2).

5. Depicted as a series of triangular *nagû* and described in the text as "seven outer regions beyond the encircling ocean." The term *nagû* may refer to islands as in *The Gilgamesh Epic* but may also be used for "distant unspecified areas" (Horowitz, "Babylonian Map," 157). The text describes the third to seventh *nagû* respectively as: a place where "the winged bird ends not his flight"; where "the light is brighter than that of sunset or stars"; a land "where one sees nothing" and "the sun is not visible"; "where a horned bull dwells and attacks the newcomer"; and "where the morning dawns." See "Babylonian Map."

6. In terms of both cognitive limitations and constraints imposed by a dominant ideology.

7. The Babylonian text states that "only two mythical kings, *Nurdagan* and *Gilgamesh*, ever passed across the floods of death to the region of the island mountains and the heavenly fields beyond them" (Keel, *Symbolism*, 22).

8. The Second Lagrangian Point (L2) of the Earth-Sun system is a location in space where spacecraft can "hover," staying fixed in the system as gravitational forces and the orbital motion of a body balance each other (see "L2, the Second Lagrangian Point").

9. Residual radiation from the Big Bang.

10. See "Planck Reveals."

entering the unknown territory of interstellar space[11] while, on "an inward voyage of discovery,"[12] the mapping of the genes that make up the human genome has revealed a text three billion letters long, written in a cryptographic four-letter code.[13]

These remarkable journeys of discovery were and are radical departures into the unknown, revealing new and once unthinkable conceptions of reality; conceptions that challenge previously held beliefs and provide new ways of explaining and understanding both the human condition and the world within which humans exist. They are journeys enabling mappings that, in the words of Denis Cosgrove, "Take the measure of a world . . . in such a way that it may be communicated between people, places or times." It is a measure that is not, however, "restricted to the mathematical," and he makes the significant point that

> it may equally be spiritual, political or moral . . . It includes the remembered, the imagined, the contemplated . . . Acts of mapping are creative, sometimes anxious, moments in coming to knowledge of the world, and the map is both the spatial embodiment of knowledge and a stimulus to further cognitive engagements.[14]

This is, therefore, knowledge that, according to Niran Abbas, is not simply about "*something*" but about "*how* ideas and concepts interact."[15] It is a perspective of knowledge that the book will explore by investigating how Nagel's work might offer hermeneutical insight into *how* ideas and concepts emerging from scientific endeavor might interact with ideas and concepts emerging in biblical narrative. This is to consider how the focus of his most recent book on the limitations of reductive attempts to understand both mind and cosmos might have hermeneutical significance for contemporary interpretation of biblical narrative. Three narratives will then be considered from the perspective of a constructive theological space and a hermeneutic which, in being productive

---

11. See "NASA Spacecraft." Voyager 2 was recorded leaving the heliosphere on November 5, 2018, at a distance of about eighteen billion kilometers from Earth. See "Voyager 2."

12. Heralded as one of "the great feats of exploration in history." See "Human Genome Project."

13. The mapping of the human genome was completed in 2003 (Collins, *Language of God*, 1).

14. Cosgrove, *Mappings*, 1–2.

15. Abbas, *Mapping Michel Serres*, 1.

rather than reductive, is able to embrace possibility.[16] This is possibility that emerges from what Richard Bauckham describes as "the points of challenging interplay between the Bible and our own context."[17] It is this interplay that the book will explore by engaging with some of the ideas and concepts arising from the search to understand consciousness and the advances in quantum mechanics, astrophysics and cosmology.

The selected narratives have played a significant role in the development of Christian tradition and doctrine—and, therefore, in the articulation of Christian belief—but each contain conceptions of reality that, in moving beyond the experiential and known world of the reader or hearer, challenge perceptions of conceptual boundaries. These are boundaries that have emerged as:

> Anthropology and psychology have thrown doubt on revelation and religious experience. Philosophy has mounted some considerable challenges against the meaningfulness of religious language in general and the concept of God in particular. The notion that basic reality is material and that all mental and spiritual facts are parasitic on this, has become the unexamined assumption underlying the world-view of most educated Western people, and has been through them diffused into popular culture.[18]

Forty years after this statement, it is a diffusion that remains apparent. This is both explicitly and implicitly, not only in popular culture but also in the theology of increasing numbers within Western church communities,[19] as advances in science and technology and unprecedented

---

16. This is space that Catherine Keller describes as being shaped by the subtle, indefinite and opaque cloud from within which possibility can emerge: possibility that "may present as the impossible . . . or as the possible clings softly, subtly, to the actual losses knotted round every terrestrial event. So in its very nuance (from the French *nuage*, cloud) this possibility billows into dense ecologies, personal, political, planetary. These materializations shiver with their own endings and rumors of endings. They will not reduce to theory or to fact. They do not finally dissolve. Yet they also shimmer with life, with difference, with relation" (Keller, *Cloud of the Impossible*, 15–16).

17. Bauckham, *Bible in the Contemporary World*, ix.

18. Baker, "Carried about," 278.

19. James C. Livingston and Francis Schüssler Fiorenza note that while Christian thought in the twentieth century took new directions, "especially in the latter half of the century, many of the questions that emerged during the Enlightenment, and often were pursued more deeply in the nineteenth century, remain vital issues today . . . the epistemological and metaphysical issues having to do with our knowledge of God and God's relation to the world, and the hermeneutical or interpretive questions involving the reading of a sacred text such as the Bible" (Livingston et al., *Twentieth Century*, 1). A popular reference is found in the *State of Theology* survey, undertaken by Ligonier

access to information appear to challenge the enduring meaningfulness of the language of biblical narrative and particularly its supernatural[20] content. In this respect, as Robert Robinson suggests, this may, therefore, be an age of "the greatest paradox in biblical studies":

> At no time in history have we known more about the ancient world, about the processes that produced the Bible, about the groups that shaped the biblical traditions and received the final texts . . . Yet at few times has the Bible generally seemed so obscure. The great power of our research capabilities is nearly precisely matched by a practical confusion over the meaning and theological significance of the biblical texts.[21]

In 2003, John Haught referred to the "reading problem" of how we are "to read sacred writings in an age of science";[22] a problem that, two years later, Kevin Vanhoozer described as "the present crisis in biblical interpretation—the confusion not only over what the Bible means but also over how to read it."[23] It is a crisis that he believed extended to the Church whose history, according to Gerhard Ebeling, is essentially the history of biblical interpretation.[24] In this respect, it is also, therefore, a theological crisis regarding the understanding and articulation of Christian belief and the role of the biblical narratives in formulating this belief

---

Ministries in the US in 2020, which concluded that almost a third of American evangelicals now believed Jesus to be a great teacher but not God (see www.thestateoftheology.com).

20. In the sense of its apparent incompatibility with our empirical understanding and knowledge of the natural world. This is due to what Philip Clayton and Steven Knapp describe as a methodological "presumption of naturalism"—a presumption that cannot accommodate the supernatural events in the Bible (Clayton and Knapp, *Predicament of Belief*, 7). The vulnerability of this sense of the supernatural to the criteria of modern historical method and particularly form criticism led Bultmann to his interpretive approach of demythologization, "stripping the Kerygma" from an obsolete "mythical framework" and focusing on the New Testament as kerygma rather than history or metaphysical doctrine. While he argues for an embodiment of truth in the New Testament that is "quite independent of its mythological setting," he acknowledges, however, that "it may equally well happen that truths which a shallow enlightenment had failed to perceive are later rediscovered in ancient myths" (Bultmann, "New Testament and Mythology," 3).

21. Robinson, "Narrative Theology," 130.

22. Haught, *Deeper than Darwin*, 13.

23. Vanhoozer, "What Is Theological," 21.

24. When the concept of history is "the dialogue between the objective event in the past and the subjective understanding of the past event in the present" (Gerhard Ebeling in Parris, *Reception Theory*, x).

through the development of doctrine. Sixteen years later, the crisis appears to be still present, with continuing doubt and suspicion about any biblical claim to authority[25] and an increasing cognitive dissonance arising from what Thomas Ekstrand refers to as a "dual citizenship of Western Enlightenment culture and Christian religious tradition."[26] Lieven Boeve describes cognitive dissonance as a state of discomfort, embarrassment or unpleasant tension arising when beliefs and behaviors conflict with the reality that is experienced. It is a state that may consequently lead to an alteration or even abandonment of beliefs in order to reconcile with this reality and restore balance,[27] but it can also lead to the hardening of belief into rigid fundamentalism. As expression of Christian belief emerging from this tension increasingly appears to be assigned the label of either liberal abstraction or conservative literalism,[28] declining church attendance indicates that both have limited appeal.[29] This is not only for those of dual citizenship but also for the steadily growing number whose citizenship status is now that of Western Enlightenment culture alone, with no direct ties to any form of Christian religious tradition.[30]

This is a culture that has been shaped by the remarkable progress of science, particularly in the fields of quantum mechanics, astrophysics, and cosmology. In 1983, astrophysicist Paul Davies noted that the radical reorientation of society by science had resulted in a biblical perspective of the world seeming to be "largely irrelevant," rooted in the past and unable to adapt to the changing times.[31] He suggested that adapting to the "space age" would be a difficult task for "any comprehensive philosophy based on ancient concepts" but also noted the rise in popularity of cults associated with UFOs (Unidentified Flying Objects), ESP

---

25. Ricoeur attributed this to the impact of the "three masters" of suspicion: Marx, Nietzsche, and Freud (Ricoeur, *Freud and Philosophy*, 32).

26. Ekstrand, *Max Weber*, 1.

27. Boeve, *Theology at the Crossroads*, 222. See also Festinger, *Theory of Cognitive Dissonance*.

28. For a critique of this simplistic but common distinction, see O'Callaghan, "Is the Christian Believer."

29. New Gallup research has shown that church membership in the US has now dropped below 50 percent (Jones, "US Church Membership").

30. Other than the increasingly secularized festivals of Christmas and Easter. In 2018, research showed that in the past year approximately 19 percent of Australians attended a Christmas service and 16 percent attended an Easter service (Pepper and Powell, *Religion, Spirituality*, 17).

31. Davies, *God and the New*, 2.

(Extrasensory Perception), spirit contacts, scientology, and transcendental meditation.[32] Regardless of the scientific advances in this space age, by 2013, the growing popularity of elements of ancient eastern traditions, which include mindfulness and meditation, led to yoga becoming a twenty-seven billion dollar industry in the United States; an industry described as reinventing spirituality and encouraging non-judgmental acceptance, compassion and community.[33] In appearing to be "a panacea for the ailments of modern society—tech overload, disconnection and alienation, insomnia, stress and anxiety,"[34] it therefore appeared to exacerbate the crisis in biblical interpretation by offering more relatable and seemingly baggage free options; options which appeared to be more in tune with the immediate needs of a world whose boundaries were now extending into interstellar space.

RATIONALE

While the context of the book is the apparent ongoing "crisis" in biblical interpretation in a seemingly post-secular and space-age world, its rationale is that Nagel's thinking has the potential to offer a response to this crisis in the form of a constructive interpretation[35] of his work that looks for implications beyond his original intent. Despite the teleological undertones in his most recent book, Nagel does not consider theism to be a viable epistemological option as a comprehensive worldview.[36]

---

32. With specific emphasis on seeking spiritual comfort rather than intellectual enlightenment. See Davies, *God and the New*, 2; Berger, *Rumor of Angels*.

33. Gregoire, "How Yoga." The growth of yoga has been followed by the growth of the meditation market, which was estimated to be valued at $1.8 billion USD in 2022 and forecast to grow to $2.5 billion by 2025 (LaRosa, "$1.8 Billion").

34. Gregoire, "How Yoga." In an update on January 20, 2020, before the rapid spread of COVID-19, the World Health Organization stated that globally there are more than 264 million people of all ages suffering from depression, the "leading cause of disability worldwide and is a major contributor to the overall global burden of disease." The report also highlights the link to suicide, with nearly 800,000 deaths annually and suicide being the second leading cause of death in fifteen to twenty-nine-year-olds (see "Depressive Disorder").

35. Or "theory extension," following the thinking of Ekstrand, *Max Weber*, 4. This is a variant of what Swedish philosopher Anders Wedberg has called the extension of theories (*teoriutbyggnad*) (Wedberg, *Filosofins historia*, 203).

36. Nagel, *Mind and Cosmos*, 22. He explores instead the possibility of a naturalistic or "Aristotelian" teleology in which certain organizational and developmental principles are "an irreducible part of the natural order, and not the result of intentional or purposive influence by anyone" (Nagel, *Mind and Cosmos*, 92–93).

The intention of this book is not, therefore, to misappropriate his thinking for apologetic enterprise, as is feared by many of his detractors. The outraged and at times vitriolic response to the publication of *Mind and Cosmos* came predominantly from a group of scientists and philosophers whose polemical opinions about what they believe to be the travesty of organized religion appear frequently in the public domain.[37] While their opinions do not represent the wider and more considered views of many other scientists and philosophers,[38] they have, however, been granted considerable space in the media.[39] This is as the authors of popular science books, articles and podcasts that are aimed at lay readers and hearers and it is space that has resulted in their wide sphere of influence in the public domain, with an apparent assumption of the authority of their definitive statements about both science and religion.

It is the crisis for biblical interpretation in this public domain, in which a plethora of alleged facts, theories, and opinions compete for the attention of the layperson in what has been termed the "Information Age"[40] that undergirds the rationale of the book. The formulation of a response to this crisis will, therefore, begin by examining Nagel's unapologetic critique of contemporary epistemology regarding the ongoing search for "a systematic understanding of how we and other things fit into the world."[41] This is to consider whether he inadvertently provides significant critical insights for hermeneutical endeavor. His concluding thoughts in *Mind and Cosmos* will then be explored as a framework

---

37. Which includes those referred to as the "new atheists," such as Richard Dawkins, Sam Harris, and Daniel Dennett.

38. Whose thinking echoes the words of Albert Einstein in a personal letter to Guy Raner, dated September 28, 1949: "I do not share the crusading spirit of the professional atheist whose fervor is mostly due to a painful act of liberation from the fetters of religious indoctrination received in youth. I prefer an attitude of humility corresponding to the weakness of our intellectual understanding of nature and of our own being" (Einstein in Raner, "Einstein"). See also the work of physicist Alan Lightman, a self-declared atheist who is also troubled by a "wholesale dismissal of religion and religious sensibility" as "we have beliefs and experiences that exist beyond the reach of rational analysis" and include "the extremely personal and immediate nature of the transcendent experience" (Lightman, *Accidental Universe*, 37, 65).

39. This is despite what atheist philosopher Michael Ruse describes as a schism in the ranks of atheists with many being more "modest" in their unbelief and prepared to take "scholarship seriously" in trying to understand Christian claims (Ruse, "Dawkins").

40. Characterized by the gathering and almost instantaneous transmission of vast amounts of information and by the rise of information-based industries. See "Information Age."

41. Nagel, *Mind and Cosmos*, 128.

within which to develop a biblical hermeneutic. This is a hermeneutic that is able to facilitate an engagement with biblical narrative which enables a biblically informed perspective of reality to make a unique and significant contribution to the furthering of knowledge and understanding about the complexities of the human condition and relationships within the twenty-first-century world; relationships that appear, in many respects, to be broken, not only between human beings, both locally and globally but also between humankind, the environment in which we live and the other species with which we coexist.

The significance of the contribution of a biblically informed perspective of reality relates to three issues that emerge from the context of both a hermeneutical crisis and a need to restore these broken relationships in an increasingly troubled world. The first concerns whether this restoration can be achieved by an understanding of the human condition that is based on the fundamental elements and laws of physics and chemistry or if, in the words of Nagel, something more is needed.[42] The second involves how a biblical perspective of human fallibility and the subsequent fractured relationships, that emerges in the early chapters of the book of Genesis and continues throughout biblical narrative, might contribute to this "something more." This is by offering insights into the human condition that originate from a sense of the biblical metanarrative as

> a story about the whole of reality—or at least about the whole of human history—providing the meaning and purpose by which people and societies can live in relation to that whole.[43]

The third issue subsequently concerns how confidence in the potential of these insights might be restored in the context of twenty-first-century epistemology. The methodology and structure of the book will, therefore, aim to address these issues from a perspective developed from Nagel's thinking; a perspective that will be extrapolated from *Mind and Cosmos* but also be informed by his earlier work.

---

42. Nagel suggests that while these elements and laws "have been inferred to explain the behavior of the inanimate world," something more "is needed to explain how there can be conscious thinking beings whose bodies and brains are composed of these elements" (Nagel, *Mind and Cosmos*, 20).

43. Bauckham, *Bible*, x.

METHODOLOGY AND STRUCTURE

In attempting to examine how biblical narrative might make a significant contribution to addressing the challenges of the twenty-first-century world, the methodology of the book appears to enter the realm of constructive theology. While there may be "wildly divergent views" within this realm,[44] this will be in the sense of taking an approach that is "theologically traditional" while also being "intellectually critical" and "connected to the present-day world and its pressing concerns."[45] It is an approach that therefore involves conversation with other disciplines[46] in order to discover what Caird describes as "cuttings" that might take root in theological soil. From the perspective of the methodology, these cuttings may, however, be better be described as *threads* that are woven into the fabric of the book. This is as threads that are introduced at various stages but do not always travel on the surface. As interwoven threads they are not always in direct sight but remain as a supporting part of the structure and resurface when they are once again an appropriate part of an unfolding pattern. This is a pattern that does not exclude the now seemingly problematic doctrine that has been developed from biblical narrative[47] but offers an alternative to their representation as "ironclad statements" of "carefully calculated, highly abstracted, and tightly regulated truth claims or propositions . . . that represent the timeless data of faith."[48] This is in the form of a hermeneutical approach that enables both the narratives and the subsequent doctrines to be understood as opening

---

44. With constructive theologians differing "on whether they see constructive theology as being an expansion or redefinition of systematic theology, a subset of systematic theology, or an entirely new method" (Wyman Jr., *Constructing Constructive Theology*, 156).

45. Jones and Lakeland, *Constructive Theology*, 2–4.

46. Wyman suggests that constructive theology is "inherently interdisciplinary . . . incorporating insights from other disciplines into its corpus," with the potential for limitless engagement with other disciplines (Wyman Jr., *Constructing Constructive Theology*, 83, 87).

47. Constructive theology does not "accommodate itself to the methods and assertions of other disciplines" but seeks to "find a way to offer insights back in a fashion that other disciplines find compelling and impossible to ignore" (Wyman Jr., *Constructing Constructive Theology*, 116). See also Rieger, who describes constructive theology as "a discourse that is always in process and open to interaction with other forms of knowledge, including knowledge produced in the social and natural sciences." It therefore "links doctrines and concepts with particular expressions of life" (Rieger, "Constructive Theology," 483–84).

48. Jones and Lakeland, *Constructive Theology*, 8.

"onto vaster worlds of meaning and possibilities," with the doctrines representing maps or "theological geographies" that enable the navigation and clarification of the complex landscape of belief and faith.[49]

The book is divided into two parts, with the first chapter in each taking the form of what Nagel refers to as a "stepping back" to "place ourselves in the world that is to be understood." This is a process that he advocates in order to acquire a more objective understanding of a particular aspect of the world[50] and is a process that, from a hermeneutical perspective, is also advocated by Bauckham, who suggests that "in order to relate the Bible to the contemporary world we need both an interpretation of Scripture and an interpretation of the contemporary world."[51]

PART I

In chapter 1, this is a stepping back to explore the impact of perceptions of reality emerging from twentieth and twenty-first-century "Information Age" epistemologies, on the perspective of the layperson; the person who may not have professional or extensive theological and/or scientific knowledge but for whom access to information is increasing exponentially and challenging how concepts of truth and, in Nagel's words, "real belief" might now be understood. These are perceptions arising from developing technology and a variety of disciplines but in particular the rapidly expanding realms of quantum mechanics, astrophysics, and cosmology. Specific focus will be on responses to these perceptions and their impact on biblical hermeneutics, Christian tradition, and the articulation of Christian belief. This is to provide a foundation upon which selected insights from Nagel's thinking can be examined.

Chapters 2–6 focus on the potential implications for biblical hermeneutics of five insights extrapolated from both *Mind and Cosmos* and a selection of earlier works. Each insight is examined firstly, in the context of Nagel's work and secondly, from a hermeneutical perspective to

---

49. Jones and Lakeland, *Constructive Theology*, 8–9. See also Marion Grau, who suggests, "Theologies manifest as stories and narratives of the sacred and of divine action in the world. Constructive theologians are invested in tracing and mapping such histories, translations and shifts in meaning. To give a more reflective account of the narrations of the sacred" (Grau, "Methodological Themes," 54).

50. Nagel states that "to acquire a more objective understanding of some aspect of the world, we step back from our view of it and form a new conception which has that view and its relation to the world as its object" (Nagel, "Limits of Objectivity," 77).

51. Bauckham, *Bible*, ix.

consider what it might offer as both a critique of, and way forward for, interpretive endeavor. In chapter 2, the first insight emerges from his skepticism about the assumptions of an epistemological climate currently dominated by a scientific naturalism[52] and materialist reductionism,[53] which he believes will not be able to account for the reality of features such as consciousness, intentionality, meaning, value, thought, and purpose.[54] This leads him to suggest that "something more" may be needed to understand the reality of subjective experience; a reality in which there are "facts" that expose the limits of human language and may, therefore, be beyond not only the current boundaries of human understanding but also beyond our conceptual and cognitive ability. His subsequent advocacy of the need to move from reductionist or eliminative revisions of current concepts to expansionist revision that is open to new discoveries while still preserving features of the old, is then considered in relation to biblical hermeneutics.

In chapter 3, the second insight arises from Nagel's concern about "a defensive world-flattening reductionism"[55] that he attributes to a "fear of religion." Starting with his definition of this fear, the chapter explores how his concern has been substantiated by reactions to his work; reactions that have made a seemingly widespread impact in the populist domain but appear to ignore more considered and scholarly responses. The impact of reductionist approaches to knowledge and understanding are traced from their roots in the fifth century BCE to the appearance of the term "reductionism" in the mid-twentieth century. This is in order to consider Nagel's warning about the potentially detrimental consequences for modern intellectual life, in relation to reductionist approaches to both theology and biblical hermeneutics. These approaches are examined; firstly, in the light of what he refers to as the "God hypothesis" and the possibility that he raises of an alternative teleological approach to explain

---

52. That he believes is "heavily dependent on speculative Darwinian explanations of practically everything" (Nagel, *Mind and Cosmos*, 127).

53. This is reductionism that Nagel describes as "the hope that everything can be accounted for at the most basic level by the physical sciences, extended to include biology," referencing the work of Daniel Dennett (Nagel, *Mind and Cosmos*, 13). See also Philip Clayton's discussion of the rise and fall of reductionism, in which he refers to "the project of explanatory reductionism—explaining all phenomena in the natural world in terms of the objects and laws of physics" as being "finally impossible" (Clayton, *Mind and Emergence*, 2).

54. Nagel, *Mind and Cosmos*, 13.

55. Nagel, *Secular Philosophy*, 25.

Introduction   13

the existence of living things; secondly, in relation to how biblical narrative might resist reductive methods of interpretation; and finally, from the perspective of his advocacy for a new conceptual framework. This is a framework within which we can understand ourselves as "specific expressions simultaneously of [*both*] the physical and mental character of the universe."[56]

Chapter 4 explores the third insight arising from his subsequent emphasis on acknowledging what he calls the "true extent of reality" in a world that is independent of and extends beyond the reach of our minds.[57] This is a world in which ongoing attempts to map and explain both consciousness and the cosmos have exposed the limitations of not only technology but also language in the struggle to articulate concepts that appear to defy traditional forms of understanding.[58] In the first part of the chapter, the concept of ancient light and its seemingly paradoxical wave-particle duality is explored as an aspect of reality that challenges what Nagel calls our intuitive conception of the world, and subsequently demands the expansion of language for its accommodation. This is to consider how some of the conceptual challenges that have emerged in cosmology and quantum mechanics might resonate with those emerging in the interpretation of biblical narrative. A scientific approach to the mapping of consciousness is then explored to consider how a biblical perspective of a developing state of consciousness might offer a unique mapping of the human condition and thus contribute to a deeper understanding of what Nagel calls the "affliction" of "the pervasive self-consciousness that makes us human."[59]

---

56. Nagel, *Mind and Cosmos*, 69.

57. Nagel, *View from Nowhere*, 9.

58. In 1922, Werner Heisenberg cited Niels Bohr as stating that all existing concepts were proving inadequate as explanations for atomic physics, with a lack of "a language in which we can make ourselves understood." Current theories were, therefore, unable to offer explanation in a "strictly scientific sense" by describing facts, leading Bohr to suggest that in the present epistemological climate, "when it comes to atoms, language can be used only as in poetry" in the sense of "creating images and establishing mental connections" (Heisenberg, *Physics and Beyond*, 40–41). Nearly one hundred years later, in a lecture on quantum behavior, Richard Feynman stated: "We choose to examine a phenomenon which is impossible, *absolutely* impossible, to explain in any classical way, and which has in it the heart of quantum mechanics. In reality, it contains the *only* mystery. We cannot make the mystery go away by 'explaining' how it works. We will just *tell* you how it works" (Feynman, "Quantum Behavior").

59. Nagel, "Analytic Philosophy."

In chapter 5, the fourth insight concerns Nagel's focus on maintaining a good understanding of problems that are encountered in the search for understanding. This is in order to recognize "what can and cannot in principle be understood by certain existing methods"[60] and be able to ask the right questions. The chapter begins with a story that he relates to highlight the hazards of combining perspectives that are radically distinct; hazards that will be considered in relation to the interpretation of biblical narrative. Nagel's concern to understand the complexity and what he describes as the absurdity of human life is then examined in relation to the human capacity for self-transcendence and the consequential collision of subjective and objective viewpoints. His rejection of "solutionism" and suggestion that we do not yet have the methods needed to understand ourselves and our place in the world, is considered from the perspective of hermeneutical endeavor. This leads to an exploration of his emphasis on the need to ask the right questions and its significance for the interpretation of biblical narrative, particularly in relation to the impact of reductive critical methods. The development of language is then considered as the acquisition of a system of concepts that enable an understanding of reality which extends beyond the world of appearances.[61] The corresponding challenge to articulate such reality in the narratives of both science and the Bible, in what Nagel calls "ordinary natural language," is then considered in order to explore the potentially unique nature of biblical language.

The fifth insight and focus of chapter 6, is Nagel's advocacy for the development of new tools to enable new forms of understanding. This chapter looks firstly at his belief that a significant conceptual shift is necessary for an integrated theory of reality that is able to accommodate the development of mind. His call for the creation of new intellectual tools to enable this shift is then examined in relation to the conceptual shift instigated by the biblical writers. This is to consider both the impact of using the wrong interpretive tools and the subsequent need to create new ones in a process that recognizes the hazards of, but also the possibilities in, combining perspectives that are radically distinct. These are possibilities that emerge from what physicist and theologian John Polkinghorne describes as an "unexpected kinship" between quantum physics and

---

60. Nagel, *Mind and Cosmos*, 3–4.

61. In Nagel's words, as "we come to recognize the distinction between appearance and reality, and the existence of objective factual or practical truth that goes beyond what perception, appetite, and emotion tell us" (Nagel, *Mind and Cosmos*, 73).

theology; a kinship that is found in their confrontation with mystery that appears to demand new ways of thinking to accommodate new perspectives of reality. This kinship is explored in order to consider how it might contribute to the development of a hermeneutical approach that enables contemporary understanding of a biblical perspective of reality; a perspective that appears to challenge distinctions between fact and fiction and sets its own unique terms for interpretation. An investigation into these terms introduces the thinking of philosopher Paul Ricoeur which is used to provide a foundation on which a contemporary hermeneutical approach to biblical narrative might be developed.

Chapter 7 integrates the five insights extrapolated from Nagel's work with four insights from Ricoeur's phenomenological hermeneutics. The first relates to his shared concern about the complexity of the human condition and the absurdity of human life due to the conflict arising from the phenomenological characteristics of consciousness which cannot be resolved with a reductionist methodology. The second concerns Ricoeur's advocacy of an interpretive stance of critical "second naïveté" which is examined and adapted to a stance of "informed receptivity." The third insight, arises from his decision to develop his work by taking the "long route" of multiple detours investigating other disciplines to break new paths.[62] These are the detours of a patient topographical tracking[63] across the often contentious territory of interdisciplinary debate to enable degrees of understanding that are achieved "little by little" in the successive investigations,[64] but gradually provide deeper insight into the new possibilities that subsequently emerge.[65] They are detours that enable the fourth insight which concerns the role of the productive imagination in relation to Ricoeur's understanding of the referential world of narrative, his belief in the "functional unity" of the multiple narrative modes and

62. Ricoeur, *Conflict of Interpretations*, 448.
63. Wallace, "Introduction," in Ricoeur, *Figuring the Sacred*, 1.
64. Ricoeur, *Conflict of Interpretations*, 6.
65. Insight that resonates with the constructive and interdisciplinary nature of the book's methodology in seeking to discover new possibilities from hermeneutical endeavor; possibilities which include science being understood as "a tool within the larger theological enterprise" or "source within theology." See Watson, "Transversal Rationality"; Huyssteen, *Alone in the World?*, 21. Huyssteen uses Calvin Schrag's "rich and multidimensional notion of transversal rationality" to argue for "the idea of transversality as a heuristic device that opens up new ways for crossing boundaries between disciplines, and for identifying those interdisciplinary spaces where the relevance of scientific knowledge can be translated into the domain of Christian theology, and vice versa" (Huyssteen, *Alone in the World?*, 21, xv).

genres within seemingly diverse disciplines, and the irreducibility of "the various uses of language."[66]

The insights from both Nagel and Ricoeur are then incorporated in the development of a hermeneutical approach to biblical narrative that is constructed within the framework of three concepts that emerge at the conclusion of *Mind and Cosmos*. In his closing chapter, Nagel suggests that an understanding of the universe as "basically prone to generate life and mind"[67] will probably require a much more radical departure from "the familiar forms of naturalistic explanation" than he is currently able to conceive.[68] It is a departure that he believes will be necessary in order to explore imaginative alternatives that will enable the current boundaries of "what is not regarded as unthinkable"[69] to be extended. These three concepts of *radical departure from the familiar, imaginative alternatives* and *extending the boundaries of the thinkable* will provide the framework for the development of a biblical hermeneutic which will be applied to three biblical narratives in Part II.

PART II

Prior to this application, chapter 8 offers a second "stepping back" to consider biblical narrative in the context of ancient Near-Eastern mythology and how the three concepts may be an innate and integral part of biblical narrative. The role of the imagination, as a tool for both theological and scientific endeavor, is then examined as a link between the ancient and contemporary world. In the following chapters, the three concepts are applied both individually and collectively to three biblical narratives to enable an interweaving of, and convergence between, theological and scientific endeavor. This is to investigate; firstly, how radical departure from the familiar might function in biblical narrative, both literally and figuratively, as a departure *to* rather than *from* reality; secondly, whether the imaginative epistemological alternatives offered by the biblical writers imply that, rather than being redundant fantasists from an age of ignorance and superstition, they may instead be the "realists of a larger

---

66. Ricoeur, *Philosophy in France*, 175–76.

67. See Davies, *Goldilocks Enigma*, xi. Davies follows the development of physicist Brandon Carter's anthropic principle, focusing on "the Goldilocks factor" or "the fitness of the universe for life." See also McGrath, *Fine-Tuned Universe*.

68. Nagel, *Mind and Cosmos*, 127.

69. Nagel, *Mind and Cosmos*, 127.

reality" that, in 2014, author Ursula Le Guin suggested might be needed for the "hard times ahead." These are times in which

> we'll be wanting the voices of writers who can see alternatives to how we live now, can see through our fear-stricken society and its obsessive technologies to other ways of being, and even imagine real grounds for hope. We'll need writers who can remember freedom—poets, visionaries—realists of a larger reality.[70]

The third aspect of the investigation subsequently concerns how the narratives might serve to extend the boundaries of the thinkable in a world that may, as Nagel suggests, contain "not only what we don't know and can't yet conceive, but also what we never could conceive."[71]

The narratives have been selected because of their contribution to the development of Christian doctrine. This is in the sense of their portrayal of a developing concept of evil, its impact on the human condition, the consequential fractured relationships, and the possibility of their restoration through a process of incarnation and redemptive action. The narratives are also linked by the features of radical departure into unknown territory which occurs as both physical and epistemological boundaries are crossed, within the presence of a supernatural being and a theme of transformational new life. A third link concerns their subsequent potential for cognitive dissonance as they appear to challenge assumptions of current boundaries of the thinkable.

In chapter 9, the departure from Eden in Genesis 3:23–24 is used as an event from which to explore a biblical perspective of the development of human consciousness, the introduction of the concept of evil and the subsequent broken relationships resulting from the misuse of reason. It is a perspective that unfolds as a woman is expelled from the safety, comfort, and nurturing abundance of a home in a paradisiacal garden to a new life of hardship in an unfamiliar and potentially threatening world; a world in which there will be a loss of security, unrelenting toil, and the pain of childbirth, with the way ahead unknown but the way back barred by the presence of cherubim and a flaming sword. Chapter 10 focuses on the narrative of Luke 1:26–38 in which a woman is now in a more familiar scenario of everyday life. Here, however, there is also confusion, with the presence of a supernatural being and another radical departure from a virgin state of purity to one in which there will be a loss of innocence and

---

70. Le Guin, "Speech."
71. Nagel, *View from Nowhere*, 108.

security, the pain of childbirth, and future hardship. The former physical image of radical departure from the familiar in the expulsion from Eden, is now expanded to include a new *conception*. This is a conception that is both literal and figurative, with the boundaries of the thinkable extended by the supernatural presence of an angel and a holy overshadowing that will result in the bearing of a new "word" within a virgin birth. Chapter 11 then explores the narrative of Revelation 12:1–5 as a new conception of the Lukan narrative which is birthed amidst the high drama of mythological tradition, with a woman crying out in the promised birth pangs and agony of giving birth as a hostile supernatural creature in the form of a dragon threatens to devour her child. It is a tradition from which the narrative will radically depart as a vivid eschatological image of liberating new life that emerges as the force of evil, that was introduced in the Eden narrative, is finally and definitively overcome.

The concluding chapter 12 summarizes the exploration into and utilization of Nagel's work in the context of responses that are emerging within the sciences to a view of the universe as devoid of meaning, and evidence of "re-enchantment" that can be linked to both the development of and withdrawal from technology. This is technology that includes the increasing connectivity of the Internet providing wider access to manipulated perspectives of reality and thereby enabling and sustaining a consumer-driven culture; a culture that is putting unprecedented and unsustainable demands upon the environment, the preservation of which is increasingly under threat. The chapter suggests, however, that this context provides an inflection point for the contribution of biblical narrative to an understanding of the human condition that will assist in addressing the broken relationships in an increasingly fragile world. This is through the development of a hermeneutical approach that enables the narratives to offer a "something more" that Nagel suggests is needed for "an expanded conception of the natural order";[72] an expanded conception that is enhanced rather than inhibited by the *super*natural components of the narratives. This is when these components are approached, not with empirical questions, but as important tools that are used to address the issue of the limitations of language and the concomitant struggle to articulate concepts that challenge assumptions about the boundaries of the thinkable.

---

72. Nagel, "Letter to the Editor [2009]."

PART I

Thomas Nagel and Biblical Hermeneutics?

Bat and Apple[1]

Reflection on what it is like to be a bat seems to lead us ... to the conclusion that there are facts that do not consist in the truth of propositions expressible in a human language. We can be compelled to recognize the existence of such facts without being able to state or comprehend them.[2]

1. Dr. Nachum Ulanovsky and Dr. Yossi Yovel, Weizmann Institute of Science.
2. Nagel, *Mortal Questions*, 171.

1

Belief and the Pursuit of Truth
An Epistemological Dance

Once we enter the world for our temporary stay in it, there is no alternative but to try to decide what to believe and how to live, and the only way to do that is by trying to decide what is the case and what is right.[1]

Most of our beliefs at any time must in some degree be regarded as provisional since they may be replaced when a different balance of reasons is generated by new experience or theoretical integrity.[2]

Pursuit of the truth requires more than imagination: it requires the generation and decisive elimination of alternative possibilities until, ideally, only one remains, and it requires a habitual readiness to attack one's own convictions. That is the only way real belief can be arrived at.[3]

NAGEL'S STATEMENTS ABOUT THE "pursuit of truth" and "real belief" in "trying to decide what is the case and what is right" regarding how we should conduct our limited life-span, reflect the complexity of these

1. Nagel, *Last Word*, 143.
2. Nagel, *Concealment and Exposure*, 168–69.
3. Nagel, *View from Nowhere*, 9.

overlapping and sometimes seemingly interchangeable concepts.[4] In the closing sentence of *Mind and Cosmos*, he describes the human will to believe as inexhaustible[5] but he has previously warned that this inherent hunger for belief[6] can result in a captive mind that is controlled or coerced by the will.[7] This is a mind that, in being uncomfortable without convictions, may resist a condition of suspended judgment and become attached to systematic theories that produce conclusions. It may also have a "penchant for clear-cut dichotomies" that force a choice between a right and wrong alternative or adopt a view simply because all others appear to be refuted. Alternatively, if the truth seems undecided, it may lead to a position of detachment and the belief that there is no right or wrong.[8] Nagel's concern, throughout his career, has been that these responses all fail to acknowledge the ontological and epistemological difficulties arising from a recognition of the restrictions and, therefore, potential limits to our capacity to discover and understand what he describes as the "true extent of reality";[9] discovery and understanding that is directed towards living as closely as possible to what he refers to as "the light of the truth" amidst the complexities of human existence.[10] He is supported in this concern by theoretical physicist Marcelo Gleiser for whom the "truths" that are obtained from scientific endeavor can only be partial and of limited validity as there is always more to explain beyond the reach of a theory.[11] These are, therefore, potentially unstable truths that will always

---

4. For philosopher Donald Davidson, belief has an "essential veridical nature" (Davidson, "Empirical Content," 332, in Nagel, *Concealment and Exposure*, 176).

5. Nagel, *Mind and Cosmos*, 8.

6. See also Ward, *Unbelievable*. For Graham Ward, belief is a primordial disposition.

7. Which, for Nagel, occurs in both politics and religion (Nagel, *Mortal Questions*, xi).

8. Nagel, *Mortal Questions*, xi.

9. Nagel, *Mind and Cosmos*, 14.

10. The concluding words in Nagel, *View from Nowhere*, 231, which examines the tension within the human condition due to the possibility of both objective/external and subjective/internal standpoints.

11. Gleiser, *Edge of Creation*, 6. In a more recent article (and subsequent workshop), Gleiser, in collaboration with astrophysicist Adam Frank and philosopher Evan Thompson, adds to this concern the issue of the *Blind Spot*. This is described as "the existential and spiritual crisis of modern scientific culture" arising when the primacy of the "life-world" of human experience as the "grounding soil" of science is forgotten. They warn that when "we lose sight of the necessity of experience, we erect a false idol of science as something that bestows absolute knowledge of reality, independent of how it shows up and how we interact with it" (Frank et al., "Blind Spot").

be vulnerable to either revision or even complete change if the acquisition of new information exposes them as false or invalid hypotheses.

In the porous, "enchanted" world of the pre-modern social imaginary,[12] the association of Christian truth claims and subsequent belief, with terminology such as instability, "limited validity," "theory" or "false and invalid hypotheses" revealed by new information, would have been unthinkable for many living in societies within which the concept of timeless and unchangeable Christian truth was the default condition; societies which George Lindbeck describes as living in the "linguistic and imaginative world of the Bible," with its stories, images, and conceptual patterns permeating the culture both directly "by its reading, hearing, and ritual enactment" and also indirectly "by an interwoven net of intellectual, literary, artistic, folkloric, and proverbial traditions."[13] Within this culture, Nagel's call for "a habitual readiness to attack one's own convictions" would have been regarded by many as not only unthinkable but also as a heretical and potentially dangerous anomaly. The increasingly secular climate of the modern enlightened Western world led, however, to the Church losing its monopoly on what Lonnie Kliever describes as "defining the nature of reality, the order of society, and the destiny of individual"[14] and thus the loss in modern Christianity of its potency "as both explanatory paradigm for the visible worlds and universal belief system for Western culture."[15] The way was then open for a habitual readiness to attack traditional Christian convictions and a growing hostility toward them, with "decisive elimination" often appearing as a primary goal.[16] This is hostility that Nagel suggests stemmed from

> a deep-seated aversion in the modern 'disenchanted' *Weltanschauung* to any ultimate principles that are not dead—that is, devoid of any reference to the possibility of life or consciousness.[17]

---

12. As described by Charles Taylor in *Secular Age*.

13. There were also many other worlds ranging from those of hobgoblins, fairies, necromancy, and superstition to the pagan classics of the Greeks and Romans. See Lindbeck, "Church's Mission," 38.

14. Kliever, *Shattered Spectrum*, 9.

15. Tarnas, *Western Mind*, 307.

16. As seen in Richard Dawkins, *God Delusion*, Sam Harris, *End of Faith*, Christopher Hitchens, *God is not Great*, and Daniel Dennett, *Breaking the Spell*. They have been referred to as the "four horsemen" of new atheism following a 2007 filmed discussion about their hard-hitting critique of religion.

17. Nagel, *Last Word*, 133.

It is, therefore, hostility toward not only the existence of a personal god but also any form of what Nagel describes as "mind-friendly cosmology" within which mind exists as an irreducible and non-accidental part.

NO ECHO OUTSIDE:[18]
THE LOSS OF THE TRANSCENDENT

The fate of our times is characterized by rationalization and intellectualization and above all, by the "disenchantment" of the world.[19]

The words of Max Weber, written in the second decade of the twentieth century, introduced the concept of developing "disenchantment"; a disenchantment that would relentlessly challenge the credibility of the supernatural[20] components of Christian belief. From the perspective of the book, this is in the sense of components that are deemed unnatural in

---

18. Taylor, *Secular Age*, 376.
19. Weber, "Science as a Vocation," 155.
20. This is "supernatural" in the sense of what George T. Knight rather whimsically referred to in 1910 as "the common sense of the word" or "every-day usage among people of ordinary intelligence and generally among their superiors" (Knight, "Definition of the Supernatural," 310). It is a sense that accepts the existence of phenomena which, in transcending the laws of nature, are unable to be explained by science. Benson Saler suggests that the supernatural "is our culture-bound category for anything that transcends the immanently principled operations of nature 'as we understand them'" and it is this category that will be used in the book (Saler, "Supernatural," 51). The term is, however, contentious, and Saler argues that it is better understood in ethical rather than cosmological terms. Stephen Clark also refers to the supernatural having "a significance other than the cosmological," with its "real beginning" found in the "'supernatural' demand that brought Abram out of Haran, and the people of Israel out of Egypt . . . [and] broke the social bonds of ordinary civilized life for followers of Christ." This was by refusing to follow "the obvious, natural and eclectic religion of the Roman world, refusing to accept the names and natures expected of them" and insisting "that it was their novel duty to be loyal to an agent 'from outside,' and so assist in the creation of a new humanity" (Clark, "Supernatural Explanations," 57–60). Another perspective is offered by Branden Thornhill-Miller and Peter Millican, who distinguish between a dogmatic *first-order supernaturalism*, which invokes the role of supernatural agents in accounting for the world and human religious experience, and a more abstract and "tolerant" *second-order supernaturalism*. This is a supernaturalism which "maintains that the universe in general, and the religious sensitivities of humanity in particular, have been formed by supernatural powers, *working through natural processes*." In this respect, "intimations of divinity" can be found "in the general structures of the world and in our own religious instincts, while remaining fully committed to the enterprise of natural science" (Thornhill-Miller and Millican, "Common-Core/Diversity Dilemma," 3, 46).

"going beyond" our conceptual grasp[21] and consequently relegated to the realm of the unthinkable.[22] This was, therefore, a challenge arising from what Hans Frei refers to as the "fact" issue[23] and Nicholas Wolterstorff calls the "evidentialist challenge to religious belief," which is rooted in classical foundationalism[24] and deeply embedded in the mentality of the *Aufklärung* or Enlightenment;[25] a mentality prizing reason as its most precious possession, with freedom from dogmatism and social authoritarianism only obtainable through the submission of thoughts and actions to its "common court."[26] It was, therefore, a mentality that would significantly undermine the validity of biblical perspectives of reality in narratives within which natural and supernatural "accounts and explanations are constantly intermingled."[27] To believe without objective evidence now appeared to violate human dignity at a fundamental level and as "childish pusillanimity"[28] was seen to be unworthy of an adult human being.[29] Theistic belief without sufficient evidence cannot be what Nagel terms "real belief" as, in failing to meet the evidentialist challenge, it appears to be unable to compete with alternative possibilities and is exposed as being unreasonable or irrational and, therefore, intellectually irresponsible.[30] It also falters at another significant hurdle as, within the *Aufklärung* mentality of an unprecedented secular age,[31] Nagel points out:

21. Armstrong, *Lost Art*, 2. For Charles Taylor, this is a "going beyond" the natural so only makes sense "within a world in which natural and supernatural are distinguished" (Taylor, "What Is Secularity?," 59).

22. Arkoun argues that at any particular time and place within specific linguistic communities some things are "unthinkable" due to the cognitive limits of the social-cultural system or remain "unthought" due to the internalization of constraints imposed by the dominant ideology (Robinson, "Arkoun Mohammad," 67).

23. Elevated by eighteenth-century realism to prime importance in religious argument. See Frei, *Eclipse*, 138.

24. Which insists that "beliefs, to be justified, must be grounded in the certain" (Wolterstorff, "Migration," 55). Wolterstorff sees this challenge arising from Locke and argues that it is profoundly different to "the medieval project of natural theology" (39).

25. Wolterstorff, "Migration," 38–39.

26. Wolterstorff, "Migration," 44. In 1784, Kant declared that what was needed for enlightenment was "freedom to make *public* use of one's reason in all matters," with the motto of enlightenment being "*Sapere aude* [Dare to be wise!] Have courage to use your *own* understanding" (Kant, *Answer to the Question*, 3, 1).

27. Frei, *Eclipse*, 14.

28. Taylor, "What Is Secularity?," 63.

29. Wolterstorff, "Migration," 44.

30. Plantinga, "Coherentism," 109.

31. Taylor argues that it is one of the most important and remarkable transformations

> In belief, as in action, rational beings aspire to autonomy. They wish to form their beliefs on the basis of principles and methods of reasoning and confirmation that they themselves can judge to be correct, rather than on the basis of influences that they do not understand, of which they are unaware, or which they cannot assess. That is the aim of knowledge.[32]

Nagel's statement names another key participant, "understanding," in the increasingly complex epistemological dance within which belief and truth are often intertwined but can also appear to operate independently, following steps that send them on different trajectories. The rapid growth of knowledge in the twentieth century served to continually refuel the already significant force of factually based materialist scientism; a force which Charles Taylor suggests united with the developing moral outlook of exclusive humanism to make a further shift in the conditions of belief.[33] For Taylor, this shift led to the emergence of closed world structures (CWS) rendering the transcendent inaccessible, incomprehensible and, therefore, unthinkable. It was a shift that consequently heralded the emergence of the "buffered self";[34] an enlightened and internalizing identity replacing the "porous self" of the enchanted world and no longer open to the exteriorized concepts of spirits, moral forces and "causal powers with a purposive bent."[35]

Taylor's explanation of secularization resists what he describes as a simplistic reduction to a "subtraction story"[36] in which everything is attributed to disenchantment. His focus is on what he believes to be a fundamental shift in naïve understanding[37] and his identification of three stages in the development of contemporary secularity.[38] These are the

---

in human history as it is unprecedented for a civilization to take this kind of "secular" turn. See Taylor, "What Is Secularity?," 57.

32. Nagel, *View from Nowhere*, 118.

33. Taylor, *Secular Age*, 12. See also Taylor's *Sources of the Self* (1989); *Ethics of Authenticity* (1992); and *Dilemmas and Connections* (2011).

34. Taylor, "What Is Secularity?," 57.

35. Taylor, *Secular Age*, 539. Richard Tarnas traces the origin of the modern self to 1486 in Pico della Mirandola's *Oration on the Dignity of Man*. See Tarnas, *Cosmos and Psyche*, 3.

36. Taylor, *Secular Age*, 26–27. A reduction made by "Lucretian dissidents" (267).

37. Taylor, *Secular Age*, 31.

38. For an examination of ongoing research into, and debate over, multiple forms of secularism and related terms see the series of essays in Calhoun et al., *Rethinking Secularism*. For the purpose of this book, the term secular will refer to what Taylor describes as the affirmation that "the 'lower,' immanent or secular, order is all that there

growth of exclusive humanism, the fractured "nova effect" of the "ever-widening variety of moral/spiritual options across the span of the thinkable," and the resulting "generalized culture of 'authenticity' or expressive individualism";[39] a culture within which

> each one of us has his/her own way of realizing our humanity, and . . . it is important to find and live out one's own, as against surrendering to conformity with a model imposed on us from outside, by society, or the previous generation, or religious or political authority.[40]

Boeve uses the terms "detraditional*ization*," "individual*ization*" and "plural*ization*" to define the sociocultural processes that have shaped and continue to change this culture;[41] processes in which traditions no longer transfer to the next generation naturally and in their original form, identity "is no longer assigned but is actively taken on or constructed," and there is a demand for equal and reciprocal recognition of different philosophical and religious positions.[42]

This aspiration to autonomy presents a significant challenge to traditional Christian belief but, as Nagel suggests, it is a challenge arising from the rejection of models or influences not simply because of their imposition by an outside authority but also because they are no longer understood and consequently have no meaning.[43] Nagel states that he is "not tempted to belief in God"[44] as he has "never been able to understand the idea of God well enough"[45] or "understand the idea" of the role of God as ultimate explanation.[46] He is, though, prepared to concede that this may

---

is and that the higher, or transcendent, is a human invention" (Taylor, "Western Secularity," 33).

39. Taylor, *Secular Age*, 299.
40. Taylor, *Secular Age*, 475.
41. Boeve, *Theology at the Crossroads*, 44. Boeve believes that there is a fundamental difference between the processes or *izations* and the specific strategies or *isms* with which they are evaluated.
42. Boeve, *Theology at the Crossroads*, 45.
43. See also Van A. Harvey who states that much unbelief is driven by a fierce sense of honesty, desire for intellectual responsibility and respectability, suspicion of the desire to believe and a sense of resentment against obscurantism (Harvey, *Historian and the Believer*, 104).
44. Nagel, "Letter to the Editor [2009]."
45. Nagel, *Last Word*, 75–76.
46. Nagel, *What Does It All Mean?*, 100.

be due to his "inadequate understanding of religious concepts"[47] as he is "just failing to understand religious ideas."[48] This is, however, a failure that now appears to be pandemic within contemporary Western society due to both the shift in the conditions of belief and an accompanying "Information Age" ideology articulated in varying formulations of, "now we know 'x'"—with x being perceived developments in scientific knowledge, "we can no longer believe 'y'"—with y being the supernatural elements of biblical narrative. These are elements that appear to have become for many, inside as well as outside church communities, redundant baggage from a pre-scientific age, with phenomena such as cherubim, angels, and dragons consigned to the fantasy worlds of seemingly impossible things such as vampires, werewolves, and superheroes with magical powers.[49]

BELIEF IN IMPOSSIBLE THINGS

"I can't believe that!" said Alice

"Can't you?" the Queen said in a pitying tone. "Try again: draw a long breath and shut your eyes."

Alice laughed. "There's no use trying," she said: "one can't believe impossible things."[50]

The carefully formulated creeds and doctrines that emerged within the early Christian church once served to define and unify Christian communities,[51] with communal declarations of belief and participation in meaningful rituals that immersed the participants in the biblical world. William Abraham describes the creedal formulas as designed to provide an indispensable mapping of this world;[52] a mapping that Paul Gavri-

---

47. Nagel, *Last Word*, 75–76.

48. Nagel, *What Does It All Mean?*, 100.

49. Langdon Gilkey refers to this shift as an inner change of feelings, attitudes, and convictions within individuals expressed as, "I just can't believe any longer what my church [or synagogue] teaches; it seems so anachronistic, so unreal, so unrelated to everything else" (Gilkey, *Naming the Whirlwind*, 3).

50. Carroll, *Alice's Adventures*, 140.

51. Prior to the early Church councils, the Christian movement included groups such as Montanists, Manichaens, Gnostics, Ebionites, Donatists, Docetists, Arians, and Nestorians. See Prothero, *God Is Not One*, 66.

52. Abraham, "Canonical Theism," 291–92.

lyuk, using Irenaeus's analogy of the Scriptures as a mosaic, describes as the fitting together of the various biblical tesserae to form a harmonious whole.[53] This is to prevent the rearrangement of biblical texts and verses to fit other patterns, as when this occurs,

> various parts of scripture become like pieces of dismembered mosaic. One can make all sorts of theological animals out of those pieces, either Gnostic foxes and dogs, or, more fashionable in modernity, historically reconstructed Jesuses.[54]

The loss of such harmony now appears, however, to be widespread, with discord more prevalent than unity due to a growing perception and subsequent rejection of a seemingly irrational requirement to profess belief in impossible physical realities such as supernatural beings, a virgin birth, bodily resurrection of Jesus, and three-tiered universe.[55]

To remove this burden of an unscientific and potentially primitive grounding for Christian belief, one option has been to refer to a spiritual as opposed to physical reality within the biblical text; a reality accessed by the use of symbol and metaphor[56] and thus resolving the hermeneutical controversy arising from a variety of often competing *isms* such as historicism, empiricism, rationalism, and literalism. This is reality that appears to be connected to and, therefore, can be sought within the individual psyche in a form of Jungian depth psychology responding to an abstracted concept of God, now articulated as "universal mind," "ultimate reference point" or "serendipitous creativity."[57] The way ahead is then

---

53. Gavrilyuk, "Scripture and the *Regula Fidei*," 37.

54. Gavrilyuk, "Scripture and the *Regula Fidei*," 40.

55. A perception articulated by John Hick in 1977 in stating that, "to say, without further explanation, that the historical Jesus of Nazareth was also God is as devoid of meaning as to say that this circle drawn with a pencil on paper is also a square" (Hick, *Myth*, 178). In reviewing this book, Lindbeck describes it "as a unified attack on the doctrine of the incarnation" (Lindbeck, "Review," 248).

56. This was advocated by Hick and is the approach of a recent book by David Tacey for whom the current "crisis of faith" is a literary problem. He argues that "true" faith must be rescued from "the absurdities of the Church councils" as Western religion has confused faith with belief in impossible events (Tacey, *Religion as Metaphor*, 213).

57. Gordon Kaufman suggests this is manifest "in many different trajectories through the universe" and is a more appropriate construction of God for the current understanding of the world and human existence. It is a necessary "contemporary, comprehensive, fresh reinterpretation of the received Christian symbol-system" that allows for what we have learned about the evolutionary character of our world and ourselves in the modern astrophysical, geological, biological, ecological, social, and historical sciences" (Kaufman, *In the Beginning*, 117, 123).

clear for a focus on the practical and more epistemologically palatable teaching of Jesus as a paradigmatic advocate for the vulnerable and oppressed, with his primary role as the instigator of transformational social justice and corresponding societal reform.[58] This *natural* as opposed to a *supernatural* theology[59] is thus able to break free from the traditional and epistemologically problematic seemingly *literal* interpretation of the biblical Christ-figure and, in the words of John Hick, "make Christian discipleship possible for our children's children."[60] Whether it is then legitimately able to remain under the mantle of "Christian" belief remains, however, open to debate, with Roberto Unger warning that

> once we start to expunge from the narratives any elements that are offensive to modern understanding, there is a risk that we will be left with a bland mixture of moral ideals that might just as well be expressed in the language of conventional secular humanism.[61]

Such accommodation to contemporary culture,[62] in the discarding of both tradition and a significant portion of biblical testimony, may, therefore, lead only to a potentially fatal weakness, with Christian organizations becoming indistinguishable from secular social welfare groups.[63]

---

58. Maurice Wiles refers to Jesus as embodying "openness to God," with his life as a "profound human response to God," becoming a "parable of the loving outreach of God to the world" (Wiles, "'Myth' in Theology," 243). In the 1960s, Gilkey saw this manifest in "the development of new forms and views of the ministry; in the new-worldly activism of religious leaders in civil-rights protests and peace movements; in the organization of new training centers for ministry in the cities; in the heated arguments about a new sex ethic and drugs" as well as in "the upheaval more conservatively reflected in most of documents of Vatican II on the Church, its liturgy, authority, and relation to the world" (Gilkey, *Naming*, 5).

59. In the sense of what Thornhill-Miller and Millican refer to as *first-order supernaturalism*. See footnote 20 above.

60. Hick, *Myth*, x.

61. Unger, *Religion of the Future*, 224–25.

62. It can of course be argued that there has always been an inevitable accommodation to cultural change, particularly the paradigm shifts in philosophical thought. Hans Küng describes the positive aspects of such accommodation but also highlights the negative in referring to the impact of the legalism and externalized ritualism of Judaism; the intellectualistic theorizing, "trite rationalistic formulas," "idiosyncratic conceptual casuistry," anti-materialistic and anti-physical dualism of the Greek world; the secular political power, authoritarian traditionalism, formalism, judicialism, and triumphalism of the Roman world; and the disintegrating subjectivism, naturalistic superstition and unfruitful mysticism, ecclesiastical particularism, and tendency towards revolutionary individualism within German thought. See Küng, *Church*, 320–21.

63. William Placher critiques Christian apologists who "adopt the language and assumptions of their audience so thoroughly that they no longer speak with a distinctively

Gavrilyuk compares the disintegration of the iconic Christ of canonical theism into critically deconstructed "cubist Jesuses," with the cutting of the nervous system that is integral to the health of an organism.[64] In this respect, it appears to be the severing of traditional Christology[65] as the climax of a redemptive process; a process that is revealed throughout the biblical narrative and dependent on an empirical, historical intervention in which God came into the world to live a mortal life in human form. An alternative option has, therefore, appeared to demand a concomitant and non-negotiable responsibility to vigorously defend a literal interpretation of historical *facts*; facts that are believed to be foundational to Christian truth claims and discerned from varying degrees of adherence to scripture, tradition, reason, and experience. Between these seemingly polar perspectives of what will appear to their adversaries as either an almost total succumbing to the demands of contemporary culture or a rigid, literalistic and, therefore, anachronistic fundamentalism, there are, however, many variations, as the Christian faith has not been immune to the "nova effect," with multiplying manifestations of Christian belief emerging over recent centuries.

SEEING THE LIGHT

In 1800, the number of Christian denominations/organizations was estimated to be 1,600 but this rose to 45,000 by 2014 and is predicted to reach 55,000 by 2025,[66] indicating the wide-ranging diversity within the global Christian community. The mantle of Christian belief now consists of not *many* but a *myriad* of colors with often conflicting theologies and approaches to hermeneutical endeavor coexisting as uneasy and sometimes incompatible shipmates; shipmates that continually jostle for a position of dominance as they attempt to navigate through both the turbulent seas of hostile atheism and the becalmed waters of secular-humanist indifference.

Christian voice. As a result, they not only cease to give a faithful account of the Christian tradition, they cease to be interesting to their non-Christian listeners because they do not seem to have anything new or different to say" (Placher, *Unapologetic Theology*, 11).

64. Gavrilyuk, "Scripture," 40.

65. Found in the cross and resurrection that formed the center of early Christian confession. See Küng, *Christianity*, 49.

66. Johnson, "Christianity Is Fragmented."

The temptation to classify and attach labels to differing hermeneutical approaches is indicated when they are perceived to be located on a spectrum of multicolored theological *light* that ranges from the seemingly polar perspectives of *conservative* fundamentalism to seductively baggage-free *liberal* abstractions; abstractions that, at their most extreme, could be labeled as forms of secularized Christianity or even quasi-spiritualized humanism.[67] It is a classification that is, however, problematic, as the meaning of a label may be unclear, mean many different things to different people[68] or even be inappropriate and misleading as a reference point. In 1963, Roger Shinn wrote about the shattering of this theological spectrum which he believed started to disintegrate when the thinking of Karl Barth and Reinhold Niebuhr defied classification by offering, in different ways, penetrating critiques of liberalism while manifesting their own liberal strains. Appearing to be "in some ways more biblical and orthodox than most conservatives, they were in other ways more liberal and radical than the liberals they attacked."[69] Later developments would, according to Shinn, smash the spectrum completely when the original and unconventional thinking of Paul Tillich, Rudolf Bultmann and Dietrich Bonhoeffer found no home on the spectrum, thus breaking it "at both ends."[70]

The imagery of the spectrum may, however, have more to offer if it is reconstructed from a different perspective. The opening lines of Walter Smith's 1876 hymn, *Immortal, invisible God only wise, In light inaccessible hid from our eyes*[71] serve as a reminder that, just as our eyes are only sensitive to a tiny portion of the electromagnetic spectrum, our knowledge about an immortal and invisible God hidden within inaccessible light may also be very limited. This is a God who may, therefore, resist location at either end of, or even any specific point on, a theological spectrum. It might also, however, be a spectrum on which the most extreme liberal and conservative theologies are located, not as polar opposites but at the

---

67. Which could be argued to be the position of United Church of Canada minister Greta Vosper who, as a self-declared atheist, has replaced the literal sense of a "theistic supernatural being," with "god" as a "metaphor for goodness and love lived out with compassion and justice, no more and no less" (Vosper, "Little Bit About Me"). See also Berger, "Secular Theology"; Cottingham, *How to Believe*.

68. Placher, *Domestication of Transcendence*, 1.

69. Attempts to locate them in a middle ground of neo-orthodoxy were, therefore, questionable. See Shinn, "Shattering," 169.

70. Shinn, "Shattering," 169.

71. Smith, *Hymns of Christ*.

same end, as the most energetic wavelengths with the highest and hottest energies. The salutary warning from an electromagnetic comparison may, consequently, be that this ultraviolet end of the light spectrum is also the most destructive with rays that can be deadly to humankind.

For Shinn, the emergence of seemingly unclassifiable theologies forced Christianity to "seek its vocation in a careening world"[72] and in 1975 he revisited this article stating that "the world still careens" with the current state of theology being "a mixture of the vital and the frenetic, the relevant and the faddish, the profound and the escapist, the pace-setting and the ephemera."[73] It is a situation that is not unfamiliar over forty years later in a world that is still careening in the emerging age of the Zettabyte.

BELIEF IN THE AGE OF THE ZETTABYTE

In the streets and online, there is an atmosphere of confused expectancy mixed with concern; an awareness of exciting, bottom-up changes occurring in our views about the world, ourselves, and our interactions with the world and each other . . . the alterations in our views of the world are the result of our daily adjustments, intellectually and behaviorally, to a reality that is fluidly changing in front of our eyes and under our feet, exponentially and unremittingly.[74]

The rapid and ongoing development of information and communication technologies (ICTs) has led to unprecedented access to vast quantities of information that are now shaping perceptions and perspectives of reality.[75] This is not only for those in the academy but also for those in the public square who may be witnessing "the fastest growth of knowledge in the history of humanity."[76] The current production of information has now reached the level of zettabytes,[77] with an estimate in 2015 that enough new data was being generated on a daily basis to fill all the libraries in the United States at least eight times.[78] There is now access to previously

---

72. Shinn, "Shattering," 170.
73. Shinn, "Whatever Happened," 112.
74. Floridi, *Fourth Revolution*, viii.
75. See Floridi, *Fourth Revolution*; Jackelén "Knowing Too Much," 149–63.
76. Floridi, *Fourth Revolution*, 81.
77. A zettabyte has the storage capacity of 1 sextillion bytes.
78. It has been estimated that before the commodification of computers humanity had, throughout history, accumulated the equivalent of twelve exabytes of data. By

unthinkable realities which include the hidden realities[79] of subatomic "ghost" particles,[80] galactic superclusters[81] and multi-dimensional space-time, as well as the virtual reality of the Internet and the developing concept of augmented reality in which computer graphics are integrated into real-world environments to enhance sensory perception.[82]

The island of knowledge[83] is now a continent, within which the boundaries between different disciplines appear to be in constant flux as a whirlwind of scientific and technological progress sweeps across its landscape; a whirlwind within which the entangled concepts of knowledge, explanation, understanding, belief, and truth have left the dance floor to take the form of epistemological tumbleweed unable to find a secure base in the shallow soil of what Nagel describes as the "extreme intellectual laziness of contemporary culture and the collapse of serious argument throughout the lower reaches of the humanities and social sciences."[84] The perception of increasing knowledge does not always equate to increased understanding or meaning and Nagel has been scathing in his critique of what he describes as the "oversimplification" and "fake profundity" of popular philosophy,[85] as well as the "magical flavor" of popular presentations of fundamental scientific discoveries given out

---

2015, the total amount had risen to approximately eight zettabytes. See Floridi, *Fourth Revolution*, 13.

79. Some of which—though not all—are only detectable with artificial devices.

80. The neutrinos that pervade the universe, travelling through space and barely interacting with matter so they are able to pass though the earth's core. Their presence is revealed when they collide with molecules of water creating a momentary flash of light that can be captured by the artificial eyes or strings of optical modules on an underwater neutrino telescope. See Ananthaswamy, *Edge of Physics*, 5, 80.

81. On March 3, 2016, it was announced that NASA's Hubble Space Telescope had sighted the farthest galaxy (GN-z11) ever seen, looking back through time to observe it as it was 13.4 billion years ago. See "Hubble Team."

82. While it may be thought that virtual reality is fictional or illusionary, philosopher David Chalmers argues that it is "a sort of genuine reality, virtual objects are real objects, and what goes on in virtual reality is truly real" (Chalmers, "Virtual and the Real," 309).

83. Kant, *Critique of Pure Reason*, 294–95.

84. Nagel, *Last Word*, 6; cf. Baggott, *Farewell to Reality*.

85. Nagel, *Other Minds*, 9. In an ironic endorsement of this critique, a supposed accolade from *The New York Times* is printed on the cover of the 1989 edition of Richard Dawkins's *Selfish Gene*, describing it as "the sort of popular science writing that makes the reader feel like a genius."

as propositions to which one must subscribe without really understanding them.[86]

Abraham is equally scathing in his critique of both "the contemporary church and its theologians" for their "ignorance and shortsightedness in the matter of Christian initiation."[87] He believes that "proper catechetical instruction" is an intellectually and spiritually demanding exercise and cannot be reduced to what he describes as "the thin, emaciated affair it became in the modern period"; a period in which he suggests the church still believed that it could "rely on the culture of Christendom to carry the central themes of faith."[88] The demise of this culture has, however, resulted in a church whose theology, once the queen of the sciences, is now for many no more than a "Wonderland" queen demanding a blinkered belief in impossible things from a society that can only echo Alice in its response. Gordon Kaufman is more severe in suggesting that the loss of intellectual integrity and meaning has reduced the queen to "a common prostitute";[89] a judgment that may seem harsh but, if she is not without her clothes as either courtesan or Empress, there appears to be an increasing perception that "certain vital areas of the royal anatomy" are now covered with only a "transparent tissue of ideology" rather than "a stout weave of convincing argument."[90]

The new culture that has seen through this transparent tissue and emerged embracing the apparent liberation of secular humanism has not, however, managed to construct its own utopia. Nagel offers the sobering comment that, despite our aspirations to autonomy, "we remain, as pursuers of knowledge, creatures inside the world who have not created ourselves."[91] We may, therefore, believe that we are following the path that appears to lead to freedom and knowledge but at the end we may find ourselves in a landscape dominated by skepticism and helplessness.[92] This

---

86. Nagel, *Mortal Questions*, 177. Echoing Ludwig Wittgenstein's statement in 1929 that the popular science lecture is "a lecture intended to make you believe that you understand a thing which in actuality you don't understand, and to gratify what I believe to be one of the lowest desires of modern people, namely the superficial curiosity about the latest discoveries of science" (Wittgenstein, "Lecture on Ethics," 3–4).

87. Abraham, "Canonical Theism," 310.

88. Abraham, "Canonical Theism," 310.

89. Kaufman, "Whatever Happened to Theology," in Kliever, *Shattered*, 17.

90. I have borrowed and adapted this revealing imagery from Wick, *Infamous Boundary*, xiii.

91. Nagel, *View from Nowhere*, 118.

92. Nagel, *View from Nowhere*, 119.

is in part because it is a landscape in which the speed and unprecedented scope of what philosopher Luciano Floridi terms the "information revolution" has "greatly outpaced our understanding of its nature, implications and consequences, and raised conceptual issues that are rapidly expanding and evolving."[93] It is, therefore, perhaps unsurprising that the frontiers of this landscape appear to be in a state of upheaval due to what Floridi suggests is the widespread and sometimes radical influence of ICTs on "our moral lives and on contemporary ethical debates."[94]

UNQUIET FRONTIERS

While there may appear to be strong incentives to remain within the bounds of the human domain, it is a domain that Taylor described in 2007 as having "unquiet frontiers." The cross-pressures of a secular age in which "the draw of the narratives of closed immanence" is continually challenged by "the sense of their inadequacy,"[95] have not allowed its inhabitants to settle into comfortable unbelief.[96] There is a growing discomfort that Langdon Gilkey, in the early 1980s, referred to as an "autumnal chill" of cultural decline that was evident in the air of Western culture as

> the intellectual and spiritual heart of the culture, its confidence in science, technology and expanding industrialism, has come upon difficult if not self-contradictory and self-destructive days ... The culture as a whole is thus entering a "time of troubles" of very deep scope.[97]

The depth and scope of these troubles has not lessened in the third decade of the twenty-first century which began with the chaos of a global pandemic. Existential comfort and security remain for increasing numbers elusive despite, but in some ways because of, extraordinary scientific and technological progress. Ethicist Wendell Wallach warns that while there is increasingly rapid development in the production of new tools for communication, education, research, productivity, and entertainment, there is also a concomitant pressure to "absorb, assimilate ... engage and

---

93. Floridi, *Ethics*, xii.
94. Floridi, *Ethics*, xiii.
95. Taylor, *Secular Age*, 595.
96. Taylor, *Secular Age*, 727.
97. Gilkey, *Society and the Sacred*, xi.

make choices with little opportunity to reflect on the ramifications and human costs of selecting unwisely."[98]

Philosophers Ingmar Persson and Julian Savulescu question, however, whether, even if the opportunity arises, constructive reflection might occur. In an interesting contemporary twist on the concept of original sin, they argue that the radical transformation of our social and natural environments[99] by advanced scientific technology has exposed a fundamental flaw in the human condition as "human beings are not by nature equipped with a moral psychology that empowers them to cope with the moral problems that these new conditions of life create."[100] This is a flaw that was highlighted by Nagel early in his career, with the closing paragraph of his first book suggesting that:

> To say that altruism and morality are possible in virtue of something basic to human nature is not to say that men are basically good. Men are basically complicated; how good they are depends on whether certain conceptions and ways of thinking have achieved dominance, a dominance which is precarious in any case. The manner in which human beings have conducted themselves so far does not encourage optimism about the moral future of the species.[101]

Validation for his conclusion can be found in the ongoing manipulation of our environment that, as Persson and Savulescu point out, has led to significant challenges; challenges which include global climate change, the existence of weapons of mass destruction and widening economic inequality which will require major behavioral adjustments involving some sacrifice of personal welfare to "promote the interests of future generations and non-human animals." These are, however, adjustments that they believe, to be not only at odds with our "moral dispositions" but also antithetical to liberal democracies in substantially restricting consumerist lifestyles and curtailing privacy with the intensified surveillance of citizens.[102]

98. Wallach, *Dangerous Master*, 8.

99. Savulescu and Persson, "Moral Enhancement."

100. Savulescu and Persson, *Unfit for the Future*, 1. It is an argument that has echoes of the thinking of Reinhold Niebuhr who, while denying the historicity of "the fall of Adam in the garden" and the conception of original sin passed down by Paul and Augustine, suggests that this is the only doctrine of the Christian faith that can be empirically verified (Niebuhr, *Man's Nature*, 23–24).

101. Nagel, *Possibility of Altruism*, 146.

102. Savulescu and Persson, *Unfit for the Future*, 2.

In 1991, Nagel addressed these issues in his book *Equality and Partiality*, making the thought-provoking claims that not only do we not yet "possess an acceptable political ideal"[103] for economic equality but also that "we really do not know how to live together"[104] and "have been given ample reason to fear human nature."[105] He had already provided an example of such reason in a lecture in 1979:

> we are at a very primitive stage of moral development. Even the most civilized human beings have only a haphazard understanding of how to live, how to treat others, how to organize their societies. The idea that the basic principles of morality are known, and that the problems all come in their interpretation and application, is one of the most fantastic conceits to which our conceited species has been drawn.[106]

Forty years later, his sobering indictment appears to remain relevant, endorsed by Persson and Savulescu's contention that while the necessary adjustments to combat contemporary societal challenges could, in part, be achieved by traditional methods of moral education, this will not be sufficient due to our natural focus on the near future and immediate circle of family and friends. They therefore suggest, with Huxleyan[107] undertones, that "[we] must now consider applying technology to our own nature" in the form of "moral bioenhancement," an option made possible by developing knowledge in human biology,

> in particular of genetics and neurobiology . . . [which] is now beginning to supply us with means of directly affecting the biological or physiological bases of human motivation, e.g., by the use of pharmacological and genetic methods, like genetic selection and engineering.[108]

For Wallach, this is technosolutionism at its most extreme, with the potential to pathologize human nature and reduce attributes such

---

103. Nagel, *Equality and Partiality*, 3.
104. Nagel, *Equality and Partiality*, 5.
105. Nagel, *Equality and Partiality*, 7.
106. Nagel, "Limits of Objectivity," 136.
107. In Aldous Huxley's 1931 novel *Brave New World*, embryos are chemically conditioned to provide social stability in a futuristic society dominated by science and technology.
108. Savulescu and Persson, *Unfit for the Future*, 2.

as compassion and self-sacrificing love to biochemistry.[109] Persson and Savulescu acknowledge the issues that it raises, not least in who would administer such enhancement, but the premise of their argument does at least reflect the profundity of the potential issues ahead. In the words of Wallach:

> A juggernaut of change in the form of genetic engineering, mood and character-altering drugs, nanotechnology, and advanced forms of artificial intelligence threaten to redesign our minds and bodies and redefine what it means to be human.[110]

Floridi may, therefore, be correct in suggesting that the second decade of the twenty-first century experienced a fourth revolution "in the process of dislocation and reassessment of our fundamental nature and role in the universe."[111] It is a process in which understanding and intelligibility appear to remain elusive as, in a somewhat ironic twist, the invisible and mysterious reality of Christian belief is replaced by the invisible, mysterious but also often unintelligible reality of contemporary science and technology. Floridi makes the significant point that much of the data processing that we now rely on is invisible to us, with our smartphone automatically connecting to our home wireless service, downloading updates and "talking" to other ICT devices in the house. He therefore believes that we are still living in a "classic Renaissance house," where we

> inhabit the upper, noble floor, not even knowing what happens on the ground floor below us, where technologies are humming in the service rooms. Unless there is something malfunctioning, we may not even know that technologies are in place.[112]

In this respect, he can suggest that the new priests are the specialists in the temple of technology who have to take care of both sides of the interface, with their power increasing as we rely more and more on higher-order technologies.[113] Autonomy, intelligibility, and also explanation and

---

109. Wallach, *Dangerous*, 189.

110. Wallach, *Dangerous*, 8. See also Kass, whose work in bioethics has led him to suggest that the boundaries between healing and enhancement are vanishing and warn that an increasing reliance on genetics, neuroscience, a perfected educational psychology and pharmacology that deals with the miseries of the human condition may lead to "creatures of human shape but greatly stunted humanity" (Kass, "On Bioethics").

111. Following those initiated by Copernicus, Darwin, and Freud. See Floridi, *Fourth Revolution*, 90.

112. Floridi, *Fourth Revolution*, 37.

113. Floridi, *Fourth Revolution*, 37.

understanding are, therefore, still elusive concepts that may have been sacrificed on an altar of perceived progress. It is an altar that appears, however, to have shallow foundations raising the question of what tools might be necessary for stabilization to occur.

THE METANARRATIVE OF PROGRESS

Bauckham suggests that a defining characteristic of modernity has been its metanarrative of progress with the overriding idea that "the extension of human knowledge and the application of human reason are able to shape the world and human society in a process of constant improvement of the human condition."[114] The application of reason and achievements in science and technology, in enabling the mastery of both the natural world and human history, will, therefore, "direct history towards the greatest human good," with "an expectation of unending economic growth" and a "strong sense of moral superiority over the past."[115] As Bauckham points out, the concept of freedom is a primary value in both modernity and postmodernity, with the latter retaining a focus on moral progress but seeking liberation from metanarrative which, as "a global or totalizing cultural narrative schema which orders and explains knowledge and experience,"[116] can become a deceptive and oppressive ideology giving specific goals and values as the only valid ones.[117] The apparent freedom in the independence and individualism of postmodern relativity consequently offers a considerable challenge, not only to the biblical metanarrative but also in relation to Nagel's ultimatum that "once we enter the world . . . there is no alternative but to try to decide what to believe and how to live, and the only way to do that is by trying to decide what is the case and what is right."[118]

These appear to be decisions that will necessitate an understanding of what Nagel refers to as the complicated human condition in what appears to be an increasingly complicated world. This is understanding that is now being sought in emerging disciplines such as cyberpsychology[119]

114. Bauckham, *Bible*, 27–28.
115. Bauckham, *Bible*, 28–29.
116. Stephens and McCallum, *Retelling Stories*, 6.
117. Bauckham, *Bible*, 31.
118. Nagel, *Last Word*, 143.
119. Encompassing all psychological phenomena associated with or affected by emerging technology. See "What Is Cyberpsychology."

and behavioral economics which incorporates ideas from psychology, neuroscience and microeconomics to better explain the "real world" of human behavior in which economic decision making may be emotional or based on external factors rather than on impersonal logic and rational thought.[120] The challenges of this "real world" were exposed in thought-provoking detail in Gilkey's personal account of the struggle to build a society in a World War II internment camp in the early 1940s. His observations of "human behavior under pressure" led him to conclude that "our problems were created more by our own behavior than by our . . . captors"[121] when, under circumstances of increasing vulnerability, the "thin polish of easy morality and of just dealing was worn off."[122] As a result of his experience, he was forced to radically revise his ideas about human nature and motivation; a revision which anticipates Nagel's reflection on moral development, with Gilkey stating that:

> People generally—and I knew that I could not exclude myself—seemed to be much less rational and much more selfish than I had ever guessed, not at all the "nice folk" I had always thought them to be. They did not decide to do things because it would be reasonable and moral to act that way: but because that course of action suited their self-interest. Afterward they would find rational and moral reasons for what they had already determined to do.[123]

Gilkey's conclusions appeared to be endorsed by the work of Richard Dawkins in his 1976 book *The Selfish Gene*. Dawkins argued that "a predominant quality to be expected in a successful gene is ruthless selfishness," which "will usually give rise to selfishness in individual behavior" as "universal love and the welfare of the species as a whole are concepts that simply do not make evolutionary sense."[124] He therefore suggested that we are "born selfish" requiring generosity and altruism to be taught.[125] In the 2006 preface to the thirtieth anniversary edition of the book he expressed, however, regret for this misleading "rogue" statement that he now believed should be "mentally deleted" as it had been

---

120. Samson, "Behavioral Economics."
121. Gilkey, *Shantung Compound*, ix.
122. Gilkey, *Shantung Compound*, 92.
123. Gilkey, *Shantung Compound*, 89–90.
124. Dawkins, *Selfish Gene*, 2.
125. Dawkins, *Selfish Gene*, 3.

misunderstood.[126] As the book "devotes more attention to altruism,"[127] he stressed that an equally appropriate title could have been *The Cooperative Gene*; *The Altruistic Vehicle*; or even *The Immortal Gene*. This is because a central part of the book argues "for a form of cooperation among self-interested genes" and the term "immortal" captures "a key part of the book's argument" about the immortality of genetic information.[128]

Dawkins's later comments reflect the increasing opposition to *Veneer Theory*,[129] a term used by primatologist Frans de Waal to describe the assumption that human kindness and morality are just a thin veneer as a "cultural overlay" disguising an otherwise "selfish and brutish nature."[130] This assumption has now been challenged, with de Waal arguing in favor of a Darwinian view of morality as "a natural outgrowth of the social instincts," which have resulted in the evolution of altruism and cooperation.[131] In his recent book, *Humankind: A Hopeful History*, Rutger Bregman develops this view with the claim that his book is offering the "radical idea" that "most people, deep down, are pretty decent."[132] He acknowledges, however, that the capacity for kindness can be overcome by the capacity for cruelty, which leads him to what he calls the fundamental

---

126. Dawkins, *Selfish Gene*, x.

127. The "critical question" for Dawkins concerned which level in the hierarchy of life—in terms of the species, group, organism, or ecosystem—was the "inevitable 'selfish' level, at which natural selection acts" (Dawkins, *Selfish Gene*, ix). His conclusion was that it was the level of the gene. "The gene is the basic unit of selfishness" as "at the gene level, altruism must be bad and selfishness good," but he notes that genes are not "free and independent agents in their control of embryonic development. They collaborate and interact in inextricably complex ways, both with each other, and with their external environment" (46).

128. Dawkins, *Selfish Gene*, x, 347. The defining property of a gene (as a long-lived replicator) is its "potential near-immortality . . . in the form of copies" (44–45).

129. Which appeared to find support from the 1963 *Milgram Shock Experiment* at Yale University, supervised by psychologist Stanley Milgram, and the 1973 *Stanford Prison Experiment* at Stanford University, supervised by psychologist Philip Zimbardo.

130. An assumption that he suggests was once "the dominant view within evolutionary biology and other science writers popularizing this field" (Waal, "Morality," 6).

131. Instincts that we share with many other animals and a view which now appears to find support from disciplines such as, neuroscience, moral psychology, anthropology, primatology, and economics. See also Midgley, *Beast and Man*; Haidt, *Righteous Mind*, in which Haidt argues that the human mind is intrinsically moral with moral intuitions arising "automatically and almost instantaneously, long before moral reasoning has had a chance to get started." It is, however, also, "intrinsically moralistic, critical and judgmental" (Haidt, *Righteous Mind*, xx).

132. Bregman, *Humankind*, 2.

question: "Why do people do evil things?"¹³³ While evil appears in this question as an adjective, its use as a noun in his following sentence and question is an interesting, although perhaps inadvertent, development, with Bregman suggesting that "humans may be tempted by evil when it masquerades as good." This is temptation which he believes raises the question of "why . . . evil has grown so skilled at fooling us over the course of history."¹³⁴ The presentation of evil as an entity has biblical undertones, with *The Dictionary of Biblical Imagery* suggesting that the Bible "tells the story of evil—its origin, its battle against good and its ultimate defeat at the hands of an eternally good God"¹³⁵ but, while Bregman does infrequently use biblical references, it is a presentation that is not, however, explained or followed up.¹³⁶

With an echo of Persson and Savulescu's concerns about the inability of human nature to adapt to the conditions of twenty-first-century life, one of the themes running through Bregman's book is that our distant hunter-gatherer ancestors may "have understood the human condition better than we do today" and that we are consequently neither physically nor mentally prepared for "modern times."¹³⁷ In the closing sentences of the book, he therefore suggests that it is "time for a new view of humankind"; a view which offers hope in a "new realism" that sees people as being "deeply inclined to be good to one another."¹³⁸ Regardless of whether the grounds for this new realism are based on morality being an evolved social instinct or a cultural innovation and choice, this is a new view that may, however, be hard to achieve if Nagel is correct in suggesting that "the methods needed to understand ourselves do not yet exist."¹³⁹ An emerging question appears to be whether such methods will be found in the future or whether they can be rediscovered, at least in a partial sense, in the past; rediscovered through a growing sensitivity to the abuses of

---

133. Bregman, *Humankind*, 198.
134. Bregman, *Humankind*, 198.
135. Ryken et al., *Dictionary of Biblical Imagery*, 248.
136. Although Bregman refers to religion as fiction that only exists in our minds and "the clichéd lessons" he heard as a child at church, he still uses biblical references to support some of his arguments stating in one case that he recently realized that "Jesus was advocating a quite rational principle!" (Bregman, *Humankind*, 233, 322).
137. Bregman, *Humankind*, 72.
138. Bregman, *Humankind*, 397.
139. Nagel, *View from Nowhere*, 10.

colonialism[140] and increasing attempts to better respect and understand the interconnection of indigenous groups, both physically and spiritually, with the environment.[141] This raises the possibility that Nagel's call to extend the boundaries of the thinkable "in light of how little we really understand about the world"[142] may require an initial revision of where these boundaries might actually lie.

To move forward it may, therefore, be necessary to address the issue of perceptions of contemporary epistemological boundaries that, in appearing to disconnect us from the past, serve only to limit understanding of both the human condition and the world in which we live. It is this limited understanding of the world that is the focus of Nagel's latest book and the first insight that his thinking offers to hermeneutical endeavor concerns the issues that he raises about what he believes to be the unsupported assumptions of contemporary epistemology. It is an insight emerging from his willingness, at considerable personal cost, to cross disciplinary boundaries in his search for understanding. This is a crossing that acknowledges the overlap within the landscape of knowledge between different disciplines and the possibility of borderlands around which boundaries are becoming increasingly blurred. It is here that the issue of cognitive dissonance[143] arises in the challenge to traditional forms of understanding but it is also territory that may facilitate the discovery of what Nagel describes as "real truth" that may be "somewhat different from what is easiest for us to grasp."[144]

---

140. This can be seen in the growing field of post-colonial scholarship. For a theological perspective, see Heaney, *Post-Colonial Theology*; Kwok, *Postcolonial Imagination and Feminist Theology*; Keller et al., *Postcolonial Theologies*.

141. In 2014, the New Zealand *Te Urewera Act* changed the status of *Te Urewera* National Park to a "legal entity, with all the rights, powers, duties, and liabilities of a legal person." As a "place of spiritual value," it was returned to the *kaitiakitanga* (guardianship) of her *Tūhoe* descendants as their place of origin and return. See "Te Urewera Act"; Gilbert, "Custodians of the Land."

142. Nagel, *Mind and Cosmos*, 127.

143. As defined by Lieven Boeve and referenced in the introduction. See footnote 27 in the Introduction.

144. Nagel, "Reductionism and Antireductionism," 9.

2

The Dragons Take Flight in the Realm of the Unbelievable

Our beliefs about the properties of the physical elements and their constituents are based on what is needed to account for their contemporary observable behavior and interaction and the results of their combination into molecules and larger structures. The materialist form of naturalism assumes that the history of the universe since the big bang, including the origin and evolution of life, can be explained by those same properties. This is a very large assumption.[1]

It seems to me that, as it is usually presented, the current orthodoxy about the cosmic order is the product of governing assumptions that are unsupported, and that it flies in the face of common sense.[2]

NAGEL'S SELF-DECLARED FAILURE "to understand the idea of God" is given validation by philosopher Mary Midgley's suggestion that, for many today, theology and religion are the dragons that are found on the beyond of the map representing the senselessness outside the realm

---

1. Nagel, *Mind and Cosmos*, 65.
2. Nagel, *Mind and Cosmos*, 5.

of the objective and rational.³ Her work also supports his critique of a material orthodoxy that adds the dragon of reductionism and its rambunctious offspring scientism to the herd. This is because he believes it to be a speculative worldview embracing unsupported assumptions that are also flying into the realm of the unbelievable. In *Mind and Cosmos* he describes this as "a particular naturalistic *Weltanschauung*" postulating a hierarchical relationship between the natural sciences, with Darwinian materialist reductionism providing the key to achieving the goal of a comprehensive and systematic understanding of the world extrapolated from the discoveries of biology, chemistry, and physics.⁴ He acknowledges the achievements of reductionism which he believes will remain an important source for both "concrete understanding and control of the world around us,"⁵ but he believes that it has become a "prevailing doctrine" that is "ripe for displacement"⁶ as there is a lot that it is unable to explain.

For Nagel, this is specifically the problem of mind, with psychophysical reductionism failing to account for the reality of features such as consciousness, intentionality, meaning, value, thought, and purpose. These are features that he believes must be more than incidentally generated "epiphenomenal ripples" on the "surface of physical substrates"⁷ and more than a process that can be entirely explained by the operation of the nonteleological laws of physics on the material of which we and our environment are composed.⁸ It is, therefore, a failure that Nagel believes has the potential to infect "our entire naturalistic understanding of the universe, not only our understanding of consciousness"⁹ as it implies that

---

3. Midgley, *Science as Salvation*, 182.

4. Nagel, *Mind and Cosmos*, 4. See also Midgley, who refers to *reductivism* as the belief that materialist reduction is the only or at least the best way of understanding the world (Midgley, "Atomistic Visions," 320).

5. Nagel, *Mind and Cosmos*, 12. Achievements that have led to molecular biology and the Human Genome Project.

6. Nagel, *Mind and Cosmos*, 12.

7. As described in Polkinghorne, *One World*, 102.

8. Nagel, *Last Word*, 131. In *Mind and Cosmos*, Nagel posits that teleological principles may be part of the natural order. This is in the sense of a "natural teleology," with the universe being "rationally governed in more than one way—not only through the universal quantitative laws of physics that underlie efficient causation but also through principles which imply that things happen because they are on a path that leads toward certain outcomes—notably, the existence of living, and ultimately of conscious, organisms" (Nagel, *Mind and Cosmos*, 67).

9. Nagel, *Mind and Cosmos*, 43.

"something more is needed";[10] a something more that "must be added to the physical conception of the natural order . . . to explain how it can give rise to organisms that are more than physical."[11]

MIND AND COSMOS

Speculation about what this "something" might be, is a focus in his latest book in which he addresses what he believes to be the assumptions of contemporary epistemology, with skepticism and increasing impatience. Although he concludes with a claim to have "argued patiently" against the ability of reductive materialism to explain both life and mind,[12] there are both hints and explicit evidence of an ongoing frustration throughout the book. This is found in the inclusion of statements which are grounded, either indirectly, or often directly, in appeals to intuition and commonsense. He declares that he finds the materialist account of how we came to exist and the standard version of how the evolutionary process works implausible and, therefore, "hard to believe" as, "the more details we learn about the chemical basis of life and the intricacy of the genetic code, the more unbelievable the standard historical account becomes."[13] He extends this to a critique of presentations of the current orthodoxy about the cosmic order, claiming that, "almost everyone in our secular culture has been browbeaten into regarding the reductive research program as sacrosanct, on the ground that anything else would not be science."[14] He suggests, however, that this present "right-thinking" consensus may seem laughable to future generations and therefore concludes with the somewhat ironic call to both the "secular theoretical establishment" and "contemporary enlightened culture which it dominates" to wean themselves "of the materialism and Darwinism of the gaps";[15] a call that he acknowl-

10. Nagel, *Mind and Cosmos*, 20.
11. Nagel, *Mind and Cosmos*, 46.
12. Nagel, *Mind and Cosmos*, 128.
13. Nagel, *Mind and Cosmos*, 5.
14. Nagel, *Mind and Cosmos*, 7.
15. Nagel, *Mind and Cosmos*, 127. It is a call that appears, however, to have already been heeded by those within the scientific domain for whom the concept of emergence has renewed interest. This is due, in part, to the rise of the sciences of complexity which include chaos theory, network theory, non-linear, and self-organizing systems. See Clayton and Davies, *Re-Emergence of Emergence*, in which physicists, biologists, and philosophers discuss emergence. In the preface to the book, Davies suggests that the concept of emergence does not reject the power of reductionism as a methodology that

edges to be an adaptation of their own pejorative terminology in order to highlight the rise of scientism and accompanying belief that the natural sciences are the only valid source of explanation and understanding.

Nagel's frustration is evident in earlier works in which there are references to a "ludicrous overuse" of evolutionary biology to explain everything,[16] exercises "in utopian theorizing on the basis of available information," and the production of "purposive-sounding Just-So stories" that explain evolutionary theory by obscuring its radical contingency.[17] He endorses the assumption that the world is intelligible, as he believes it to be a prerequisite in the pursuit of knowledge and a successful fuel for scientific endeavor. It has, however, led to what he believes to be the ungrounded assumption that this intelligibility has a particular form, which is found in "the simplest and most unified physical laws."[18] The claim can then be made that "the appearance of life from dead matter and its evolution through accidental mutation and natural selection to its present forms has involved nothing but the operation of physical law."[19] This is, however, a claim that may lead to a scientism that is exemplified in the writing of physical chemist Peter Atkins who considers that there is nothing that science cannot illuminate as "the reach of its beam is boundless."[20] Atkins acknowledges that we live within an extraordinary and wonderfully rich "Technicolor" world but has previously described this world as the result of "growth from the dunghill of purposeless interconnected corruption."[21] It is a description that provokes, however, the question of whether a "dunghill" that could also be described as a heap of compost consisting of the decomposing remnants of organic materials

---

enables an understanding of the properties of matter and the fundamental forces shaping it. It instead "recognizes that in physical systems the whole is often more than the sum of its parts [as] . . . at each level of complexity, new and often surprising qualities emerge that cannot . . . be attributed to known properties of the constituents" (Clayton and Davies, *Re-Emergence of Emergence*, xi).

16. Nagel, *Last Word*, 130–31.
17. Nagel, "Why So Cross?," 22–23.
18. Nagel, *Mind and Cosmos*, 20.
19. Nagel, *Mind and Cosmos*, 11.
20. Atkins, *On Being*, x. The opening line of the prologue claims that "the scientific method can shed light on every and any concept, even those that have troubled humans since the earliest stirrings of consciousness and continue to do so today. It can elucidate love, hope and charity. It can elucidate those great inspirations to human achievement, the seven deadly sins of pride, envy, anger, greed, sloth, gluttony and lust."
21. Atkins, *Creation Revisited*, 127–28.

packed with rich minerals and natural fertilizer[22] can, in providing nourishment for future growth, be described as purposeless. This is with purposeless origins leading to the purposeless end envisaged by scientists such as Steven Weinberg, Sam Harris and Richard Dawkins. For Nagel, such claims are "a heroic triumph of ideological theory over common sense"[23] as he does not believe that the assumption of an intelligible underlying order can be reconciled with the potentially meaningless universe revealed by chemistry and physics; a universe that "however beautiful and awe-inspiring, is meaningless in the radical sense that it is incapable of meaning."[24] His "guiding conviction," that he declares in the first chapter of *Mind and Cosmos* is, therefore, that mind "is not just an afterthought or an accident or an add-on, but a basic aspect of nature";[25] a fundamental feature of "rational intelligibility" rather than "a byproduct of contingent developments," allowing nature to give rise, and be comprehensible, to conscious beings with minds.[26] It is a conviction that, in presenting a direct challenge to reductionism as a universal panacea, provoked an immediate and at times vitriolic response.

THE HORSE IN THE ZEBRA PEN

In explicitly targeting what he refers to as the "orthodox view" of the dominant place of the physical sciences in describing the natural order, Nagel knew that he was entering hallowed ground in daring to challenge a conception that he suggests is widely regarded as being both scientifically and politically correct.[27] His barbs have inevitably caused consid-

---

22. Tomlinson, *Re-Enchanting Christianity*, 23. Tomlinson uses the metaphor of compost in relation to the biblical text citing Frederick Buechner's description of the Bible as "a swarming compost of a book" (Buechner, *Beyond Words*, 43).

23. Nagel, *Mind and Cosmos*, 128. As "in order to understand our questions and judgments about values and reasons realistically, we must reject the idea that they result from the operation of faculties that have been formed from scratch by chance plus natural selection, or that they are incidental side effects of natural selection, or are products of genetic drift" (124–25).

24. Nagel, *Secular Philosophy*, 7. Citing theoretical physicist Steven Weinberg, for whom "the more the universe seems comprehensible, the more it also seems pointless" (Weinberg, *First Three Minutes*, 155, in Nagel, *Secular Philosophy*, 9n3).

25. Nagel, *Mind and Cosmos*, 16.

26. Nagel, *Mind and Cosmos*, 17.

27. Nagel refers to Richard Dawkins's *Blind Watchmaker* as a "canonical exposition" of the current orthodox view about the cosmic order which "seems to convince practically everyone" (Nagel, *Mind and Cosmos*, 5).

erable irritation, not least because he has dared to enter the domain of specialist scientific debate confessing to holding only the "untutored" credentials of "a layman who reads widely in the literature that explains contemporary science to the nonspecialist."[28] For this effrontery, he was accused of being "the horse in the zebra pen,"[29] but this proprietary territorial response appears to overlook some of the sources of such literature and the possible motivations that underlie the promulgation of the vast quantities of now easily accessible explanatory information entering the public domain.

The populist writing of scientists such as Dawkins and Akins is often polemical, attacking what they believe to be the "time-wasting" delusions of religious belief and the "stifling grip of religion" that is driven by "muddle-headed sentiment and intellectually dishonest emotion" that contaminates truth.[30] In seemingly ironic moves, both frequently appear, however, to leave their specialist domains to break into the theological *pen* in order to wreak havoc before returning triumphant to the higher ground of their "kingdom of science."[31] Atkins accuses theologians of inventing a world and language of their own but, as Nagel points out, scientists have also constructed their own language to describe a world within which they are the new lofty saviors. These are scientists who, according to Atkins, "have had and are continuing to have to scrape away the detritus of religious obfuscation before they can begin their own elucidation" which he claims will "liberate truth from prejudice, and . . . lend wings to society's aspirations."[32] This appears to be liberation from the oppressive realm of religion and flight from what is now unbelievable Christian belief into the ever-expanding and believable realm of science.[33] The

---

28. Nagel, *Mind and Cosmos*, 5. Nagel acknowledges that such literature may be over-simplistic in not reflecting the most sophisticated scientific thought. He has also previously highlighted his awareness that "it is dangerous to enter into discussion of a topic on which one is not an expert" (Nagel, *View from Nowhere*, 78).

29. Michael Chorost, citing philosopher of science Michael Ruse in Chorost, "Where Thomas Nagel Went Wrong."

30. Atkins, "Limitless Power," 123. See Dawkins, *God Delusion*, as well as responses from biologist Rupert Sheldrake, *Science Delusion*, and theologians Alister McGrath and Joanna Collicutt McGrath, *Dawkins Delusion*.

31. Atkins, "Limitless Power," 130.

32. Atkins, "Limitless Power," 130.

33. This is, however, a realm with its own form of "magic and alchemy," which Haught suggests is present in the "gratuitous leaps" in the "naturalist's account of the origin of mind . . . in which I am asked to believe that the lustrous gold of critical intelligence 'emerges' from the dross of pure mindlessness" (Haught, *Is Nature Enough?*,

attempts to broadcast this enlightened stance through popular science writing appear, however, to suggest that, rather than the fences of the scientific pen being breached by unqualified and therefore unwelcome intruders, the gate to the pen has actually been opened and the intruders ushered in by the gate-keepers themselves.

Nagel is, therefore, unapologetic in his challenge to the conception of the dominant role of the physical sciences as it is a conception that he believes to be not only the product of unsupported assumptions but also increasingly driven by an infectious scientism rampant throughout both specialist and non-specialist domains; a dogma that he defines as a special form of idealism, assuming that

> empirical science is the one secure, privileged form of understanding and that we can trust other forms only to the extent that they can be validated through a scientific account of how and when they work.[34]

It is a dogma that he subsequently charges with being unable to recognize both its limitations and the consequent need for other forms of understanding that must expand beyond materialism to "render intelligible what physical science does not explain."[35] For Nagel, the subjectivity of consciousness and the subsequent mind-body problem[36] is, therefore, not only "the most conspicuous obstacle to a comprehensive naturalism that relies only on the resources of physical science,"[37] but also one of

---

135–36).

34. Nagel, *Mind and Cosmos*, 27. See also Haught, who argues that scientism is "a supposition that has no basis in science" and is, therefore, "literalist" in being "more akin to biblical creationism than to the open-minded, depth-seeking quest for truth" (Haught, *Deeper*, 48).

35. Nagel, *Mind and Cosmos*, 18. In taking this stance, Nagel is supported by Midgley, whose writing shows a similar level of frustration with the issues arising from scientism and a reductionist approach to understanding. This led her write her most recent book, *Are You an Illusion?*, at the age of ninety-four, in which she cites Nagel several times without agreeing with all his conclusions.

36. Which he also refers to as "conceiving the impossible" in terms of the current explanatory gap (Nagel, "Conceiving the Impossible," 337–52). His thinking has influenced and is supported by the work of philosopher David Chalmers, who cites Nagel's work when arguing that consciousness "poses the most baffling problems in the science of mind," as there is nothing that we know more intimately than conscious experience, but there is nothing that is harder to explain. Chalmers differentiates between the "easy" problems which can be explained in terms of neural mechanisms and the "hard" problems related to subjective experience that appears to resist the methods of cognitive science (Chalmers, "Facing Up," 200).

37. Nagel, *Mind and Cosmos*, 35.

considerable significance. This is because he believes that the existence of subjective experience at "the core of everyday life"[38]

> seems to imply that the physical description of the universe, in spite of its richness and explanatory power, is only part of the truth, and that the natural order is far less austere than it would be if physics and chemistry accounted for everything.[39]

Understanding this obstacle, to what might be an enlarged conception of reality, has consequently been a driving force throughout his career in relation; firstly, to explaining the appearance of the mental phenomena associated with the mind and their relationship to the physical status that neurological sciences ascribe to the brain; secondly, to understanding what we can and cannot know about the world that exists beyond our own minds which includes the minds of others and is the subject of his seminal paper, "What is it like to be a bat?"[40]

THE BATS TAKE FLIGHT IN THE REALM OF THE BELIEVABLE

In 1974, Nagel used the example of the phenomenology of bats to explore the subjective character of experience and articulate the issue of what he believes to be the impossibility of knowing what it is like to *be* another person, or creature, and what an experience might be like *for* them. Five years later, he would turn to the insect world to explain that we may never "know exactly how scrambled eggs taste to a cockroach even if we develop a very complete objective phenomenology of his sense of taste."[41] There are facts, therefore, whose exact nature we are currently unable to conceive or even accommodate within the scope of human language. There may, however, also be facts that Nagel believes are not only beyond the current limits of our understanding and articulation but also potentially permanently beyond the scope of our conceptual and cognitive abilities.[42] This raises the issue of what Nagel refers to as "the relation

---

38. With the objective view developing "initially as a form of extended understanding" (Nagel, *View from Nowhere*, 210).
39. Nagel, *Mind and Cosmos*, 35.
40. Nagel, *Mortal Questions*, 166–70.
41. Nagel, "Limits of Objectivity," 89.
42. Nagel, *Mortal Questions*, 170–71.

between facts . . . and conceptual schemes or systems of representation"[43] and the potential dangers of reductive approaches that limit perceptions of reality by denying "the reality or logical significance of what we can never describe or understand";[44] a denial that he suggests exhibits "the crudest form of cognitive dissonance."[45]

In an essay published in 1979, Nagel considered a proposal with potential significance for biblical hermeneutics. If facts exist that are impossible to include in a physical conception of the world,[46] the objective picture of reality may not be simply incomplete but rather in essence only a partial conception. Reality may, therefore, contain aspects that are beyond not only our current limited understanding but also beyond the limits of our minds. The phenomena of consciousness and its on-going resistance to what he called the "modern weakness for reduction" that attempts to "beat everything into its shape and deny the reality of anything that cannot be so reduced,"[47] remained a focus. A decade later, in a lecture at the Royal Institute of Philosophy, he made "a plea" for it to be recognized as

> a conceptually irreducible aspect of reality that is necessarily connected with other equally irreducible aspects—as electromagnetic fields are irreducible to but necessarily connected with the behavior of charged particles and gravitational fields with the behavior of masses, and vice versa.[48]

---

43. Nagel, *Mortal Questions*, 171.
44. Nagel, *Mortal Questions*, 170–71.
45. Nagel, *Mortal Questions*, 171.
46. Nagel, *Mortal Questions*, 212.

47. Nagel, "Limits of Objectivity," 80–81. His anti-reductionist stance differentiates between epistemological and the more controversial ontological anti-reductionism, with the latter being of greater interest to him in terms of understanding that will always only be partial as opposed to temporarily incomplete. See Nagel, "Reductionism and Antireductionism," 3–10.

48. Nagel, "Conceiving the Impossible," 337. Those who offer at least partial support for Nagel's stance include philosopher David Chalmers (see footnote 36 above); philosopher Colin McGinn, who argues that the "mystery" of consciousness cannot be resolved as it is an ultimate mystery that the human mind will never unravel (see McGinn, *Problem of Consciousness*); and biophysicist Christof Koch, for whom consciousness is a "simple substance" or fundamental, "an elementary, property of living matter" that is "ontologically distinct from its physical substrate" (see Koch, *Consciousness*). Strong opposition to Nagel's stance can be found in the work of philosopher Daniel Dennett, who, from a materialist perspective, describes human consciousness as an "evolved user-illusion" and "a system of virtual machines that evolved genetically and memetically, to play very specialized roles in the 'cognitive niche' our ancestors have

He did not, however, believe that analogies from within physical science would assist in connecting subjective experience with the physical, which he referred to as a "new ballgame."[49] He suggested that the ongoing lack of "an intelligible conception of the relation between mind and body" indicated the ongoing inadequacy of present concepts and the limits of our understanding as "we do not at present possess the conceptual equipment to understand how subjective and physical features could both be essential aspects of a single entity or process."[50] He therefore called for an "expansionist" revision of current concepts as opposed to a reductionist or eliminative revision; an expanded revision that would allow for "the possibility of a successor concept of mind which will . . . preserve the essential features of the original" but also be open to new discoveries. In this way:

> A new concept is developed to talk about the same things as the old, one that includes most of the features of the old concept but puts them in a relation to one another and to other features that is new, and that makes it possible to see or explore further connections.[51]

The development of a new concept is, however, only possible when obstacles or barriers are dismantled and it is this dismantling that is a goal of *Mind and Cosmos*; a goal seeking to explore and develop the themes that emerge in the enterprise of "imagining possibilities."[52] This, for Nagel, involves firstly, a rethinking "in the light of evidence, about the subject we want to understand" and secondly, devising concepts that "do better justice to it than the ones we have" by searching for "something more unfamiliar."[53]

AN EXPANSIONIST REVISION

There are several potentially important implications for a critique and revision of hermeneutical endeavor if Nagel's argument about the limitations of reductionist approaches to reality are turned in this direction.

---

constructed over the millennia" (Dennett, *From Bacteria to Bach and Back*, 335).

49. Nagel, "Conceiving the Impossible," 337.
50. Nagel, "Conceiving the Impossible," 340.
51. Nagel, "Conceiving the Impossible," 341.
52. Nagel, "Conceiving the Impossible," 342.
53. Nagel, "Conceiving the Impossible," 342.

This is firstly, in relation to the need to dismantle perceived obstacles to the interpretation of biblical texts that appear to be problematic in the light of contemporary knowledge and secondly, in the possibility of developing a new hermeneutical concept or approach. This is an approach which, using Nagel's words, does "better justice" to the text by preserving "most of the features of the old" and being able "to talk about the same things" but "puts them in a relation to one another and to other features that is new, and that makes it possible to see or explore further connections." It is a hermeneutical approach which, therefore, involves a rethinking that aims at an expansionist rather than a reductive or eliminative revision; a rethinking that, in recognizing the potential limits of understanding, is able to enter into new and perhaps unfamiliar territory. In describing expansionist revision as an enterprise of "imagining possibilities," Nagel makes the challenging observation that the physicalist-functionalist movement in philosophy of mind has failed because it is too *conservative* in trying "to reinterpret mental concepts so as to make them tractable parts of the framework of physical science."[54] This provides an interesting, if unintentional, critique of assumptions underlying reductive hermeneutical approaches that may be perceived to be more liberal in enabling biblical texts to become "tractable parts" of the framework of contemporary epistemology. For Nagel, conceptual intelligibility demands instead, a move beyond reductionism to consider imaginative and unfamiliar alternatives that might enable the development of explanation and understanding. It is a move that is supported by theoretical biologist Stuart Kauffman for whom reductionism alone is inadequate, either as a way of doing science or a way of understanding reality.[55]

In some respects, *Mind and Cosmos* reveals a surprisingly antagonistic, and also courageous, stance from someone who has previously claimed to have no appetite for the role of public intellectual or desire to enter "the arena" to either compete for popular approval[56] or combat what he believes to be "debased philosophy."[57] The inevitability of him setting foot on this frequently bloodied ground is, however, indicated throughout his career with his admission that his 1986 book, *The View From Nowhere*, is "in some respects a deliberately reactionary work" in attacking

---

54. Nagel, "Conceiving the Impossible," 334.

55. Kauffman, *Reinventing the Sacred*, 3.

56. As competing for the approval of those who don't understand the issues is "a great burden for a field of theoretical inquiry" (Nagel, *Other Minds*, 9).

57. Such as behaviorism and logical positivism.

the prevalence of scientism and calling for what he believes to be "an overdue downward revision of the prevailing intellectual self-esteem."[58] His latest book continues in this vein reflecting his longstanding conviction that "one should trust problems over solutions, intuitions over arguments and pluralistic discord over systematic harmony"[59] and, therefore, anticipating the discordant response to his speculation. The nature of this response confirms that this may be a conviction that is not widely shared and that, for some, the boundaries of the thinkable remain closely guarded. This raises the potentially significant questions for biblical hermeneutics of why and by whom, and leads to the second insight from Nagel's thinking which involves his concern about the defensive world-flattening reductionism that he attributes to a fear of religion.

---

58. Nagel, *View from Nowhere*, 9–10.

59. Declared in his first collection of essays, published in 1979 (Nagel, *Mortal Questions*, x).

3

Guardians of the Thinkable

The thought that the relation between mind and the world is something fundamental makes many people in this day and age nervous. I believe this is one manifestation of a fear of religion which has large and often pernicious consequences for modern intellectual life.[1]

The fear of religion leads too many scientifically minded atheists to cling to a defensive, world-flattening reductionism... hobbled by the assumption that the only alternative to religion is to insist that the ultimate explanation of everything must lie in particle physics, string theory, or whatever invariant spatiotemporal laws govern the elements of which the material world is composed.[2]

IN REFERRING TO A "fear" of religion, Nagel explicitly states that this is not what he believes to be "the entirely reasonable hostility towards certain established religions and religious institutions" holding "objectionable moral doctrines, social policies, and political influence." Neither is it "the association of many religious beliefs with superstition and the acceptance

---

1. Nagel, *Last Word*, 130.
2. Nagel, *Secular Philosophy*, 25. This comment was directed at biologist Richard Dawkins in a review of his book *God Delusion*.

of evident empirical falsehoods."³ It is rather what he calls the "fear of religion itself" or the "cosmic authority problem," which he believes to be a much deeper and widespread phenomenon. It is a phenomenon that he identifies with and articulated in 1997:

> I want atheism to be true and am made uneasy by the fact that some of the most intelligent and well-informed people I know are religious believers. It isn't just that I don't believe in God and, naturally, hope that I'm right in my belief. It's that I hope there is no God! I don't want there to be a God; I don't want the universe to be like that.⁴

In *Mind and Cosmos*, he attempts to explain this by stating that he lacks "the *sensus divinitatis*" that he believes enables and often "compels" many people to see an expression of divine purpose in the world⁵ and confirms in a footnote that he is "not just unreceptive but strongly averse to the idea." He has, however previously admitted, to having spent several years "occupied mainly with thoughts about the relation between science and religion."⁶ This is because he believes that the "What am I doing here?" question does not disappear when science replaces a religious worldview,⁷ particularly when an explanation of how the natural order is "disposed to generate beings capable of comprehending it"⁸ remains elusive. Nagel is aware of the controversial nature of the language that he is using and, therefore, clearly states that he rejects any theistic understanding of this disposition.⁹ In the often acrimonious space within which this

---

3. Nagel, *Last Word*, 130.

4. Nagel, *Last Word*, 130.

5. Nagel, *Mind and Cosmos*, 12. A sense that is not unique to atheists and agnostics as there are echoes here of theologian Gordon Kaufman's declaration in the later years of his life: "I seem to be 'tone deaf' with respect to so-called religious experience. When others speak of their 'experience of God,' or of 'God's presence,' or of the profound experience of 'the holy' or of 'sacredness,' I simply do not know what they are talking about" (Kaufman, *In the Beginning*, 109–110).

6. Nagel, *Secular Philosophy*.

7. Nagel, *Secular Philosophy*, 8. See Mark C. Taylor, who argues that there is a religious dimension to all culture in Taylor, *After God*, 3.

8. Nagel, *Mind and Cosmos*, 86. See also Haught's conclusion that "scientific naturalism is finally incoherent since its formal view of nature is not large enough, logically speaking to encompass either the fact of critical intelligence or the infinite horizon of being and truth anticipated by the desire to know" (Haught, *Is Nature Enough?*, 130).

9. He admits however that it would provide an easier solution than the possibility that he explores in *Mind and Cosmos* of giving current physical reductionism an expanded metaphysical base in which the physical and mental are ontologically

scientific replacement has occurred, he has, however, shown an unusual, and at times costly, willingness to engage with and commend work that he believes might make a contribution to further understanding. This is even when he disagrees with the underlying motivation as well as the conclusions.[10] His belief that "a greatly expanded base" is needed to achieve intelligibility,[11] has led him to endorse the potential contribution to epistemological debate from exponents of intelligent design and in 2009, he included Stephen Meyer's *Signature in the Cell: DNA and the Evidence for Intelligent Design*, in his selection for *The Times Literary Supplement*'s "Books of the Year." By praising Meyer's careful presentation of the "fiendishly difficult problem" of life coming into existence from lifeless matter,[12] he came under a volley of fire as, in the words of Plantinga:

> For that piece of blasphemy Nagel paid the predictable price; he was said to be arrogant, dangerous to children, a disgrace, hypocritical, ignorant, mind-polluting, reprehensible, stupid, unscientific, and in general a less than wholly upstanding citizen of the republic of letters.[13]

In a subsequent exchange of letters to *The Times*, Nagel responded to organic chemist Stephen Fletcher's dismissive critique of his endorsement of Meyer's work, by stating that Fletcher's tone "exemplifies the widespread intolerance of any challenge to the dogma that everything in the world must be ultimately explainable by chemistry and physics." Nagel once again stressed that his doubts about reduction are not dependent on theism as he "is not tempted to belief in God,"[14] but added that his honesty compels him to admit his belief that theism, atheism, and agnosticism are all rationally possible positions that cannot be clearly ruled out by either empirical evidence or *a priori* argument. While he does not support

---

inseparable. See chapter 3 in *Mind and Cosmos*.

10. In a review of philosopher Alvin Plantinga's book *Where the Conflict Really Lies*, Nagel acknowledges the "huge epistemological gulf" between their perspectives but concludes that he makes a "valuable contribution" to the debate: "It is of great interest to be presented with a lucid and sophisticated account of how someone who holds these beliefs understands them to harmonize with and indeed to provide crucial support for the methods and results of the natural sciences" (Nagel, "Philosopher Defends Religion").

11. Nagel, *Mind and Cosmos*, 32.

12. Nagel, "Books of the Year."

13. Plantinga, "Secular Heresy."

14. Nagel, "Letter to the Editor [2009]."

Meyer's conclusions, he believes that "the problems he poses are real" and lend support to the view that physics is not "the theory of everything."[15]

A SECULAR HERETIC

Nagel reentered the arena with *Mind and Cosmos* by reiterating that he finds the arguments from intelligent design stimulating in offering empirical arguments that are of great interest. He does not believe them to be real options but admits that this is also "an ungrounded assumption"[16] and suggests that they should be taken seriously as the scorn with which they are commonly met is "manifestly unfair."[17] He is also open about his agreement with Plantinga's suggestion that, "unlike divine benevolence, the application of evolutionary theory to the understanding of our own cognitive capacities should undermine, though it need not completely destroy, our confidence in them."[18] For Nagel there is, therefore, an overconfidence in the construction of the "evolutionary story" as he believes that it weakens both the authority of reason and "the natural conviction that our moral judgments are true or false independent of our beliefs."[19]

The critical response to his skepticism about what he refers to in *Mind and Cosmos* as the assumptions of an epistemological climate currently dominated by scientific naturalism[20] was, from some within both scientific and philosophical circles, swift, disparaging, and in some cases vitriolic.[21] It was, however, a response that he might have anticipated in penning the provocative subtitle, *Why the Materialist Neo-Darwinian Conception of Nature Is Almost Certainly False*. Despite the provisional "almost certainly" and perhaps because of its possible parody of a chapter

---

15. Nagel, "Letter to the Editor [2010]."
16. Nagel, *Mind and Cosmos*, 12.
17. Nagel, *Mind and Cosmos*, 10.
18. Plantinga in Nagel, *Mind and Cosmos*, 27.
19. Street, "Darwinian Dilemma," in Nagel, *Mind and Cosmos*, 28.

20. That he believes is "heavily dependent on speculative Darwinian explanations of practically everything" (Nagel, *Mind and Cosmos*, 127).

21. While the focus of this chapter is on the initial and widely publicized negative response, more considered views can be also found. Jon Fennell describes Nagel's work as "courageous and honest" (Fennell, "Plausibility and Common Sense," 52). See also reviews by Bremer, "Mind and Cosmos"; Yates, "Mind and Cosmos"; Plantinga, "Secular Heresy." Essays include Cutting et al., "Nagel's Untimely Idea"; Baggett, "On Thomas Nagel's Rejection"; Glouberman, "Being of Mind."

title in Richard Dawkins's book *The God Delusion*,[22] Nagel was depicted on the cover of one publication as a heretic burning at the stake while surrounded by red-robed, hooded figures representing currently prominent scientists and philosophers.[23] Cognitive scientist Steven Pinker is reputed to have tweeted that the book exposed "the shoddy reasoning of a once-great thinker."[24] Philosophers Brian Leiter and Michael Weisberg referred to it as "an instrument of mischief" containing arguments that, in being "quixotic" and "unconvincing," were aimed at a market of "evolution deniers, intelligent-design acolytes, religious fanatics and others who are not really interested in the substantive scientific and philosophical issues."[25] *The Guardian* writer Mark Vernon awarded *Mind and Cosmos* its prize for "The Most Despised Science Book of 2012" which was frequently quoted by its antagonists. Their outrage appeared, however, to overlook his offsetting comments suggesting that in attempting to confront and even "break" scientific taboos it is a book worth reading as it is "a model of carefulness, sobriety and reason" and that "those prepared to face the flak" are needed as many contemporary philosophers bow too low to science.[26]

The "flak" that Nagel had to face was considerable but in an article responding to the hostile critique he was once again unapologetic, declaring that the reaction was "not surprising," given the ongoing entrenchment of the worldview that the book attacks;[27] a view that he describes as embracing an "authoritative form of explanation that has defined science since the revolution of the seventeenth century."[28] It is a form of explanation that has also had an impact on biblical hermeneutics, but Nagel's belief that it is now outdated has potentially significant consequences for

---

22. A chapter entitled, "Why There Almost Certainly Is No God." Nagel reviewed *The God Delusion* in 2006.

23. Ferguson, "Heretic."

24. Pinker, "What Has Gotten into Thomas Nagel?"

25. Leiter and Weisberg, "Do You Only Have a Brain?"

26. Vernon, "Most Despised." See also Ferguson, who refers to Daniel Dennett as one of a group of philosophers who have "turned their field into a handmaiden of science: meekly and gratefully accepting whatever findings the scientists come up with—from brain scans to the Higgs boson—which they then use to demonstrate the superiority of hardheaded science to the airy musings of old-fashioned 'armchair philosophy'" (Ferguson, "Heretic").

27. Nagel, "Core."

28. Nagel, *Mind and Cosmos*, 92.

not only contemporary epistemology as he suggests, but also for hermeneutical endeavor.

THE HEGEMONY OF REDUCTIONISM

The whole method consists entirely in the ordering and arranging of the objects on which we must concentrate our mind's eye if we are to discover some truth. We shall be following this method exactly if we first reduce complicated and obscure propositions step by step to simpler ones, and then, starting with the intuition of the simplest ones of all, try to ascend through the same steps to a knowledge of all the rest.[29]

Nagel suggests that a dominant tone of twenty-first-century epistemologies, in relation to both the nature and extent of propositional knowledge,[30] has remained in thrall to the seventeenth-century Cartesian idea of the world as a machine made up of pieces functioning like clockwork mechanisms that can be taken apart and studied to advance understanding. This "reductive" approach to understanding reality can be traced back to the fifth century BCE when Greek philosophers Democritus and Leucippus proposed that all matter consisted of tiny, indivisible atoms in varying shapes and textures;[31] a proposition that was immortalized in the first century BCE by Roman poet Lucretius in his description of "the nature of things."[32] It was, however, the holistic and teleological approach of Aristotle, in which the whole is different from the sum of its parts,[33] that dominated Western philosophy until the revolutionary thinking of Descartes, Galileo, Kepler, and Newton[34] heralded the dawn of modern science in the

---

29. Descartes, "Rules," 20.

30. Both the "rationalist" non-empirical or *a priori* knowledge requiring only the use of reason, and the "empiricist" empirical or *a posteriori* knowledge based on sense experience.

31. From the Greek *atomos*, meaning indivisible. See Lightman, *Accidental Universe*, 3, 7.

32. A poem described as aiming "to bury all superstitious speculation and philosophical dogma by outlining the scope of a purely materialistic doctrine" (Barrow and Tipler, *Anthropic Cosmological Principle*, 41–42).

33. "In the case of all things which have several parts and in which the totality is not, as it were, a mere heap, but the whole is something beside the parts, there is a cause" (Aristotle, *Metaphysics* 8.6).

34. Kauffman, *Reinventing*, 10.

sixteenth and seventeenth centuries. The term *reductionism* only appeared in the mid-twentieth century[35] but by 1981, philosopher Robert Nozick could claim that "ours can be aptly named the Age of Reductionism"[36] due to the widespread belief that reality, in terms of "true" understanding, lies at the source or substance of a phenomenon which must, therefore, be reduced to its smallest parts before an explanation can be formulated.[37] In the current intellectual climate that Nagel describes as having a fear of religion and subsequently being "armed to the teeth" against its attacks,[38] reductionism appears to still be a significant force.[39] This is not only ontologically in focusing on the breakdown through *downward* causation of physical entities, but also epistemologically in relation to concepts and theories, descriptions and explanations.[40]

The impact of reductionism on theology can be seen in attempts to reduce it to a single discipline such as history, anthropology, psychology, or sociology,[41] but its infiltration into hermeneutical endeavor has also been significant. Nagel's warning that "a defensive, world-flattening reductionism" has had "large and often pernicious consequences for modern intellectual life" has, therefore, potentially important implications for both theology and biblical interpretation where there is evidence that it is not restricted to scientifically minded atheists. This is evidence that can

35. Jones, *Analysis*, 25–26.

36. Nozick, *Philosophical Explanations*, 630, in Jones, *Analysis*, 1.

37. Stemming from methodologies of the natural sciences in which the reduction of the human sciences to the natural sciences and then biology to chemistry and chemistry to physics aims at a starting point of a simple mathematical equation that will encompass a "Theory of Everything."

38. Nagel, *Mind and Cosmos*, 127.

39. Despite the fact that, as Brian Leiter and Michael Weisberg point out, "most philosophers, [believe] that Nagel is right to reject theoretical reductionism, because the sciences have not progressed in a way consistent with it. We have not witnessed the reduction of psychology to biology, biology to chemistry, and chemistry to physics, but rather the proliferation of fields like neuroscience and evolutionary biology that explain psychological and biological phenomena in terms unrecognizable by physics" (Leiter and Weisberg, "Do You Only Have a Brain?"). There are also a significant number of scientists and mathematicians who question the reach of reductive approaches, examples of which can be found in Cornwell, *Nature's Imagination*. See also Paul Davies who refers to "a growing dissatisfaction with sweeping reductionism, a feeling that the whole really is greater than the sum of its parts. Analysis and reduction will always have a central role to play in science, but many people cannot accept that it is an exclusive role. Especially in physics, the synthetic or holistic approach is becoming increasingly fashionable in tackling certain types of problem" (Davies, *Cosmic Blueprint*, 8).

40. Jones, *Analysis*, 13.

41. McKenzie, "Emergence," 226.

be found in diametrically opposed but equally reductive approaches to the commonly labeled *supernatural* features within the biblical narratives that appear to reduce them to either elements of myth and story in the sense of "useful fiction"[42] or factual historical phenomena.

THE GOD HYPOTHESIS

Nagel's antireductionist stance therefore offers a potentially important critique of interpretive approaches to biblical narrative that appear, for increasing numbers, to be unable to address the failure to understand Christian belief and doctrine. It is a failure that often appears to transmute into misunderstanding which has considerable implications for the corresponding issue of whether the biblical narratives can contribute to the search for an answer to what Nagel believes to be the persistent "What am I doing here?" question. For Nagel, as for his detractors, these ancient, prescientific and, therefore, now anachronistic "stories" do not appear to merit consideration. His thinking contributes, however, an insight into this lack of understanding which is found in his explanation of what he calls the "God hypothesis"; an explanation which highlights some of the assumptions that appear to underlie contemporary approaches to, and interpretations of, the biblical text. Nagel states that

> God, whatever he may be, is not a complex physical inhabitant of the natural world. The explanation of his existence as a chance concatenation of atoms is not a possibility for which we must find an alternative, because that is not what anybody means by God.[43]

While it may be undisputed that Nagel is biblically correct in rejecting the explanation of God's existence as "a chance concatenation of atoms," the hermeneutical conundrum arising from contemporary interpretations of the biblical depiction of God is reflected in his use of both objective and subjective reference in declaring *whatever he* may be.[44] It

---

42. Ian Barbour suggests that a "useful fiction" can fulfil an important function in human life but is neither true nor false (Barbour, *Myths*, 5). For John Polkinghorne, useful fictions serve as "rafts to float on seas too deep for other forms of knowledge" and are, therefore, a "seductive opportunity to retain the power of biblical narrative without embarrassment to a scientific world-view" (Polkinghorne, *Reason and Reality*, 33).

43. Nagel, *Secular Philosophy*, 22.

44. While Nagel uses the more common male pronoun in referring to God, this is a contested area, with increasing support for both female and gender-neutral language

is a conundrum that raises the question of the nature, specificity, and purpose of biblical language in referring to potentially indescribable and even unthinkable concepts. Nagel's statement is indicative of an increasing hermeneutical tendency to reject the anthropomorphism of God in favor of an abstracted concept such as an orientating symbol.[45] This is a tendency that dismisses propositional approaches to biblical and doctrinal language that interpret it as factual in representing or referring to that which, in some sense can be held to be literally true.[46] What this sense is may be fiercely contested but such rejection appears to present limited options for the interpretation of the physicality in the concrete language of both the narratives and the accompanying literary genres that comprise the biblical canon. This is a physicality that includes not only the anthropomorphic imagery of a God who walks in the garden that he has created (Genesis 3:8) and in which he has formed human beings in his image (Genesis 1:26), but also the subsequent and often contrasting portrayals of a God who is variously referred to as being, or having the attributes of, an eagle (Deuteronomy 32:11), lion (Genesis 49:9), dove (Matthew 3:16) lamb (John 1:29), rock (Deuteronomy 32:4;1 Peter 1:4) and vine (John 15:5) or present within, and represented by,

---

that moves away from gender stereotypes. It should, however, be noted that twelfth-century-medieval writers, such as Bernard of Clairvaux and Hildegard of Bingen as well as the later Julian of Norwich, used the feminine imagery of Jesus as "mother." For contemporary debate, see Sallie McFague's advocacy of the metaphors "Mother, Friend, and Lover" in referencing God in McFague, *Metaphorical Theology*. Elizabeth A. Johnson suggests that "naming God SHE has profound theological significance for human understanding of God . . . releasing divine mystery from its age-old patriarchal cage so that God can be truly God," thus setting free "a greater sense of the mystery of the living God." She warns, however, that "seeking the female face of God" and using the "category of the feminine can ensnare women in a patriarchally generated gender stereotype" (Johnson, *Naming God She*, 14–16). Johnson makes the salient point that "no expression for God can be taken literally" as "we are always naming *toward* God" (Johnson, *Quest for the Living God*, 18, 20). See also Elisabeth Schüssler Fiorenza, for whom concerns about an exploitative patriarchy have led to the more comprehensive term "kyriarchy" as "an intersectional pyramidal social order traversed by gender/race/class/colonial domination, exploitation and subordination" (Schüssler Fiorenza, *Jesus*, x).

45. See Kaufman, for whom "it is not the existence of some being, but rather an adequate God-concept that is essential for human flourishing" (Kaufman, *In the Face of Mystery*, 42).

46. See Murphy, *Beyond Liberalism*, 36–61, esp. 41. Murphy calls this an "experiential-expressivist" approach using Lindbeck's terminology and citing his focus on the experiential-expressive dimension of religion that "interprets doctrines as noninformative and nondiscursive symbols of inner feelings, attitudes, or existential orientations" (Lindbeck, *Nature of Doctrine*, 16).

wind (2 Samuel 22:11), water (Jeremiah 2:13), fire, cloud (Exodus 13:21) and bread (John 6:35).

This is language that therefore appears to resist the reduction of God to *either* abstraction, articulated as the more intellectually palatable "creativity," "godness," or "sacredness" in the universe, *or* to anthropomorphism. It also appears to resist the reductive categorization of grammatical terminology, as literal and figurative language often seem to be inextricably intertwined. It serves instead to challenge linguistic boundaries by holding, in considerable tension, the mystery of a transcendent and radically unfamiliar being, manifest in often dramatic theophanies involving natural cataclysms, with an immanent and more familiar, relational being;[47] a being that bears both the physical attributes of sight, hearing, and speech, and the emotional qualities of sensing what is good and expressing anger at what is not. This is a tension that prepares for and culminates in the climactic Gospel accounts in which, contra Nagel, God does become, for a limited period, "a complex physical inhabitant of the natural world." It is a becoming that arises not, however, from "a chance concatenation of atoms" but from the predetermined mystery of a holy overshadowing, thereby enabling the biblical narratives to provide a unique, unified concept of God represented in the comprehensible forms

---

47. Gunton refers to the "mine-field" to be crossed in clarifying transcendence, with the word "transcendent" having "widely different meanings" for different theologians and philosophers. He argues from a late Barthian perspective for a dynamic (qualitative) rather than spatial (quantitative) conception. This is so that transcendence is not "something that God possesses in greater or lesser quantity, at the expense of his immanence, but rather something he *is* and *does*." In this respect, it is a transcendence "of act, event, of identity in difference . . . that comes to expression when the story of Jesus of Nazareth, crucified and risen is narrated." God's transcendence thus becomes "the ground of immanence" by providing "the ontological basis for the events in which he becomes immanent" (Gunton, "Transcendence, Metaphor," 511–13). See also Grenz and Olson, who refer to the destabilizing Enlightenment effect on "the classic quest for a transcendent-immanent theology" in which there is a biblically based, balanced creative tension between "the twin truths of the divine transcendence and the divine immanence." These are the "truths" of God being transcendent in the sense of apart from or "beyond" the world but also immanent in being present and active within the world's processes and history. They describe the Enlightenment effect as "binding God so closely to nature and human reason that God's transcendence came to be dissolved in the immanence of the divine within the orderly realm of creation and reason. Rather than looking beyond the world to find God, the Enlightenment ultimately turned within." They suggest, however, that "a proper relation between theology and reason or culture," requires a balanced affirmation of both truths. This is because "an overemphasis on transcendence can lead to a theology that is irrelevant to the cultural context in which it seeks to speak, whereas an overemphasis on immanence can produce a theology held captive to a specific culture" (Grenz and Olson, *Twentieth-Century*, 11–23).

of both mind and body. Nagel is, therefore, correct in both acknowledging the significance of the "God hypothesis" being able to offer "a different kind of explanation from those of physical science" and in concluding:

> The point of the hypothesis is to claim that not all explanation is physical, and that there is a mental, purposive, or intentional explanation more fundamental than the basic laws of physics, because it explains even them.[48]

He is, however, entering more contentious territory in his assumption that the *only* way that the hypothesis can make sense is as the "purpose or intention of a mind without a body, capable nevertheless of creating and forming the entire physical world." This is an assumption that is in itself reductive in limiting interpretation of the biblical text to a concept of God that appears to be barely, if at all, distinguishable from a teleological principle or bias within nature. The "God hypothesis" then serves simply as an opening to what Nagel hopes to be the possibility of teleological principles that do not require either intentional design, chance or purposeless physical law but provide instead "an independent end point of explanation for the existence and form of living things."[49] This is an alternative end point that he argues might be better equipped to provide the elusive comprehensive worldview. He develops this argument further in *Mind and Cosmos* admitting that teleological explanation "may have serious problems"[50] and "is in many ways obscure"[51] but he believes that these are also features of existing alternatives. He acknowledges that it is "a throwback to the Aristotelian conception of nature" and anticipates the alarm that this might generate[52] in offering the defense that he has been persuaded that "the idea of teleological laws is coherent, and quite different from the idea of explanation by the intentions of a purposive being who produces the means to his ends by choice."[53] The critical response

---

48. Nagel, *Secular Philosophy*, 22.
49. Nagel, *Secular Philosophy*, 23.
50. Nagel, *Mind and Cosmos*, 88.
51. Nagel, *Mind and Cosmos*, 67.
52. As a return to the naiveté of a pre-scientific age.
53. Nagel, *Mind and Cosmos*, 66. A holistic teleological approach that incorporates both science and theology in a psychic/physical perspective of the unfolding universe can, however, be found in the thinking of Pierre Teilhard de Chardin and Thomas Berry. See Teilhard, *Phenomenon of Man*; Berry, "New Story"; Swimme and Berry, *Universe Story*. For a comprehensive analysis of the development of their thinking, see Tucker and Brim, "Evolutionary and Ecological." They suggest that, for both Teilhard and

to *Mind and Cosmos* indicates, however, that others are not persuaded about the sufficiency of this difference, which raises a potentially important consideration for hermeneutical endeavor. While those who "fear" religion, in the sense that Nagel describes, may be concerned that a teleological approach might lead in that direction, there is also the potential for the opposite to occur when contemporary reworkings of Christian tradition appear to result in the morphing of theology into teleology.

BREAKING THE GALILEAN SPELL

This is exemplified in the approach of United Church of Canada minister Greta Vosper who advocates the letting go of the "religious detritus of our traditions"[54] to liberate Christianity as a "values-based alternative" embracing the attributes of love, compassion and justice, with the concept of God becoming an optional extra.[55] For Vosper, the relevant question and related problem is

> no longer about the existence of a God . . . [but] about how we live together, fragile life forms that we are, as we seek to coexist on an equally fragile planet. Belief in a supernatural God has only ever managed to get in the way of addressing that question as fully and deeply as we need to.[56]

In this respect, she is in partial agreement with the thinking of biologist Stuart Kauffman who, from a different perspective, also believes that the "Galilean spell" must be broken and "the sacred" reinvented as a global ethic, with "one view of God as the natural creativity in the universe."[57] In referring to the Galilean spell, Kauffman is not, however, alluding to the

---

Berry, matter "is not dead or inert, but a numinous reality possessing both a physical and spiritual dimension. Consciousness, then, is an intrinsic part of reality and is the thread that links all life-forms" (Tucker and Brim, "Evolutionary and Ecological," 404).

54. Vosper, *With or without God*, 197.

55. Vosper, *With or without God*, 100. Vosper argues that, as these attributes are the core values of early Christianity, it is legitimate to reject what she believes to be subsequent, and now irrelevant, developments of concepts that we created but no longer understand—such as the Bible as the authoritative word of God and the divinity of Jesus—but still retain the title Christian. See Vosper, *With or without God*, 192–93. Philip Kitchen suggests that this is a form of "refined religion" in which "religion is not understood as primarily a collection of doctrines about the transcendent, but as a system of practices and commitments" (Kitchen, *Life after Faith*, 61).

56. Vosper, "What's God."

57. Kauffman, *Reinventing*, xiii.

anachronistic hold of an ancient prophet whose ministry on the shores of Lake Galilee is recorded in the biblical text, but rather to that of Galileo and the belief that "the universe and all in it are governed by natural laws, Newton's, Einstein's, Schrödinger's."[58] This remains, though, a spell that reflects a worldview that he also believes we have moved beyond to "an entirely new philosophic and scientific worldview" of an emergent and partially lawless "ceaseless creativity in the universe, biosphere and human life."[59] Kauffman rejects intelligent design as a valid theory as he believes "God" to be a human construct, invented to "serve as our most powerful symbol to orient our lives and civilizations."[60] In similar fashion to Nagel's acknowledgment that we live in an "astonishing" world,[61] he concludes, however, that we "confront something amazing" in the construction and evolution of the biosphere. He therefore also suggests that a new conceptual framework is needed to both see and articulate this new worldview and "then to understand and orientate ourselves in our ever creative world" as; "We find ourselves far beyond reductionism, indeed."[62]

For Nagel, this must be a framework within which a form of understanding can be developed "that enables us to see ourselves and other conscious organisms as specific expressions simultaneously of the physical and the mental character of the universe."[63] The interesting hermeneutical question that this provokes is whether the biblical depiction of humankind, created by God *"in his image"* (Genesis 1:27) and formed from both *"the soil"* or dust of the ground and *"the breath of life"* which God *"blew into his nostrils"* (Genesis 2:7),[64] already provides its own unique framework for this form of understanding. It is a question that a fear of religion and subsequent scientism may inevitably suppress, but it is also of interest that twenty years ago Nagel suggested that this was a fear that had resulted in an ideology that might be premature in

58. Kauffman, *Reinventing*, 131.

59. Kauffman, *Reinventing*, 142.

60. Kauffman, *Reinventing*, xiii. Kauffman's thinking and his consequent book were motivated by his attendance at a conference in 1992, the purpose of which was to identify and discuss, "What is the most important question confronting mankind?" A suggestion that "stunned" Kauffman was that there was a need to "reinvent the sacred" as a "new transnational mythic structure," created to sustain and guide the emerging global civilization (Kauffman, *Reinventing*, 291n1).

61. Nagel, *Mind and Cosmos*, 7.

62. Kauffman, *Reinventing*, 6.

63. Nagel, *Mind and Cosmos*, 69.

64. Alter, *Five Books*, 21.

heaving "a huge sigh of collective relief" that Darwinism has provided a way "to eliminate purpose, meaning, and design as fundamental features of the world."[65] It is relief that is evident in Atkins's 1992 conference paper making the triumphant claim that science had finally discarded its "chrysalis" of antireductionist "religious obfuscation" and emerged as its present liberated butterfly;[66] a perhaps unfortunate choice of metaphor as the average lifespan of the butterfly is only about a month.[67] In promoting a scientism that Nagel describes as extending "far beyond a rejection of the existence of a personal god, to include any cosmic order of which mind is an irreducible and nonaccidental part,"[68] reductionism appears, therefore, to have the potential to become a doctrine that is potentially at odds with science itself; a "reductive megalomania"[69] ignoring an increasing shift by scientists to what Nancey Murphy terms "nonreductive physicalism."[70]

As science struggles to articulate what Nagel terms the "true extent" of the "astonishing world"[71] that is opening up to new technology, and as new perceptions of reality emerge from quantum mechanics and astrophysics, he acknowledges the need to move beyond the "evolutionary hand waving" resulting from "the pervasive and reductive naturalism of our culture."[72] It is a move that may be overdue according to the mid-twentieth-century words of anthropologist Loren Eiseley:

> I have come to suspect that this long descent down the ladder of life, beautiful and instructive though it may be, will not lead us to the final secret. In fact I have ceased to believe in the final brew or the ultimate chemical. There is, I know, a kind of heresy, a shocking negation of confidence in blue-steel microtomes and

---

65. Nagel, *Last Word*, 131.

66. Atkins, "Limitless Power," 125.

67. According to Lepidopterists.

68. Nagel, *Last Word*, 133. He attributes this to what he describes as "a deep-seated aversion in the modern 'disenchanted' *Weltanschaaung* to any ultimate principles that are not dead—that is, devoid of any reference to the possibility of life or consciousness."

69. See Midgley's response to Atkins in Midgley, "Reductive Megalomania."

70. Following the development by Roy Wood Sellars of a position called emergent realism, emergent naturalism or evolutionary naturalism. See Murphy, *Beyond Liberalism*, 136.

71. Nagel, *Mind and Cosmos*, 7.

72. Nagel uses the term "evolutionary hand waving" to refer to "the tendency to take a theory which has been successful in one domain and apply it to anything else you can't understand" (Nagel, *View from Nowhere*, 78).

men in white in making such a statement. . . . It is only that somewhere among the seeds and beetle shells and abandoned grasshopper legs I find something that is not accounted for very clearly in the dissections to the ultimate virus or crystal or protein particle. Even if the secret is contained in these things, in other words, I do not think it will yield to the kind of analysis our science is capable of making.[73]

It is a move that may, however, have an ancient precedent in the alternative conceptions of reality within biblical narrative; conceptions that also attempt to accommodate the wonder and mystery within the existential reality of an astonishing world that was acknowledged by the biblical psalmists long before the development of the sophisticated technology that is currently increasing, but also revealing the limits of, contemporary knowledge and understanding. This is revelation that provides the third insight which emerges from Nagel's subsequent emphasis on acknowledging what he calls the "true extent of reality" in a world that is independent of and extends beyond the reach of our minds.

---

73. Eiseley, *Immense Journey*, 202.

4

An Astonishing World

Any conception of the world must include some acknowledgment of its incompleteness: at a minimum it will admit the existence of things or events we don't know about. The issue is only how far beyond our actual conception of the world we should admit that the world may extend. I claim that it may contain not only what we don't know and can't yet conceive, but also what we never could conceive—and that this acknowledge of the likelihood of its own limits should be built into our conception of reality.[1]

The world is an astonishing place, and the idea that we have in our possession the basic tools needed to understand it is no more credible now than it was in Aristotle's day. That it has produced you, and me, and the rest of us is the most astonishing thing about it.[2]

THE ISSUE THAT NAGEL raises about potential limits to our conception of reality and how far the world that we exist within may extend beyond these limitations, emerges from a growing awareness of the complexity and only partial understanding of both consciousness and cosmology,

---

1. Nagel, *View from Nowhere*, 108.
2. Nagel, *Mind and Cosmos*, 7.

or in Nagel's words, mind and cosmos. As increasingly sophisticated technology confirms his claim that there are aspects of reality that are currently, and may always be, inaccessible to what he describes as the voracious objective appetite[3] and fetish for facts,[4] it also supports his belief that the world remains "an astonishing place"; a belief that leads him to suggest that we still lack some of the "basic tools" needed to understand it.[5]

There are, however, tools that are now in our possession that have enabled a series of extraordinary mappings which shed light on realities that challenge our current conceptual abilities and stretch the boundaries of what is regarded as thinkable. This includes the problem of quantum gravity and ongoing attempts to comprehend what quantum space and time are; a problem that physicist Carlo Rovelli suggests will require both an in-depth revision of the way in which we conceive things and a rethinking of "the grammar of our understanding of the world"[6] as "in seeking a coherent vision of the world in keeping with what we have learned about it, our ideas about the nature of reality have to change."[7] What this change will involve appears to be open to imaginative speculation which includes the possible realities of "string" theory[8] and multiple existences in "many worlds" or "multiverses."[9] The acknowledgment of a need for change raises, however, two potentially important questions for biblical hermeneutics and Christian theology. The first is in relation to the ongoing problem of attempting to comprehend not only the world but also what Nagel refers to as its most astonishing feature—its "production" of the human condition. It subsequently asks; how might the biblical text provide its own in-depth revision of the way in which we conceive things

---

3. An appetite that is revealed in the tendency "to seek an objective account of everything before admitting its reality" (Nagel, *Mortal Questions*, 196, 211).

4. Nagel, "Facts Fetish."

5. A suggestion that, in making a comparison to the limited resources of Aristotle's day, has been described as "perhaps the most startling sentence in all of *Mind and Cosmos*" (Leiter and Weisberg, "Do You Only Have a Brain?").

6. Rovelli, *Reality*, 127.

7. Rovelli, *Reality*, 128.

8. String Theory proposes a seven-dimensional world within which the smallest constituents of matter are not subatomic particles but tiny (10^{-33} centimeter) string-like vibrations of energy (Lightman, *Discoveries*, 473). It has been estimated that the "string landscape" has the potential to contain 10^{500} different possible universes (Lightman, *Accidental*, 21).

9. Theories that attempt to explain the appearance of "fine-tuning" or "design" in the physical constants from which life and complex levels of consciousness emerged.

through a rethinking of the grammar of our understanding of the world in order to both supplement and expand our ideas about the nature of reality? The second is the interrelated question of how the contribution of a biblical revision and rethinking to contemporary epistemology might be seen as relevant in an age in which, as Thomas Hosinski points out, science "is widely regarded as the surest way to knowledge of the truth."[10] Hosinski does not believe science to be either the source or "ultimate criterion" for the formulation of Christian doctrine and understanding of God but is convinced that

> Christian theology, today . . . must work out its interpretations of God and God's relation to the universe in conversation with the sciences or it runs the risk of being regarded as irrelevant to our understanding of reality.[11]

This is a conversation and understanding that is, however, increasingly challenged as, in the words of Nagel: "Science penetrates to less and less intuitively imaginable accounts of the reality that lies behind the familiar manifest world; accounts that rely more and more on mathematics that only specialists can learn."[12] These are accounts that have had to develop their own unique language to articulate the measurement and mapping of both the macro and microscopic elements of our world; a world in which there are over forty-five orders of magnitude between the largest and smallest measurements that are currently possible,[13] with human beings situated approximately in the middle on a logarithmic scale, between the quantum world and our universe.[14] This is a universe in which the astonishing extremes of measurement can be found in the extraordinary

10. Hosinski, *Image of*, 63.

11. Hosinski, *Image of*, 63.

12. Nagel, *Concealment and Exposure*, 173.

13. When the orders increase or decrease in powers of ten. The scale of these measurements has necessitated the use of symbolic language such as: AU (Astronomical Unit, the average distance between the Earth and the Sun which is about 150 million kilometers); LY (Light Year: the distance light travels in a year: 9,460,000,000,000 kilometers or 63,240 AU); and PC (Parsec: equivalent to 3.26 light years and equalling 30.8 trillion kilometers). Within the language of atomic physics, a length unit called the *angstrom* (Å) is one ten-billionth of a meter (10^{-10}m) and roughly the size of a hydrogen atom. In nuclear physics, a *fermi* (fm) or quadrillionth of a meter (10^{-15}m) is about the size of a proton or a neutron. But even more astonishing is the fact that quarks are known to be smaller than 10^{-18}m, with a language of measurement that must consequentially include trillionths and quintillionths in its vocabulary (Smith, *How Big*, 1, 2, 7, 31).

14. Gribbin, *Schrödinger's Kittens*, 18.

phenomenon of radiant energy or electromagnetic radiation that we call light; a phenomenon of quantized photons which, in traveling at a speed of about 300,000 kilometers per second and, therefore, nearly 9.5 trillion kilometers in a year, enables the map of the observable universe[15] to become larger every day as the light emitted from slightly more distant objects has the required time to reach the range of our telescopes.[16]

MAPPING THE COSMOS: A UNIVERSE OF ANCIENT LIGHT

We are immersed in a sea of light, emanating from ordinary matter that is floating, as it were, on an ocean of dark matter. The dark matter itself floats on the dark energy of the particle vacuum that in turn is embedded within the scaffolding of space-time—which is shaped by the dark gravity effects from all matter and energy.[17]

In February 2008, the ground-based six hundred-ton Large Binocular Telescope, located in the rarified air of Mount Graham in the Pinaleño Mountains of southeast Arizona, achieved first binocular light,[18] with a spiral galaxy detected at a distance of over 102 million light years from the Milky Way galaxy. Heralded as "breaking boundaries in astronomy and related fields" by peering into history, its two 8.4 meter mirrors were described as "eyes" with the light gathering power to "provide new and more powerful views of deep space" and the potential to answer "fundamental questions about the origins of the universe and mysterious worlds in other planetary systems."[19] Physicist Alan Lightman describes this peering out to increasingly greater distances in space as travelling back in time because when a galaxy is discovered over 102 million light years away it is observed as it was 102 million years ago.[20] This is, therefore, the observation of ancient light that has been travelling for 102 million years from a distant galaxy.

    15. Containing between 100 billion and 200 billion galaxies (Howell, "How Many Galaxies").
    16. Lightman, *Ancient Light*, 42.
    17. Perrenod, *Dark Matter*, 7.
    18. The first scientific images.
    19. Strittmatter, "Large Binocular Telescope."
    20. Lightman, *Ancient*, 31–32.

In early 2011, further evidence of Nagel's astonishing world was captured with the sighting of an even more distant galaxy when the image of a faint red dot was received at the University of California from the Hubble Space Telescope orbiting the Earth once every ninety-seven minutes.[21] This tiny dot, given the disappointingly unimaginative name UDFj-39546284 for a compact galaxy of young, hot, blue stars, is believed to be one of the first galaxies to form in the universe[22] and, as Lightman explains, only appears to be red because the light has been stretched to longer and longer wavelengths as it has traveled through space for about 13.2 billion years.[23] The wave-like nature of light corresponds to our instinctive sense that light is "a continuous fluid of energy, completely filling the space that it occupies"[24] but the discovery, in the early twentieth century, that light is made up of tiny individual quanta[25] or photons, introduced the seemingly paradoxical concept of wave-particle duality. Astrophysicist John Gribbin describes the behavior of light, as both a wave and particle, as the phenomenon at the heart of physicists' understanding of the two pillars upon which twentieth-century-physics developed; relativity theory and quantum mechanics.[26] These are pillars that, as Rovelli points out, reveal a paradox at the heart of our understanding of the world as the theory of general relativity reveals a world of "curved space-time where everything is *continuous*" while the theory of quantum mechanics[27] reveals a flat world "where *discrete* quanta of energy leap and interact."[28]

The theory of general relativity has led to extraordinary progress in cosmology and astrophysics, but the developing field of quantum mechanics has introduced concepts at the microscopic level of reality that continue to challenge what Nagel describes as "our intuitive conception of the world." He explains this conception as a "natural idea" which conforms to "the scale of ordinary experience" where "things happen in a

---

21. Lightman, *Accidental*, 87.
22. Lightman, *Accidental*, 88.
23. Lightman, *Accidental*, 88.
24. Lightman, *Discoveries*, 43.
25. The idea of the quantum as an elemental drop of energy was proposed by Max Planck in 1900, but it was Albert Einstein who argued that light exists in individual, indivisible units called quanta or photons in 1905 (Lightman, *Discoveries*, 44).
26. Gribbin, *Schrödinger's Kittens*, 30.
27. The laws of the fundamental behavior of matter and light.
28. Rovelli, *Reality*, 125.

An Astonishing World

unique, three-dimensional space and along a unique, one-dimensional time order."[29] In this respect, he can state that

> contemporary scientific theories describing the invisible physical reality that underlies the appearances no longer represent a world that can be intuitively grasped, even in rough outline, by the human imagination. Newtonian mechanics, the atomic theory of matter, and even the basic principles of electricity and magnetism can be roughly visualized by ordinary people. Quantum theory and the theory of relativity cannot be so visualized, because they introduce concepts of space, time, and the relation between observed and unobserved states of affairs that diverge radically from the intuitive concepts that we all use in thinking about our surroundings.[30]

This is a statement that offers a potential hermeneutical resonance with the radical divergence of supernatural concepts in biblical narratives from our intuitive thinking and understanding about our surroundings. These are narratives that, consequently, exploit the human imagination in their representation of invisible realities which, in transcending the reach of the human senses and extending the boundaries of what is presumed to be thinkable, also expose the limitations of language; an exposure that leads Dan Stiver to suggest that "language is notoriously unstable when applied to God" as we are "stretching it to breaking point—and perhaps beyond."[31] It is an exposure of limitations that has, however, interesting parallels with the emergence of quantum theory which provides a contemporary example of what Nagel describes as the ongoing compulsion, despite the risks involved, to repeatedly "use existing language to reach beyond its existing limits . . . however inadequately, in our recognition that our understanding of reality is so limited."[32]

In 1955, physicist Werner Heisenberg referred to the difficult and "really serious" problems of language that emerged in quantum theory when common or intuitive concepts could not be applied to the structure of atoms, stating, "We wish to speak in some way about the structure of the atoms and not only about the 'facts.' . . . But we cannot speak about the atoms in ordinary language."[33] This was because

---

29. Nagel, *Concealment and Exposure*, 172.
30. Nagel, *Concealment and Exposure*, 171.
31. Stiver, *Philosophy of Religious*, 20.
32. Nagel, *Secular Philosophy*, 31.
33. Heisenberg, *Physics and Philosophy*, 154.

no language existed in which one could speak consistently about the new situation. The ordinary language was based upon the old concepts of space and time and this language offered the only unambiguous means of communication about the setting up and the results of the measurements. Yet the experiments showed that the old concepts could not be applied everywhere.[34]

Heisenberg therefore points out that, as scientific knowledge expanded, language also had to expand with new terms introduced and "the old ones . . . applied in a wider field or differently from ordinary language." He consequently describes scientific language developing as "a natural extension of ordinary language adapted to the added fields of scientific knowledge,"[35] raising the questions of how theological language develops and how biblical narrative might also use old concepts in a different way to introduce new ones by a natural extension of ordinary language.

The discovery of quantum reality has introduced terminology such as complementarity,[36] superposition[37] and entanglement[38] to explain the strange counterintuitive nature of wave-particle duality and the behavior of separated but still connected particles. It is terminology that is unique to the concepts of a microscopic quantum world but the challenge of articulating these concepts is not in some ways dissimilar to the challenge faced by the biblical writers in attempting to articulate their new and at times counterintuitive perspective of the nature of the world with ordinary language; a world in which God is revealed firstly as a transcendent creator and sustainer but then as incarnate in the life of Jesus, revealing a paradox at the heart of the Christian faith. To articulate this extraordinary claim within the limitations of existing language, the biblical writers borrowed some concepts from the language of ancient Near-Eastern mythology but, like the quantum physicists of the future, they also had to make a radical divergence or departure from familiar ways of

---

34. Heisenberg, *Physics and Philosophy*, 151.

35. Heisenberg, *Physics and Philosophy*, 149.

36. A "situation in which it is possible to grasp one and the same event by two distinct modes of interpretation. These two modes are mutually exclusive, but they also complement each other, and it is only through their juxtaposition that the perceptual content of a phenomenon is fully brought out" (Heisenberg, *Physics and Philosophy*, 79).

37. The ability of a quantum system to be in multiple states at the same time.

38. The possibility of entanglement was discovered in 1926 by Erwin Schrödinger, who first used the term in 1935 (Aczel, *Entanglement*, 69).

An Astonishing World

understanding to introduce new and unprecedented ideas about a reality that would extend the boundaries of what was believed to be thinkable.

Despite the remarkable and ongoing discoveries about the wonders of the cosmos, it is the existence and complexity of consciousness that is, for Nagel, "one of the most astonishing things about the world."[39] In *Mind and Cosmos*, he describes its appearance as a development of life that "casts its shadow back over the entire process [of cosmological history] and the constituents and principles on which the process depends."[40] This is a shadow arising from what he believes to be the difficulty of integrating the appearance of mind in terms of "consciousness, perception, desire, action, and the formation of both beliefs and intentions on the basis of reasons,"[41] into the perspective of a mindless universe. It is, however, a perspective that has driven, and to a great extent is still driving, the development of the physical sciences, leading him to make the thought-provoking comment that it is a shadow under which

> we go on using perception and reason to construct scientific theories of the natural world even though we do not have a convincing external account of why those faculties exist that is consistent with our confidence in their reliability.[42]

MAPPING CONSCIOUSNESS: A UNIVERSE OF NEURONS

That ... [the world] has produced you and me, and the rest of us is the most astonishing thing about it.[43]

In the 1937–1938 Gifford Lectures, neurophysiologist Charles Sherrington used a cosmological analogy in his poetic, if not entirely accurate, description of the human brain awaking from sleep:

---

39. Nagel, *Mind and Cosmos*, 53. A conclusion that is reinforced in a recent paper in which Chalmers states that "the problem of phenomenal consciousness, or the reality of subjective experience and its relation to physical processes" is still one of the hardest philosophical problems arising from contemporary science (Chalmers and McQueen, "Consciousness and the Collapse," 12).

40. Nagel, *Mind and Cosmos*, 8.

41. Nagel, *Mind and Cosmos*, 32.

42. Nagel, *Mind and Cosmos*, 31.

43. Nagel, *Mind and Cosmos*, 7.

> The brain is waking and with it the mind is returning. It is as if the Milky Way entered upon some cosmic dance. Swiftly the head-mass becomes an enchanted loom where millions of flashing shuttles weave a dissolving pattern, always a meaningful pattern though never an abiding one; a shifting harmony of subpatterns.[44]

It is an analogy that is also used over seventy years later by physicist Leonard Mlodinow in stating that the brain contains at least a hundred billion neurons,[45] which is roughly the number of stars in our galaxy. Mlodinow's emphasis is, however, that while there is little interaction between the stars "the average neuron is plugged into thousands of others." He therefore concludes that the human brain is "far more complex and difficult to fathom than the universe of galaxies and stars" and believes this to be an example of why great leaps have been made "in our understanding of the cosmos, while knowledge of ourselves proceeds at a relative crawl."[46] For Nagel, this snail-like progress is attributed in part to his belief that attempts to accommodate mind in the materialist world picture "all appear . . . to reduce the true extent of reality to a common basis that is not rich enough for the purpose."[47] It is, therefore, impoverished reduction, an example of which can be found in the prosaic words of DNA (deoxyribonucleic acid) pioneer Francis Crick:

> You, your joys and your sorrows, your memories and your ambitions, your sense of personal identity and free will, are in fact no more than the behavior of a vast assembly of nerve cells and their associated molecules. As Lewis Carroll's Alice might have phrased it: "You're nothing but a pack of neurons."[48]

Crick calls this the "The Astonishing Hypothesis" which, with the subtitle, *The Scientific Search for the Soul*, is the title of a book in which he explores the mystery of consciousness in an attempt to find a scientific explanation.[49] It is an explanation that, for his collaborator Christof Koch,

---

44. Sherrington, *Man on His Nature*, 178.
45. Koch puts this figure at about 86 billion (Koch, *Consciousness*, 16).
46. Chopra and Mlodinow, *War of the Worldviews*, 16–17. Although in 2010, using data and methods emerging from the *Human Connectome Project*, researchers produced a new intricate mapping of the landscape of the human cortex delineating 180 areas, 97 of which were characterized as new. See Saemz, "NIH Awards."
47. Nagel, *Mind and Cosmos*, 14.
48. Crick, *Astonishing Hypothesis*, 3.
49. Crick, *Astonishing Hypothesis*, xi.

remains elusive after a twenty-five-year search for its physical, neurobiological base. Koch pioneered the use of physics to describe what he calls the "habitat of consciousness"[50] but his work has led him to reject reductionism and emergence as an all-encompassing explanation. Like Nagel, he now believes that science is "inadequate to the task of fully understanding the mind-body divide" and the "essential mystery at the heart of phenomenal existence."[51] His conclusion that consciousness is a "simple substance" or fundamental, "an elementary, property of living matter" that is "ontologically distinct from its physical substrate"[52] adds support to what Nagel declares to be his guiding conviction. This is that mind is "not just an afterthought or an accident or an add-on, but a basic aspect of nature" and fundamental feature of the universe.[53] It is a feature that he has described, however, as the "'affliction' of 'the pervasive self-consciousness that makes us human'";[54] a self-consciousness that occurs as:

> We wake up from our familiar surroundings to find ourselves, already elaborately formed by biology and culture, amazingly in existence, in the midst of the contingency of the world, and suddenly we do not know where we are or what we are. We recognize that we are products of the world and its history, generated and sustained in existence in ways we hardly understand.[55]

It is an affliction which has an interesting, if unintended, resonance with the development of a new level of pervasive self-consciousness within the human condition that occurs in the narrative of the third chapter of Genesis as *"the eyes of the two were opened, and they knew they were naked"* (Genesis 3:7).[56]

---

50. A habitat in which: "Neurons are highly diverse and sophisticated processors that collect, process, and broadcast data via synapses, or contact points with other nerve cells. They receive input via their finely branched dendrites, which are studded with thousands of synapses.... Our nervous system has perhaps 1,000 trillion synapses linking about 86 billion neurons" (Koch, *Consciousness*, 16).

51. Koch, *Consciousness*, 5. Koch has also rejected his once held Catholic faith, which he believes to be "an inescapable part of growing up and maturing and seeing the world as it is" (166).

52. Koch, *Consciousness*, 119, 132. As "experience, the interior perspective of a functioning brain, is something fundamentally different from the material thing causing it and that it can never be fully reduced to physical properties of the brain" (119).

53. Nagel, *Mind and Cosmos*, 16–17.

54. Nagel, "Analytic Philosophy."

55. Nagel, *Secular Philosophy*, 9.

56. Alter, *Five Books*, 23.

WAKE UP AND DIE

In the Genesis narrative, the opening of their eyes to the knowledge of both good and evil is a form of awakening, presenting the human couple with a new awareness of their vulnerability as they are "afflicted" firstly with shame and an accompanying fear which causes them to hide and attempt to cover their nakedness (Genesis 3:7–8). This is no longer the innocent or naïve self-awareness that emerged with the naming of the animals (Genesis 2:19–20) and was evident in the statement that *"the two of them were naked . . . and they were not ashamed"* (Genesis 2:25).[57] It is rather, "the movement from a primordial innocence to an existential deviation"; a movement in which humankind deviates from an "originally good destination through an act of will . . . by accepting a temptation."[58] From a biblical perspective, it is, therefore, deviation that occurs through an act of defiance portrayed in the narrative as emerging from manipulative reasoning in the form of persuasive rhetoric that occurs in the encounter between the woman and a serpent (Genesis 3:1–6). It is an encounter that will result in the couple becoming definitively human, but this is not, as in Nagel's sense, through a differentiation from other creatures due to a developing sense of self-consciousness within the human condition. This has already been established when *"the human called names to all the cattle and to the fowl of the heavens and to all the beasts of the field"* (Genesis 2:20).[59] The presence in the biblical narrative of a *knowing* serpent exhibiting the human characteristics of speech and a self-consciousness that is intimated in its introduction as *"the most cunning of all the beasts of the field"* (Genesis 3:1),[60] indicates that more is at stake and the unfolding events reveal this to be the differentiation between the humans and God in whose image they have been created (Genesis 1:27).

Although the serpent's promise, that in eating the forbidden fruit the human couple *"will become as gods knowing good and evil"* (Genesis 3:5),[61] is confirmed by God's statement that the human is now godlike, becoming *"like one of us"* (Genesis 3:22),[62] from the perspective of the

---

57. Alter, *Five Books*, 23.
58. Ihde, *Hermeneutic Phenomenology*, 120–21.
59. Alter, *Five Books*, 22.
60. Alter, *Five Books*, 24.
61. Alter, *Five Books*, 24.
62. Alter, *Five Books*, 27.

human couple this "becoming" is manifest as an awakening to a fearful awareness of their vulnerability. This is not only because they now "*knew they were naked, and they sewed fig leaves and made themselves loincloths*" (Genesis 3:7).[63] It is also in the affliction of the knowledge of their mortality and subsequent forced departure from the paradisiacal garden within which body and mind have been generated within a harmonious, unified and potentially infinite order. They must now find their place in the new reality of a world of fractured relationships and begin the ongoing search to find answers to what Nagel refers to as the "mortal questions" about human life—about "its end, its meaning, its value, and about the metaphysics of consciousness."[64] These are questions that, for Nagel, are philosophical rather than theological, but his emphasis on the need to understand the problems that this search might encounter has potentially important implications for both theology and biblical hermeneutics if, as he suggests,

> progress in philosophy consists not in answering questions definitively, but in deepening our understanding of the problems that inevitably arise in the attempt to find our place in the world, once we become afflicted with the pervasive self-consciousness that makes us human.[65]

From this perspective, if biblical narrative is to offer its own unique mapping of both our human "affliction" and subsequent attempts to find our place in an astonishing world, hermeneutical endeavor may be less about seeking definitive answers from the narrative and more about searching for a deeper understanding of these problems. This is understanding that emerges from the fourth insight from Nagel's work which relates to what he identifies as the hazards of combining perspectives that are radically distinct, with the subsequent need to ask the right questions and recognize "what can and cannot in principle be understood by certain existing methods."[66]

---

63. Alter, *Five Books*, 25.
64. Nagel, *Mortal Questions*, ix.
65. Nagel, "Analytic Philosophy."
66. Nagel, *Mind and Cosmos*, 3–4.

5

A Spider's Story

There is more to the basic substance of the world than can be captured by physics and chemistry.[1]

Our understanding is limited so there will not always be solutions to philosophical problems which will only show us the limits. The insight that we can achieve will therefore depend on maintaining a strong grasp of the problem and coming to understand the failure of each new attempt at solution.[2]

IN THE CONCLUDING SECTION of *The View From Nowhere*, entitled *Birth, Death, and the Meaning of Life*, Nagel reflects on his failed attempt to solve what he perceived to be a life-threatening problem for a large spider living a precarious existence trapped in a drain. The spider was continually tumbled and drenched as torrents of water were flushed through the drain, with the ongoing threat of being washed away. Its life appeared to be both "miserable" and "exhausting" in the relentless struggle to survive but his attempt to liberate the spider, from what seemed to be an avoidable, unnecessary but ultimately fatal struggle, by placing it in what he

---

1. Nagel, *Mind and Cosmos*, 64.
2. Nagel, *Mortal Questions*, xii.

assumed to be a more hospitable environment, soon ended in disaster. The spider, once freed from what to the onlooker appeared to be a desperate and perilous existence, was unable to adapt to its new "safe" home and after initially appearing to be in a state of paralysis, slowly shriveled to a premature demise on the exact spot where liberation was supposed to occur.[3]

Nagel uses this encounter to illustrate what he refers to as "the hazards of combining perspectives that are radically distinct"[4] but such combinations appear to be endemic, although often unnoticed, within contemporary culture and the impact on biblical narrative has been significant. When developments in science and technology are perceived to confine biblical perspectives of reality to an increasingly limited and potentially precarious space, the narratives also appear to be in constant danger of being swept away as victims of the currents of contemporary thought; currents that seem to render them to redundant waste products devoid of any nutritional content that might contribute to the growth of knowledge or understanding. To preserve their life and give them contemporary relevance, they therefore appear to need rescuing from this environment, with salvage attempts taking different but often equally problematic reductive forms. When "safe-houses" of historical evidence, demythologization, metaphor or analogy are constructed for the narratives to ward off potential threats, they also create their own dangers by often accommodating only limited and potentially misguided perspectives; perspectives that might, as with Nagel's approach to the spider, underestimate both their resilience and their need to remain in what might be their natural environment. The question that then arises concerns whether biblical narrative may, in similar fashion to the spider, contain inherent qualities that enable its ongoing existence within the often turbulent flow of everyday life and its enduring resilience to the forces of changing contemporary contexts, even when it might appear to be threatened by the process. These are qualities that may, however, be overlooked, with potentially fatal consequences unless there is a strong grasp of the "problem," which Nagel suggests is imperative in order to recognize "what can or cannot in principle be understood by certain existing methods."[5]

---

3. Nagel, *View from Nowhere*, 209.
4. Nagel, *View from Nowhere*, 209.
5. Nagel, *Mind and Cosmos*, 3–4.

UNDERSTANDING THE PROBLEMS

Identifying and understanding the problems that may inhibit the search for an intelligible, systematic understanding of a universe that is somehow prone to generating life and mind[6] has been a driving force in the Nagel's work for over forty years. Initially majoring in physics, he soon turned to philosophy after the realization that it better suited his aim of discovering "whether there was such a thing as objective reality."[7] In the preface to his first collection of essays, *Mortal Questions*, he describes his central interest and motivation as the understanding of the place of subjectivity in an objective world: "the point of view of individual human life and the problem of its relation to more impersonal conceptions of reality."[8] In a complex world of both feelings and facts, he identified an important concern of philosophy as the understanding and living of mortal life amidst the "absurdity" of the two inescapable but colliding viewpoints of the subjective and the objective that arise from the capacity for self-transcendence.[9] He addresses the difficulties of reconciling these two viewpoints more fully in *The View from Nowhere* but admits in the introduction that it contains "a great deal of speculation about the world and how we fit in to it" as "the methods needed to understand ourselves do not yet exist."[10]

The high probability that Nagel would not consider biblical narrative as a possible method for understanding ourselves and contributing to an intelligible, systematic understanding "about the world and how we fit in to it," raises a significant problem for both biblical hermeneutics and Christian doctrine as their intelligibility and subsequent relevance or value are increasingly questioned. How well this problem is understood may, however, be the more significant hermeneutical issue that Nagel's thinking inadvertently raises and offers insight into. This is through his

---

6. Nagel, *Mind and Cosmos*, 3, 127.

7. Nagel, *Other Minds*, 4.

8. Nagel, *Mortal Questions*, xii. Nagel will later argue that our understanding of ourselves must be part of our understanding of the world of which we form a part (see Nagel, *Last Word*, 74) and that the mind-body problem goes beyond the relation between mind, brain and behavior to invade "our understanding of the entire cosmos and its history" (Nagel, *Mind and Cosmos*, 3).

9. Nagel argues that this absurdity is one of the most human things about us and describes its main condition as "the dragooning of an unconvinced transcendent consciousness into the service of an immanent, limited enterprise like a human life" (Nagel, *Mortal Questions*, 22).

10. Nagel, *View from Nowhere*, 10.

work displaying, both directly and indirectly, an ongoing resistance to, and consequent attempt to raise awareness of, presumptive approaches to complex epistemological concepts, such as understanding, explanation, meaning, belief, and truth; approaches that he believes "miss the real problem" and, in using "limited materials" to find solutions, reflect "an impatience with demands for rigor."[11] Amidst the gathering momentum of rapidly developing information and communication technologies, he has continually opposed what he recognized as a growing trend towards a "solutionism" which, in setting the resolution of problems as its primary goal, fails to have a strong enough grasp of the problem and is presumptive rather than investigative in its approach.[12] He therefore placed himself in a potentially adversarial position early in his career by admitting that he does not offer solutions to the problems that he identifies as he does not regard this as the role of philosophy. This stance was based on his belief that the deepest and oldest philosophical problems may have no solutions but only show us the limits of our understanding.[13] He would later expand on this:

> The search for a physicalistic understanding of the mental is due to a natural human weakness: the desire for closure—to reach a solution using the tools available before one departs from the scene—and a refusal to recognize that we are at an early stage in the progress of human understanding.[14]

For Nagel, "it is certain forms of perplexity—about freedom, knowledge, the meaning of life—that embody more insight then supposed solutions."[15] His work has consequently maintained an ongoing focus on what he believes to be the often neglected task of establishing a deeper understanding of the epistemological issues at the heart of the problems;

---

11. Nagel sees this occurring in the reductive attempts of philosopher Daniel Dennett to explain consciousness. See Nagel, *Other Minds*, 87.

12. In 2012, Evgeny Morozov used the term "solutionism" to represent an ideology that has "an unhealthy preoccupation with sexy, monumental, and narrow-minded solutions—the kind of stuff that wows audiences at TED Conferences—to problems that are extremely complex, fluid, and contentious." He cites design theorist Michael Dobbins in stating that "solutionism presumes rather than investigates the problems that it is trying to solve, reaching 'for the answer before the questions have been fully asked.' How problems are composed matters every bit as much as how problems are resolved" (Morozov, *To Save Everything*, 6).

13. Nagel, *Mortal Questions*, xi.

14. Nagel, "Analytic Philosophy."

15. Nagel, *View from Nowhere*, 4.

issues which need to be addressed before any solution can be sought. He reiterates this belief in *Mind and Cosmos* stating that "all that can be done at this stage in the history of science is to argue for recognition of the problem, not the solution."[16] Without this recognition and deeper understanding there is the likelihood of not only using the wrong tools to find answers but also formulating questions to either suit the tools at hand or fit existing solutions, with the potential danger of ignoring or suppressing the questions that refuse any such reshaping.[17]

ASKING THE RIGHT QUESTIONS

In the mid-twentieth century, Heisenberg suggested that in order to progress with quantum mechanics, physicists had to learn to ask the right questions. It is a suggestion that is endorsed over fifty years later by physicist and theologian John Polkinghorne who describes this as "one of the greatest gifts that a scientist can possess" requiring "a sense of what is significant and attainable at a particular time in the development of a subject."[18] For Heisenberg, these were questions about the strange apparent contradictions between the results of different atomic experiments leading him to conclude that "asking the right questions is frequently more than halfway to the solution of the problem."[19] The impact of materialist reductionism has led, however, to what Nagel describes as an accompanying scientism which assumes that "the natural sciences, mathematics, and logic both define the questions that it makes sense to ask and provide the only methods of true understanding, whatever the subject matter." It is an assumption that he suggests is "an obstacle to full understanding of ourselves" as it "limits the capacity to explore seriously questions of value of all kinds."[20] If, therefore, as Nagel suggests, objectivity is not reality but "only one way of understanding it,"[21] the "right" questions to address to biblical narrative may not be those emerging from modern historical criticism concerning its objective factual content and relating to the perceived issue of whether and where the labels of history

---

16. Nagel, *Mind and Cosmos*, 33.
17. Nagel, *Other Minds*, 87.
18. Polkinghorne, *Quantum Physics and Theology*, 28.
19. Heisenberg, *Physics and Philosophy*, 38.
20. Nagel, "Analytic Philosophy."
21. Nagel, "Limits of Objectivity," 90.

or fiction can be applied. As Northrop Frye points out, the Bible's answer to this question "is a curiously quizzical one; so quizzical that there must be something wrong with the either-or way of formulating it."[22] For Frye, there is not only no clear boundary line in the narratives between what might be identified as the "obviously legendary" and the "possibly historical" but also an "exuberant repudiation of everything we are accustomed to think of as historical evidence" leading him to conclude that, "perhaps we should be looking for different categories and criteria altogether."[23]

The advent of a literary approach, focusing on treating the biblical text as a whole,[24] has provided a significant challenge to the dominance of what Robert Alter terms "atomistic" critical approaches which have been principally occupied with taking narratives apart. He suggests that this has been the result of a hidden imperative, "the more atomistic, the more scientific," leading to a focus on "dissected elements" of the text; a focus that he describes as a "nervous hovering over its various small components," with the consequent discovery of "discontinuities, contradictions, duplications and fissures."[25] In this respect, biblical narrative appears to have become the victim of not only a reductive approach but also one that appears to be presumptive rather than investigative. This is an approach which, in experiencing discomfort with the seeming perplexity of a biblical perspective of freedom, knowledge, value, and the meaning of life, turns to a potentially premature solutionism in the search for insight. The "right" question emerging from Alter's observations may, therefore, concern how the narrative might be read in a way that is not focused primarily on "sorting out its components, reconstructing it, and looking for some textual or historical reality that lies behind the text we have"[26] in order to establish its meaning.

---

22. As the text itself often frustrates a search for a context of descriptive accuracy. Frye, *Great Code*, 39, 62.

23. Frye, *Great Code*, 40–42.

24. As "finished texts without regard to their composite origins or prior recensions" (Kugel, "On the Bible," 218). Kugel lists the other three senses in which literary criticism is currently used as source criticism (analysis in terms of original sources or documents and the various redactions these documents went through); form criticism (isolating the Bible's significant literary units and establishing the conventions governing their form); and the application of "the tools of literary analysis" to biblical criticism. He also points out that it can be argued that the Bible has been read as literature, "according to the norms of secular texts," since Greek and Roman times and as a human text in addition to or as opposed to Scripture since the sixteenth century (217–18).

25. Alter, *World*, 70.

26. Alter, *World*, 1.

It is perhaps symptomatic of increasing epistemological overlap between seemingly conflicting disciplines[27] that the answer to this question might be initiated in the discipline of physics and the words of Heisenberg suggesting that to progress with quantum mechanics, physicists had to learn not only how to ask the right questions but also how "to get into the spirit of quantum theory."[28] It is a suggestion that raises the potentially provocative issue of whether there is a contemporary need to learn how to re-enter "into the spirit" of biblical narrative to understand the unique nature of both its truth claims and the language that is used to articulate them. This is an issue concerning the perplexity arising from its seemingly audacious and outlandish truth claims if its language is perceived to be literal in the sense of referring to an historical reality behind the text. It is a perception that has taken a considerable battering by the forces of logical positivism, with its emphasis on a generally univocal approach to language and scientifically verified depiction of reality.[29] A literary approach that does not presume that the pre-scientific and often historically unverifiable biblical narratives are now epistemologically redundant has, therefore, considerable appeal but it may, however, make its own presumptions in bracketing "the question of history, not necessarily out of indifference to history but because it assumes that factual history is not the primary concern of the text and that it is . . . largely indeterminable, given the scant data."[30]

While there may be "scant data" to substantiate factual history, this assumption appears to be at odds with the proclivity of the text for historical pointers. These are frequently seen in the genealogies, the experiences of the prophets and the eye-witness accounts of the apostles, declaring, "*This Jesus God raised up, and of that all of us are witnesses*" (Acts 2:32); "*We did not follow cleverly devised myths when we made known to you the power and coming of our Lord Jesus Christ, but we had been eyewitnesses of his majesty*" (2 Peter 1:16); "*We declare to you what was from the beginning, what we have heard, what we have seen with our eyes, what we have looked at and touched with our hands, concerning the word of life*" (1 John 1:1). An emerging and potentially key question therefore concerns how it might

---

27. A conflict accentuated by Enlightenment epistemology, within which science and Christianity appeared to be increasingly incompatible.

28. Heisenberg, *Physics and Philosophy*, 38.

29. Stiver, *Philosophy of Religious*, 6.

30. Alter, *World*, 203.

be possible to re-enter what Barth described as the "strange new world"[31] of the narratives in order to encounter a biblical perspective and implication of this "word of life;" a world and word that might require both the suspension of the often pressed question of whether the narratives should be interpreted as history, myth or fictional story and a renewed focus on identifying the epistemological foundations upon which the narratives are constructed. For Barth, the "paramount question" is "whether we have understanding for this different new world, or good will enough to meditate and enter upon it inwardly"; to enter into a wholly new world of God containing a "history with its own distinct grounds, possibilities and hypotheses" and projecting itself into our old ordinary world.[32] In this sense, Barth can acknowledge that the Bible may be full of multiple forms of human history that include religious, literary, cultural, and world history but also claim that it resists the questions of *how* events happened, *what* the causes were and *why* they occurred, by responding to them "at the most decisive points of its history," with "silences quite unparalleled."[33] He consequently concludes that

> the presumed equation of the Word of God with a "historical" record is an inadmissible postulate which does not itself originate in the Bible at all but in the unfortunate habit of Western thought which assumes that the reality of a history stands or falls by whether it is "history". . . . as the witness of God's true Word, the Bible is forced to speak also in the form of saga precisely because its object and origin are what they are, i.e., not just "historical" but also frankly "nonhistorical."[34]

In this respect, it is, therefore, in Alter's words a "peculiar literature"[35] that makes unique demands of its readers or hearers[36] by presenting narratives in which, according to Meir Sternberg, the dichotomy between fact and fiction appears to be suspended,[37] with the consequence that the

---

31. Barth, "Strange New World," 33.
32. Barth, "Strange New World," 37.
33. Barth, "Strange New World," 36.
34. Barth, *Church Dogmatics*, 82.
35. This is the title of his first chapter and relates to the peculiar circumstances of the text's composition and evolution, its peculiar aims and objects of representation. See Alter, *World*, 1–24.
36. Frye describes it as "more" than a work of literature as it "both disregards and exhibits unity evading all literary criteria" (Frye, *Great Code*, xvi).
37. Sternberg, *Poetics*, 46.

idea that "history-writing is wedded to and fiction-writing opposed to factual truth . . . forms a category mistake of the first order."[38] If this is correct, a response to these textual demands that respects the reader's corresponding demands for intelligibility in the form of conceptual coherence, may need to begin in an investigation of the nature of language which, in the words of Nagel, "is often the best place to begin when clarifying our most important concepts."[39]

THE ACQUISITION OF LANGUAGE

To acquire a language is in part to acquire a system of concepts that enables us to understand reality.[40]

Nagel describes the acquisition of language as an important aspect in explaining our ability to distinguish between appearance and reality and "the existence of objective factual or practical truth that goes beyond what perception, appetite, and emotion tell us." It also facilitates the possibility of forms of "interpersonal communication, justification and criticism"[41] that are not limited to basic forms of perception, appetite, and emotion as language develops to articulate reality beyond the world of appearances. It is a development that can, however, be traced in biblical narrative in which the acquisition of language appears when reality is perceived in its most basic objective form and naming of the animals occurs: "*And whatever the human called a living creature, that was its name. And the human called names to all the cattle and to the fowl of the heavens and to all the beasts of the field*" (Genesis 2:19–20).[42] Dru Johnson describes this act of naming as the "first epistemological act in human history" as God leads the man "through a process of coming to know something, and the man poetically articulates 'something known' only after he discovers it."[43]

---

38. Sternberg states that "history-writing is not a record of fact—of what 'really happened'—but a discourse that claims to be a record of fact. Nor is fiction-writing a tissue of free invention but a discourse that claims freedom of invention. The antithesis lies not in the presence or absence of truth value but of the commitment to truth value" (Sternberg, *Poetics*, 25).

39. Nagel, *Last Word*, 37.

40. Nagel, *Mind and Cosmos*, 73.

41. Nagel, *Mind and Cosmos*, 73.

42. Alter, *Five Books*, 22.

43. Johnson, *Epistemology*, 19. Caird refers to "naming things" as the simplest and

The creation of the second human being then leads to the first recorded human speech as discourse in the sense of a communicative action (Genesis 2:23), but almost immediately another dimension of language appears. This is as the words of a serpent introduce and add the concepts of justification and criticism to initiate an action following the woman's observation that *"the tree was good for eating... lust to the eyes... and... lovely to look at"* (Genesis 3:6).[44] In the terms of J. L. Austin's "speech act" theory, the locutionary act of uttering words is now one of both illocutionary and perlocutionary force[45] as the serpent uses subtle rhetoric to inform but also persuade the woman into a course of action; action that will expose not only the humans' vulnerability, as their eyes are opened to a reality beyond the world of appearances, but also the challenges of articulating this reality in what Nagel terms "ordinary, natural language."

Nagel's philosophical career was formed at the universities of Cornell, Oxford, and Harvard in the analytic tradition, which he describes as having a conspicuous "focus on language, both as a subject of great philosophical importance in itself, and as a path into the philosophical understanding of other topics, from metaphysics to ethics." This included exposure to the writings of Wittgenstein and his emphasis on the root of many philosophical problems being "misunderstandings about the way language functioned;" Austin's focus on the functioning and subtleties of "ordinary, natural language ... in contrast with the oversimplification of general theories expressed in artificial and often obscure vocabulary;" and the systematic, logically based approach to language of W. V. Quine.[46] Without claiming to be a follower of any of these traditions, Nagel has, consequently, developed his work within an analytic framework[47] and a belief that the history of philosophy is

---

most fundamental of all linguistic acts. "To name is to give identity and character, in some sense even to create" (Caird, *Language and Imagery*, 8).

44. Alter, *Five Books*, 24.

45. Austin's theory distinguishes between the locutionary act of uttering words, the illocutionary act of what is done with words as greeting, informing, or instructing, and the perlocutionary act of what is activated by speech in terms of persuading. See Austin, *How to Do*, 94–131.

46. Nagel, "Analytic Philosophy."

47. Nagel highlights three developments of analytic philosophy that have been important influences on his work as "the close connection between philosophy and science," the "great revival of moral, political, and legal philosophy" and "the return to at least partial respectability of *Lebensphilosophie*—philosophical reflection on basic questions of life and death" (Nagel, "Analytic Philosophy").

a continual discovery of problems that baffle existing concepts and existing methods of solution. At every point it faces us with the question of how far beyond the relative safety of our present language we can afford to go without risking complete loss of touch with reality.[48]

The problems emerging in the history of science, as the instruments of modern technology penetrated a quantum world that baffled the existing Newtonian concepts, also raised the issue of the adequacy of what Heisenberg referred to as the "language of daily life."[49] This was because, while the patterns of order within the quantum world could be represented and understood in mathematical forms, they were much more difficult to articulate in ordinary language. In this respect, the question appears to be less about how far we can afford to go beyond this language before losing touch with reality and more about how we might understand and use ordinary language to access reality that is epistemologically confronting, challenging, and confounding in appearing to be beyond what Alter terms human ken.[50] Alter's identification of this issue with the articulation of biblical rather than quantum reality is, therefore, a reminder that the biblical authors were the scientists' precursors in grappling with the nature and limitations of language. There is also, however, a significant hermeneutical challenge for modern epistemology in his suggestion that the literal force of their narrative details might be crucial to the reader and that it is now becoming feasible to think about the "literal meaning" of the Bible[51] as "the life of narrative inheres in the potency of the literal, and also, paradoxically, it is the literal that creates the potential of narrative to mean many things."[52]

THE NATURE OF BIBLICAL LANGUAGE

Frei describes the *sensus literalis* as being "at the heart of the Christian interpretive tradition of its sacred text,"[53] with a strongly realistic reading of the biblical narratives that was both literal and historical being

---

48. Nagel, *View from Nowhere*, 11.
49. Heisenberg, *Across the Frontiers*, 226.
50. Alter, *World*, 23.
51. Alter, *World*, 87–88.
52. Alter, *World*, 106.
53. Frei, *Theology and Narrative*, 113.

preeminent up until the eighteenth century. In a 1976 lecture, he suggested that this was a sense that, for Luther and Calvin, was not "*grammatical*-literal" but "*literary*-literal" as, rather than every word being "the precise name for whatever thing it named . . . breathed directly into the writer by divine inspiration," the words are instead "the right description," neither allegory nor symbol, meaning exactly what they say, with the narratives describing and depicting "precisely what they mean to describe and depict."[54] The impact of the eighteenth-century rise of historical criticism[55] led, however, to what Childs describes as a total commitment to the literal sense in terms of meaning as historical reference; a commitment that in undermining the coherence between the verbal sense and real reference of the text also undermined the integrity of the literal sense.[56] It heralded the beginning of what Frei termed the eclipse of biblical narrative[57] and in a 1983 conference essay suggested that the current hermeneutical theory, in attempting but failing to defend the tradition of the *sensus literalis* in a revised form, was serving only to break literal reading apart.[58] As Garrett Green points out, a legacy of modern epistemology has, subsequently, been that

> from one end of the theological spectrum to the other, virtually all have assumed that taking the stories literally means affirming their historical veracity. For the supernaturalists or fundamentalists, the identification of literal and historical has meant defending the ostensive historical truth of the texts. Theological liberals . . . also assume the identity of literal meaning and historical reference, but they have sought to detach the meaning of texts from their literal-historical sense.[59]

For Frei, reducing biblical narratives to either history[60] or myth and allegory revealing timeless truths and moral lessons, is not simply to eclipse but also to distort the literal sense. This is because their "realistic

---

54. Frei, *Writings from the Archives*, 75.

55. Within which the "goal posts of historical reality moved" (Vanhoozer, *Is There a Meaning*, 306).

56. Childs, "Sensus Literalis," 88–89. See also Fabiny, "Literal Senses."

57. Robinson describes this eclipse as "the dark shadow thrown by questions of truth and accurate reference [which] occluded the biblical narratives" (Robinson "Narrative Theology," 136).

58. Frei, *Theology and Narrative*, 118–19.

59. Green, "Bible As," 79–80.

60. In terms of being an accurate historical source.

character" and "history-likeness" are not "identical with affirming a degree of historical likelihood of the stories."[61] A dependence on historical veracity as an interpretive tool to determine the nature of the texts serves only to confuse

> history-likeness (literal meaning) and history (ostensive reference), and the hermeneutical reduction of the former to an aspect of the latter, meant that one lacked the distinctive category and the appropriate interpretive procedure for understanding ... the high significance of the literal, narrative shape of the stories for their meaning.[62]

The result of this confusion is what Rowan Williams calls a "disastrous shrinkage" in terms of "narrow and sterile definitions of the literal sense"[63] and Vanhoozer refers to as a fatal distortion "condemning interpretation to offering only thin, literalistic descriptions of empirical referents."[64] Vanhoozer distinguishes between an unimaginative and *"empirically minded" literalistic* reading that disregards illocutionary intent and insists on remaining at the "level of ordinary usage, even when another level is intended,"[65] and a *literal* reading that is able to include a figurative sense.[66] In combining historical reference, storied referent and canonical sense as three partial dimensions of the literal sense,[67] he thus defines literal meaning as literate meaning in "the sense of the literary act," with literal interpretation being less "a matter of identifying objects in the world than it is specifying communicative acts—their nature and

---

61. Frei, *Eclipse*, 11–12.

62. Frei, *Eclipse*, 12.

63. Williams refers to Aquinas's insistence on the priority of the literal sense in *Summa Theologiae* 1.10.3 to point out that: "The literal sense is not dependent on a belief that all scriptural propositions uncomplicatedly depict real states of affairs detail by detail; it can and does include metaphor with the literary movement that leads us into the movement of God within the time of human biography. In this way, Thomas sketches an understanding of the literal that allows for a plurality of genres within it" (Williams, "Literal Sense," 123–24).

64. Vanhoozer, *Is There a Meaning*, 308.

65. Vanhoozer, *Is There a Meaning*, 311. See also Hyers, who refers to a literalist "lack of imagination" pervading contemporary culture. Hyers, "Biblical Literalism," 823–27.

66. Citing the Antiochene perspective of John Chrysostom that, "We must not examine the words as bare words, else many absurdities will follow, but we must mark the mind of the writer" (Regina Schwartz in Vanhoozer, *Is There a Meaning*, 117).

67. Vanhoozer, *Is There a Meaning*, 307–9.

their objects."[68] Within this definition, there may, therefore, be a sense of an historical kernel within the biblical narratives but it may function only as the seed from which meaning emerges from the text as a continuously unfolding process that is not static or fixed.[69] In this respect, the tools of philology that have been used to penetrate to this historical kernel and excavate the truth behind the text, discovering in Alter's words "a welter of E, J, P, and D documents, scribal glosses, editorial bridges, redactional revisions, shards, and fragments pasted together from a hundred conjectured ancient sources,"[70] may not be the right tools with which to excavate the meaning of narratives; narratives in which the concept of history is used in a unique way to facilitate their unique perspective of reality. The fifth potential contribution that Nagel's thinking offers to biblical hermeneutics therefore concerns the implications of using the wrong tools and, as new perspectives of reality arise from developing knowledge and the use of increasingly sophisticated technology, the way in which these perspectives might provide new tools. These are tools which are able to avoid the hazards of combining perspectives that appear to be radically distinct but also identify when such combinations might actually be beneficial and able to offer new insight.

---

68. Vanhoozer, *Is There a Meaning*, 304.
69. Fabiny, "Literal Senses," 20–21.
70. Alter, *World*, 192–93.

6

From the Known into the Unknown
Reflection on the Impossible

Humans are addicted to the hope for a final reckoning, but intellectual humility requires that we resist the temptation to assume that the tools of the kind we now have are in principle sufficient to understand the universe as a whole.[1]

Whenever we proceed from the known into the unknown we may hope to understand, but we may have to learn at the same time a new meaning of the word "understanding."[2]

NAGEL ACKNOWLEDGES THAT HIS doubts about the ability of chemical and physical laws to provide a "fully mechanized" explanation of the origin and evolution of life, and his consequent suggestion that some form of teleological principles[3] may be at work within developing natural history, will appear "outrageous" to many who live in a secular and

---

1. Nagel, *Mind and Cosmos*, 3.
2. Heisenberg, *Physics and Philosophy*, 172.
3. As the basis for our identity as "large-scale, complex instances of something both objectively physical from outside and subjectively mental from inside" may pervade the world (Nagel, *Mind and Cosmos*, 42).

scientifically-orientated culture.[4] He believes, however, that the concept of historical understanding that has emerged as a part of science through evolutionary theory and "big bang" cosmology has raised the significant issue of how "mind," as a development of life, can be included in an understanding that has an underlying perspective of a "mindless" universe. This is understanding that Nagel suggests must make two questionable assumptions, the first being that evolving physical systems have supposedly formed from dead matter. The second is that there has been sufficient geological time for an adequate supply of viable mutations that, as a result of chemical accident, have led to complex cognitive capacities such as thought, reasoning, and evaluation;[5] capacities that have enabled humans to "transcend the perspective of the immediate life-world given to us by our senses and instincts, and to explore the larger objective reality of nature and value."[6]

Nagel does not believe that a physically reductive theory can fully explain the generation of these capacities[7] as the difference between the mental and the physical is so great. A significant and potentially radical conceptual shift is therefore necessary to achieve an integrated theory of reality that may require the creation of new concepts.[8] In *The View From Nowhere*, Nagel used the nineteenth-century acceptance of the electromagnetic field as an irreducible feature of physical reality, and the subsequent conceptual shift from the mechanical universe of Newtonian physics, as an example of the need to develop new forms of understanding; a need already acknowledged by Heisenberg as twentieth-century advances in quantum mechanics led physicists further into the realm of

---

4. Nagel, *Mind and Cosmos*, 7.

5. Nagel, *Mind and Cosmos*, 9. Nagel cites Stuart Kauffman, who suggests that variation is not due to chance, with "principles of spontaneous self-organization" playing a more important role in evolutionary history than natural selection. Nagel also refers to Kauffman, *At Home in the Universe*; Kauffman, *Investigations*; and Kauffman, *Reinventing the Sacred*.

6. Nagel, *Mind and Cosmos*, 71. As complex, biologically generated physical systems with rich nonphysical properties. See Nagel, *View from Nowhere*, 51.

7. In terms of the sources of both phenomenological consciousness, that includes sensation, perception and emotion, and what he describes as the "active capacity" of humans to "think our way beyond these starting points" (Nagel, *Mind and Cosmos*, 72).

8. Which Nagel believes to be "at least as radical as relativity theory, the introduction of electromagnetic fields into physics—or the original scientific revolution itself" (Nagel, *Mind and Cosmos*, 42). In *The View from Nowhere*, Nagel describes these as "new types of concepts" that are specifically devised to explain "newly explored phenomena" (52).

the unknown. Nagel believes, however, that the difference between the physical and the mental is even greater than between the mechanical and electrical, leading him to conclude:

> To insist on trying to explain the mind in terms of concepts and theories that have been designed exclusively to explain non-mental phenomena is, in view of the radically distinguishing characteristic of the mental, both intellectually backward and scientifically suicidal ... We need entirely new intellectual tools, and it is precisely by reflection on what appears impossible ... that we will be forced to create such tools.[9]

Nagel's focus is on the seeming impossibility of the recombination of matter to generate mind, but the question could also be raised about whether the biblical writers were also "forced" to create new intellectual tools; tools that were needed to introduce concepts that, while appearing impossible in a secular and scientifically orientated culture, might also have appeared impossible in the context of both ancient Near-Eastern and Classical epistemology. For Nagel, the complexity of the mind-body problem has led him to advocate for both *suspicion* regarding any attempts to solve it with "the concepts and methods developed to account for very different kinds of things," and an *expectation* that "theoretical progress in this area" will require "a major conceptual revolution at least as radical as relativity theory."[10] While there may be debate about whether contemporary interpretation of biblical narrative is a complex problem,[11] it is an advocacy with potentially important hermeneutical considerations in relation to understanding how the biblical writers may have instigated their own major conceptual revolution that remains as radical today as it did in its initial context. The first consideration therefore concerns Nagel's suspicion regarding the use of tools that, while providing a useful starting point for explanation, may also have significant limitations.

---

9. Nagel, *View from Nowhere*, 52.

10. Nagel, *Mind and Cosmos*, 42.

11. In being, for some, a "minefield" of "potentially competing orientations, assumptions and foundations for determining meaning" (Porter and Stovell, "Trajectories," 19). For others, however, it appears to be a "green pasture" of unambiguous clarity as "God's Word makes it plain enough what it is there for and how we may make proper use of it" and requires no supplementation from other disciplines (Linnemann, *Historical Criticism*, 155–56).

USING THE RIGHT TOOLS

The success of a particular form of objectivity in expanding our grasp of some aspects of reality may tempt us to apply the same methods in areas where they will not work, either because those areas require a new kind of objectivity or because they are in some ways irreducibly subjective.[12]

The relevance for biblical hermeneutics of Nagel's concern about the misapplication of intellectual tools, is highlighted by M. D. Hooker's critique of form criticism as a precision tool able to uncover the "authentic" teaching of Jesus, and her questioning of the value of classifying a miracle story or paradigm as such. While acknowledging that it can be a potentially "invaluable" tool,[13] her concern is with tools or critical methods that cannot do what is required of them, and New Testament scholars who, even when recognizing the inadequacy of their tools, "go on, hammering or chiseling away with their pet tools, and using the pieces which are left as the sure foundation on which to erect their edifices."[14] Of equal concern is that they will use whatever tools are available but that, in throwing down one and picking up another, they may be in danger of selecting the tool which fits the desired conclusion resulting from their own presuppositions and prejudices.[15] The increasing awareness in the 1970s of the potential limitations of the tools of historical criticism[16] provoked responses that ranged from Eta Linnemann's impassioned critique and rejection of historical criticism as ideology rather than methodology,[17] to advocates of literary approaches, looking within and beyond rather than

---

12. Nagel, *View from Nowhere*, 87.

13. In attempting "to discover the way in which the material was being used and applied to the life of the community at a time when it came into the written tradition" (Hooker, "On Using," 571).

14. Hooker, "On Using," 578.

15. Hooker, "On Using," 581.

16. When "it came under attack from many different sources, including within the discipline itself" (Bray, *Biblical Interpretation*, 461).

17. A former student of Rudolf Bultmann and Ernst Fuchs, Linnemann was a professor at German universities until a theological *volte-face* led to her renunciation of her previously held approach to the historical-critical method and rejection of and attempts to destroy her previous work.

behind the text.[18] The rise of narrative criticism,[19] as a branch of modern literary criticism that moved away from authorial intention and historical background to an emphasis on poetics, narrative and textual unity, with "all of the elements of the text, even those in tension" contributing to its overall sense,[20] subsequently offered to some an alternative tool but to others a complementary one with the ability to provide important additional insights.

A second hermeneutical consideration arises from Nagel's advocacy of an expectation that "entirely new intellectual tools," in terms of a radical conceptual revolution, may need to be created as a result of "reflection on what appears to be impossible" and outside "the scale of ordinary experience."[21] In an essay published in 1998, Nagel used the conceptual problems of special relativity and quantum theory to explain this need; problems concerning "how to conceive the underlying reality that the theory describes, which is so different from the observed reality that it explains,"[22] which he relates to the conceptual problems regarding the mind-body problem. In making this association between the problems of two seemingly very different disciplines which both appear to require radical conceptual revolution, a hermeneutical question emerges. This concerns whether the conceptual tools developed to articulate an invisible quantum reality that cannot be grasped intuitively by the human imagination, may offer insights into a contemporary approach to interpreting the apparent impossibility of a biblical perspective of reality; a perspective that also introduces what Nagel describes as "concepts of space, time, and the relation between observed and unobserved states of affairs that diverge radically from the intuitive concepts that we all use in thinking about our surroundings."[23] It is an approach that can, however, only be undertaken in light of the suspicion raised by Nagel concerning the use of "concepts and methods developed to account for very different

---

18. Taking a synchronic approach in ascertaining how characters and actions fit together in the time frame of the narrative as a unified whole rather than a diachronic approach determining how the various sources, forms, traditions and redactions of the narratives have developed through time. See Spencer, "Literary/Postmodern View," 49–50.

19. Developing from a hermeneutical tradition that "focused on the text as an autonomous means of transmitting meaning" (Porter and Stovell, "Trajectories," 17).

20. Porter and Stovell, "Trajectories," 17.

21. Nagel, *Concealment and Exposure*, 172.

22. Nagel, *Concealment and Exposure*, 172.

23. Nagel, *Concealment and Exposure*, 171.

kinds of things" and the hazards of combining perspectives that are radically distinct; issues that are highlighted in his review of physicists and philosophers of science Alan Sokal and Jean Bricmont's critique of the misuse of scientific concepts and terminology in their book, *Fashionable Nonsense: Postmodern Intellectuals' Abuse of Science*.[24]

USING THE WRONG TOOLS

In 1996, Sokal submitted a hoax article to the American cultural-studies journal *Social Text*. The article, entitled "Transgressing the Boundaries: Toward a Transformative Hermeneutics of Quantum Gravity," was a parody of postmodernism[25] and social constructivism, containing "absurdities and blatant non-sequiturs" and asserting "an extreme form of cognitive relativism."[26] The parody was constructed around quotations from eminent intellectuals in both France and the United States about the alleged philosophical and social implications of mathematics and the natural sciences to which "whimsical glue" was applied to join them together.[27] The follow-up book, written in collaboration with Bricmont, aimed to draw attention to what the authors believe to be the repeated, if often clever, abuse of concepts and terminology emerging from mathematics and physics. This related to the misuse of scientific terminology in contexts beyond their validity, the extrapolation of concepts from the natural sciences into the humanities or social sciences without conceptual or empirical justification,[28] and a fondness for the most subjectivist writings of Heisenberg and Bohr, interpreted in a radical way that goes far beyond their own views.[29] This is, therefore, abuse that, in too often displaying "a superficial erudition by shamelessly throwing around technical terms in a context where they are completely irrelevant," simply

---

24. Sokal and Bricmont, *Fashionable Nonsense*.

25. Defined as "an intellectual current characterized by the more-or-less explicit rejection of the rationalist tradition of the Enlightenment, by theoretical discourses disconnected from any empirical test, and by a cognitive and cultural relativism that regards science as nothing more than a 'narration,' a 'myth' or a social construction among many others" (Sokal and Bricmont, *Fashionable Nonsense*, 1).

26. Sokal and Bricmont, *Fashionable Nonsense*, 1–2.

27. Sokal and Bricmont, *Fashionable Nonsense*, 3.

28. Sokal and Bricmont, *Fashionable Nonsense*, 4.

29. Sokal and Bricmont, *Fashionable Nonsense*, 261.

exploits the prestige of the natural sciences,[30] provoking Nagel to hope that

> incompetents who pontificate about science as a social phenomenon without understanding the first thing about its content are on the way out and that they may one day be as rare as deaf music critics.[31]

Sokal and Bricmont do, however, offer criteria for a legitimate use of scientific concepts which include, having a genuine and relevant intellectual goal in mind, a good understanding of the science that is being applied and justification of its relevance, making no "gross mistakes," and providing a clear explanation of technical notions that is understandable to the intended reader.[32] With these in mind it may, therefore, be possible to extrapolate some of the concepts and terminology associated with quantum theory for hermeneutical endeavor and avoid the hazards of what Gell-Mann, refers to as a "flurry of flapdoodle"[33] and Polkinghorne describes as

> the disagreeable appearance of trying to appeal to . . . quantum hype—the invocation of the peculiar character of quantum thinking as if that were sufficient licence for lazy indulgence in playing with paradox in other disciplines . . . the strangenesses encountered at different levels of reality have characters that are idiosyncratic to those levels, and no facile kind of direct transfer is possible between physics and theology.[34]

While Polkinghorne therefore rejects the label "Quantum Theology" he does, however, acknowledge that there is an "unexpected kinship" between quantum physics and theology particularly in the area of paradox and the difficulty of reconciling the seemingly irreconcilable dualities that appear in both disciplines. In discussing the quest to understand the New Testament phenomena that led to an incarnational understanding of the presence of both divine and human natures in Christ[35] he makes

---

30. Sokal and Bricmont, *Fashionable Nonsense*, 5.

31. Nagel, *Concealment and Exposure*, 163.

32. Sokal and Bricmont, *Fashionable Nonsense*, 9.

33. Resulting from the misappropriation of quantum theory. See Gell-Mann, *Quark*, 172.

34. Polkinghorne, *Quantum Physics & Theology*, ix.

35. In 451 CE, the Council of Chalcedon defined the unity of two distinct natures in the incarnation which "concur" into one *prosopon* or "appearance" and one *hypostasis* or "underlying entity," thus proclaiming Jesus Christ to be one individual reality who is

a comparison with physicist Richard Feynman's reference to atomic behavior as a phenomenon

> which is impossible, *absolutely* impossible, to explain in any classical way, and which has in it the heart of quantum mechanics. In reality it contains the *only* mystery. We cannot make the mystery go away by "explaining" how it works. We will just *tell* you how it works.[36]

This is a "telling" that, in being related to seemingly irreducible mystery, demands the adoption of "new and unanticipated ways of thought"[37] as physicists attempt to distinguish between empirical and ontological reality[38] and to understand the ontological flexibility of the quantum world; ways of thought that include concepts such as the superposition principle which, in asserting the counterintuitive formulation of quantum states,[39] is able to dissolve the paradox of wave/particle duality by revealing the intrinsic indefiniteness of wave functions which express only "present potentiality rather than persistent actuality."[40] In replacing Newtonian clarity with Heisenberg uncertainty,[41] they are ways of thought that appear to be at odds with the Christian sense of conviction and certainty that emerges from texts such as Luke 1:4; John 17:7–8; Romans 8:38 and Hebrews 11:1. In attempting to articulate mystery that resists physical explanation, it is thinking that raises, however, two potentially important considerations for hermeneutical endeavor.

This is firstly, in relation to whether there might be an ontological flexibility within a biblical perspective of the world that enables rather than threatens Christian conviction and certainty and, secondly, in relation to how this flexibility is manifest; how biblical testimony and particularly biblical narrative might be interpreted as an often counterintuitive form

---

both "truly divine" and "truly human" (Need, *Truly Divine*, 93–107).

36. Feynman in Polkinghorne, *Quantum Physics & Theology*, 18.

37. Polkinghorne, *Quantum Physics & Theology*, 18.

38. French philosopher and quantum theorist Bernard d'Espagnat refers to empirical reality as "the set of phenomena, that is, the totality of what human experience, seconded by science, yields access to" and ontological reality as "the notion referred to when 'what exists independently of our existence' is thought of or alluded to" (d'Espagnat, *On Physics*, 4).

39. By "adding together, in a mathematically well-defined way, physical possibilities that Newtonian physics and common sense would hold to be absolutely incapable of mixing with each other" (Polkinghorne, *Quantum Physics*, 18).

40. Polkinghorne, *Quantum Physics*, 92.

41. Polkinghorne, *Faith, Science*, 18.

of discourse that also resists generic categorization in order to introduce a new perspective of reality. This is a formulation that, in dissolving the paradox of history/fiction duality, is not reductive in being dependent on persistent actuality but is able to be open to the present potentiality of narrative that exhibits history-like and fiction-like behavior[42] while resisting the constraints of being labeled as *either* essentially history *or* fiction. In this respect, while quantum physics does not provide a new tool for biblical hermeneutics, it may provide the conceptual means to develop a tool that is able to meet, not only the needs of the twenty-first-century interpreter whose epistemology has been shaped by reductive materialism, but also "the need of the material";[43] a material that, in similar fashion to quantum physics, presents a reality that demands to be met on its own terms[44] as, in the words of Polkinghorne, there is

> no universal epistemology applicable to all entities. They can only be known in a manner that conforms to their actual and individual natures. Different kinds of entities can be expected to be knowable in different kinds of ways.[45]

CREATING A NEW TOOL TO ENABLE A NEW FORM OF UNDERSTANDING

Realism is most compelling when we are forced to recognize the existence of something which we cannot describe or know fully, because it lies beyond the reach of language, proof or evidence, or empirical understanding.[46]

Nagel's commitment to realism[47] has led him to his belief in a "strong sense" of the world extending beyond the reach of our minds, with our understanding not only limited to what we can "know" but also in

---

42. Barbour points out: "We do not say that an electron is both a wave and a particle, but only that it exhibits wavelike and particle-like behavior" (Barbour, *Religion and Science*, 170).

43. Mettinger, *Eden Narrative*, xi.

44. Polkinghorne, *Faith, Science*, 7.

45. Polkinghorne, *Faith, Science*, 15.

46. Nagel, *View from Nowhere*, 108.

47. Defined as "the view that the world is independent of our minds" (Nagel, *View from Nowhere*, 90).

relation to what we can "conceive."⁴⁸ It is a strong sense that is, however, also evident in the biblical book of Job in which God's response from the whirlwind exposes the limits of human understanding. Beginning with the question, *"Where were you when I founded earth?"* and the challenge to, *"Tell, if you know understanding"* (Job 38:4), the highly poetic series of questions that follow, relentlessly challenge the extent of not only human knowledge about the natural order but also our conceptual ability. While we may now know much about this order and the effect on earth of the *"laws of the heavens"* (Job 38:33) in terms of astronomical laws, our knowledge and understanding of *"the way that light dwells"* and *"the place of darkness"* (Job 38: 19) remain limited and conceptually challenging. This is as we have become aware that it is a "way" that includes the dwelling and distribution of ancient light that has been traveling for over 13 billion years through a universe in which only 4.9 percent is currently visible matter; 68.3 percent is dark energy that, according to NASA, currently remains "a complete mystery," and 26.8 percent⁴⁹ is apophatic dark matter about which we are currently "much more certain" about what it *is not* than about what it is.⁵⁰

Over two millennia after the book of Job was written,⁵¹ there remains, therefore, despite, and in some ways because of, developments in scientific knowledge, an ambiguity about reality that resonates with what Stephen Prickett describes as an intrinsic indefiniteness in biblical narrative; narrative that he suggests does not convey its own frame of reference to allow the reader to know whether it is "fact" or "fiction."⁵² In this respect, it is narrative that appears to demand a tolerance of ambiguity which also appears to have been forced upon scientific endeavor. Prickett uses the account of Elijah on Horeb (1 Kings 19) as an example of an event "of such complexity and mystery that it resists translation into any of our preconceived categories or disciplines (as it resisted Elijah's own)."⁵³ It is an account that is enigmatic and puzzling as no answers are given to what might appear to be "'obvious' circumstantial and naturalistic

---

48. Nagel, *View from Nowhere*, 90.

49. According to data from the Planck satellite in 2013 (Amos, "Planck Telescope").

50. See "Building Blocks" (italics added).

51. Most scholars appear to place the majority of the book, if not its final form, between the seventh and fourth centuries BCE. See Coogan, *New Oxford Annotated Bible*, 726.

52. Prickett, *Words*, 8.

53. Prickett, *Words*, 242.

questions"[54] and Prickett is, therefore, critical of modern translations of the "mysteriously suggestive Hebrew" that reduce it to either an implicitly natural *or* supernatural reading.[55] In similar fashion, Alter refers to an "unacknowledged heresy" that he believes underlies "most modern English translations of the Bible"; a heresy manifest in "the use of translation as a vehicle for *explaining* the Bible instead of representing it in another language."[56] This is translation that ignores the "strangeness" of Hebrew narrative prose; prose that cultivates "certain profound and haunting enigmas" and delights in "leaving its audiences guessing about motives and connections," setting "ambiguities of word choice and image against one another in an endless interplay that resists neat resolution."[57] He consequently claims that the impulse of the philologist in search of clarity of meaning serves only "'to disambiguate' the terms of the text"[58] reducing and simplifying it and thereby narrowing its potential vision of reality; a vision that, regardless of the cultural context that it is projected into, will challenge the current boundaries of the thinkable.

In this respect, the creation of a new hermeneutical tool requires an understanding of both what the terms of the biblical text might be and of how these terms might be realized in the context of twenty-first-century epistemology; terms that, while emerging out of and retaining a potentially vital connection to the "strangeness" of Hebrew narrative prose, developed further in the Hellenistic world of the New Testament to enable the articulation of Barth's "strange new world within the Bible." It is a world that he suggests "meets the lover of history with silences quite unparalleled,"[59] but it is a world that also appears to meet the lover of science in similar fashion. This is a silence that Barth attributes to its content as history with a "strong wrapping of saga" and also "a good deal of saga with historical wrappings," but "little pure 'history' and little pure saga, and little of both that can be unequivocally recognized as the one or the other as the two elements are usually mixed."[60] In a similar sense Barr

---

54. Prickett, *Words*, 6.

55. Prickett, *Words*, 8. Citing translations that endeavor to "use language that is natural, clear, simple and unambiguous" (*Good News Bible*, viii).

56. Warning that "in the most egregious instances this amounts to explaining away the Bible" (Alter, *Five Books*, xix).

57. Alter, *Five Books*, xviii.

58. Alter, *Five Books*, xviii.

59. Barth, "Strange New World," 36.

60. Barth, *Church Dogmatics*, 81–82.

refers to "biblical story" which is neither simply the reporting of history nor fictional story with no historical contact. It is rather a tangential relationship in which biblical story functions as "a spiral which runs back and forward across history, sometimes touching it or coinciding with it" but without revealing how close or far apart they might be.[61] If both are correct in suggesting that this is a mixing that resists disentanglement, the question arises of whether and how biblical narrative, in having properties of both history and fiction but resisting reduction to either, might present its own unique terms for interpretation. The particle and wave properties of light led Einstein to state:

> There seems no likelihood of forming a consistent description of the phenomena of light by a choice of only one of two possible languages. It seems as though we must use sometimes the one theory and sometimes the other, while at times we may use either. We are faced with a new kind of difficulty. We have two contradictory pictures of reality; separately neither of them fully explains the phenomena of light, but together they do![62]

The interpretation of the "phenomena" of biblical narrative that appear to resist reduction to either the language of history or fiction may, therefore, benefit from the conceptual developments in quantum theory and astrophysics although not perhaps in the way expected by reductive interpretive enterprises such as the Jesus Seminar continuing the quest for the historical Jesus;[63] a seminar and subsequent book that were driven by the belief that historical knowledge is "an indispensable part of the modern world's basic 'reality toolkit'" and that "the Christ of creed and dogma . . . can no longer command the assent of those who have seen the heavens through Galileo's telescope."[64]

---

61. Barr, "Some Thoughts," 65–66.

62. Einstein and Infeld, *Evolution of Physics*, 263.

63. Two significant contributions to this quest are David Friedrich Strauss's *The Life of Jesus, Critically Examined* (1835) and Albert Schweitzer's *The Quest of the Historical Jesus* (1906).

64. Funk and Hoover, *Five Gospels*, 2. The aim of the seminar and subsequent book was to discover the "authentic" voice of Jesus by color-coding and classifying the words attributed to an "enigmatic sage from Nazareth" from whom the gospel writers would create "an imaginative theological construct"; writers whose faith had "overpowered their memories" (Funk and Hoover, *Five Gospels*, 4).

SHEDDING LIGHT: VISIONS OF THE HEAVENS

The refracting telescope designed by Galileo in the early seventeenth century enabled the observation of astronomical targets that were visible within its magnification factor of twenty. Over four hundred years later, the HARMONI (High Angular Resolution Monolithic Optical and Near-infrared Integral field spectrograph) project is heading towards completion as one of the "first-light instruments" for the Extremely Large Telescope (ELT); a reflecting telescope that will enable the observation of "an astronomical target in four thousand different wavelengths simultaneously."[65] On December 25, 2021, the infrared James Webb Space Telescope was launched on a course to the second Lagrangian point in space, 1.5 million kilometers away from the earth, to start its orbit around the Sun. Designed as a successor to the Hubble Telescope[66] and searching for the first galaxies to form in the universe, it will "look to longer wave-lengths" in order to examine more distant objects whose light has been pushed from optical and ultraviolet wavelengths into the near-infrared.[67] This is, therefore, a vision of "the heavens" that is looking *back* in time and while it indicates great progress in cosmology it may not be the best analogy with which to invalidate a forward-pointing Christ of creed and doctrine emerging from the biblical text. Ricoeur refers to the new worlds that open up in *front* of a narrative text when a hermeneutical approach adopts a broader concept of truth than one within which "true" history with a direct referential claim and "fictional" story with an indirect referential claim are opposed.[68] For Ricoeur, it is both the telling of stories *and* the writing of history that provides shape to what would otherwise remain "chaotic, obscure and mute"[69] and it is, therefore, in the interweaving of history and fiction and the non-ostensive referential

---

65. The ELT, situated over three thousand meters above sea level on top of Cerro Armazones in the Atacama Desert of northern Chile, will be the largest optical telescope with a main mirror thirty-nine meters in diameter. See "Latest Step."

66. Orbiting the Earth from a distance of five hundred and seventy kilometers.

67. As the universe expands and the space between objects stretches, causing them to move away from each other, the light also stretches with its wavelengths becoming longer and reaching us as infrared light. The instruments on Hubble can observe a small portion of the infrared spectrum from 0.8 to 2.5 microns, but its primary capabilities are in the ultra-violet and visible parts of the spectrum from 0.1 to 0.8 microns. See "Webb vs Hubble."

68. Ricoeur, *Ricoeur Reader*, 116.

69. Ricoeur, *Ricoeur Reader*, 115. See also Stiver, *Ricoeur and Theology*, 16.

function of the narrative text that new worlds are opened up in front of, rather than behind, the text.

While an historical perspective may be an important and even indispensable part of the modern world's basic hermeneutical toolkit for the interpretation of a biblical perspective of reality, it might, therefore, be important to consider Nagel's concluding comment in *Mind and Cosmos* that decisive proof or refutation are not always the most credible form of progress.[70] Acknowledging how little we "really understand" about the world, he suggests that a "radical departure from familiar forms of naturalistic explanation"[71] might be needed. It is a departure that, in exploring imaginative alternatives, is able to extend the boundaries of the thinkable and it is here that the possibility appears to emerge for the creation of a tripartite hermeneutical approach that, while new in some respects, is also an inherent part of biblical narrative. It is an approach that is, therefore, able to incorporate Nagel's "expansionist" revision of existing concepts; a revision that is able to include "most of the features of the old concept but puts them in a relation to one another and to other features that is new, and that makes it possible to see or explore further connections."[72] These are connections emerging from features of the unfolding quantum world; features indicating that from the perspective of both quantum and biblical depictions of reality, "the last word" regarding where understanding and justification come to an end[73] may come not from physics but rather from the poetic, as in the words of Annie Dillard:

> I cannot cause light; the most I can do is try to put myself in the path of its beam. It is possible, in deep space, to sail on solar wind. Light, be it particle or wave, has force: you rig a giant sail and go. The secret of seeing is to sail on solar wind. Hone and spread your spirit till you yourself are a sail, whetted, translucent, broadside to the merest puff.[74]

---

70. Nagel, *Mind and Cosmos*, 127.
71. Nagel, *Mind and Cosmos*, 127.
72. Nagel, "Conceiving the Impossible," 341.
73. In terms of either "objective principles whose validity is independent of our point of view" or "within our point of view . . . so that ultimately, even the apparently most objective and universal principles derive their validity or authority from the perspective and practice of those who follow them" (Nagel, *Last Word*, 3).
74. Dillard, *Pilgrim*, 38.

7

No Way Back
A Hermeneutic of Radical Departure from the Familiar

In the present climate of a dominant scientific naturalism . . . I would like to extend the boundaries of what is not regarded as unthinkable, in light of how little we really understand about the world. . . . However, I am certain that my own attempt to explore alternatives is far too unimaginative. An understanding of the universe as basically prone to generate life and mind will probably require a much more radical departure from the familiar forms of naturalistic explanation than I am at present able to conceive.[1]

THE FIVE INSIGHTS EXTRAPOLATED from Nagel's thinking about contemporary epistemology, are precursors to a hermeneutical framework that he inadvertently offers at the end of *Mind and Cosmos*; a framework for a tripartite hermeneutic that is based on the concepts of radical departure from familiar forms of naturalistic explanation, exploring imaginative alternatives, and extending the boundaries of the thinkable. Foundational to this framework is his skepticism about the assumptions of an epistemological climate currently dominated by scientific naturalism and materialist reductionism, which offers a partial explanation of perceptions

1. Nagel, *Mind and Cosmos*, 127.

of incompatibility between religious concepts and contemporary epistemology. His suggestion of a "fear of religion" from which "a defensive world-flattening reductionism"[2] has emerged, adds an additional consideration for hermeneutical endeavor. This is regarding interpretive approaches that appear to have fallen prey to a defensive reductionist impulse in offering apologetic responses to manifestations of this "fear"; responses that can be found at both ends of the theological spectrum when biblical narrative is reduced to specific genres and categorized in a way that may serve only to violate the text by restricting its potential for meaning. His focus on the ongoing mystery of both *mind* and *cosmos* has led him to consider the potential limits of both knowledge and conceptual ability. These are limits that present significant challenges to the identification and articulation of what he calls the "true extent of reality" in a world that is independent of, and extends beyond, the reach of our minds. He consequently believes that understanding the nature of this world will require the recognition of both "what can and cannot in principle be understood by certain existing methods" and the significant "hazards" that arise when perspectives that may be radically distinct are combined. He therefore offers a potentially important warning about the issue of solutionism and the implications of using the wrong tools in its pursuit, suggesting that alternative forms of understanding are needed as new perspectives of reality arise from the developing knowledge made possible by the use of increasingly sophisticated technology.

A hermeneutical challenge arising from Nagel's thinking is, therefore, to discover the tools that this developing knowledge may offer to enable the construction of a contemporary interpretive approach to biblical narrative that is able to function with integrity within the current epistemological climate. This is integrity that respects the tension between the critical consciousness that has emerged from this climate, and a biblical perspective of reality that appears to demand independence from it. This is by presenting narratives that Auerbach describes as seeking to overcome the reality of the reader or hearer, drawing them into its world as "elements in its structure of universal history."[3] The challenge for the contemporary reader or hearer of these narratives is, therefore, considerable as, in the words of Nagel:

---

2. Nagel, *Secular Philosophy*, 25.

3. As opposed to narrative that simply seeks to make the reader forget their own reality for a limited time. See Auerbach, *Mimesis*, 15.

> Once innocence has been lost and reflective consciousness has begun . . . there is no way back to a merely biological view of one's own thoughts in general—nor a merely psychological, or sociological, or economic, or political view.[4]

There are echoes of the Eden narrative in Nagel's reflection on lost innocence and the emergence of reflective consciousness; a narrative presenting the unfolding consequences of a new perspective of reality as *"the eyes of the two were opened, and they knew they were naked"* (Genesis 3:7).[5] There is also a significant resonance with Ricoeur's belief that, in modern hermeneutical endeavor, there is no way back to a state that he refers to as a first or primitive naïveté.[6] His thinking consequently offers four insights that, in conjunction with the insights from Nagel, might serve as building blocks for a contemporary approach to biblical narrative; an approach that acknowledges the narratives' potential to extend the boundaries of the thinkable about not only the human condition but also a world within which life and mind have been generated. These are insights that concern; firstly, Ricoeur's approach to the complexity of the human condition;[7] secondly, his advocacy of an interpretive stance of critical "second naïveté"; and thirdly, his preference for a long route of multiple detours. The fourth insight that is enabled by these detours concerns the role of the productive imagination, the "functional unity" of the multiple narrative modes and genres within seemingly diverse disciplines,[8] and the referential world of narrative within which "new modes of being" are disclosed.[9]

---

4. This is because "all such external forms of understanding are themselves examples of thought, and in the end, any understanding we may achieve of the contingency, subjectivity, and arbitrariness of our desires, impressions and intuitions (whether or not it is accompanied by acceptance) has to depend on thoughts that are not so qualified—thoughts whose validity is impersonal and whose claim to our assent rests on their content alone" (Nagel, *Last Word*, 142).

5. Alter, *Five Books*, 25.

6. Ricoeur, *Symbolism*, 351.

7. In relation to fallibility and the propensity for evil which he explores in *Fallible Man* (1965) and *The Symbolism of Evil* (1967).

8. Ricoeur, "On Interpretation," 175–76.

9. Ricoeur, *Interpretation Theory*, 94.

BOOKS, BRICKS, GOLD, PEANUT BUTTER, A GRAND PIANO: THE COMPLEXITY OF THE HUMAN CONDITION

An animal organism is composed of ordinary elements, which are in turn composed of subatomic particles found throughout the known physical universe. A living human body can therefore be constructed out of a sufficient quantity of anything—books, bricks, gold, peanut butter, a grand piano. The basic constituents just have to be suitably rearranged.[10]

For Nagel, the question emerging from an objective understanding of physical reality concerns how a complex arrangement of basic physical elements can result in not only "remarkable physical capacities" but also a human mind that he believes resists all forms of psychophysical reductionism as "there is no way of constructing subjectivity out of two hundred pounds of subatomic particles."[11] The first connection with, and insight from, Ricoeur's thinking therefore arises from a shared concern for a better understanding of the complexity of the human condition, a significant feature of which, for both philosophers, is the "feeling" of the absurdity of life in its often perceived ambiguity and futility. It is a feature that Nagel describes as one of the most human things about us, occurring due to our capacity to transcend ourselves in thought:[12]

> We take some things more seriously within our human life than others but we always have available a point of view from outside our lives from which the seriousness can seem gratuitous. These two inescapable viewpoints collide making life absurd; absurd because we ignore the doubts that we know cannot be settled and continue to live with nearly undiminished seriousness in spite of them.[13]

For Ricoeur, it is a feature that he identifies in the course of history and the cruelty of nature and humankind which he suggests results in "a

---

10. Within the "natural biological process of nourishment and growth, beginning with conception" (Nagel, *View from Nowhere*, 28).

11. Nagel, *View from Nowhere*, 29.

12. With its main condition being "the dragooning of an unconvinced transcendent consciousness into the service of an immanent, limited enterprise like a human life" (Nagel, *Mortal Questions*, 22).

13. Nagel, *Mortal Questions*, 14.

feeling of universal absurdity" inviting man "to doubt his destination."[14] The phenomenological characteristics of consciousness can lead to both external and internal conflict arising from the tension between our capacity to take both what Nagel terms an objective, impersonal "view from nowhere" and a subjective, personal view arising from what we experience; capacities that, with reference to Nagel, Ricoeur states "leave us divided within ourselves" and attempting to "restore unity."[15] It is restoration that he did not believe could be achieved through reductionism which, in a conversation with neuroscientist Jean-Pierre Changeux, he refers to as being an issue "at the heart of Anglo-American philosophical discussion."[16] This is because the two "distinct discourses" of firstly the "body and the brain," in the sense of neural connections, and secondly, the "mental" regarding knowledge, feelings, intentions, motivations, and values, cannot be either reduced to or derived from each other.[17]

Ricoeur's interest in and engagement with the natural sciences stemmed from the recognition that, as Nagel suggests, they offer important ways of revealing the intelligibility of the world.[18] He is, however, in similar fashion to Nagel, prepared to raise the issue of the potential limits of these sciences in the sense of what they may "never succeed in explaining"[19] as "we have to struggle with the believable and the unbelievable of our time in order to make a place for intelligent discourse."[20] In 1967, Ricoeur referred to the "prejudice" in modern times of an "exclusive respect" for observable facts, with objects considered as the "correlates of a theoretical consciousness" and reducible to a physic-mathematical model. As a consequence:

> What we call experience is a product of such a reduction to the objective fact which is mathematized and inserted into a system which can be, in addition, formalized and axiomatized."[21]

---

14. Ricoeur, *Symbolism*, 258.

15. Ricoeur, *Reflections*, 68, citing Nagel's question, "How can we put ourselves back together?" (Nagel, *Equality and Partiality*, 16). It is a question that Marc de Leeuw sees as summing up "Ricoeur's entire philosophical anthropology" (Leeuw, "Anthropological Presupposition," 44).

16. Changeux and Ricoeur, *What Makes us Think?*, 25.

17. Changeux and Ricoeur, *What Makes Us Think?*, 14.

18. Nagel, *Mind and Cosmos*, 18.

19. Changeux and Ricoeur, *What Makes Us Think?*, 69.

20. Ricoeur, *Philosophy of Paul Ricoeur*, 224.

21. Ricoeur, *Philosophy of Paul Ricoeur*, 70.

It is "prejudice" that therefore serves to hide the phenomenological and "proper" characteristics of consciousness that includes both human perception and will or action. For Ricoeur, the "perceived" and "willed" are the "original contours of the world" in the sense of being part of an initial state of pre-critical "naïve" awareness within which "reality has already become a meaningful world." They are consequently "dimensions of a reality more original than the scientific object, which appears later at a second level of elaboration."[22] In this respect, he is able to state that phenomenology "represents a return to naïveté," liberating sight and rendering it "attentive to all the richness of the real."[23] This is a return to a position that is prior to the total objectification of the sciences but provides its preliminary ground in being a position within which "the world is not reduced to physical nature, but where it is still—following the expression of a pre-Socratic thinker—the gathering of gods and men and things."[24]

NAÏVETÉ OR RECEPTIVITY?

We . . . [cannot] go back to a primitive naïveté? Not at all. In every way, something has been lost, irremediably lost; immediacy of belief. But if we can no longer live the great symbolisms of the sacred in accordance with the original belief in them, we can . . . aim at a second naïveté in and through criticism.[25]

For Ricoeur, while it is no longer possible to return to a first, original stage of naïveté, a stage of second "mature" or more "sophisticated" naïveté is achievable through the hermeneutics of both suspicion and faith and the corresponding hermeneutical arc,[26] which is able to point to new existential possibilities within which the absurdity of life can be understood. It is a stage which, if enabling the recovery of an openness to the world

---

22. Ricoeur, *Philosophy of Paul Ricoeur*, 70.

23. Ricoeur, *Philosophy of Paul Ricoeur*, 70.

24. For Ricoeur, there is "a world of *praxis*, of which *theoria* is a second level" (Ricoeur, *Philosophy of Paul Ricoeur*, 70).

25. Ricoeur, *Symbolism*, 351. "The second naivete aims to be the postcritical equivalent of the precritical hierophany" (352).

26. Ricoeur's three-stage hermeneutical arc moves from the "precritical naïveté" of a first (literal) understanding through "critical explanation" to a "postcritical mature naïveté" or second understanding. This is comprehension that is a "sophisticated" mode of understanding supported by explanatory procedures (Ricoeur, *Interpretation Theory*, 74).

of biblical narrative, holds considerable hermeneutical significance. A potential stumbling block lies, however, in his references to a first "primitive" naïveté and the maturity and sophistication that are part of a second, "critically informed" naïveté.[27] It is terminology that is not intentionally pejorative[28] but has the potential to support claims of contemporary intellectual superiority. This is superiority emerging from a perception that the acquisition of empirical, factual knowledge leads to intellectual maturity; a maturity that consigns not only a biblical perspective of reality to an uninformed past but also other ancient traditions belonging to indigenous communities. It is, therefore, at odds with growing attempts to address the historic repression of these communities and assumptions of their epistemological inferiority;[29] assumptions that fail to recognize what such communities might offer to contemporary societies wrestling with relational issues that are both interpersonal and environmental. This is not least in relation to indigenous understanding of interconnectivity in which human lives "are part of, and inseparable from, the natural world," with protecting the environment a "sacred duty" rather than an "intellectual exercise," and stories and ceremonies providing continual reminders of responsibilities to the land.[30]

In her recent book *The Lost Art of Scripture*, Karen Armstrong traces the development within the human condition of a perception of transcendence and "an instinctive appetite for a more enhanced state of being."[31] She questions current assumptions of spiritual maturity stating that "in the modern West we have developed an inadequate and ultimately unworkable idea of the divine, which previous generations would have found naïve and immature."[32] She is supported in this claim by Midgley who describes the notion of "primitive animism" as arising from

---

27. Barth used similar terminology in calling for a direct reading of the biblical text with a "tested and critical naivety" (Barth in Frei, *Writings from the Archives*, 59).

28. As Ricoeur questions critical thinkers who abandon their normally suspicious nature and capitulate to an assumed verdict of modernity by adopting "the ideology of science and technology in a most naïve fashion" (Ricoeur, *Figuring the Sacred*, 63).

29. As either "troubled descendants of savage peoples" or "innocent children of nature, spiritual but incapable of higher thought" (Mankiller, "Being Indigenous").

30. Mankiller, "Being Indigenous."

31. Armstrong suggests that this is evident in the earliest known stages of human existence and in "all cultures until the modern period, it was taken for granted that the world was pervaded by and found its explanation in a reality that exceeded the reach of the intellect" (Armstrong, *Lost Art of Scripture*, 2).

32. Armstrong, *Lost Art of Scripture*, 9.

a familiar Enlightenment myth which compares the intellectual development of the human race to that of an individual. That myth gave the name "animism" to a supposedly childish "primitive" phase, followed, firstly by more organized religions, then by metaphysics, and finally, in the adult state, by science, which made all its forebears obsolete.[33]

It is a myth that is, however, challenged by the Eden narrative which does not appear to equate the acquisition of knowledge and emergence of reflective consciousness with a move to adulthood or maturity, focusing instead on the motivating forces that drove the actions of the human couple; a couple who were not children but already functioning adults. In this respect, Mark Wallace's substitution of "the first innocence of original understanding"[34] for Ricoeur's initial state of pre-critical naïve awareness or naïve realism, appears better suited to both biblical narrative and Armstrong's claim. It is, however, a substitute that leaves Wallace returning to Ricoeur's terminology in referring to a second critically "naïve" reading of the text. To avoid this potentially misleading term it therefore appears that *receptivity*, in the sense of an openness that is constrained by neither the limited knowledge of an immature childhood nor the developing knowledge of mature adulthood, may be a more positive concept to include in a contemporary hermeneutic. This is as a concept that is able to express both a pre-critical state of receptivity to transcendent dimensions of reality and also a receptive state that can in some form be rediscovered after critical reflection. In this respect, it is an *original receptivity* that is able to transmute into an *informed receptivity* able to acknowledge not only the new theories that are emerging within science and technology but also that they are subject to change as new discoveries are made. It becomes, therefore, a *receptivity* that is enhanced by interdisciplinary engagement and what Ricoeur refers to as the long route of multiple detours.

---

33. Midgley, *Science as Salvation*, 170.
34. Wallace, *Second Naiveté*, xiv–xv.

THE LONG ROUTE OF MULTIPLE DETOURS: A CRITICAL JOURNEY OF RADICAL DEPARTURE FROM THE FAMILIAR

The third insight arises from the acknowledgment of a need for intelligible articulation of what Ricoeur terms the "richness of the real"[35] and Nagel refers to as "the true extent of reality"[36] which they both believe resist reductive approaches to explanation. It is an insight that, therefore, concerns Ricoeur's decision to ground his hermeneutics in phenomenology[37] by taking the "long route" of multiple detours investigating other disciplines to break new paths.[38] The concept of a long route that may begin with a radical departure from the familiar and involve detours onto new and unknown ground, is one that plays a significant role in biblical narrative in both a physical and abstract sense. The dramatic departure of the Edenic couple from the familiarity of their paradisiacal home, is the first in a series of radical physical departures from the familiar into unknown and potentially hostile territory that are recorded in narratives that follow. These are narratives that, in varying amounts of detail, trace the steps of individuals such as Cain (Genesis 4), Noah (Genesis 7–10), Abraham (Genesis 12–25), Joseph (Genesis 37–50), Moses (Exodus–Deuteronomy), David (1 Samuel–2 Samuel), Elijah (1 Kings 17–19) and Jeremiah (Jeremiah) as well as large groups of people in radical departures that include escape from captivity in Egypt and exile in Babylon. From the opening chapters of Genesis, there is also, however, a sense of radical departure from contemporary thought as a new creation narrative emerges that reworks and challenges existing mythology by presenting a new and unique perspective of the cosmos.[39] It is departure that, in both senses, continues throughout the Old Testament in narratives that critique and offer insight into the human condition. In exposing both its weakness in the potential for self-serving gratification and its strength

---

35. Ricoeur, *Philosophy of Paul Ricoeur*, 70.

36. Nagel, *Mind and Cosmos*, 14.

37. Following and extending the phenomenological method developed by Husserl, which "starts from the position that whatever I perceive I perceive through the senses" (Simms, *Paul Ricoeur*, 11).

38. Even at the risk of them becoming winding paths that go astray. See Ricoeur, *Conflict of Interpretations*, 448.

39. A perspective which, in stripping the cosmos of the multitudes of gods affiliated with the natural environment, appears to be more closely aligned with modern cosmology than ancient mythology. See Kass, *Beginning of Wisdom*, 28.

in the potential for self-sacrificing altruism, they provide a foundation for the New Testament narratives; narratives in which the two forms of radical departure from the familiar are exhibited both ontologically and epistemologically in the life and teaching of Jesus and then, through his spirit, in the lives of his followers.

It could, therefore, be argued that, in rejecting the short and less arduous route taken by an "ontology of understanding"[40] for a longer route of multiple detours, Ricoeur is following biblical principles in his search for clarity. As with Nagel, intelligibility is an important issue for Ricoeur in addressing the conflicting viewpoints that can arise from the collision of objective and subjective perspectives.[41] A specific focus in his work is, consequently, on the dialectic between the search for "explanation" affiliated with the objective, empirical methodology of the natural sciences and the search for the more subjective existential "understanding" which is sought by the human sciences.[42] For Ricoeur, a central problem of hermeneutics is what he believes to be the "disastrous" opposition between explanation and understanding which should instead be viewed as complementary.[43] This is because explanation and understanding are not distinct and irreducible modes of intelligibility but overlap and pass into each other,[44] with explanation functioning as "the mediation between two stages of understanding."[45] His preferred route is, therefore, one of degrees of understanding that are achieved "little by little" through a deeper methodology of successive investigations.[46] Through these inves-

---

40. Following Heidegger, this understanding is a mode of "being" rather than "knowledge" (Ricoeur, *Conflict of Interpretations*, 6).

41. For Ricoeur, this occurs within hermeneutics when the immanence of structural linguistics as a closed system opposes the potential transcendence of discourse when language attempts to leap across the thresholds of "ideality of meaning" and "reference" to "take hold of reality" (Ricoeur, *Conflict of Interpretations*, 84). As a result, Ricoeur resists a structuralism that reduces language to the functioning of a system of signs and the object of empirical science with no reference to anything outside itself. A full interpretation requires both "the objective analysis . . . and also acknowledgment that there is always a surplus of meaning to be found in discourse when language goes beyond itself becoming a *mediation* rather than an object" (Ricoeur, *Conflict of Interpretations*, 85).

42. Ricoeur, *Hermeneutics and the Human Sciences*, 209.

43. Ricoeur, *Hermeneutics and the Human Sciences*, 43. This is because, "ultimately," the correlation between them is the "hermeneutical circle" (Ricoeur, *Hermeneutics and the Human Sciences*, 221).

44. Ricoeur, *Interpretation Theory*, 72.

45. Ricoeur, *Interpretation Theory*, 72.

46. Ricoeur, *Conflict of Interpretations*, 6.

tigations, new possibilities in the form of Nagel's imaginative alternatives are able to emerge; possibilities which Ricoeur describes as the work of the productive imagination in its capacity to offer an "expanded vision of reality"[47] and let new worlds shape our understanding of ourselves.[48] It is imagination and an expanded vision that are not, however, confined to the arts, as the sciences continue to be confronted by the mysterious new world that is being opened up by the challenges of quantum reality.[49]

THE ROLE OF THE PRODUCTIVE IMAGINATION: A NEW VISION OF REALITY

The layman always means, when he says "reality" that he is speaking of something self-evidently known; whereas to me it seems the most important and exceedingly difficult task of our time is to work on the construction of a new idea of reality.[50]

The words of physicist Wolfgang Pauli[51] were written in 1948 as the discoveries of the mysterious quantum world challenged both existing ideas of reality and the ability of language to articulate emerging concepts; concepts that seemed to be only expressible in mathematical equations. It was a world that appeared to demand the construction of a new idea of reality; a demand that still prevails due not only to the data emerging from the advanced technology of particle accelerators, laser interferometers, and neutrino telescopes as well as the research into quantum gravity, but also as scientists still struggle to understand quantum mechanics. In the 1980s, Feynman extended Nagel's suggestion of the absurdity of the

---

47. Ricoeur, *Ricoeur Reader*, 123.
48. Ricoeur, *Hermeneutics and the Human Sciences*, 181.
49. Initially confined to the realm of physics, but moving into the realm of biology as it became evident that there was "growing evidence that a number of specific mechanisms within living cells make use of the non-trivial features of quantum mechanics, such as long-lived quantum coherence, superposition, quantum tunnelling and even quantum entanglement—phenomena that were previously thought to be relevant mostly at the level of isolated molecular, atomic and subatomic systems, or at temperatures near absolute zero, and were thereby not thought to be relevant to the mechanisms responsible for life" (McFadden and Al-Khalili, "Origins of Quantum Biology," 1).
50. Pauli in Gieser, *Innermost Kernel*, 268.
51. Pauli has been described as "the architect behind wave-particle complementarity" (Beller in Gieser, *Innermost Kernel*, 6).

human condition into the natural world by claiming that nobody understood the theory of quantum electrodynamics as it "describes Nature as absurd from the point of view of common sense" and we therefore must "accept Nature as She is—absurd."[52] Nearly forty later, it appears that, while we are able to *use* quantum mechanics[53] we are still unable to fully understand it,[54] with ongoing debate as to whether the concept of wave function is *epistemic*, in referring only to a state of knowledge about a system of observation and measurement, or *ontic* in being directly related to an underlying objective reality.[55]

For science writer Philip Ball, quantum mechanics, in "profoundly confronting our expectations," remains "a beguiling, maddening, even amusing gauntlet thrown down to challenge the imagination" and it is "quite possible that only an imagination sufficiently broad and liberated will come close to articulating what it is about."[56] An example of such imagination can be found in the attention now directed towards the *Many Worlds* theory[57] of quantum mechanics, which suggests that reality as a whole is a state of superposition described by "a smoothly evolving wave function," with decoherence causing it to split into multiple realities or worlds.[58] The implications of the theory are profound as the observer or human being, as part of this reality, must consequently also branch into multiple copies with each copy appearing in a separate world with some particular measurement outcome.[59] What the possibility of an individual existing simultaneously in multiple worlds might offer in terms of the meaning or purpose of the human condition is as yet unclear, but a significant question appears to concern whether it is a theory that can,

52. Feynman, *QED*, 10.

53. The equations of quantum physics are used for the operation of computers, smartphones, telecommunication lasers, atomic clocks, GPS (Global Positioning Systems), and MRI (Magnetic Resonance Imaging).

54. According to physicist Sean Carroll, "We *use* quantum mechanics to design new technology and predict the outcomes of experiments. But honest physicians admit that we don't truly *understand* quantum mechanics" (Carroll, *Something Deeply Hidden*, 2).

55. Ball, *Beyond Weird*, 54.

56. Ball, *Beyond Weird*, 12, 10.

57. First proposed by physicist Hugh Everett in 1957 and initially attracting little interest. It remains controversial but some scientists now argue that the theory is supported by the phenomenon of *decoherence*; a state in which interference cannot occur and superposition cannot be maintained, which was introduced in 1970 by physicist Hans Dieter Zeh. See Carroll, *Something Deeply Hidden*, 117.

58. See chapter 2 in Carroll, *Something Deeply Hidden*.

59. Carroll, *Something Deeply Hidden*, 119.

in Ricoeur's words, contribute to the shaping of our understanding of ourselves.[60] This is understanding that may require an expanded vision of the scientific reality of both the human condition and the world in which we live, as in the words of Nagel:

> We don't want an understanding of everything in terms of particle physics. We wouldn't feel we understood biological processes if someone were to give us a particle physics account of them because we don't see the world in those terms: instead, we want to understand the world in the categories in which we perceive it and carve it up naturally.[61]

For Nagel, the issue that this raises concerns how what he terms the "real truth about the causal order of the universe" may challenge our conceptual ability,[62] but this is a challenge that was also faced by the biblical writers in presenting their unique perspective of reality. There appears, therefore, to be an interesting hermeneutical convergence with the ongoing struggle to articulate quantum reality which, according to Ball, arises as we have mathematics but not "stories," leading him to conclude that "we can hardly talk about quantum theory at all unless we find stories to tell about it: metaphors that offer the mind purchase on such slippery ground."[63] His conclusion is reinforced by physicist Christopher Fuchs who believes that

> we will one day tell a story about quantum mechanics—"literally a story, all in plain words"—that is "so compelling and so masterful in its imagery that the mathematics of quantum mechanics in all its exact technical detail will fall out as a matter of course." That story, he says, should not only be crisp and compelling. It should also "stir the soul."[64]

---

60. It is a question that could be applied to the many existing interpretations of quantum theory, which include "the Copenhagen, the many worlds (Everett 1957; De Witt and Graham 1973), the realistic statistical (Ballentine 1970), the (nonlocal) hidden variables (Bohm 1952; Vigier 1982), the modal (van Fraassen 1981, 1991; Kochen 1985; Dieks 1994; Bub 1992; Healey 1989), the quantum logical (Finkelstein 1965; Putnam 1968; Friedman and Putman 1978)" (Geiser, *Innermost Kernel*, 106). This leads Gleiser to refer to the polyphony of the *notion* of interpretation, with there being "no agreement on the basic question: what does it mean to interpret a mathematical-physical theory?"

61. Nagel, "Reductionism and Antireductionism," 9.

62. In terms of "what is easiest for us to grasp" (Nagel, "Reductionism and Antireductionism," 9).

63. Ball, *Beyond Weird*, 45, 12.

64. From a personal communication between Ball and Fuchs (Ball, *Beyond Weird*, 324).

The imagination and the concept of "story" appear, therefore, to be re-emerging as significant forces for contemporary scientific endeavor[65] in a search for a description of reality that can accommodate the overlapping goals of explanation and understanding. According to cognitive scientist Mark Turner, story or "narrative imagining" is a fundamental instrument of the mind and a literary capacity that is "indispensable to human cognition" as both a fundamental form of predicting and a fundamental cognitive instrument for planning and explanation.[66] Story and projection are, therefore, "the root of and essential to human thought" and two of our basic forms of knowledge.[67] If this is correct, a key question that a contemporary approach to biblical narrative must address concerns how a deeper understanding of the purpose of "story" might facilitate a renewed appreciation for how the biblical writers' "plain words" and "compelling and masterful" imagery resulting from a "broad and liberated" imagination might be able to once again "stir the soul." This is in order to allow the narratives to contribute to the search for a better understanding of the human condition and, in Nagel's words, how we fit into the world in which we live.

THE WORLD OF BIBLICAL NARRATIVE: REALITY IN SUPERPOSITION

Nobody really knows what a superposition is, but we can think of it as a sort of refusal on the part of reality to be definitely one way or the other.[68]

Hermeneutics is not confined to the *objective* structural analysis of texts or to the *subjective* existential analysis of the authors of texts; its primary concern is with the *worlds* which these authors and texts open up. It is by an understanding of the worlds, actual and possible, opened by language that we may arrive at a better understanding of ourselves.'[69]

---

65. Although it can be argued that they have always been a significant force, with Einstein suggesting in 1931 that; "Imagination is more important than knowledge. For knowledge is limited, whereas imagination embraces the entire world, stimulating progress, giving birth to evolution. It is, strictly speaking, a real factor in scientific research" (Einstein, *On Cosmic Religion*, 97).

66. Turner, *Literary Mind*, 4–5, 20.

67. Turner, *Literary Mind*, 12, 5.

68. Goff, *Galileo's Error*, 41.

69. Ricoeur, *Ricoeur Reader*, 490.

In his essay "On Interpretation,"[70] Ricoeur refers to "the game of story-telling." This has diverse forms and modes that, in the process of cultural development, have branched out into "increasingly well-determined literary genres," thereby fragmenting the narrative field. In an earlier lecture he described this as an "overwhelming proliferation" of narrative forms that include myth, folk-tale, fable, epic, tragedy, drama, novel, movies, comics as well as history, autobiography, analytical case-histories, testimonies of witnesses, and ordinary conversation.[71] It is fragmentation that he believed to be problematic as, within Western culture, it has led to a "major dichotomy" between the concepts of history and story. History, as "an explanatory endeavor" that had "severed its ties with story-telling,"[72] was now perceived to be articulated in narratives which, in being comparable to "the descriptive forms of discourse in the sciences," could claim to be empirically verifiable or falsifiable and therefore "true." Conversely, "fictional stories" that ignored "the burden of corroboration by evidence" were perceived to renounce the possibility of truth claims.[73] He therefore sought a hermeneutical approach that had a broader concept of truth than one within which "true" history with a direct referential claim and "fictional" story with an indirect referential claim are opposed.[74] It was a search that was driven by his belief in the "functional unity" of the multiple narrative modes and genres within seemingly diverse disciplines and also in the irreducibility of "the various uses of language."[75] It is, therefore, both the telling of stories *and* the writing of history that provides clarity to the "chaotic, obscure and mute,"[76] with an interwoven history and fiction and subsequent non-ostensive referential function of the narrative text that opens up new worlds before, rather than behind, the text.

The concept of narrative within which history and fiction are interwoven to open up new worlds may be a potentially important key to an understanding of the unique nature of biblical discourse that challenges

---

70. Ricoeur, "On Interpretation," viii. Ricoeur was asked to present his view of his work in relation to both the context in which he was currently working and the reactions which he might expect it to provoke.

71. Ricoeur, *Ricoeur Reader*, 103.

72. Ricoeur, *Ricoeur Reader*, 104.

73. Ricoeur, *Ricoeur Reader*, 103. See also Ricoeur, "On Interpretation," 176.

74. As history-writing is more fictional and fiction is more mimetic than positivistic trends of thought would acknowledge. See Ricoeur, *Ricoeur Reader*, 116.

75. Ricoeur, "On Interpretation," 175–76.

76. Ricoeur, *Ricoeur Reader*, 115.

conventional concepts of narrative in a perhaps not dissimilar way to which quantum mechanics has challenged the conventional concepts of classical physics. While Nagel rightly warns of the dangers of combining perspectives that are radically distinct,[77] some thought-provoking conceptual parallels appear to emerge, firstly in the discovery that a quantum entity is neither particle nor wave but rather exhibits either *particle-like* or *wave-like* characteristics to an observer when measurement occurs. This raises the question of whether biblical narrative has an inherent duality in being both *history-like* and *fiction-like* in nature; a nature within which the two forms of discourse are complementary and entangled to enable multiple possibilities of transformational story. In this respect, the second conceptual parallel concerns the implications of the nature of biblical narrative being considered from the perspective of a wave function that is able to hold not only history and fiction but also a proliferation of narrative forms in a state of superposition until "measurement," or the attempt to "collapse"[78] or reduce the narrative to a single specific form, occurs. This is reduction that is made by both defenders of and detractors from biblical narrative particularly in relation to historical truth claims,[79] but the nature of quantum reality suggests that it may serve only to limit the reference of biblical language and thus narrow the scope of a biblical vision of reality.

In this respect, as some physicists consider a move beyond a mathematical description of reality,[80] Ricoeur's concern to move beyond or "eclipse" the "narrow boundaries" of the ostensive or "first order reference" of language which seeks to describe reality,[81] appears to have con-

---

77. Although some assumed distinctions may be challenged, with Chalmers suggesting that if experience, as the "hard" problem of consciousness, is a non-reductive fundamental property, "then in some ways a theory of consciousness will have more in common with a theory in physics than a theory in biology" (Chalmers, "Facing Up," 200–219).

78. Heisenberg's original word was "reduces" (Ball, *Beyond Weird*, 97).

79. Leading Frei to suggest: "It cannot be said often and emphatically enough that liberals and fundamentalists are siblings under the skin in identifying or rather confusing ascriptive as well as descriptive literalism about Jesus at the level of understanding the text, with ascriptive and descriptive literalism at the level of knowing historical reality" (Frei, *Types of Christian Theology*, 84).

80. Moving from the Platonist concept of mathematics having its own existence, with mathematical forms underpinning the physical universes, to the opposing concept of mathematical forms as objects of the human imagination that "we make . . . up as we go along, tailoring them to describe reality" (Abbott, "Reasonable Ineffectiveness").

81. Ricoeur, *Interpretation Theory*, 36.

siderable significance for the building of a biblical hermeneutic that is also seeking to extend the boundaries of the thinkable. For Ricoeur, this is a move to liberate "a power of reference to aspects of our being in the world that cannot be said in a direct descriptive way."[82] This is "productive reference" that is both non-ostensive and non-descriptive and therefore able to enlarge our concept of the world by pointing to both a "possible world" and a "possible way of orienting oneself in it";[83] a world that is opened up by the text with the result that

> a new vision of reality springs forth, which ordinary vision resists because it is attached to the ordinary use of words. The eclipse of the objective, manipulable world thus makes way for the revelation of a new dimension of reality and truth.[84]

This is a new vision or dimension of reality that demands an understanding of language as discourse that operates not only on the boundary between the expressible and inexpressible[85] but also on the boundary of the thinkable and unthinkable; a boundary that ordinary language must therefore attempt to "push back" or, in Nagel's terminology, "extend."

A NEW HERMENEUTIC

A hermeneutic that is developed in response to the epistemological impact of what Nagel describes as the hegemony of "a defensive world-flattening reductionism," with an accompanying fear of and failure to understand "religious ideas" must, therefore, serve to enable biblical narrative to extend the boundaries of the thinkable. This is by revealing an alternative perspective of reality; a perspective that, through the imaginative use of language, will radically depart from familiar forms of naturalistic explanation. It is a hermeneutic that will, firstly, require the reader to adopt a position of "informed receptivity." This is a position that, in being "informed" but not constrained by critical inquiry, is able to heed Nagel's warning about asking the wrong questions and using the wrong tools. The reader is then able to be receptive or open to a biblical perspective of reality that emerges from narratives that embark both

---

82. Ricoeur, *Interpretation Theory*, 37.
83. Ricoeur, *Interpretation Theory*, 87–88.
84. Ricoeur, *Interpretation Theory*, 68.
85. Ricoeur, *Hermeneutics and the Human Sciences*, 176, citing the thinking of Wilhelm von Humboldt.

ontologically and epistemologically on a journey towards an extended form of knowledge and understanding; a form that is able to incorporate *meaning* and *purpose* as vital concepts in the ongoing search for what Nagel highlights as "how we and other things fit into the world."[86]

It is a hermeneutic that, therefore, attempts to give the text what Frei refers to as "breathing space"[87] by approaching the narratives as "transformational story" in which history and fiction are merged and thus able to refer to an expanded rather than reductive vision of reality; a vision that is enabled by what Ricoeur calls the productive imagination and the concept of productive reference which enable the narratives to offer imaginative alternatives in order to "discover," "redescribe," and thereby even "increase" reality.[88] This is imagination that is, therefore, productive in being able to provide both "insight into the nature of things"[89] and the means of presenting ideas which constantly "strain after something lying outside the limits of experience,"[90] with the imagination being the "condition" rather than the "cause" of truth.[91] In this respect, it is a hermeneutic that allows the biblical text to function on its own unique and often genre-defying terms in combining differing narrative forms to enable "ordinary" language to extend conceptual boundaries. This is by articulating the possibilities of an invisible and transcendent reality beyond an assumed range of human knowledge and experience. The ongoing challenges within quantum mechanics to articulate the possibility of invisible and transcendent quantum reality also lying beyond current epistemological and experiential boundaries offer some interpretive insights as to how biblical narrative might function and how its reference might be understood. The challenge of extending conceptual boundaries in attempts to understand the human condition and the world within which we live is not, however, a new problem, and before applying the hermeneutic to the selected texts it is necessary to take another "stepping

---

86. Nagel, *Mind and Cosmos*, 128.

87. Frei suggests that "a good interpretation of a text is one that has 'breathing space,' one in which finally no hermeneutic allows you to resolve the text. There is something that is left to bother; something is wrong; something is not yet interpreted" (Frei, "Conflicts in Interpretations," 353).

88. Ricoeur, *Ricoeur Reader*, 121–28.

89. Warnock, "Imagination," 408.

90. After Immanuel Kant in Warnock, "Imagination," 404.

91. Lewis states, "For me, reason is the natural organ of truth; but imagination is the organ of meaning. Imagination, producing new metaphors or revivifying old, is not the cause of truth, but its condition" (Lewis, "Bluspels and Flalansferes," 265).

back" to examine the role of ancient imagination as, in the words of Midgley:

> We need to understand the human imagination rather than predicting the progress of the cosmic Heat Death. What is needed when new scientific facts clash with beliefs formerly held is not to declare war, not to bend the facts, it is to rethink that significance, to look much deeper into what underlies the symbols.[92]

---

92. Midgely, *Science as Salvation*, 54.

PART II

Into the Light

Extending the Boundaries of the Thinkable

Splendid you rise in heaven's lightland,
O living Aten, creator of life!
When you have dawned in eastern lightland,
You fill every land with your beauty.[1]

Compact Muon Solenoid Tracker Outer Barrel (Large Hadron Collider)[2]

   1. Opening lines of *The Great Hymn to the Aten*, attributed to the Egyptian Pharaoh Akhenaten (r. 1353–1336 BCE), in Lichtheim, *Ancient Egyptian Literature*, 96.
   2. The Compact Muon Solenoid experiment Tracker Outer Barrel, which is one of two general purpose Large Hadron Collider experiments designed to explore the physics of the Terascale. Maximilien Brice/CERN.

8

Ancient Light
Into the Remote Mists of the Ancient Imagination

If we want to dream of Eden, we had better go back to sleep. But if we want to understand the dream, we had better learn something of the past from which it sprang. Only then can we hope to divine its meaning for the hard daylight hours ahead.[1]

Human life is not lived in a realm of "raw experiences" that serve as the foundation for knowledge and action. Rather, human life is lived in a world of inherited meanings that profoundly shape cognition and praxis. We are not rigidly bound by these meanings; our own thoughts and actions are not mere repetitions of what has gone before. Yet we are placed in a situation by these meanings, so that the things that we know and do, as well as how we know and do them, receive an indelible stamp from what has come to us from the past. The categories by which we think, what we tend to deem important, the aspects of things that stand out for us, how we relate to others and to things in the world—all these and much more besides are given to us from the past.[2]

---

1. Eisenberg, *Ecology of Eden*, xx.
2. Bryant, *Faith and the Play*, 86.

THE SECOND STEPPING BACK, that Nagel suggests is necessary to "place ourselves in the world that is to be understood,"[3] concerns the world within which biblical narrative emerged. This is the mythical world of the ancient imagination; a world in which the perennial search for an understanding of the human condition can be seen in the stories, hymns, and laments of the ancient Near East (ANE). Beginning with the fourteenth-century BCE *Hymn to the Aten* and moving to laments and incantations from the Classical or Old Babylonian Period between ca. 1850 and 1500 BCE, the opening sections of this chapter will consider what Nagel refers to as the human will to "believe" and to "make sense of" the challenges of being human in an often hostile world. This is from the perspective of the ancient imagination and in relation to what Mary Midgely describes as the vital human function of myth-making in order to interpret the world and provide a sense of meaning to human life and death. The impact of scientific development on this potentially vital human function will then be considered; firstly, from the negative stance of what Assyriologist Wilfred Lambert referred to as the "the strait jacket of twentieth-century thinking";[4] secondly, from a more positive position emerging from the rediscovery of interconnection and coherence as important features of the world.[5] This position will be explored in relation to the biblical creation accounts and their radical departure from other ANE accounts. The role of the imagination and its relationship to the concept of revelation will then be considered through an investigation of Ricoeur's concept of the creative and thereby productive imagination which will be incorporated with the thinking of Hans Frei and Garrett Green. In the final section, potential links between the ancient and contemporary world regarding the role of the imagination in enabling understanding will be explored. These are links emerging from developments in particle physics, with a particular focus on the hermeneutical possibilities arising from the increasing convergence of theoretical physics with other disciplines in attempts to explain the mysteries of existence.

---

3. Nagel, "Limits of Objectivity."
4. Lambert, *Babylonian Wisdom*, 2.
5. Joseph Bracken uses the term "intersubjectivity" as "the common denominator in our human understanding of the world around us, both the starting point and the goal for resolving the tension between subjectivity and objectivity, the Many and the One, at all different levels of existence within Nature as well as within the world of human discourse and action" (Bracken, *Subjectivity, Objectivity*, 5).

INTO THE LIGHT

A primal desire of man is the imaginative impulse—working under the special conditions of our time... to visit strange regions in search of such beauty, awe or terror as the actual world does not supply.[6]

Myth intends to talk about a reality which lies beyond the reality that can be objectified, observed and controlled, and which is of decisive significance for human existence.[7]

The brief period of monotheistic worship of the solar disc *Aten*, in the fourteenth-century BCE reign of the Egyptian Pharaoh *Akhenaten*, was a radical departure both physically, from the inside of darkened temples to beneath the open sky,[8] and philosophically, from the polytheism, anthropomorphism, and theriomorphism of the ancient world.[9] The radical nature of this departure is also evident in the declaration by nineteenth and early twentieth-century Egyptologists that the veneration of the sun disc *Aten*, as the visible emanation of a transcendent "unnamed and unnameable Deity,"[10] was "an absolutely rational religion,"[11] with a scientific conception[12] as its characteristic feature. This feature, extrapolated from both the content of the hymn and the naturalistic qualities of some of the contemporary artwork was, according to Flinders Petrie, the "abstraction" of regarding the radiant energy of the sun as the life-giving and life-sustaining force that regulates all existence, leading him to conclude in the 1890s that:

> If this were a new religion, invented to satisfy our modern scientific conceptions, we could not find a flaw in the correctness of this view of the energy of the solar system. How much

---

6. Lewis, *Other Worlds*, vi.

7. Rudolf Bultmann, "On the Problem," 160.

8. In a "classical" Egyptian temple, halls of graduated light led to the total darkness of the Holy of Holies sanctuary. The open-air temples following the Great Temple of *Aten* had no roof to allow worship to be directed toward the light in the sky.

9. Petrie, *History of Egypt*, 218.

10. The "window in heaven through which the unknown God, the "Lord of the Disk," shed a portion of his radiance on the world" (Hall, *Ancient History*, 300).

11. Given an "ignorance of the true astronomical nature of the sun" (Hall, *Ancient History*, 300).

12. Petrie, *History of Egypt*, 214.

Akhenaten understood, we cannot say, but he certainly bounded forward in his views and symbolism to a position which we cannot logically improve upon at the present day.[13]

Despite, however, the possible correctness of this view of the energy of the solar system and the potential satisfaction of nineteenth-century scientific conceptions, the *Aten* worship introduced by *Akhenaten* was a radical departure that was short-lived as, after his death, Egypt reverted to the polytheistic tradition and the old gods were reinstated. Rationality and scientific conceptions did not prove to be necessary features of an enduring religion in the fourteenth century BCE, raising the issue of their relevance to religion in the twenty-first—a century within which human pain and suffering continue and science, despite its remarkable progress, appears unable to fully meet what Midgley calls "our imaginative needs,"[14] which include a sense of meaning and purpose.

BLEATING GOATS AND FRETFUL BABIES

Nagel describes the biological evolutionary process that has given rise to self-conscious human beings as a story that includes "huge quantities of pain" and often "horrible misery."[15] It is also a story of what appears to be the inexhaustible human will to not only *believe*, as Nagel suggests, but also to make sense of such experiences, with both pain and misery evident in some of the earliest forms of literary expression that emerged on the clay tablets of the ANE.[16] In the cuneiform texts of the second millennium BCE, human fears and concerns about life and death were expressed not only in epics such as *Gilgamesh* and *Atrahasis* but also in emotive incantations for the everyday experiences of calming fretful babies,[17] rabid dog bites,[18] swatting flies,[19] the frustration resulting

---

13. Petrie, *History of Egypt*, 214.
14. Midgely, *Science as Salvation*, 2.
15. Nagel, *Mind and Cosmos*, 120.
16. See also Berger, who suggests, "It is possible to argue that the human condition that is fraught with suffering and the finality of death demands interpretations that not only satisfy theoretically but also give inner sustenance in meeting the crisis of suffering and death" (Berger, *Rumour of Angels*, 40).
17. See "To Calm a Baby," in Foster, *Before the Muses*, 172.
18. See "Swift Dog," in Foster, *Before the Muses*, 190.
19. See "Against Flies," in Foster, *Before the Muses*, 195.

from a bleating goat that is "keeping me awake at night"[20] and the "stabbing" pain of stomach ache caused by inflamed intestines.[21] A deeper level of human suffering and misery is, however, revealed in the anguish of a lament that reflects the perennial issues relating to the challenges of the human condition; of being human in an often hostile world and of trying to make sense of the difficulties, fears, insecurities and often extreme hardship of human existence.[22]

> A young man was imploring his god as a friend,
> He was constantly supplicating, he was [praying to(?)] him.
> His heart was seared, he was sickened with his burden . . .
> His burden had grown too heavy for him,
>   he drew near to weep.[23]

As Thomas Howard suggests, in the search for features such as tranquility, permanence, order, health, strength, and beauty in human life, we more often find instead those of tumult, decay, chaos, sickness, weakness, and horror,[24] resulting in the ongoing aspiration to understand this turmoil. As a result, "myth-making," in the sense of an imaginative guiding vision at the core of every thought-system,[25] has always been a "vital human function"[26] in providing a sense of meaning to human life and a way of interpreting the world that is both around and within us;[27] a world which despite the advances in science and technology, remains for many the "chancy progress towards inevitable death," that it appeared to be in the ancient world where the same hopes were held for good health, longevity, an abundant family, and financial success.[28] In

---

20. See "Against a Bleating Goat," in Foster, *Before the Muses*, 198.

21. See "Against Stomach Ache," in Foster, *Before the Muses*, 185.

22. Haught describes the questions of "why suffering" as irrepressible and, with the prospect of death, as "the main stimulus to the countless stories about the origin and end of evil that humans have been telling . . . for thousands of years" providing "reassurance that life is not absurd" (Haught, *Is Nature Enough*, 171).

23. See "Dialogue between a Man and His God," in Foster, *Muses*, 148.

24. Howard, "Myth," 337.

25. A vision which appeals to the deepest needs of our nature. See Midgley, *Science and Poetry*, 277–78.

26. Midgley, *Science as Salvation*, 2.

27. Midgley, *Science as Salvation*, 93. See also Haught, who proposes that "our sacred symbols and myths may, at a certain level of understanding, come closer than science to registering what is *really* going on in the narrative depths of the universe" (Haught, *Deeper*, 45).

28. Foster, *Muses*, 80.

an increasingly complex and improbable world revealed by quantum mechanics, the hopes and fears of humankind have not changed. While developing knowledge and advanced technology have improved life for many, they have also resulted in further challenges. Philosopher Renata Salecl suggests that the current glorification and ideology of choice in the developed world has been an illusion, disguising its tyrannical aspect that makes us "more anxious and more acquisitive rather than giving us more freedom."[29] Closely linked to the concept of choice is the desire for control with the paradoxical consequence of a growing industry of self-help manuals promising structured strategies for positive change and the associated comfort of being told what to do in order to achieve this goal. As Salecl points out, while choice should involve the freedom of an individual to determine the direction of their life, all too often this freedom is relinquished in the search for an authority to help deal with all the options and the individual retains only the power to choose which authority to consult.[30]

The hope for liberation resulting from the promise of multiple possibilities within an ideology of choice is, therefore, illusory, not least in the midst of the current global pandemic and the struggle for racial and gender equality that are challenging the concepts of both choice and control. In this respect, the perception that the extraordinary scientific progress of the twentieth century[31] has led to a better informed and consequently superior modern mind freed from what Sam Harris describes as the "ancient confusion" and "perennial lies" of "our ignorant ancestors,"[32] may also be illusory. While there may, justifiably, be no doubt that the modern mind is better informed in a scientific and technological sense, it is also possible that this may actually serve to limit understanding, with Fernando Canale stating:

> The legacy of the twentieth century is anxiety over both humanity's place in the universe within an increasingly recognized environmental crisis and also revealed in new searches for transcendence, for a source of meaning and hope beyond

---

29. Salecl, *Choice*, 9.

30. Salecl, *Choice*, 33.

31. Which includes, the publication of the theory of relativity and the discoveries of the first quantum model of the atom, the particle nature of light, the expansion of the universe, how nerves communicate with each other, the first human hormone, and the structure and secret code of DNA. See Lightman, *Discoveries*.

32. Harris, *Waking Up*, 203.

the self-enclosed world described by Enlightenment science and philosophy.[33]

THE STRAIGHT JACKET OF A SELF-ENCLOSED WORLD

In 2008, Nagel referred to the desire for closure as a "natural human weakness"[34] but in 1974 he had raised the issue of what he described as "reductionist euphoria" in relation to the mind-body problem and "the general human weakness for explanations of what is incomprehensible in terms suited for what is familiar and well understood, though entirely different."[35] Just over a decade earlier, Lambert had identified such human weakness in the inability of the modern mind to accommodate ancient intuitions or cognitions on their own terms and in consequent attempts to fit them into what he believed to be "the strait jacket of twentieth-century thinking."[36] As Conrad Hyers warns, mythic expression then comes to be seen as "simpleminded or simplistic" while it may be that it is instead "our own understanding and interpretation which is simpleminded and simplistic."[37] It is a position that is given support by Armstrong's more recent comment that many today

> live in a society of scientific logos, and myth has fallen into disrepute. In popular parlance, a "myth" is something that is not true. But in the past, myth was not a self-indulgent fantasy; rather, like logos, it helped people to live creatively in our confusing world, though in a different way. Myths may have told stories about the gods, but they were really focused on the more elusive, puzzling and tragic aspects of the human predicament that lay outside the remit of logos.[38]

From these perspectives, the issue is not the cognitive or epistemological limits of social-cultural systems but rather the impact of the

33. Canale, *Back to Revelation-Inspiration*, 5.
34. Nagel, "Analytic Philosophy."
35. Nagel, *Mortal Questions*, 166.
36. Lambert, *Babylonian Wisdom Literature*, 2.
37. Hyers, *Meaning of Creation*, 109. See also Jung, who suggests, "It would be a ridiculous and unwarranted presumption on our part if we imagined that we were more energetic or intelligent that the men of the past—our material knowledge has increased, but not our intelligence. We have become rich in knowledge, but poor in wisdom" (Jung in Tacey, *Religion as Metaphor*, 50).
38. Armstrong, *Case for God*, 3.

internalization of constraints imposed by a dominant ideology.[39] These are constraints that can bar the door to further discovery but, as Taylor suggests, they are not only imposed by those in thrall to a reductive scientism but also by those in faith communities who are also seeking closure through an adherence "to their own hard-edged truths."[40] In this respect, Hyers offers two potentially important considerations in stating; firstly, that it is possible to cling to myth "in such a way as to subject it to the charge of being primitive superstition and archaic fantasy";[41] secondly, in the reminder that

> myths represent human language and natural imagery and narrative form operating at their limits, pushed actually beyond their limits, in an effort to approach and respond to the mysteries of existence.[42]

Lambert, therefore, makes a salient point in suggesting that it is important to understand the context from which the worlds of the ancient texts emerged and highlighting the need for immersion in the literature before any sense of the spirit that moved the writer could be discovered.[43] It is a suggestion which may be key for a contemporary biblical hermeneutic operating in a post Enlightenment world within which the skies above and earth below[44] are no longer perceived as being inhabited by

---

39. Islamic scholar Mohammad Arkoun refers to the consequent "unthought" and "unthinkable" (Robinson, "Arkoun," 67).

40. Taylor, *Secular*, 769.

41. Hyers, *Meaning of Creation*, 109.

42. Hyers, *Meaning of Creation*, 109. Hyers highlights the challenge to respond to these mysteries and the inadequacy of words and images at the limits of understanding that is also found in science: "Where the 'is' gives way to the 'as if.' Quarks are described as blue and green. Light is both 'wavelike' and 'particle-like,' and yet neither, for the 'wavicle' character of light carries us beyond picturability. . . . Chemical compounds are represented by tinkertoy models, with colored balls to depict the configuration of different elements. And the beginning of the universe is characterized, in analogy with a large firecracker, as a 'big boom.' . . . Scientific description begins to have the sound of a child's first words: things begin with a 'big boom' and disappear in a 'dark hole'" (110).

43. Lambert, *Babylonian Wisdom Literature*, 2.

44. One of the oldest recorded cosmologies, the second millennium BCE Babylonian creation epic *Enûma Elish* begins, "When skies above were not yet named, nor earth below pronounced by name" (Dalley, *Myths*, 233). Copies exist from the first half of the first millennium BCE, but the language suggests that it was composed during the middle of the latter half of the second millennium. See Jacobsen, *Treasures of Darkness*, 167.

invisible gods, devils, angels and demons.[45] It remains, however, a world in which entities exist beyond both direct experience, visualization and common sense as, in moving away from the Newtonian concepts of space and time, science reveals it to be populated by invisible and unpicturable micro particles, multi-dimensional space-time and "a plethora of fields and forces";[46] entities which also demand a vision of a mutually interdependent system of continual interconnection and interaction. This is a system that is not simply made up of its individual parts but is rather a whole which influences and constitutes its parts.[47] It is, therefore, as Ervin Laszlo suggests, potentially "in line with ancient intuitions"[48] that understood the coherence that science is now rediscovering.

IN THE BEGINNING

The desire to understand and form beliefs about a world which, as Nagel points out, we have not created and are products of,[49] is reflected in the creation stories of the ANE but there are significant differences between the attempts of the biblical writers and their predecessors to address what Leon Kass refers to as "some of the most important and enduring questions of human existence."[50] *Enûma Elish* is in part a creation story in which the order of the universe is established. The initial watery chaos, unlike the "formless void" in the opening verses of Genesis where "darkness covered the face of the deep" (*těhôm*), is comprised of *Apsû* and *Ti'âmat* as the primeval sweet-water and salt-water oceans[51] and ancestors of the Babylonian and Assyrian divinities.[52] While the *těhôm* of Genesis has no literal "face" or mythological associations referring only to a vast expanse of water,[53] *Ti'âmat*[54] appears to take the form

---

45. See Laszlo, *Science and the Reenchantment*, 79.

46. Laszlo, *Science and the Reenchantment*, 79.

47. For Green, it is therefore "illegitimate to examine the 'parts' in abstraction from the whole pattern that makes them parts in the first place" (Green, *Theology, Hermeneutics*, 77).

48. Laszlo, "Interview." See also Laszlo, *Connectivity Hypothesis*.

49. Nagel, *View from Nowhere*, 118–19.

50. Kass, *Wisdom*, 13.

51. Heidel, *Babylonian Genesis*, 88.

52. Heidel, *Babylonian Genesis*, 96.

53. Heidel, *Babylonian Genesis*, 99.

54. A name developed from the noun *tiāmtu* (sea) (Millard, "New Babylonian," 7).

of a terrifying serpent-like monster capable of cunning deception and wild, uncontrollable rage.[55] A main focus of the epic's first four tablets is consequently a battle between the god *Marduk* and *Ti'âmat* who has created a monstrous army:

> Contributed an unfaceable weapon: she bore giant snakes,
> Sharp of tooth and unsparing of fang (?).
> She filled their bodies with venom instead of blood.
> She cloaked ferocious dragons with fearsome rays,
> And made them bear mantles of radiance, made them godlike . . .
> Their bodies shall rear up continually and never turn away!" . . .
> Bearing merciless weapons, fearless in battle.[56]

The ancient imagination is in full flight, but there is a much closer resemblance to the imaginative constructions of the twenty-first-century fantasy world in which the heroes of film and electronic games battle supernatural forces of evil and chaos with weapons of supernatural power,[57] than to the opening chapters of Genesis. In the Hebrew creation account, which Ricoeur describes as effecting "a vigorous demythologization" of Babylonian sacred cosmology,[58] there is no conflict but an orderly progression of creation, by separation and naming; a progression that the nineteenth and early twentieth-century Egyptologists might also have been tempted to identify as pointing to "an absolutely rational religion," with a scientific conception as its characteristic feature. Kass describes this feature as the reining in of the mythic imagination to give "an *intelligible* account of a cosmic order based on noetic . . . principles" rather

---

55. Although Mary Ann Beavis points out that the idea of *Ti'âmat's* portrayal as a serpentine monster in *Enûma Elish* is contested by scholars of the ancient Middle East, with Heidel suggesting that *Ti'âmat* is only said to have given birth to monster-serpents while also giving birth to good and benevolent gods. See Beavis, "Jezebel Speaks," 136; Heidel, *Babylonian Genesis*, 83.

56. Dalley, *Myths*, 239–40.

57. An interesting comparison can be made between the "unfaceable weapon" that *Marduk* receives from the gods (Tablet 4) with which to defeat the "unfaceable weapon" created by *Ti'âmat*, (Tablet 1) and the mythical weapons of power, violence and destruction in modern electronic games. Weapons such as: Ashbringer (*World of Warcraft*), Wabbajack (*The Elder Scrolls V: Skyrim*), Gravity Hammer (*Halo*), and the Moonlight Greatsword (*Dark Souls*).

58. Ricoeur, *Conflict of Interpretations*, 388.

than "mythic or sensual ones";[59] an account which he suggests is in "substantial agreement with the world as we experience it and as we reflect on it."[60] Consequently, it is an account which functions in one sense to refute the polytheism of the ANE,[61] denying "the alternative of *generative beginnings*"[62] but, as Umberto Cassuto points out, it does not do so as a polemic, with the "controversial note" being heard indirectly through "deliberate, quiet utterances . . . which sets the opposing views at naught by silence or by subtle hint."[63]

In the first biblical creation story God (*Elohim*),[64] in similar fashion to the kings of the ANE, pronounces his will and sees it accomplished.[65] There is no need for the "unfaceable weapon,"[66] "cloak of awesome armor"[67] and "frightful, unfaceable storm-chariot" drawn by terrifying creatures[68] that *Marduk* must use to defeat *Ti'âmat*. Through a series of tests and a climactic battle *Marduk* must earn his sovereignty in superhero fashion, by claiming the Tablet of Destinies and sealing it with his own seal.[69] It is only then that he can begin the process of creation by dividing up the body of *Ti'âmat*, but it is a creation primarily for the gods, in which Babylon is heralded as the "home of the great gods" and the "centre of religion" where *Marduk* has established his private quarters and confirmed his kingship.[70] In this sense the epic can be seen as being "first and foremost a literary monument in honor of *Marduk* as the champion of the gods and the creator of heaven and earth" offering a cosmological explanation for his status as "head of the entire Babylonian pantheon."[71] There is, therefore, a political dimension to the epic, with this status supporting Babylon's claim to "supremacy over all the cities of

---

59. Kass, *Wisdom*, 33.
60. Kass, *Wisdom*, 33.
61. See Hyers, "Biblical Literalism."
62. Kass, *Wisdom*, 27.
63. Cassuto in Kass, *Wisdom*, 28.
64. As the sovereign creator of the universe. See Wenham, *Genesis*, 15.
65. Hyers, *Meaning of Creation*, 180.
66. Dalley, *Myths*, 250.
67. Dalley, *Myths*, 251.
68. Dalley, *Myths*, 251.
69. Dalley, *Myths*, 254.
70. Dalley, *Myths*, 259.
71. Heidel, *Babylonian Genesis*, 11.

the land"[72] as the city of *Marduk*, with its origin at the beginning of time and foundations laid by the *Anunnaki* or gods.[73]

A NEW PERSPECTIVE

The second biblical creation story opens with humankind already identified as being made in God's image and given dominion over every living thing (Genesis 1:26–27), with provision for all (Genesis 1:29–30). In a radical departure from earlier ANE accounts, such as *Enûma Elish*[74] and *Atrahasis*,[75] humans are not created to be providers for the gods but are nourished and sustained by God who is now the named as the more personal YHWH Elohim.[76] A second radical departure occurs with the removal of any hierarchical status within humankind as "a mere handful of deftly ordered words [disassemble] the lofty bearing, stature and commission of ancient, oriental kingship" and place the royal crown "on the sturdy heads of everyman and everywoman."[77] Within this new form of kingship there is also an element of dependence as the relational aspect of creation is developed. As the living image of the living God, humankind "in general, as opposed to a selected few," is made for "intimate, reciprocal relationship with God, designed for relationship with . . . created others and born to the divine and creative vocation of earth-care and earth-filling."[78]

This relational perspective is reinforced by the intimacy of the second biblical creation story in which the man is personally shaped by God from the dust of the ground, with his relationship to the earth "subtly reinforced for the Hebrew ear in the assonance of ʾāḏām 'human' and ʾaḏāmâ 'ground'"[79] (Genesis 2:7). Humans, who appeared to be the "crowning

72. Heidel, *Babylonian Genesis*, 11. Foster suggests that the epic was primarily intended to place Babylon at the center of the universe, as seen in the oldest extant "world" map, and should therefore be read as a "document of Babylonian nationalism" rather than as a creation story (Foster, *Muses*, 436).

73. Heidel, *Babylonian Genesis*, 11, referring to Tablet 6.

74. "Let me create a primeval man. The work of the gods shall be imposed (on him), and so they shall be at leisure" (Dalley, *Myths*, 261).

75. "And let man bear the load of the gods" (Dalley, *Myths*, 15).

76. Suggesting covenantal intimacy as Yahweh is unique to Israel (Cassuto in Baker, "God," 367).

77. Ryken et al., *Dictionary of Biblical Imagery*, 10.

78. Ryken et al., *Dictionary of Biblical Imagery*, 9.

79. Ryken et al., *Dictionary of Biblical Imagery*, 9.

act of God's creativity" in the first account, are now "merely dust and ashes"[80] animated by God breathing *"into his nostrils the breath of life"* (Genesis 2:7).[81] This life force of divine breath is in marked contrast to the divine flesh and blood of a slaughtered god which is mixed with clay to create humankind in the *Atrahasis* epic, or the blood of the traitorous god *Qingu* which is used for the same purpose in the Babylonian creation epic. The humans in Genesis are more than ghosts "come into existence from the god's flesh"[82] as they are bound in relationship with both God and the earth as creatures of the ground, from which trees will also grow that are good for food (Genesis 2:9). They are also more than servants of the gods as, while the human will till and keep the earth (Genesis 2:15), it will be for his own benefit, and he will also be responsible for the naming of every living creature (Genesis 2:19–20).

In this respect, the biblical creation stories appear to be less concerned with demythologizing or polemic than with the presentation of a radically new vision for humanity; a vision that makes a radical departure from the familiar ANE creation stories to present an alternative vision that will extend the boundaries of the thinkable.[83] In so doing, it is a vision that is able to both counter and look beyond the possible motivations, agendas and foci of the ANE communities within which it appeared. The indication is, therefore, that the seemingly remote mists of the ancient imagination, within which the biblical texts emerged, may consist of a very different substance, in terms of the source of their inspiration, from the billowing fog created by *Marduk* from *Ti'âmat's* poisonous spittle.[84]

---

80. Shulman, *Genius*, 57.

81. Alter, *Five Books*, 21.

82. *Atrahasis* in Dalley, *Myths*, 15.

83. Tom McLeish describes this perennial vision as "a grounding of the present predicament of humankind within the history and fabric of the material world—it begins but, does not finish—an *explanation* of the relationship of toil and pain humans have with the material world" (McLeish, Faith & Wisdom, 72).

84. *The Epic of Creation* in Dalley, *Myths*, 256.

Part II: Into the Light: Extending the Boundaries of the Thinkable

REVELATION AND THE ROLE OF THE IMAGINATION

If the Bible may be said to be revealed this must refer to what it says, to the new being it unfolds before us. Revelation, in short, is a feature of the biblical world proposed by the text.[85]

Ricoeur describes the question of revelation as formidable[86] and the history of its development as a doctrine is outside the scope of this book.[87] In developing a contemporary approach to the interpretation of biblical narrative, it is, however, an important feature in relation to the unique nature of a biblical perspective of reality that is opened up by the text; a proposed world which Ricoeur suggests is, in biblical language, a new creation, new covenant or new birth that unfolds in front of the text.[88] Another important feature is the related idea of inspiration,[89] particularly in light of the explicit assertion in 2 Timothy 3:16: "*All scripture is inspired by God.*" Ricoeur resists the "imprisonment" of the idea of revelation in the "double authorship of speech and writing" evident in prophetic discourse, as he believes it to be too narrow a concept that diminishes the idea of inspiration in narrative texts where authorship is not an emphasis.[90] This is because he believes that the events recounted in narratives take on more significance than the author and their prompter, with God often being the "ultimate *actant*" in the story as "he is one of

---

85. Ricoeur, "Toward a Hermeneutic," 26.

86. As he believes that while it can be seen as "the first and last question for faith" it has also been obscured by false debate (Ricoeur, "Toward a Hermeneutic," 1).

87. Ronald Thiemann suggests that many discussions of revelation have "created complex conceptual and epistemological tangles that are difficult to understand and nearly impossible to unravel," with some arguing that the term is "unbiblical," "unintelligible," and "incoherent." He consequently rejects the concept of the doctrine as an epistemological theory and presents an argument suggesting that "the category of 'narrated promise' offers a way of reconceptualizing the Christian doctrine of revelation" so that it can "assert the intelligibility and truth of Christian claims" (Thiemann, *Revelation and Theology*, 1, 7).

88. See Ricoeur, "Toward a Hermeneutic," 26; *Figuring the Sacred*, 44.

89. Thiselton notes, "Karl Barth, Emil Brunner, and Bernard Ramm argue that questions about revelation are prior to questions about inspiration. Revelation constitutes a major biblical theme from the revelation to Abraham and certainly to Moses at the burning bush (Exodus 3). Only in the light of God's self-revelation can we then discuss theories of biblical inspiration by the Holy Spirit" (Thiselton, *Thiselton Companion*, 485).

90. He suggests that it binds prophecy to the "literary genre of the oracle" and the idea of the unveiling of the future (Ricoeur, "Toward a Hermeneutic," 3–4).

the personages signified by the narration itself and intervenes among the other actants of the goings on."[91] It is the nature of these "goings on" from which the idea of revelation can also emerge in enabling them to become transcendent events; events that, in not simply occurring and passing away, "mark an epoch and engender history" by the arrangement of "sagas, traditions and stories around a few kernel events from which meaning has spread out through the whole structure."[92]

For Ricoeur, what must be understood in a narrative text and the consequent object of a biblical hermeneutic is not, therefore, primarily the presumed intention of the author but "the sort of world intended by the text as its reference."[93] To expand his concept of the referential function of the biblical text and "restore the concept of biblical revelation to its full dignity,"[94] Ricoeur turned to what he terms the "areligious" revelatory function of poetic language which is language that he does not define in opposition to prose. He suggested that its revelatory function has a significant resonance with aspects of revelation in biblical narrative, because poetic discourse also embodies a concept of truth which, in suspending descriptive reference to "objects that we can manipulate," replaces the "criteria of falsification and verification" with manifestation.[95] This is manifestation in the form of an opening that breaks through the closed world of ordinary experience to project and open up a new world. It is a new world that is accessed by a "conjunction of fiction and redescription, of *mythos* and *mimesis*";[96] a concept that Ricoeur develops from the paradigm of Aristotle's *Poetics* in which the essence of *poiesis*, as

---

91. Ricoeur, "Toward a Hermeneutic," 5, following the actantial model of A. J. Greimas.

92. Gerhard von Rad in Ricoeur, "Toward a Hermeneutic," 6.

93. Ricoeur, "Toward a Hermeneutic," 23. It is a hermeneutic that must seek a path between what he believed to be the "intentional fallacy" which overlooks the semantic autonomy of the text and the opposite fallacy which "forgets that a text remains a discourse told by somebody, said by someone to someone else about something" (Ricoeur, *Interpretation Theory*, 30). In a 1946 essay "The Intentional Fallacy," W. K. Wimsatt Jr. and Monroe C. Beardsley state that meaning cannot be established by discovering "what the author would have liked the words to mean" (Barton, *Reading the Old Testament*, 150).

94. Ricoeur, "Toward a Hermeneutic," 26.

95. Ricoeur refers to reference with a descriptive function as "first degree" reference as it is dominant in daily life and supported by modern science. He suggests that its suspension can liberate "a more primitive, more originary referential function" of "second order" reference (Ricoeur, "Toward a Hermeneutic," 24–25).

96. Ricoeur, "Toward a Hermeneutic," 24.

a creative act of "bringing into being," is the *mythos* of a narrative, in the sense of the joining of speech, fable and plot.[97] The aim of a narrative is able to remain the *mimesis* or imitation of human action as, for Aristotle, this was a creative imitation not simply a copy of an existing model. The conjunction of *mythos* and *mimesis* are thus able to offer a way of seeing things differently with a new vision in which fiction becomes an "instance" of productive rather than reproductive imagination.[98]

In this way, Ricoeur is able to declare that the term "fiction" is his "name for the imagination," when imagination is both a "rule-governed form of invention" and "the power of redescribing reality."[99] Fiction in this sense is not in opposition to factual reality but, as creative imagination with the ability to "invent" and "discover," is able to act where understanding fails by forcing conceptual thought to "*think more*"[100] or, in the words of Nagel, extend the boundaries of the thinkable. If fiction can be identified as the creative and revelatory imagination at work then Frei may be correct rather than controversial in suggesting that, with regard to the Gospels and particularly the passion-resurrection narratives

> we are actually in a fortunate position that so much of what we know about Jesus . . . is more nearly fictional than historical in narration . . . It is precisely the fiction-like quality of the whole narrative, from upper room to resurrection appearances, that serves to bring the identity of Jesus sharply before us and to make him accessible to us . . . fictional description, providing direct knowledge of his identity in, with and through the circumstances, merges with factual claim . . . The narration is at once intensely serious and historical in intent and fictional in form.[101]

For Green, building on Frei's thinking, the imagination is, therefore, "an organ of faith"[102] which he describes as "the anthropological point of contact for divine revelation," using the term *Anknüpfungspunkt* for the place where this contact happens and enables the Word of God to become

---

97. Ricoeur, *Hermeneutics and the Human Sciences*, 292.
98. Ricoeur, *Hermeneutics and the Human Sciences*, 292–93.
99. Ricoeur, *Figuring the Sacred*, 144.
100. Ricoeur, *Rule of Metaphor*, 358.
101. Frei, *Identity of Jesus Christ*, 144–45. See also Allison, *Constructing Jesus*. In chapter 6, "Memory and Invention: How Much History?," Allison concludes that the Gospel authors believed that they were reporting a true story, with the Synoptic writers reconfiguring memories of Jesus rather than inventing theological tales. See Allison, *Constructing Jesus*, 458.
102. Green, *Imagining God*, 144.

effective in human lives.[103] Green builds a carefully constructed argument for this theory to avoid an association with the illusory attributes of the imagination claimed by Feuerbach and Marx and to address the concerns expressed by Barth about any concept that might contradict the character of revelation as grace.[104] The imagination is not the foundation or ontological base for revelation but the place or way in which it happens, with how it is used or "what it means to imagine" becoming the crucial issue. This is in relation to doing justice to revelation as both a "divine act of grace" that is not reducible to human "ability, attribute or need" and as "a human act of faith."[105] In this respect, Green can offer a potentially important suggestion:

> The uniqueness of the revelation to which Christians bear witness is best served, not by trying to immunize it against criticism by isolating it conceptually, but rather by freely exploring its manifold relations with other human phenomena.[106]

This is exploration that is enabled by the renewed appreciation of the role of the imagination in both philosophy and contemporary science as "an essential component in conceptual thinking and a complementary approach to reality";[107] an appreciation that was highlighted on the first CERN[108] website citing Einstein's aphorism that "imagination is more important than knowledge."[109]

---

103. Green, *Imagining God*, 40.

104. Green, *Imagining God*, 32. In "Die Frage nach dem 'Anknüpfungspunkt' als Problem der Theologie," Emil Brunner argued that there is a point of contact (*Anknüpfungspunkt*) within human nature for divine revelation. Barth, however, strongly refuted this position arguing that the point of contact was not inherent but the result of divine revelation and established by the Holy Spirit (Barth, *Nein!*).

105. Green, *Imagining God*, 40.

106. Green, *Imagining God*, 40.

107. Viladesau, *Theological Aesthetics*, 83.

108. The French acronym for the European Organization for Nuclear Research, where the world's largest and most complex scientific instruments are used to study fundamental particles (https://www.home.cern/about).

109. See "Subatomic Venture."

Part II: Into the Light: Extending the Boundaries of the Thinkable

PRIMORDIAL FIRE: FROM STANDING STONES TO STANDARD MODEL STONES

> Myth... can no longer be defined in opposition to science. Myth consists in giving worldly form to what is beyond known and tangible reality. It expresses in an objective language the sense that man has of his dependence on that which stands at the limit and at the origin of his world.[110]

Ricoeur's words can perhaps find validation as, three thousand years after the veneration of the source of radiant energy within the beams of light from the solar disc, twenty-first-century awe and wonder has become focused on the mechanically generated power of high-energy particle beams or *hadrons*[111] traveling close to the speed of light.[112] It is here that the way to "a deeper, better, truer understanding about the fundamental structure and nature of existence"[113] was hoped to be found in a "$9 billion cathedral of science"[114] that exists, not in an open-air temple or within the "heaven's lightland" of the ancient hymn but in an equally "near-magical realm."[115] This new "cathedral" is home to the Large Hadron Collider (LHC)[116] and its realm is once again in a darkened temple as the CERN laboratory is one hundred meters underground, comprising subterranean caverns and twenty-seven kilometers of tunnel running between the foothills of the Jura mountains and Geneva.

Designed to recreate the conditions 10^{-43} seconds[117] after the "Big Bang,"[118] the operation of the LHC forces colliding particles to reproduce

---

110. Ricoeur, *Conflict of Interpretations*, 391.

111. Hadrons, from the Greek *adros*, meaning bulky, are particles composed of quarks.

112. Up to the record energy of 7 TeV. The unit most frequently used for energy is the electronvolt (eV). The derivative TeV = 1012 eV. See ECOG, *LHC*, 12.

113. Andersen, "Genesis 2.0," 117.

114. Andersen, "Genesis 2.0," 111.

115. The CERN Laboratory. Andersen, "Genesis 2.0," 112–13.

116. A particle accelerator that was heralded as the largest and most sophisticated machine made by humankind and the most expensive experiment in the history of science. See Henderson, "Two Tiny Dots."

117. A million, trillion, trillion trillionth of a second (Thompson, *Down to Earth*, 239).

118. The cosmic eruption, 13.8 billion years ago, of a microscopic ball of intense energy which, as it cooled, brought to life an energy field (The Higgs Field) that would give birth to our universe (Sample, *Massive*, x).

"fleeting specks of primordial fire"[119] amidst which scientists are able to detect phenomena never before observed. The goal was the discovery of the Higgs boson;[120] popularized in the media as the "God particle" and believed by some scientists to be the only missing piece of physics' Standard Model[121] or set of laws describing all the known particles in the universe. The importance of the Standard Model, as a foundational understanding of the universe at the level of fundamental principles and forces, can be seen in its inscription on a standing stone outside the CERN Control Center.

The Standard Model Set in Stone[122]

"'The top line describes the forces: electricity, magnetism, and the strong and weak nuclear forces. The second line describes how these forces act on the fundamental particles of matter, namely the quarks and leptons. The third line describes how these particles obtain their masses from the Higgs boson, and the fourth line enables the Higgs boson to do the job.'"[123]

---

119. Sample, *Massive*, ix.

120. A special particle believed to be the manifestation of a field that gives mass to elementary particles.

121. Developed in the mid-1970s, the Standard Model or "Theory of Everything" aims to explain all known matter from a small amount of elementary particles (Sample, *Massive*, 6).

122. CERN.

123. Schaeffer, "Standard Model."

The inscription is in the form of a Lagrangian,[124] or mathematical equation, representing the Standard Model which includes a description of the Higgs mechanism,[125] but it is an engraving that for most people today is as enigmatic as the information held within the ancient *menhirs* or standing stones found across the world.[126] Many appear to have functioned as astronomical observatories, with evidence of complex landscape patterning in their alignment with the movement of the Sun and Moon across the surrounding landscape and horizon.[127] For those, however, who are outside the fields of either Archaeoastronomy or Astrophysics, as the earliest known and most recent science of "stars and stones,"[128] the CERN Standard Model stone reflects simply the enigma of its ancient counterparts in the ongoing search to understand not only the cosmos but now also the possibility of a "multiverse." This is in the sense of other universes that may be far apart or even exist simultaneously in time; a phenomenon that has the potential to radically change the nature of fundamental physics.[129]

The extent of this radical change is not yet known but it is change that may offer the opportunity for interdisciplinary dialog. From a perspective of constructive theology, Jason Wyman suggests that "Christian theology . . . has new things to offer philosophy, the social sciences, literary studies, and even the sciences at this moment in history"[130] but this is not in the familiar proposition of contributing answers to the *why* rather than the *how* questions which are the concern of science. This approach now appears to be a dichotomy that is challenged by the increasing convergence of theoretical physics with disciplines that might once have been assumed to be unlikely conversationalists. Lightman describes this "deepest and purest branch of science" as the outpost of science that is closest to philosophy and religion because, unlike experimental

---

124. Named after mathematician and astronomer Joseph Louis Lagrange, a lagrangian contains the symbols representing the quantum fields for all fundamental objects—electrons and quarks, photons and gluons, and W and Z bosons. See Kane, *Supersymmetry and Beyond*, 28–29.

125. The Higgs mechanism consists of the Higgs field and its corresponding Higgs boson. See Gray and Mansoulié, "Higgs Boson."

126. The oldest recorded site is *Gobekli Tepe* on the border of Syria and Turkey and thought to be at least 12,000 years old. See "Fourteen Mind-Bending Facts."

127. Higginbottom and Clay, "Origins of Standing Stone Astronomy."

128. See Magli, *Archaeoastronomy*.

129. Steven Weinberg in Lightman, *Accidental*, 5.

130. Wyman, *Constructing*, 87.

physicists, theoretical physicists also "want to know *why*,"[131] with particular emphasis on *why* the fundamental parameters of our universe appear to be finely tuned in lying within the range needed for life to arise.[132] The still mysterious forces of nature appear, however, to retain what Nagel might describe as the last word,[133] in ongoing attempts to establish the fundamental principles that lead to the laws of nature which govern the behavior of all matter and energy underlying one self-consistent universe.

As Lightman points out, theories such as "eternal inflation"[134] and "string theory" indicate that "the *same* fundamental principles, from which the laws of nature derive, lead to many *different* self-consistent universes, with many different properties."[135] If this is correct, we may be living in one of a vast number of universes; an "accidental" universe that is, therefore, infused with mystery and ultimately incalculable by science.[136] In a seemingly ironic twist, while the multiverse theory has offered an alternative to Intelligent Design as an explanation for fine-tuning,[137] the cost appears to be high in the loss of any hope of a mathematical grand unified theory of everything. It is a loss that has, however, the potential to enable a re-connection to ancient Near Eastern thought within which, according to Othmar Keel, the desire to reach "a systematic understanding of the whole" was not a concern.[138] Keel uses the multiplicity of approaches in the iconography of the ANE to examine how its reasoning and imagination function, particularly in relation to the

---

131. Lightman, *Accidental*, 5–6.

132. Lightman, *Accidental*, 11.

133. The title of his book, in which he considers the issue "of where understanding and justification come to an end" and what he believes to be the inescapable "pretensions of human reason" (Nagel, *Last Word*, 100, 4). The last word could, however, also be applied to the *less* mysterious forces of nature as the LHC was shut down twice due to "natural causes." In 2009, it was alleged that a passing bird had dropped a "bit of baguette" into the machine, causing it to overheat, and in 2016 a beech martin was found "on the 66kV transformer in P8, causing severe electrical disturbance throughout the complex." See Gabbatt, "Big Bang Goes Phut"; Paige, "Pop Goes the Hadron Collider"; Lamont and Bertolasi, "LHC Report."

134. "In an eternally inflating universe, anything that can happen will happen... an infinite number of times. Thus the question of what is possible becomes trivial—anything is possible" (Guth, "Eternal Inflation").

135. Lightman, *Accidental*, 7.

136. Lightman, *Accidental*, 7.

137. As the likelihood of a universe with the conditions from which life can emerge increases in relation to the number of possible universes with different properties.

138. Keel, *Symbolism*, 10.

association between concrete reality and its related abstract. He highlights the fact that, rather than working almost exclusively with concepts that are *either* concrete *or* abstract, in the ANE there was a preference for "concepts which are in themselves concrete" but have a powerful associative capacity in frequently signifying "a reality far larger than their concrete meaning."[139] He therefore warns of the dangers of both "reading the pictures too concretely" and "treating them too abstractly":

> Such a (often dangerous) disassociation of concrete reality from idea is as foreign to the ancient Near Eastern perception as the dissociation of body and spirit. Ancient Near Eastern perception usually preserves the continuity between the *concretum* and its related abstract.

Keel's concern is, consequently, to show how iconography can assist with an understanding of the biblical texts whose writers and audience shared the worldview of the ANE; a worldview within which

> empirical-technical and speculative-mythical statements and conceptions are not susceptible to consistent separation. To the ancient Near East, the empirical world, as manifestation and symbol, points beyond its superficial reality. A continuous osmosis occurs between the actual and the symbolic, and conversely between the symbolic and the actual. . . . In the biblical and ancient Near Eastern conception, the world is open and transparent to things above and beneath the earth. It is not a lifeless stage.[140]

It appears, therefore, that Nagel's search for an alternative conception of the natural order that accommodates a "richer set of materials than the austere elements of mathematical physics"[141] may; firstly, find support from the theoretical physicists who are also aware of its potential limitations; secondly, and with particular relevance for hermeneutical endeavor, a connection might then be found in the conceptual similarities that appear to be emerging between the attempts of both the ancient and contemporary world to explain the mysteries of existence. This is not least because theoretical physics now appears to be entering into the domain of the *super*natural if the controversial term is understood as "an order of existence beyond the visible observable universe" and a

139. Keel, *Symbolism*, 8.
140. Keel, *Symbolism*, 56.
141. Nagel, *Mind and Cosmos*, 22.

departure from "what is usual or normal especially so as to appear to transcend the laws of nature."[142] If multiverse or *Many Worlds* theories are correct, scientific endeavor may then be faced with mystery in what Hyers describes as its ultimate sense; a sense in which it is unresolvable as "the greater the knowledge and understanding, the greater the awareness of mystery."[143] It is, however, a sense that resonates with the theological sense of mystery which R. Moberly describes as expressing "an inherent deep reality, the grasp and understanding of which intrinsically becomes ever more demanding the more fully one engages with it . . . God is not demystified by accurate knowledge."[144] The question that this sense of mystery raises then relates to the role that reason might play in this engagement and whether it might help or actually hinder understanding.

The task of a contemporary hermeneutic must, therefore, involve firstly, accepting and working with the mystery that is an integral part of reality, but which cannot be objectified, observed and controlled. It must then allow what C. S. Lewis describes as the primal imaginative impulse to continue working not only *under* but also *over* "the special conditions of our time." This is an impulse that is thus able to connect the mythic expression of the ancient world within which biblical narrative emerged, with contemporary epistemology in order to expand the concept of reality. In this respect, it is a task that must serve to free biblical narrative from the enigma of time-bound carved stones decipherable only to those with specialized knowledge and allow it to have a relevant voice in contemporary societies; societies in which there is increasing evidence of critical fractures in the relationships between humankind, the environment in which we live and the other species that exist within it.

These are fractures which suggest that there are two vital universal questions that must be addressed. The first is bipartite involving both *how* and *why* we *can* and *should* do better in addressing these fractures and the second concerns whether this can be achieved by secular humanism or even a Christian humanism that has cut its ties to the supernatural elements of biblical narrative. If Nagel is correct in suggesting that there is "ample reason to fear human nature"[145] as it is fundamentally compli-

---

142. *Merriam Webster Dictionary*, "supernatural," https://www.merriam-webster.com/dictionary/supernatural.

143. Hyers, *Creation*, 111.

144. Moberly, *Theology of the Book of Genesis*, 64.

145. Nagel, *Equality and Partiality*, 7.

cated rather than being fundamentally good[146] and that "we really do not know how to live together,"[147] then the challenge facing a contemporary hermeneutic appears to involve the explication of how biblical narrative might contribute to an understanding of this nature; understanding that offers hope in the search for a positive way forward. This is a search that, from a biblical perspective but offering support to Nagel's concerns, begins in the third chapter of Genesis with a dramatic exposé of the human condition and in particular the faculty of reason, with its vulnerability to manipulation. It is an exposé that therefore provides a starting point from which to test an interpretive approach to the narratives which will be the focus of the next three chapters. This is an approach which, in embracing the concepts of radical departure from the familiar and imaginative alternatives that extend the boundaries of the thinkable, is able to incorporate *meaning* and *purpose* as important components in the ongoing attempts to discover both *how* and *why* we fit into the world; an importance that is highlighted by Vanhoozer:

> Today we have more information about life, and more techniques for sustaining life, than ever before, but we remain flummoxed with regard to the question of life's meaning. We have mapped the galaxy, but we are still trying to get our bearings. We have mapped the human genome, but we are still trying to determine what we are.[148]

---

146. As how good one is "depends on whether certain conceptions and ways of thinking have achieved dominance" (Nagel, *Possibility of Altruism*, 146).

147. Nagel, *Equality and Partiality*, 5.

148. Vanhoozer, *Drama of Doctrine*, 1. "We have infinitely more means than ever for staying alive, but fewer reasons for doing so" (Walker Percy in Vanhoozer, *Drama of Doctrine*, 1n2).

9

Getting Our Bearings
From Eden to Interstellar Space

Arthur Boyd, *The Expulsion*, 1948, oil on hardboard, 102 x 122 cm, Art Gallery of New South Wales, Sydney, Australia[1]

1. Arthur Boyd's work is reproduced with the permission of Bundanon Trust.

Part II: Into the Light: Extending the Boundaries of the Thinkable

And He drove out the human and set up east of the garden of Eden the cherubim and the flame of the whirling sword to guard the way to the tree of life.
GENESIS 3:24[2]

IN EMPHASIZING THE NEED to understand the human imagination, Midgely makes the suggestion that:

> What is needed when new scientific facts clash with beliefs formerly held is not to declare war, not to bend the facts, it is to rethink that significance, to look much deeper into what underlies the symbols.[3]

This "looking deeper" will be the focus of the next three chapters in which Nagel's three concepts will be applied to three biblical narratives in order to explore a contemporary approach to the presence of supernatural entities and themes that appear to be at war with contemporary epistemology. This is an approach that, in not declaring war or bending the facts, is concerned with understanding the problem and a rethinking of the potential significance of the narrative that is constructive rather than reductive. From the perspective of a constructive methodological approach, it is, therefore, a rethinking that, in building on the insights extrapolated from Nagel's work, will involve interacting with, absorbing insights from, but also offering insights to, other disciplines while functioning independently from their methods and assertions. This is to identify the hazards of, but also the possibilities in, seeking conceptual similarities from perspectives that might in some ways be radically distinct, but might also find common ground in acknowledging what Nagel describes as the true extent of reality in a world that is independent of and extends beyond the reach of our minds.

Chapter 9 will begin with the theme of journeying into the unknown from the perspective of contemporary astronomy. Threads drawn from a narrative of science will then be woven into the narrative of the third chapter of Genesis in order to highlight the feature of human vulnerability in the search to find and understand what Nagel refers to as "our place" in an often hostile world. In the second section, the focus turns to the narrative's use of a supernatural, talking serpent to present a biblical

2. Alter, *Five Books*, 28.
3. Midgely, *Science as Salvation*, 54.

perspective of the development of consciousness and the presence within human nature of both a moral instinct and what Ricoeur describes as an inclination to evil. The use of ancient Near Eastern cherubim, as a second supernatural presence, will then be considered in relation to the consequences of succumbing to this inclination. The third section returns to contemporary cosmology in order to consider the concept of extending the boundaries of the thinkable in the presence of the mystery that is encountered in both science and theology. The capacity of reason will then be examined from a biblical perspective in relation to growing moral issues and the restoration of broken relationships within the twenty-first-century world.

GENESIS 3:1–24—RADICAL DEPARTURE FROM THE FAMILIAR: INTO THE UNKNOWN

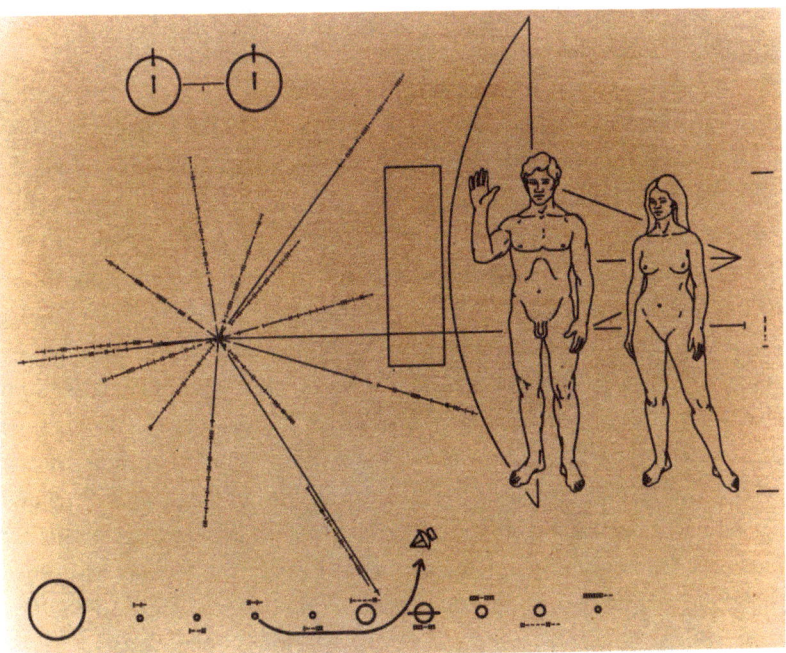

Pioneer 10 Golden Plaque[4]

In March 1972, as Nagel wrestled with the phenomenology of bats and Martians, a naked human couple, looking remarkably relaxed despite

4. NASA Ames (https://science.nasa.gov/resource/pioneer-plaque).

the inhospitable nature of the journey ahead, were launched into the unknown in a radical departure from which there would be no return. As representatives of the human race, the figures were engraved on a gold anodized plaque that was attached to the mainframe of the NASA Pioneer 10 space craft which would take them from the familiarity of our experiential reality to what could only be imagined about potential realities that were as yet unknown. Powered by four radioisotope thermoelectric generators, Pioneer 10 was the first spacecraft to fly beyond Mars, traverse through the dust particles and massive rock chunks of the Asteroid belt and pass within eighty-one thousand miles of the cloud tops of the planet Jupiter.[5] For over twenty-five years, as it journeyed into deep space, its cameras and instruments recorded images and information about radiation belts, magnetic fields, the energetic particles or Solar Wind of the sun, and the cosmic rays entering the solar system.[6] The last data was received in 2003 before the signals became too faint for NASA's antennae to locate, but in 2007 it was estimated as being over eight billion miles away coasting silently as "a ghost ship" travelling into interstellar space.[7]

In anticipation of what or whom it might encounter on its radical departure into the unknown, the gold plaque included a diagram of the solar system and the sun's position in space as well as the naked couple with the man's hand raised in a gesture of greeting. Despite the threat to human life from the inhospitable environment that they are being driven into, their fearless expressions and relaxed stance exude confidence in the technology that surrounds them; a confidence that is in marked contrast to the vulnerability and anguish that so often dominates any visual representation of the biblical couple who, in the third chapter of Genesis, were also "driven" into the unknown by a force that they could not control in a radical departure from the familiarity and security of their known world. This human couple, formed from *"the dust of the ground"* (Genesis 2:7 NRSV) or, from a contemporary perspective, the star dust of atomic particles, is also often depicted as naked despite the biblical assurance that, before their departure, *"the Lord God made skin coats"* and *"clothed them"* (Genesis 3:21).[8]

---

5. See "Pioneer 10 at Jupiter."
6. Howell, "Pioneer 10."
7. See "Pioneer 10 Sends Last Signal."
8. Alter, *Five Books*, 27.

In being "forced to leave the land from which they were formed,"[9] they are, in the words of Miguel De La Torre, the "first refugees" and the anguish of their departure from what Gordon Wenham describes as their "perfect home"[10] is captured with dramatic intensity in both Masaccio's fifteenth-century painting *The Expulsion from Paradise* and Arthur Boyd's twentieth-century depiction entitled simply *The Expulsion*. The landscapes into which the biblical humans are expelled are presented in harsh contrast to the fertile paradisiacal garden that they have been forced to leave. The reality of Masaccio's world is a barren and desert-like environment with a cloudless blue sky suggesting that the naked couple will be exposed to a searing and destructive heat from which there is no protective shade. There is a similar sense of exposure in Boyd's expulsion into the Australian bush, where the blackened trees of the sparse outback vegetation suggest the frequent ravages of fire in a landscape that is also potentially threatening and inhospitable. In similar fashion to the environs of deep space, these are not landscapes in which humans will be nurtured with an abundance of the essential water, food and shelter that will ensure their survival. They are instead environments in which they will struggle to survive and be forced to battle with the natural world which is no longer a harmonious home. For neither *pioneer* couple is there any hope of return, as a fiery threat prevents their re-entry into the rarefied atmosphere of their natural home.[11] There is no way back, which, for the biblical couple, results, not from the blazing temperatures of around 1,649 degrees Celsius that a spacecraft would face on re-entering the earth's atmosphere, but also from a life-threatening heat; a heat that is generated by *"the flame of the whirling sword"* which, together with the cherubim, guards *"the way to the tree of life"* (Genesis 3:24).[12]

AN IMAGINATIVE ALTERNATIVE: CHERUBIM AND A TALKING SERPENT

In 1901, Hermann Gunkel described the final verse of the Eden narrative as the revelation of its main point, standing "as always in the old

9. De La Torre, *Genesis*, 89.

10. Wenham, *Genesis*, 85.

11. Neither Pioneer 10 nor its expendable launch vehicle were designed to return to Earth with the launch vehicle expected to disintegrate when re-entering the Earth's atmosphere. See Gebhardt, "Pioneer 10."

12. Alter, *Five Books*, 28.

narratives, at the end," with the main point being "the expulsion from Paradise."[13] Nearly three-quarters of a century later, his words were echoed by Claus Westermann in stating that the "goal" of the second and third chapters of Genesis is "the expulsion of the man and the woman from the garden and the consequent separation from God."[14] As innocence and mutual trust are replaced by discord and suspicion,[15] it is a separation that will lead to the fracturing of the previously harmonious relationships not only between the human beings, but also with their environment and the other species within it; an environment over which the human couple were given stewardship (Genesis 1:28)[16] and within which there was provision for all (Genesis 1:29–30). The cause and impact of this separation and consequent fractures are explained by the introduction of two supernatural creatures which, while common images throughout the ancient world, are absent in the creation narratives of Genesis 1 and 2. It is an absence of potential significance if it changes the question of whether or not these creatures exist, in the sense of having ostensive reference to empirical entities, to the question of what role they might play in enabling the purpose of the narrative; a question which, if addressed from the hermeneutical approach that has been developed from the thinking of both Nagel and Ricoeur, can be seen to involve establishing how, from the narrative's perspective, such creatures might function as essential realities.

This is in the sense of their role as imaginative alternatives that enable the boundaries of the thinkable to be extended if their interpretation is constructive and expansionist rather than reductive. It is, therefore, a question that must firstly be directed towards the presence of a talking serpent that appears in Genesis 3:1–7; a creature that the narrative acknowledges as belonging to the natural order created by God (Genesis 3:1),[17] but then partially re-mythologizes in giving it speech as, in

13. Gunkel, *Genesis*, 33.
14. Westermann, *Genesis*, 277.
15. Wenham, *Genesis*, 88.
16. A provision that qualifies the controversial call to "conquer" the earth (Genesis 1:28), which Santmire suggests should not be interpreted against the "background of the ideology of modern industrial society" but in the context of the "all-pervading, harmonious world of *shalom* that Genesis 1 presupposes.... Dominion in this sense is an ecological construct. It refers to humans assuming their divinely given niche in the earth alongside of other creatures, which also have their divinely given places, and exercising special care for these creatures" (Santmire, "Genesis Creation Narratives," 374–75).
17. Information which, as Victor Hamilton points out, "Immediately removes any

the words of Ricoeur, there is a need for "a mythic residue in order to convey the unfathomable aspect of the power that perverts language and desire and thereby 'inclines' us towards evil."[18] In this respect, it therefore becomes for a limited time, a *super*natural creature but this is not the serpent-like monster Ti'âmat or as the symbol of "life, fertility and power" in Syro-Phoenician mythology.[19] Neither is it the Australian Aboriginal Rainbow Serpent which, in acts of creation and destruction, represented both fertility and punishment,[20] nor the serpent depicted in the *Gilgamesh* epic that, in carrying away the plant of life, is able to claim the secret of youth by casting off its dead skin.[21] It is a creature that is used simply to expose the fallibility of the human condition[22] and enable what André LaCocque describes as "an astonishing profound reflection on being human . . . a strikingly relevant exposition of human nature."[23]

In his book *Moral Minds*, evolutionary biologist Marc Hauser argues that a moral instinct has evolved within human nature as a capacity of the mind that "unconsciously and automatically generates judgments of right and wrong."[24] It is grounded in our biology, interacting with and adapting to changing environments,[25] leading him to conclude that it is an instinct that must, therefore, be "immune to religious doctrine."[26] For Hauser, equating religion with morality is erroneous as it makes the false assumption that moral "right and wrong" cannot be understood by those lacking religious faith.[27] This is not, however, an assumption that arises from the Eden narrative which appears to support his theory of a

---

possibility that the serpent is to be viewed as some kind of supernatural, divine force" (Hamilton, *Book of Genesis*, 188).

18. LaCocque and Ricoeur, *Thinking Biblically*, 42n20.

19. Compare Numbers 21:4–9 (LaCocque, *Trial of Innocence*, 47).

20. Taçon et al., "Birth of the Rainbow Serpent," 103.

21. Mitchell, *Gilgamesh*, 196–97.

22. Something basic is being said "about humanity that no religious or ideological, no scientific, technical or medical development or change can or will in any way alter. It is part of human existence that a person is fallible. One cannot be a human being other than a fallible human being" (Westermann, *Genesis*, 277).

23. LaCocque, *Trial of Innocence*, 11.

24. Hauser, *Moral Minds*, 4. Within this unconscious process is a hidden moral grammar evaluating the causes and consequences of actions and establishing a "range of learnable moral systems." See also Hauser, *Moral Minds*, 462.

25. Hauser, *Moral Minds*, 456.

26. Hauser, *Moral Minds*, 458.

27. Hauser, *Moral Minds*, 457.

"moral instinct" inherent in human beings who are created in the image of God and evolving as they interact with and care for their environment. Initially, this instinct takes the form of dependent obedience in the unquestioning acceptance of the role of stewardship of the earth and the command: "*From every fruit of the garden you may surely eat. But from the tree of knowledge, good and evil, you shall not eat, for on the day you eat from it, you are doomed to die*" (Genesis 2:16–17).[28] The bringing of each "*beast of the field and each fowl of the heavens . . . to the human to see what he would call it*" (Genesis 2:19)[29] then introduces the imaginative impulse as the human engages in a process of imaginative reasoning by distinguishing between and finding names for the creatures; a process from which self-awareness will develop as no "*sustainer beside him was found*" (Genesis 2:21).[30] It is, however, one of these creatures that will be used to reveal the emergence of reasoning and the evolving complexity of the human condition. As Bouteneff observes

> the scriptural account does not portray two sharply contrasted states of the human person, one (perfected, immortal, sinless, united with God) before the transgression and the (fallen, mortal, sinful, separated from God) after. It describes rather a process, whose starting point is not perfection but *nascence*.[31]

The biblical human has, therefore, a "moral instinct" that is rooted in God's holiness and righteousness[32] but also a nature that, in reflecting the nature of God, is "free, self-determining and self-transcending."[33] In this respect, the progression of the narratives in their exposition of evolving human nature appears to offer support to, rather than oppose, Hauser's belief that *all* human beings will have some level of moral understanding regardless of whether or not they have "religious faith." The concern of the biblical narrative is, however, to show how this understanding can be manipulated and how the ability to use what we might believe to be objective

---

28. Alter, *Five Books*, 21.

29. Alter, *Five Books*, 22.

30. Alter, *Five Books*, 22.

31. Bouteneff, *Beginnings*, 6. See also Fromm, who refers to a Hasidic story stating that when God created humankind he did not declare it to be good, as had occurred with the rest of creation, because humans were unfinished in the sense of being open systems that would grow and develop (Fromm, *You Shall Be as Gods*, 142).

32. Wilkinson, *Message*, 35.

33. Wilkinson, *Message*, 35.

reasoning may, in the words of Nagel, "be influenced more directly, without our knowledge, by the instinctive forces with which it coexists."[34]

The forces encountered in the narrative of Genesis 3 are described by Westermann as coming from within and approaching from without,[35] with the serpent representing the outside force in a dialogue that introduces the ability to reason and reflects "the mysterious power of enticement and temptation inherent in human existence."[36] Significantly, however, it is a force that can only function with a responsive inner force which is seen in the woman's engagement with and capitulation to the serpent's persuasive argument[37] and the man's unquestioning collusion. An important and salutary feature of the narrative appears to be how little the serpent needs to say to provoke the desired response. From a stance of apparently "innocent curiosity" using what Kass describes as the seemingly "rational power of doubt, opposition, negation, and contradiction,"[38] the serpent is able to question both the authority of God and obedience to him. This, with the suggestion of increased insight and knowledge, results in the woman seeing the world through eyes that are imaginatively transformed[39] as she now observes that *"the tree was good for eating . . . lust to the eyes and . . . lovely to look at"* (Genesis 3:6).[40] Significantly, she has also contributed to the process of temptation by extending the divine prohibition to, *"you shall not touch"* the fruit (Genesis 3:3), thus easing the way into the real transgression by allowing an intermediary step in which the possibility of threatened ill effect can be tested.[41] It is, however, a step towards the discovery that the acquisition of

---

34. Nagel, "Reason, Almost," 29.

35. Westermann, *Genesis*, 22.

36. Westermann, *Genesis*, 22.

37. Green describes the serpent as the "subtle hermeneut of suspicion" providing the "earliest recorded misrepresentation of a religious text" in its opening statement questioning the instruction concerning the forbidden fruit (Green, *Theology, Hermeneutics, and Imagination*, 1).

38. Kass, *Wisdom*, 86.

39. Kass, *Wisdom*, 87. Kass describes this transformation as a result of a "rise to self-consciousness about food and eating, about God's commands and the world's hospitality to her needs, and about herself in relation to her needs, to God and to her world." It is a transformation that is, therefore, an awakening "to herself as *mind*" and "an act of self-discovery" that is "liberating not only for thought but also for action" (Kass, *Wisdom*, 83, 84).

40. Alter, *Five Books*, 24.

41. Alter, *Five Books*, 24.

a godlike status of knowledge of good and evil[42] would initially bring only an awareness of their vulnerability as the human couple "*knew they were naked*" and "*hid from the Lord God in the midst of the trees in the garden*" (Genesis 3:7–8).[43]

The powerful impulse and capacity "to transcend oneself and one's species"[44] is, as Nagel suggests, an impulse that is "both a creative and destructive force"[45] and a capacity bringing with it "a liability to alienation";[46] alienation that Nagel describes as a loss of conviction about the meaning of life and which, from a biblical perspective, occurs as the human couple are driven from the presence of God in their natural home. Their radical departure is marked by a gift of clothing (Genesis 3:21); a gesture that also signals a radical departure from the *Gilgamesh* epic in which the "primitive man" *Enkidu* is given clothing to mark "his transition towards civilization" from "his unclothed, uncivilized state."[47] From a biblical perspective, in a challenge to the assumptions of both the ancient and modern world, the dramatic expulsion from Eden marks instead the transition *from* a civilized ideal towards a state which, in the words of Kass, will inevitably include "estrangement from the world, self-division, division of labor, toil, fearful knowledge of death, and the institution of inequality, rule, and subservience";[48] a state in which the human couple will discover, "just *what it means* to have chosen enlightenment and freedom, just what it means to be a *rational* being."[49]

The sense of alienation in this transition is highlighted by a second supernatural presence in the form of the cherubim who with "*the flame of the whirling sword*" guard "*the way to the tree of life*" (Genesis 3:24).[50] The significance of these menacing creatures emerges from their traditional

---

42. Kass suggests the substitution of "bad" for evil as the Hebrew translation has a broader meaning than moral evil and can also incorporate pain, sickness and disorder. See Kass, *Wisdom*, 63.

43. Alter, *Five Books*, 25.

44. Nagel, *Mortal Questions*, 213.

45. Nagel, *View from Nowhere*, 4.

46. Nagel, *View from Nowhere*, 214.

47. Pryke, *Gilgamesh*, 61.

48. Kass, *Wisdom*, 95.

49. Kass, *Wisdom*, 95.

50. Alter, *Five Books*, 28. Wood suggests that the flame translation is supported by an Ugaritic and an Akkadian text which seem to present "fire" and "flames" as divine beings with weapons. See Wood, *Of Wings and Wheels*.

role in the ANE as protectors of both sanctuaries and sacred trees,[51] with their biblical presence as sanctuary guardians or throne-bearers appearing in Exodus 25:18; 1 Samuel 4:4; 1 Kings 6: 2; Chronicles 3; Psalms 18:10 and 80:1b; Isaiah 37:16; and Ezekiel 1, 10 and 41. While this may serve to highlight the typology of Eden as a sanctuary that foreshadows the tabernacle,[52] the cherubim *"set up east of the garden of Eden"* (Genesis 3:24) appear to function primarily as a force with supernatural power that is, therefore, beyond the capacity of the human couple to overcome.[53] The fiery threat, whether in the form of jagged lightning,[54] an armed "animate divine being" or an "independent inanimate entity,"[55] means that there is no way back to their previous existence. In marked contrast, however, to the representatives of the human race on Pioneer 10 who are departing from our known reality into the unknown, the biblical couple are leaving our unknown to enter the reality of our known world. In this respect, the narrative is also a radical departure from the perception of myth or story as flight *from* reality as its mythical elements are reworked, with the supernatural creatures serving, not as independently functioning entities but rather to enable a trajectory that will be instead a flight *to* the reality of the hearer or reader of the biblical text.

---

51. The Hebrew word for cherubim, *kerûb*, comes from Mesopotamia, most directly from the Akkadian *karibu/kuribu*. In Assyria, fierce protective creatures, often in hybrid forms, were carved onto palace and temple walls but are also seen tending to sacred trees. Arthur and Elena George suggest that the cherubim and flaming sword are "central to the message that J sought to convey." This is as "separate but complimentary symbols, the cherubim symbolizing Yahweh's presence and association with the tree of life (by his substitution of Asherah), and the flaming sword representing again his presence but additionally his power" (George and George, *Mythology of Eden*, 170, 175).

52. Wenham, *Genesis*, 90.

53. Alter, *Five Books*, 28. Wood points out that elsewhere in the Bible cherubim are not depicted with weapons. See Wood, *Of Wings and Wheels*, 57.

54. Gunkel, *Genesis*, 25.

55. Hendel proposes that the "flame" of the whirling sword is "an independent fiery being, a divine being in service to Yahweh" with the "whirling sword" being its appropriate weapon (Hendel, "Flame of the Whirling Sword," 671–74). This is disputed by Murray Lichtenstein, for whom the reference to fire "refers to the effect or impression created by the movement of the sword's blade, perceived as blazing or flashing before one's eyes" (Lichtenstein, "Fearsome Sword of Genesis," 54).

EXTENDING THE BOUNDARIES OF THE THINKABLE: FEELING "AT HOME" IN THE WORLD

It remains unclear whether it is legitimate to seek a satisfying account of the cosmos and our place in it, one which will make us feel at home in the universe.[56]

Nagel's doubt about the legitimacy of seeking a "satisfying" account of the cosmos that will make us feel at home in the universe is supported by particle physicist Peter Bussey for whom one reason that "human beings do not easily feel 'at home' in the modern universe" is because of our awareness of its "mind-bending" size.[57] Our closest large galaxy "neighbor" and the most distant thing visible to the naked eye is the Andromeda Galaxy, about 2.3 million light years from our own Milky Way Galaxy, and it is estimated that there are around one hundred billion galaxies in the currently observable universe which has a radius of about fifty billion light years. This is an awareness that Bussey suggests has led to a feeling of insignificance arising from not only "an inability to relate to the structure as a whole" but also from the "background of blackness" that dominates the view through our telescopes; a vast expanse of dark energy and dark matter about which very little is known. Nagel's doubt also resonates with conclusions from the work of contemporary anthropology on human adaptability and the concept of our "openness to the world."[58] This "openness," described by Pannenberg as "the unique freedom of man to inquire and move beyond every regulation of his existence,"[59] is seen in our capacity for self-transcendence and ability to adapt in new ways to the environment. It is, however, an openness that Stanley Grenz suggests "lies at the foundation of our lack of a biological 'home' in the cosmos"[60] because, in lacking a "specific biological role that explains our purpose for existence," we are "never completely fulfilled by any one achievement" so are "continually shaping and reshaping our environment in an unfulfilled attempt to create a 'home' for ourselves."[61]

56. Nagel, "Analytic Philosophy."
57. Bussey, *Signposts to God*, 85.
58. Ashley Montagu in Grenz, *Theology for the Community*, 130.
59. Pannenberg in Grenz, *Theology for the Community*, 130.
60. Grenz, *Theology for the Community*, 130.
61. Grenz, *Theology for the Community*, 131.

The legitimacy of seeking a satisfying account of our place in the cosmos is also challenged by Nagel's suggestion in *Mind and Cosmos* that the appearance of reason in the world remains a mystery.[62] This is because, while we use perception and reason to construct scientific theories of the natural world and extend the boundaries of the thinkable, our confidence in their reliability is not matched by "a convincing external account of why those faculties exist."[63] The Eden narrative does not attempt to provide a scientific answer to this mystery as its focus is on the impact of reason and its potential as a destructive force. It is an impact that is clearly expressed in Denise Levertov's poem "Contraband" which refers to the potential tyranny of an excessive use or "taste" of reason.[64] In referring to the Edenic tree of *"the knowledge of good and evil"* (Genesis 2:9 NRSV) as a tree of *reason*, she suggests that its fruit would be toxic if more than a "pinch" was consumed. An overindulgence of this fruit, with what she describes as *but, how* and *if* questions would, subsequently, result in a toxicity that would both drive the human couple from Eden and form an impenetrable barrier between them and God. The biblical denial of the forbidden fruit to the biblical couple is thus validated firstly, by the warning of its potential toxicity and their inability to ration their intake; an inability that Kass relates directly to both freedom of choice and the capacity to reason:

> Because we have free choice—that is because our desires are not simply given by instinct—and because our reason, through its working on our imagination, influences and alters natural appetites, human appetite increases beyond what is necessary and good for us. Precisely because we are rational and, hence, free, we can freely desire things that are harmful to health, life and wellbeing.[65]

A second validation is found in the exposure of reason as an often tyrannical and limiting force which, in setting up its own boundaries, has

---

62. Nagel, *Mind and Cosmos*, 29.

63. Nagel, *Mind and Cosmos*, 31. He has previously stated that "an external understanding of reason as merely another natural phenomenon—a biological product, for example—is impossible. Reason is whatever we find we must *use* to understand anything, including itself. And if we try to understand it merely as a natural (biological or psychological) phenomenon, the result will be an account incompatible with our use of it and with the understanding of it we have in using it" (Nagel, *Last Word*, 143).

64. Levertov, "Contraband," 278.

65. Kass, *Wisdom*, 66.

the potential to ensnare us within a closed world and restricted sense of reality. Neuroscientist Sam Harris refers to the "shady groves of reason"[66] as a haven from the irrationality of religion but, conversely, fellow atheist and moral psychologist Jonathan Haidt might use the same term to represent what he believes to be the doubtful honesty of reason. Haidt argues against what he believes to be the current worship of reason because, in being designed to seek "justification rather than truth," it is unfit to rule;[67] "a delusion taking us to almost any conclusions that we wish if we ask the right questions and avoid others."[68] In contrast to Hauser, Haidt rejected the title *The Moral Mind* for his 2013 book in favor of *The Righteous Mind*, as he felt it necessary to highlight the sense that "human nature is not just intrinsically moral" but also "intrinsically moralistic, critical and judgmental."[69] With echoes of Nagel's belief that even "the most civilized human beings have only a haphazard understanding of how to live, how to treat others, how to organize their societies,"[70] Haidt suggests that our moral reasoning is often less about establishing truth and being "reliably or universally altruistic" than furthering our social agendas and strategic objectives.[71]

It is an aspect of the human condition that appears, however, to have been anticipated in the biblical exposure of human frailty that supports both Nagel's assessment of human nature and the suggestion of Savulescu and Persson that "[a] basic fact about the human condition is that it is easier for us to harm each other than to benefit each other." This is because they believe that "evolutionary pressures" have not enabled the development of a psychology that allows us to cope with the moral problems created by the now "overwhelming" power to harm that has resulted from the rapid advances in science and technology.[72] These are problems that they suggest are also enhanced by "our limited and parochial altruism [which] is not strong enough to provide a reason for us to give up our consumerist life-styles for the sake of our distant descendants, or our distant contemporaries in far-away places."[73] Savulescu and Persson

---

66. Harris, *End of Faith*, 161.
67. Haidt, *Righteous Mind*, 86.
68. Haidt, *Righteous Mind*, 9, 107.
69. Haidt, *Righteous Mind*, xix.
70. Nagel, *View from Nowhere*, 186.
71. Haidt, *Righteous Mind*, xx–xxi, 220.
72. Savulescu and Persson, "Moral Enhancement."
73. Savulescu and Persson, "Moral Enhancement."

conclude that a solution may only be found with the development of "specifically *biomedical* moral enhancement" for which they believe there to be "few cogent philosophical or moral objections."[74] Biotechnology may, from this perspective, appear to be our salvation as the only option that can prevent us from being "biologically or genetically doomed to cause our own destruction,"[75] but this sobering outlook is not supported by a biblical perspective of the human condition. The closure of the Eden narrative, with the expulsion of the human couple into a hostile world, offers an alternative explanation of why, in the words of Grenz,

> we no longer live in harmony with the "garden" in which the Creator placed us. Designed to enjoy fellowship with the rest of God's good creation, we now live in alienation from the natural world around us. Rather than seeing ourselves as creative beings under God, we seek to be the creator, to control nature and enslave it to serve us. We no longer see the earth as an organic whole which we serve on God's behalf. Rather, in our insatiable but misguided quest for a "home," we view the earth as the raw material for our transforming activity.[76]

It is an explanation that is also sobering but it is a perspective of the human condition that also offers hope that is not dependent on an invasive technosolutionism. The quest for the restoration of harmony, remains a theme throughout the narratives that follow; narratives in which the underlying concept of radical departure into new and unknown territory offers the prospect of transformational new life. It is in this respect, departure, both ontic and noetic, into virgin territory which is highlighted in the narrative of Luke 1:26–38 and challenges the hearer of reader to look beyond the shady groves of reason, as either intellectual haven or doubtful honesty, to a new vision in which the presence of an angel serves to further extend the boundaries of the thinkable.

---

74. Savulescu and Persson, "Moral Enhancement."
75. Savulescu and Persson, "Moral Enhancement."
76. Grenz, *Theology for the Community*, 207.

10

Virgin Territory
Beyond the Shady Groves of Reason

Fra Angelico, *The Annunciation*, ca. 1426, tempera on panel, 162 cm x 192 cm, Museo Nacional del Prado, Madrid, Spain[1]

1. © Photographic Archive Museo Nacional del Prado.

The angel said to her, "Do not be afraid Mary, for you have found favor with God. And now, you will conceive in your womb and bear a son, and you will name him Jesus."

LUKE 1: 30–31

IN THIS CHAPTER, AN approach to the interpretation of Luke 1:26–38 is explored which, in using the concepts extrapolated from Nagel's thinking, is able to contribute to a contemporary understanding of the supernatural components in the narrative. The first section examines the controversies arising from the narrative and subsequent doctrine, and differing attempts to address them. The concept of radical departure from the familiar is then applied to the narrative through a comparison with other ancient birth stories. In the second section, the concept of an imaginative alternative is used to consider the function of a supernatural being which may, from a contemporary perspective, appear to be a problematic part of the narrative. Barth's perspective of angels as a "necessary problem," is explored in order to move away from a reductive interpretive approach based on a *history or fiction* dichotomy, towards an expanded vision of a reality that demands to be understood on its own terms. This is reality that Nagel describes as not corresponding to objectivity which he suggests can lead away from the truth if it is applied to the wrong subject matter. In the final section, the narrative is considered from the perspective of extending conceptual boundaries in order to move *toward* rather than *away* from truth. This is movement away from interpretive reductionism toward an expanded vision of what Ricoeur refers to as "the richness of the real." It is movement that will, however, require the reader or hearer to enter into the spirit of the narrative, from a position of informed receptivity that is able to recognize the limitations of language in articulating reality beyond the boundaries of what may be considered thinkable.

LUKE 1:26-38—RADICAL DEPARTURE FROM THE FAMILIAR: DARING TO ASSERT MARVELS

Among the tales of those whom we call Greeks it is said that Perseus has been born of Danae, still a virgin, by him that they entitle Zeus flowing down upon her in the form of gold. And in fact you (Christians) ought to be ashamed of saying the same sorts of things as they, and should rather say that this Jesus was man of human origin, and, if you prove from the Scriptures that He is the Christ, that because of His perfect life under the Law He was deemed worthy to be chosen to be Christ. And do not dare to assert marvels, that you be not convicted of talking folly like the Greeks.[2]

The words of Trypho in Justin Martyr's second-century apologetic dialog, described by James Sweeney as "one of the earliest direct assaults on the virgin birth by a non-Christian,"[3] would resonate with many today both outside but also within Christian communities. The account of the virginal conception in Luke 1:26–38, together with the infancy narratives of Matthew 1–2 and Luke 1–2 and the seemingly conflicting chronology in Luke 3:23–38, are, according to Edith Humphrey, among "the most beloved, ignored, and debated Gospel passages"; passages that while being "a treasure-house for the liturgist," also "bring the theologian to the edge of mystery, the literary critic to the margins of genre, and the historian to the brink of a headache."[4] According to Barth, the virginal conception and birth are perhaps "*the* place, at which at all times, and even largely within the Christian community, offense has been taken."[5] It is, therefore, unsurprising that in the light of reason, due to knowledge arising from modern biology, the subsequent doctrine of the Virgin Birth[6] that developed in response to early church controversies,[7] appears for increasing numbers to be intellectual "folly" in demanding the expression of literal belief in the miraculous conception by, or of, the Holy Spirit and consequent birth of Jesus by the Virgin Mary.[8]

---

2. Justin Martyr, *Dialogue with Trypho*, 140.
3. Sweeney, "Modern and Ancient," 153.
4. Humphrey, "Infancy Narratives," 325.
5. Barth, *Dogmatics in Outline*, 95.
6. An ancient doctrine that can be traced back to the sub-apostolic period and comprises the "Virginal Conception, gestation, and Virgin Birth of Christ" (Crisp, *God Incarnate*, 78).
7. Such as Docetism (Jesus only *appears* to be human); Adoptionism (the divine *logos* takes possession of an existing human person); Nestorianism (the human and divine natures of Christ are separate so there are two persons, the man Jesus Christ and the divine *logos* dwelling in man); and Apollinarianism (Jesus had a human body but his reason or rationality took the form of the separate divine logos).
8. Hugh Mackay describes it as "the doctrine of the church most likely to strain people's credulity to breaking point" (Mackay, *Beyond Belief*, 221). See also Gerd Lüdemann, who concludes, "The statement that Jesus was engendered by the Spirit and born

Debate over the historicity of the virginal conception, more often referred to as the Virgin Birth, has included, and to some extent still includes, what Reginald Fuller describes as "violent attack," "frantic defense" and "reverent historical agnosticism."[9] In 2007, *The Spectator* magazine posed the question, "Do you believe in the Virgin Birth of Jesus Christ?" to a group that included Archbishops, Bishops, writers and politicians. A significant number were "too busy" to reply or did not respond to approaches but the answers of those who did ranged from strong affirmation to strong denial by both clergy and lay respondents. A common stance, however, was reflected in a reply from writer James Delingpole:

> Look, I've successfully survived forty-two years as a member of the Church of England without ever having to give serious thought to the Virgin Birth, and I jolly well don't see why I should be put on the spot now . . . I guess that makes me a Don't Know.[10]

While some may be prepared to take an agnostic stance on the grounds that historical evidence can neither substantiate nor disprove the biblical and doctrinal claims,[11] a significant problem for many arises from the issue of intellectual integrity in participating in what appear to be anachronistic creedal statements of belief.[12] A potentially safe haven has been found by some in seeing the virginal conception as a "literary creation" that is "profoundly true" without being "historically factual"[13] or as

---

of a virgin is a falsification of the historical facts. At all events he had a human father. From that it follows . . . that any interpretation which fails to take a clear stand here is to be branded a lie. This includes all official Catholic dogma about Mary, and also the confessions of Jesus as the virgin's son which are made every Sunday in Protestant worship" (Lüdemann, *Virgin Birth?*, 140).

9. Fuller, "Virgin Birth," 3.

10. "Do You Believe."

11. "As we do not know if eyewitness or close to eye-witness testimony stands behind any of the stories pertinent to Jesus' infancy" (Brown, "Problem," 9n18).

12. The Apostles Creed refers to "Jesus Christ . . . who was conceived by the Holy Spirit, born of the Virgin Mary," while the Nicene Creed states, "For us and for our salvation he came down from heaven, was incarnate of the Holy Spirit and the Virgin Mary and became fully human" (ACANZP, *New Zealand Prayer Book*, 48, 410).

13. For Marcus Borg, "The story of Jesus' virginal conception . . . is a metaphorical affirmation of Jesus' identity and significance . . . an early Christian narrative confession of faith and affirmation of allegiance to Jesus" (Borg, "Meaning of the Birth Stories," 185–86). David Tacey also rejects "institutional literalism" and espouses metaphor as the way to "genuine religious meaning." Through the use of metaphor as "spiritual imagining," the virgin birth can still be "real even though it never took place." This is because "a miracle such as the virgin birth is not a physical event, but a spiritual significance astir in the event" (Tacey, *Religion as Metaphor*, 18, 94, 98).

a theological or confessional statement rather than a biological fact.[14] It has not, however, been a safe haven for all as denying the factuality of a virginal conception has been and still remains in some institutions an obstacle to ordination[15] and university tenure.[16] It is, therefore, unsurprising that there have been attempts to avoid the issue; attempts that have also been driven by a fear of pastoral irresponsibility in unsettling the faithful or upsetting the masses.[17] Raymond Brown highlights the ambiguity of the 1966 *Dutch Catechism* in not explicitly stating that Jesus was born to a woman who was biologically a virgin[18] and Philip Mellor refers to the 1991 decision by the Scottish Episcopal Church to "avoid mentioning the concept, wherever possible, because people find it 'alienating.'"[19] As Brown points out, however, in some respects the faithful have already been disturbed by popularist scholarship[20] which now includes the work of those involved in the Jesus Seminar and writers such as David Tacey

---

14. John Dominic Crossan makes the declaration: "I understand the virginal conception of Jesus to be a confessional statement about Jesus' status and not a biological statement about Mary's body" (Crossan, *Jesus*, 23). See also R. Berry who states: "It is certainly correct to see the Virgin Birth as a theological necessity rather than an existential puzzle" (Berry, "Virgin Birth of Christ," 109).

15. As it is regarded as an essential criterion for orthodoxy and "doctrinal suitability for ministry" in being "essential for being identified as a Christian" (Brown, "Problem," 3).

16. In 1987, Uta Ranke-Heinemann lost her chair at the University of Essen as she was declared ineligible to teach when she refuted the Virgin Birth as an historical event.

17. Tacey traces this back to the "great minds in church history [who] have been aware of the mythic nature of dogmas" but have not wanted to "disturb the supernatural overlay that has been constructed by theology to make 'the greatest story ever told' appealing to the superstitious masses" (Tacey, *Religion as Metaphor*, 31).

18. Although a statement from the bishops' meeting in Utrecht was published in the Amsterdam newspaper *De Tijd* (August 19, 1966), stating that they "did not intend any ambiguity about Mary's corporeal virginity." After investigation by a commission of cardinals from Rome, a subsequent directive (*Acta apostolicae sedis* 60 [1968] 688) stated that "the Catechism 'must teach equally clearly [with the perpetual virginity of Mary] the doctrine of the virginal birth of Jesus, which is so supremely in accord with the mystery of the incarnation. No further occasion shall be given for denying this truth . . . retaining only a symbolic meaning [of virginal birth], for instance, that it merely expresses the gift inspired by pure grace that God bestowed upon us in His Son.' The resulting corrected text of the Catechism is now printed as a supplement" (Brown, "Problem," 4–5).

19. Mellor, "Virgin Birth," 196. In 2018, an adapted version of "Hark! The Herald Angels Sing" was reported to have incurred the ire of bishops as it removed the reference to Mary's virginity by replacing "offspring of a virgin's womb" with "offspring of the favored one." See Rouch, "Hark!"

20. Louis Evely in Brown, "Problem," 6.

seeking to recover the "true faith" from the "absurdities of the church councils."[21] Mellor may, therefore, offer an important focus in suggesting that a significant issue to be addressed concerns whether the removal of what may now appear to be an "unnecessary, elaborate ornamentation" that is obscuring "the bare structure of Christian truth," is actually the removal of a "load-bearing wall"[22] as, in the words of Nissiotis, "The Virgin Birth is the key moment within the incarnation of the Logos. Without it the whole event is perverted as a human-centred natural happening."[23]

Andrew Lincoln considers three arguments against the historicity of a virginal conception in his search for a hermeneutical approach that "is not dismissive of serious contemporary biblical criticism" and "takes account of contemporary knowledge."[24] One is based on the silence within the rest of the New Testament about the phenomenon, the "multiple and contradictory" depictions of Jesus's origins in the genealogies and references to his father Joseph in both Luke and other New Testament books.[25] He therefore suggests that this reveals the "brief" Lukan annunciation narrative to be a "minority report"[26] adhering to the literary convention of ancient biography. A second argument concerns the issue that whilst a literal interpretation of the virginal conception as historical fact once served to *refute* Docetism in establishing the full humanity of Jesus, it now appears to *promote* it. This is because, according to modern biology, his humanity is not as was previously thought "safeguarded through his mother"[27] but requires a Y chromosome to be provided by

---

21. Tacey, *Religion as Metaphor*, 18.
22. Mellor, "Virgin Birth," 196.
23. Nissiotis in Mellor, "Virgin Birth," 196.
24. Lincoln, *Born of a Virgin?*, 274.

25. Such as Mark 3:20–25; 6:1–6; John 1:45; 6:42; Acts 2:30; 13:23; Romans 1:3; Galatians 4:4; 2 Timothy 2:8; Hebrews 7:14; Revelation 22:16. See also Brown who states that: "The NT material that rests in some way on apostolic witness (Pauline letters, Gospel traditions of the ministry) offers no support for the virginal conception" (Brown, *Birth of the Messiah*, 626).

26. As opposed to a "main or normative New Testament source for the conception of Jesus." Lincoln stresses that the narrative should still be treated with "full seriousness as part of the New Testament's authoritative witness to the person of Christ" but whether his argument supports or challenges this authority is open to debate (Lincoln, *Born of a Virgin*, 39).

27. Due to the ancient assumption based on Aristotelian theory that Jesus' full bodily humanity could come from Mary alone as "the bodily substance necessary for a human fetus comes from the mother while the life force originates with the father" (Lincoln, "How Babies Were Made," 44).

a human male in order for him to be fully human.[28] It is an issue that is also raised by Arthur Peacocke who concludes that the "hard questions" raised by modern biological science make it "impossible to see how Jesus could be said to share our human nature" and have "any salvific role for humanity" if he "came into existence by a virginal conception of the kind traditionally proposed."[29] In this respect, there is considerable appeal in Friedrich Schleiermacher's suggestion that "the assumption of a Virgin Birth is superfluous" and the setting up of a doctrine is consequently inadvisable "for this involves one all too easily in investigations of a purely scientific character which lie quite outside our sphere."[30] If, however, the "hard questions" of science are, under Nagel's terms, the wrong questions to put to the narrative then, as Oliver Crisp suggests, the narrative and subsequent doctrine of the Virgin Birth can be regarded as being "primarily concerned with demarcating the virginal conception of Christ's human nature as a miracle brought about by the Holy Spirit, and not with the biological story that explains how that may have occurred."[31] The focus is then able to turn to how and why the biblical writers portray this miracle and its potential relevance to the Incarnation in the light of Brown's observation that "in the relationship between virginal conception and incarnation, it is not the first that is essential for the second; it is the second that makes the first credible."[32]

Crisp agrees with Lincoln's suggestion that "neither the Virgin Birth nor the Virginal Conception is necessary for the Incarnation" as "Christ could have been born through natural generation, rather than via the miraculous workings of the Holy Spirit."[33] The doctrine of Incarnation does not, therefore, need a virginal conception but, as a sign indicating that a

28. Lincoln, *Born of a Virgin*, 264.
29. Peacocke, "DNA of our DNA," 65–66.
30. Schleiermacher, *Christian Faith*, 404–6.
31. Crisp, "Virgin Birth," 7.
32. Brown, "Problem," 16n34.

33. Crisp, *God Incarnate*, 77. This is also the position of other scholars, with Brown commenting that both Catholic and Protestant theologians state "clearly that the bodily fatherhood of Joseph would not have excluded the fatherhood of God" as the "idea of divine sonship is substantiated in the Synoptic account of the baptism and the transfiguration, and in Pauline and Johannine Christology; it is not dependent upon the infancy narratives" (Brown, "Problem," 16). See also John Wilkinson, who argues that "such a story was not necessary in order to prove the Messiahship of Jesus for there is no indubitable evidence that the Jews ever believed that the Messiah was to be born of a virgin, in spite of the Septuagint rendering of *'almah* by *parthenos* in Isaiah 7:14" (Wilkinson "Apologetic Aspects," 161).

"particular individual is marked out for the purposes of God," Crisp suggests contra Lincoln that it is "a fitting or suitable means by which Christ's human nature is generated."[34] He uses the concept of "fittingness"[35] to refute Lincoln's third argument, which concerns the issue of whether virginal conception can be reconciled with the pre-existence of the Son of God as referenced in texts such as John 1:1; 17:5; Philippians 2:6–7; Colossians 1:15–17; and Hebrews 1:2; texts that, in the words of Wolfhart Pannenberg, suggest:

> In its content, the legend of Jesus' virgin birth stands in an irreconcilable contradiction to the Christology of the incarnation of the preexistent Son of God found in Paul and John. For, according to this legend, Jesus first *became* God's Son through Mary's conception. According to Paul and John, on the contrary, the Son of God was already preexistent and then as a preexistent being had bound himself to the man Jesus.[36]

Crisp, however, rejects this apparent contradiction suggesting that the Virgin Birth is a "fitting" context for the incarnation as "a special birth signals the fact that it is a divine person taking on human nature, not the beginning of the life of a new individual, as a normal process of human generation from two human parents might suggest."[37] It therefore provides a "marker" that is able to "preserve the uniqueness of the event" without attempting to explain its mystery[38] as a unique event which, in radically departing from the familiar, dares to assert the marvel of an unprecedented holy overshadowing.

The sense of radical departure from the familiar in the annunciation narrative of Luke 1:26–38 is seen firstly, in its departure from the familiar ancient birth stories of world religions, Greco-Roman mythology, and the biographies of Pharaohs, emperors and philosophers,[39] with

---

34. Crisp, "Virgin Birth," 8.

35. See chapter 14 in Crisp, *God Incarnate*, 77–102. Crisp refers to Anselm's understanding of "fittingness" and cites Mozley's observation that "the fittingness of the Virgin Birth in connection with the person of Christ has been widely felt within the Christian Church" (Mozley, *Doctrine of the Incarnation*, 55).

36. Pannenberg, *Jesus*, 143.

37. Crisp, *God Incarnate*, 100. See also James Edwards, who suggests that preexistence is indicated in the wording that Jesus will be *called* Son of God (Luke 1:35) rather than *become* the Son of God (Edwards, *Gospel according to Luke*, 48).

38. Crisp, *God Incarnate*, 101.

39. Such as the births of the Buddha, Krishna, and the son of Zoroaster, the births of the Pharaohs where the god Amun-Ra acted through the father and in the marvellous

Brown suggesting that "there is no exact parallel or antecedent in the material available to the Christians of the first century who told of this conception."⁴⁰ In contrast to Brown, Lincoln argues that the Gospels can be categorized as "a subset of ancient Greco-Roman biography," with the biblical birth narratives conforming

> very closely to those of the birth of heroes or great figures in ancient biography, where there are predictions, prophecies and omens of future greatness. And their conception is traced back to a union between one of the gods and a human mother, with no male involved in the process.⁴¹

Lincoln expands his reductive argument by pointing out that in some of these biographies, such as Plutarch's biography of Alexander, a miraculous and a natural conception account are juxtaposed, with the god Apollo and Philip II of Macedonia both credited as Alexander's father.⁴² For Lincoln, the biblical narratives are, therefore, conforming not only to the ancient literary convention of the union between a god and a human mother but also to the ancient convention of dual paternity ascribed to those who would eventually achieve greatness. While this may have been a familiar concept to the biblical writers and their audience, the marked contrast between such biographies and the biblical account appears, however, to offer support to Brown and indicate the radical departure of the biblical narratives from the comparative material.⁴³ Darrell Bock and Mikel Del Rosario also point out that a close reading of Plutarch's account highlights difference rather than similarity as Alexander's mother Olympias is not a virgin when she is seduced by Apollo who takes the form of

---

births of the emperor Augustus and philosopher Plato (Brown, "Problem," 30).

40. Brown, "Problem," 30.

41. Lincoln, "How Babies Were Made," 48. See also Tacey, who refers to over "two hundred examples of historical and/or mythical figures born of a virgin," with the idea of such a birth being "a code for 'one who is favored by the gods'" therefore "an accepted literary trope at the time . . . designating the holiness of a person who impacted the world in a significant manner" (Tacey, *Religion as Metaphor*, 94–95).

42. Plutarch's biographies of Theseus and Romulus also contain accounts of both ordinary human conception and conception in which a human mother is impregnated by a god (Lincoln, "How Babies Were Made," 48).

43. See also Charles Cranfield, who suggests that "the more closely these parallels are examined, the more stark becomes the contrast between them and the narratives of Matthew and Luke" (Cranfield, "Some Reflections," 181).

a snake.[44] As Brown suggests, the supposed parallels with comparative literature are, therefore, questionable, as they appear to

> consistently involve a type of *hieros gamos* where a divine male, in human or other form, impregnates a woman, either through normal sexual intercourse or through some substitute form of penetration. They are not really similar to the nonsexual virginal conception that is at the core of the infancy narratives, a conception where there is no male deity or element to impregnate Mary.[45]

The sense of radical departure from the familiar continues in relation to other biblical birth narratives that involve supernatural intervention due to advanced age or infertility. There are parallels between the conception and birth of Isaac to the elderly Abraham and Sarah (Genesis 18:1–15), Samuel to Elkanah and the infertile Hannah (1 Samuel 1:1–20) and John the Baptist to the elderly Zechariah and Elizabeth who is also described as barren (Luke 1:5–25). Brown notes the further significant parallels between the annunciation to Zechariah and the annunciation to Mary of the birth of Jesus[46] but also the significant differences in the Lukan account from the previous narratives as it begins with the disclosure that Mary is a virgin who is engaged rather than married to Joseph. It is a disclosure that paves the way for what will follow in the imaginative and unprecedented alternative of a holy overshadowing that is presented in a

---

44. Bock and Del Rosario, "Table Briefing," 465.

45. Brown, "Problem," 30. See also Barth, who states that the biblical narrative "has nothing to do with the myths narrated elsewhere in the history of religions, myths of the procreation of men by gods . . . there is no question of a sexual event." God is not "a partner" to the Virgin (Barth, *Dogmatics in Outline*, 97). Perhaps the final word should be left with Philip Carrington, who suggests that the parallels "would never have been made if we were in the habit of using plain, straightforward language. The ladies in question were none of them virgins in any sense of the word; they have only been called so to make the myths sound respectable" (Carrington, *Meaning of The Revelation*, 205).

46. As "(a) both annunciations have an introduction that mentions the husband, the wife, and the tribal origin, (b) in both annunciations the angel is identified as Gabriel, (c) in both annunciations Gabriel addresses the visionary by name and urges 'Do not be afraid,' (d) the phrasing of the messages in 1:13 and 1:31 about the birth and naming of the son is very similar, (e) each message is followed by a poetic passage predicting the future greatness of the child, (f) in turn, this prediction is greeted by a 'How?' question posed by Zechariah and by Mary respectively, (g) finally, the 'How?' question is answered by a sign from the angel showing the power of God" (Brown, "Luke's Description," 360n5). See also Mikeal Parsons on Luke's use of the rhetorical device of "*synkrisis* in double encomium" where a comparison of two people is made for the purpose of praise but also to establish one as the superior (Parsons, *Luke*, 21–22).

story which operates at the edge of mystery and the margins of genre[47] but uses the "plain words" and compelling and masterful imagery that physicists now suggest are necessary for an understanding of quantum reality.

AN IMAGINATIVE ALTERNATIVE: A SUPERNATURAL CREATION

In Fra Angelico's painting *The Annunciation*, a supernatural being in the form of a menacing cherubim hovers in the background behind the distraught human couple forcing their departure into the unknown and preventing their return to a paradisiacal home. In contrast, the supernatural being taking center stage in the foreground appears as a benevolent angel whose posture reflects the nature of the words spoken to Mary: "*Greetings, favored one! The Lord is with you*" and "*Do not be afraid, Mary, for you have found favor with God*" (Luke 1:28–30). The presence of these supernatural creatures in biblical narratives was described by Barth as "an extraordinarily acute embarrassment"[48] because, if they are seen to denote a reality that is distinct from both God and humankind and "therefore distinct from the true and central content of the Word of God although intimately related to it," the concept of angels can lead to a step into the "sphere of the superfluous and uncertain."[49] This is a sphere that Barth believed to be "the most remarkable and difficult of all" as it has always contained "a good deal of theological caprice, of valueless, grotesque and even absurd speculation . . . and also of no less doubtful skepticism." He therefore raised the significant issues of how we can "even put the right questions, let alone give the right answers"; how we might "steer between this Scylla and Charybdis, between the far too interesting mythology of the ancients and the far too uninteresting 'demythologization' of most of the moderns"; how we are able "to be both open and cautious, critical and naïve, perspicuous and modest" without saying too much or too little.[50] Perhaps his most salutary comment, however, emerges from his concern

---

47. Whitehouse, "God's Heavenly Kingdom," 378.

48. Referring to angels and demons. Barth in Wood, "Extraordinary Acute Embarrassment," 326.

49. Barth, *Church Dogmatics*, 370.

50. Barth, *Church Dogmatics*, 369.

about a lack of a sense of humor on the part of both "those who know and say too much" and "those who deny or ignore too much."[51]

Despite their problematic nature, Barth believed angels to be a "necessary problem"[52] as "a theology which has no account of angels . . . is an impoverished theology."[53] He stressed that they are not "independent or autonomous subjects" and never "leading characters" but rather "marginal figures, who come and go in the service of God subordinated to the great events enacted between God and man."[54] They can therefore only be spoken of "incidentally" and "softly," with the awareness that

> when the Bible speaks of angels . . . it always introduces us to a sphere where historically verifiable history . . . passes over into non-verifiable saga or legend . . . when it is a matter of angels in the Bible, we are in the sphere of a particular form of history which by content and nature does not proceed according to ordinary analogies, and thus can only be grasped by divinatory imagination, and find expression in the freer observation and speech of poetry.[55]

For Barth, the biblical angels, as distinctive representatives of "the work and revelation of divine grace,"[56] therefore serve to mark the transition from the transcendent to the worldly, "the reaching of the incommensurable to the commensurable, of mystery into the sphere of known possibilities."[57] They are, in this respect, "figures of biblical saga and legend" but for Barth this labeling is not a reductionist "concession to modern thought" but rather emphasizes that the history of the work and revelation of a transcendent God is not confined to "the narrow sphere of historically verifiable occurrence" and "ordinary earthly analogies."[58] He is then able to suggest that this "real history," which "escapes ordinary analogies and cannot therefore be verified historically," can take the form

---

51. Barth, *Church Dogmatics*, 369.
52. Barth in Wood, "Extraordinary Acute Embarrassment," 333.
53. Whitehouse, "God's Heavenly Kingdom," 377.
54. Barth, *Church Dogmatics*, 371.
55. Barth, *Church Dogmatics*, 374.
56. Barth, *Church Dogmatics*, 374.
57. Barth, *Church Dogmatics*, 375. "Whereas earth is the sphere and limit of humanity's vision and comprehension, the angels stand at the boundary of knowing and unknowing, at the place where the 'unknowable waits at the limits of the knowable'" (Barth in Lindsay, "Heavenly Witness," 8).
58. Barth, *Church Dogmatics*, 375.

of saga and legend which is "true" even if this is truth that can only be "grasped by the imagination and represented by the medium of poetry."[59] From this perspective, the annunciation narrative can be interpreted as a radical departure from the familiar to an expanded vision of reality; a vision that is enabled by the overlap of, and interaction between, multiple narrative forms as a result of the productive imagination at work in a narrative that is operating at the edge of, and looking beyond, conceptual boundaries.

The supernatural presence of an angel is in this sense a fitting precursor to the supernatural event that follows, with the introduction of a radically new concept when Mary is informed that "*you will conceive in your womb and bear a son, and you will name him Jesus*" (Luke 1:30). This radical departure from the reality of the hearer or reader is, however, offset by Mary's response in asking "*How can this be, since I am a virgin?*" (Luke 1:34); a response that James Edwards describes as being "determined by *human* reality and possibility as she knows that children cannot be conceived apart from sexual intercourse."[60] It is a reaction that therefore invites and allows the hearer or reader to take a similar stance of initial incredulity to this seemingly impossible concept; a concept that is portrayed in the Fra Angelico painting by a dove representing the Holy Spirit who, according to the angel, will "*come upon*" Mary and enable "*the power of the Most High*" to "*overshadow*" her in order for the child that will be born to be holy and "*called Son of God*" (Luke 1:35). Edwards describes the word *overshadow* as "critically important" in recalling the divine cloud that overshadowed the tabernacle in Exodus 40:33 to infuse it with God's presence and glory. The cloud that established God's presence in a place now does so in a person[61] in order to enable the supernatural "marvel" of the Word becoming flesh and living among us (John 1:14) as the new Adam created in God's image and "*holy . . . called Son of God.*"[62]

The hearer or reader is then challenged to maintain a position of informed receptivity and humble acceptance that Mary adopts on being told that "*your relative Elizabeth in her old age, has also conceived a son; and this is the sixth month for her who was said to be barren. For nothing will be impossible for God*" (Luke 1:36–37). While upholding this position is a challenge that appears to be significant in the light of contemporary

---

59. Barth, *Church Dogmatics*, 374.
60. Edwards, *Gospel according to Luke*, 48.
61. Edwards, *Gospel according to Luke*, 49.
62. Edwards, *Gospel according to Luke*, 49–50.

epistemology, it does not, however, appear to be a concern of the author as there is no further elaboration of this supernatural event; an event that appears to lie beyond the assumed limits of possibility and the boundaries of the current thinkable.

EXTENDING THE BOUNDARIES OF THE THINKABLE: PREGNANT WITH MEANING

Nagel's concern about the limits of a reductive "*physical* conception of objectivity" as a method of understanding,[63] leads him to suggest that its pursuit can be "carried to excess" and that "it can lead away from the truth if carried out the wrong way or with respect to the wrong subject matter." It is, therefore, not always the best method of understanding, as it may not "correspond to reality and he makes a potentially significant point for biblical hermeneutics in stating that

> human objectivity may fail to exhaust reality for another reason: there may be aspects of reality beyond its reach because they are altogether beyond our capacity to form conceptions of the world. What there is, and what we, in virtue of our nature, can think about are different things, and the latter may be smaller than the former.[64]

If the Lukan narrative is approached in the light of Nagel's comments, the question that arises concerns how it might be seen to respond to these limitations in its presentation of a biblical perspective of reality which, in extending the boundaries of the thinkable, is able to lead *toward* rather than *away* from truth. The content of the annunciation narrative indicates that its author did not consider that the familiar human form

---

63. This is a conception that he describes as having developed as "part of our method of arriving at a truer understanding of the physical world" but he warns that "although there is a connection between objectivity and reality . . . not all reality is objective, for not everything is better understood the more objectively it is viewed." For Nagel, this relates to the issue of consciousness or mind which indicates that there is more to reality than the physical conception of objectivity can accommodate. He also points out the challenges to the idea of objective reality that have emerged in quantum physics regarding the role of the observer in the description of phenomena (Nagel, "Limits of Objectivity," 77–81). There is, therefore, a form of "objective blindness" that assumes "that what there really is must be understandable in a certain way—that reality is in a narrow sense objective reality" in the sense of being detached from a specifically human perspective (Nagel, *View from Nowhere*, 7).

64. Nagel, *View from Nowhere*, 91.

of conception was "the best mode of understanding" the reality of an incarnation in which God would take human; understanding that in the words of Barth,

> Jesus Christ is indeed ... "true man" but He is not "just" a man, not just an extraordinarily gifted or specially guided man, let alone a super-man; but, while being a man, He is God Himself. God is one with Him. His existence begins with God's special action; as a man he is founded in God, He is true God. The subject of the story of Jesus Christ is therefore God himself.[65]

The author therefore prepares the hearer or reader for this radical but fundamental aspect of a biblical perspective of reality with an account which, in also being beyond the reach of empirical evidence, will challenge their conceptual capacity. The brevity of the narrative, the following genealogy (Luke 3:23–38),[66] reference to Joseph as Jesus' parent (Luke 2:27, 33, 41–48; 4:22) and the fact that Luke does not mention the virginal conception again indicates, however, that it is an event which, for the author, serves primarily to highlight the significance of the Incarnation as a unique occurrence; an occurrence that requires a radical departure from the familiar in order to extend the boundaries of the thinkable. In this respect, the problem of a supernatural virginal conception appears to be, in the words of Barth, "a necessary problem"; a possibility that finds support from the words of Michael Polanyi:

> Recent biological suggestions ... that the virgin birth *might* take place in exceptional circumstances would, if accepted as the explanation of the birth of Christ, not confirm, but totally destroy the doctrine of the Virgin Birth. It is illogical to attempt the proof of the supernatural by natural tests, for these can only establish the natural aspects of an event and can never represent it as supernatural.[67]

The ongoing contemporary controversy about whether the meaning of the narrative is independent of, or dependent on, its historicity does not, therefore, appear to be a concern for the author. Brown suggests

---

65. Therefore, there is "no question here of conception and birth in general, but of a quite definite conception and a quite definite birth" (Barth, *Dogmatics in Outline*, 96–97).

66. Although Luke adds the enigmatic "as was thought" to his statement that Jesus was the son of Joseph (Luke 3:23).

67. Polanyi, *Personal Knowledge*, 284.

that Luke did accept "the virginal conception as historical"[68] but stresses that his primary emphasis was on presenting "a phenomenon with theological import."[69] This downplaying of the question of historicity[70] is, however, challenged by Gregory Dawes who posits that Brown's exegesis, which suggests that Luke constructed a narrative which he intended the reader to understand as referring to an actual event, is at odds with his description of the narrative as a "christological affirmation about Jesus as Son of God and son of David";[71] an affirmation that is part of a "carefully planned dramatization of the theology of salvation history."[72] Dawes believes that if Brown's exegesis is correct in suggesting that the significance of Luke's theological message "rests upon a foundation of taken-for-granted historicity,"[73] this load bearing wall and, therefore, the consequent religious significance will disappear if the events in the narrative did not actually occur.[74] Dawes does not wish to align himself with the similar concerns of "theologically conservative commentators" as he agrees with Brown that not all the "stories" in the birth narratives can be regarded as historically accurate from a modern perspective.[75] His concern is, however, with the result of redaction-critical studies that offer a less embarrassing but theologically edifying interpretation of the narratives by subordinating the issues of historical reference to the "religious

---

68. Brown states that, while it is difficult to prove that Luke believed in the virginity of Mary before the birth of Jesus, the genealogy at the end of chapter 3 indicates that he did not believe that "Joseph begot Jesus after the angel's annunciation to Mary" (Brown, "Problem," 9n17).

69. As "a sign of divine choice and grace, and as the idiom of a Christological insight that Jesus was God's Son or the Davidic Messiah from birth" (Brown, "Problem," 7).

70. Brown states his belief that "both Matthew and Luke think that Jesus was conceived without human father but are more interested in theological import than in historicity" and that "I think that both of them regarded the virginal conception as historical, but the modern intensity about historicity was not theirs." He therefore concludes that "an obsession with 'proving' historicity is regressive, forcing prolonged discussion of area in which the evangelists show no primary interest" (Brown, *Birth of the Messiah*, 140n22, 517, 576).

71. Brown, *Birth of the Messiah*, 528.

72. Brown, *Birth of the Messiah*, 346.

73. Dawes, "Why Historicity," 161.

74. Dawes, "Why Historicity," 162. Dawes suggests that Brown fails to distinguish between *intended* historical reference which may be indirect but enables a story "to be understood as having a factual basis," and *actual* historical reference which corresponds directly to actual events (Dawes, "Why Historicity," 174).

75. Dawes, "Why Historicity," 159.

message" that the author was intending to convey.⁷⁶ This leads him to the question of whether "one can claim to be expounding what the evangelists intended—while remaining indifferent to the historicity of the events they narrate"⁷⁷ if, as Brown suggests, they intended their hearers or readers to understand them as events that actually happened.⁷⁸

From a contemporary perspective and in part due to the legacy of a historical criticism which, across the theological spectrum, approaches the biblical books as historical documents,⁷⁹ the meaning of a narrative and its truth claims are often identified with the issue of whether or not a biblical event can be historically verified. It is here that the issue of interpretative reductionism resurfaces and the danger of losing what Ricoeur termed "the richness of the real" in the sense of aspects of reality that Nagel suggests are independent of their conceivability by a human mind.⁸⁰ As modern science is confronted with the existence of entities that, in the words of Nagel, "we cannot describe or fully know" as they lie "beyond the reach of language, proof, evidence, or empirical understanding"⁸¹ and, as Brown points out, the "*scientifically controllable* biblical evidence leaves the question of the historicity of the virginal conception unresolved,"⁸² reductionism does appear to be "the least adequate way" of interpreting the narrative; a narrative which, if designed to extend the boundaries of the thinkable, must, therefore, function not only at the margins of genre but also at the edge of mystery.

---

76. Dawes, "Why Historicity," 157.

77. Dawes, "Why Historicity," 158.

78. It is of course possible to argue that the original intention of an author is out of reach due to the barriers of time, language and culture. See Wimsatt Jr. and Beardsley, "Intentional Fallacy." Ricoeur warns, however, "If the intentional fallacy overlooks the semantic autonomy of the text, the opposite fallacy forgets that a text remains a discourse told by somebody, said by someone to someone else about something. It is impossible to cancel out this main characteristic of discourse without reducing texts to natural objects . . . to things which are not man-made" (Ricoeur, *Interpretation Theory*, 30).

79. "To be studied and questioned like any other ancient sources" (Krentz, *Historical-Critical Method*, 30). An approach Krentz describes as inescapable as "its results appear in our daily newspapers, in books on the paperback rack in the stores, and in the curricula of our high schools and colleges" (3–4). He points out that it is "based on a secular understanding of history," but adopted by both liberals and conservatives—although they reach different conclusions (1–2).

80. Nagel, *View from Nowhere*, 96.

81. Nagel, *View from Nowhere*, 108.

82. Brown, *Birth of the Messiah*, 527.

In his early twentieth-century response to the debate about the historicity of the Virgin Birth, J. Gresham Machen stated that "the true interpreter" must seek to enter "into the very spirit of the writer" and to enter "sympathetically into the inner spirit of the narrative";[83] a sentiment that would be echoed by Heisenberg in suggesting that to progress with quantum mechanics, physicists had to learn how "to get into the spirit of quantum theory."[84] It is a "spirit" that seems from both perspectives to be connected to a sense of reality which resists generic classification and reduction to the known and familiar. It therefore challenges the biblical interpreter to adopt a position of informed receptivity in which conceptual boundaries remain open to the focus of the Lukan narrative; a focus on a radically different form of ontic conception and birth which heralds the birth of a radically different noetic conception. Charles Cranfield describes this conception as an indication that "God himself made a new beginning in the course of the history of his creation by coming himself in person and becoming part of that history." He stresses, however, that "Jesus Christ is not a savior arising out of the continuity of our history but God in person intervening in it."[85] In this respect, while the narrative is an integral part of *biblical* history, it will not conform to modern conventions of historical authenticity and assumptions about legitimate belief. The hearer or reader is left simply to accept with Mary the reality of a supernatural event; an event which, in the conception of the Word, gives a meaningful form to the Incarnation but cannot provide answers to either the biological questions that Thomas Torrance suggests presuppose a "normal biological process" or the historical questions that are limited to the perspective of what he refers to as "causal-historical process of this world."[86]

A hermeneutic of radical departure from the familiar in which imaginative alternatives extend the boundaries of the thinkable therefore allows for the use of mythical language in the annunciation narrative to help express "what transcends our limited notions,"[87] without

---

83. Rather than impose their own predilections on the text. Machen, *Virgin Birth of Christ*, 56, 164.

84. Heisenberg, *Physics and Philosophy*, 38.

85. Cranfield, "Some Reflections," 189. See also Torrance, who states, "Jesus Christ breaks through the continuity of Adamic existence and opens up a new continuity in a new Adam, in a new humanity" (Torrance, "Doctrine of the Virgin Birth," 14).

86. Torrance, "Doctrine of the Virgin Birth," 15.

87. Fitzmyer, "Virginal Conception of Jesus," 549.

reducing it to a "mythologoumenon."[88] It also partially supports Louis Evely's proposal that the narrative is designed to "translate the mystery of the Incarnation into terms intelligible to unsophisticated people," without accepting his conclusion that it must, therefore, take the form of a "maladroit fable."[89] This is if his rather disparaging and discriminative reference *to unsophisticated people who lack knowledge* is replaced with reference *to the conceptually limited human condition*. It is a hermeneutic that allows the interpreter to absorb elements of both a form critical approach in which the narratives are interpreted as having "the mark of the legendary" and being "imaginative expansions of historical memories,"[90] and also the conclusions of redaction criticism in which the issue of historicity is subordinated to the theological message that the authors or editors intended to convey. It resists, however, a reductionist historical-critical approach that limits an understanding of history to what is perceived to be verifiable or empirical and thereby allows a place for the supernatural to exist at the boundaries of the knowable and unknowable.

The supernatural cherubim guarding the entrance to Eden and the messenger angel in Luke's annunciation are not, though, autonomous creatures as they act in the service of God's purpose for humanity. The test that remains for the hermeneutic therefore concerns the interpretation of a seemingly autonomous supernatural creature in the form of a dragon, which plays an adversarial role in the narrative of Revelation 12. It is a creature with a mythological background that has, however, contemporary resonance as modern cosmology struggles to interpret its own ancient ravenous beast that has emerged with the discovery of the black hole.

---

88. Fitzmyer, "Virginal Conception of Jesus," 549.
89. See Evely in Brown, "Problem," 5–6.
90. Dawes, "Why Historicity," 157.

11

Into the Realm of the Dragon
A Cosmic Battle

Giusto di Menabuoi, *The Woman Clothed with the Sun and the Seven-Headed Dragon*, ca. 1350, Baptistery of Padua[1]

---

1. Licensed by Bridgeman Images.

Part II: Into the Light: Extending the Boundaries of the Thinkable

A great portent appeared in heaven: a woman clothed with the sun, with the moon under her feet, and on her head a crown of twelve stars. She was pregnant and was crying out in birth pangs, in the agony of giving birth.

Revelation 12:1–2

Chapter 11 returns to the concept of ancient light in the narratives of contemporary cosmology from which threads will now be woven into the narrative of Revelation 12:1–5 in a constructive framework that seeks to "situate spiritual discourse within an irreducible sense of context."[2] This is in order to consider the theme of illumination in relation to the search for explanation and understanding in both science and theology, and how developments in the narratives of astrophysics might be shedding light on ways in which interpretation of seemingly problematic biblical narratives could be approached. The subject of birth in the heavens is explored from the perspective of both the ancient star-forming regions revealed in images captured by space telescopes, and the Revelation narrative. The depiction of a woman clothed with the sun is then considered; firstly, as a presentation of a celestial phenomenon that is a radical departure from not only images emerging in contemporary cosmology but also from comparative mythology in the ANE; secondly, in relation to the narrative's departure from, but also links to, the depiction of the woman in Genesis 3. The following section begins with a return to contemporary cosmology in order to explore the conceptual implications of the discovery of a twenty-first-century cosmic beast in the form of a black hole. Attempts to both describe and understand this phenomenon are considered to identify possible conceptual connections that might enhance understanding of the biblical destructive force that appears in the narrative as a great red dragon. The role of this supernatural creature as an imaginative alternative to the draconic creatures of ancient mythology is then explored as a development from the narrative of Genesis 3 to represent the power of evil that threatens a creation once described as being *very good* (Genesis 1:31 NRSV). The third section focuses on the concept of evil, tracing its developmental trajectory in biblical narrative before considering how it might be manifest in the twenty-first-century world. Responses to current forces of chaos are considered from a secular

2. Keller, *God and Power*, 116.

and biblical perspective and the role of the dragon is explored as what Keller describes as a meta*force* and from a position that she refers to as "apocalyptic mindfulness."³

In the last section, the biblical theme of light emerging from and overcoming darkness is explored. This is through an investigation of the composite full spectrum images of *seeing the light* that can be found in both contemporary cosmology and biblical narrative. The final thread to be drawn from contemporary cosmology concerns how the unseen reality of the cosmic landscape, revealed by the discovery of gravitational waves, may offer conceptual insight into the unseen reality of the biblical landscape that is also first encountered as darkness covering the face of the deep.

REVELATION 12:1–5—RADICAL DEPARTURE FROM THE FAMILIAR: BIRTH IN THE HEAVENS

"Pillars of Creation" in the *Eagle Nebula*, Hubble Telescope, 2014⁴

Monkey Head Nebula, Hubble Telescope, 2015⁵

The 1995 Hubble Telescope infrared image of the *Pillars of Creation* in the *Eagle Nebula*⁶ about 6,500 light-years away from Earth, reveals three towers of dust that are described as "giving birth to new stars, buried

---

3. Keller, *Facing Apocalypse*, 17.
4. NASA/ESA/Hubble Heritage Team (STScI/AURA).
5. NASA/ESA/Hubble Heritage Team (STScI/AURA).
6. Nebulae are giant clouds of dust and gas existing in interstellar space, some of which are regions where new stars are formed.

within their dusty spires."[7] The 2014 image of the *Monkey Head Nebula* reveals another stellar nursery or star-forming region about 6,400 light-years away from Earth in which "bright, new-born stars near the center of the nebula illuminate the surrounding gas with energetic radiation."[8] Light detected from these new-born stars is now, however, ancient light which has been traveling for nearly 6,500 years before reaching the "eyes" of the Hubble Telescope. The images that have been produced therefore reflect an ancient birth story that occurred nearly 6,500 years ago.

The narrative "images" of Revelation 12 also reflect an ancient birth story but the sense of radiant illumination emerges from a vision that reveals a radically different celestial phenomenon from the phenomena emerging within contemporary astronomy.[9] It is a vision that occurs after an anticipatory cosmic "drum-roll" of "*flashes of lightening, rumblings, peals of thunder, an earthquake, and heavy hail*" (Revelation 11:19), with the light that appears in the darkness radiating from a luminous woman who is "*clothed with the sun, with the moon under her feet, and on her head a crown of twelve stars*" (Revelation 12:1). The image, which could be described as a woman "bedecked with the splendor of God's celestial creation,"[10] has, however, a strong resemblance to a mythological Queen of Heaven in the form of "a high goddess, a cosmic queen conceived in astral categories: the moon is a mere footstool for her; the circle of heaven, the zodiac, her crown; and the mighty sun, her garment."[11] Adela Yarbro Collins makes a detailed comparison between the biblical depiction and descriptions of three high goddesses, the Ephesian Artemis, Atargatis (a major goddess of northern Syria in the Hellenistic period), and the Egyptian Isis. She concludes that while the vision, in some respects, reflects "the typical image of Isis,"[12] the best parallel is the Isis of

---

7. See "Eagle Nebula."

8. Bacon et al., "Evaporating Peaks."

9. G. B. Caird suggests that while John may have envisaged his portents as constellations in the sky, they belong to "the realm of vision" and are "figures of the imagination, projected on to the starry heavens" (Caird, *Revelation of St John*, 149).

10. Riley, "Who Is the Woman," 20.

11. Collins, *Combat Myth*, 71. Keller notes that no other biblical figure "comes wrapped up in so much cosmic signage . . . all at once" (Keller, *Facing Apocalypse*, 60). See also Riley, who notes, "The Seer has not only used the riches of the scriptural heritage to garb the Woman Clothed with the Sun. She is bedecked with ornaments taken from pagan myths, iconography and cultus; she reflects glints from contemporary astrological imagery; she even bears a family resemblance to certain women that appear in the Pseudepigrapha and Qumran literature" (Riley, "Who Is the Woman," 37).

12. Collins, *Combat Myth*, 71–75.

the Metternich stele[13] as it presents her as the "threatened mother of the hero" rather than as a "goddess ally."[14] The significant differences that she notes between the biblical woman and her mythic counterparts indicate, however, that the Revelation narrative, while combining material from a variety of sources, which include Jewish tradition[15] and the Old Testament, will be a radical departure from the familiar for its early hearers and readers.[16] The importance of an awareness of this sense of departure is highlighted by Mitchell Reddish in his warning about the danger of the reductive approach of

> getting so involved in trying to uncover the sources of John's images and the historical and political referents underneath the symbolism that one fails to see the overarching vision that John is presenting. One may dissect the text to such an extent that one ends up with a cadaver rather than a living text that continues to inspire, challenge, and embrace the reader.[17]

While the historical and political backgrounds of the symbols are helpful, Reddish stresses that they "do not exhaust the meaning" of the symbols which require "a creative engagement of the imagination by the reader."[18] It is an engagement that he suggests should, however, resist the temptation to submit the symbols to the subjectivity of the reader and instead allow the ancient traditions that were drawn upon and the political and historical situation against which John was writing "to serve as correctives on any reading of the visions."[19]

---

13. Made for the Egyptian priest Nesu-Atūm about 350 BCE in the reign of Nectanebo II, the stele depicts the goddess Isis fleeing into exile to protect her son Horus from poisonous reptiles. See Scott, "Metternich Stela," 201–17.

14. Collins, *Combat Myth*, 65.

15. Although "Celestial imagery was not typically used for female figures in Jewish sources" (Koester, *Revelation*, 529).

16. As the author "is not constrained" by the use of the image in other sources (Koester, *Revelation*, 530).

17. Reddish, *Revelation*, 230.

18. Reddish, *Revelation*, 230. See also Brown, who suggests, "The symbolism of apocalyptic compels imaginative participation on the part of the hearers/readers" (Brown, "Book of Revelation," 286).

19. Reddish, *Revelation*, 231. See also Keller, who suggests, "The ancient text reads the crisis of its own historical context. . . . But it discerns patterns in its own world deep enough to persist dangerously and perhaps disclosively, into our own" (Keller, *Facing Apocalypse*, 3).

A summary of historic interpretations of the identity of the woman is provided by Craig Koester[20] and includes; firstly, that of the symbolization of "the people of God," with the twelve stars representing the sons of Jacob[21] and the community of the corresponding twelve tribes; secondly, her identification with the Church, which is found in Hippolytus's early third-century *Treatise on Christ and Antichrist* §61, stating that the author

> meant most manifestly the church, endued with the Father's word, whose brightness is above the sun. And by "the moon under her feet" he referred to her being adorned, like the moon, with heavenly glory. And the words, "upon her head a crown of twelve stars," refer to the twelve apostles by whom the church was founded.[22]

The third interpretation, emerging during the patristic period, identifies the woman as Mary who is giving birth to the Messiah[23] while the fourth option identifies her as Israel; an interpretation that personifies her as "the Jewish people from whom the Messiah comes,"[24] with the sun, moon and stars recalling the dream of Joseph in Genesis 37:9–11 and the description of Israel as a woman in labor in Isaiah 26:17–18 and Jeremiah 4:31.[25]

While the first option of community of the people of God "both before and after Jesus' birth" is suggested by Koester to be the most plausible proposal,[26] he notes that John is not constrained by the use of the image in other sources.[27] In this respect, as Eugene Boring points out, the creative use of language indicates:

> The woman is not Mary, nor Israel, nor the church but less and more than all of these. John's imagery pulls together elements from the pagan myth of the queen of heaven; from the Genesis

---

20. See Koester, *Revelation*, 525–27, 541–43. For a list of bibliographical surveys of the interpretation of Revelation 12, see Fekkes, *Isaiah and Prophetic Tradition*, 177n8.

21. Following Victorius (d. 304), who suggested that she "encompassed both ancient Israel and the followers of Jesus" (Koester, *Revelation*, 525–26).

22. Hippolytus, *Fragments*, 36.

23. It was later popularized when linked to the Feast of the Immaculate Conception (Koester, *Revelation*, 543).

24. Koester, *Revelation*, 527.

25. Koester, *Revelation*, 543.

26. With her resemblance to the characteristics and experiences of ancient Israel and her child being the messianic ruler (Koester, *Revelation*, 542).

27. Koester, *Revelation*, 530.

story of Eve, mother of all living, whose "seed" shall bruise the head of the primeval serpent (Gen 3:1–16); from Israel who escapes from the dragon/Pharaoh into the wilderness on the wings of an eagle (Exod 19:4, cf. Ps 74:12–15); and Zion, "mother" of the People of God from whom the Messiah comes forth (Isa 66:7–9; 2 Esd 13:32–38). She reflects the historical experience of the people of God through the ages, Israel and the church, and yet she is the cosmic woman, clothed with the sun, with the moon under her feet, and crowned with twelve stars, who brings forth the Messiah.[28]

The radiant image of the woman, in illuminating the importance of the child that she will bear, is, therefore, secondary to the significance of her child who will provide a different form of illumination as a light that will overcome the darkness of evil. In this respect, the contrast with and radical departure from the depiction of the woman in Genesis 3 who, as the first "mother" of humankind, was clothed only with fig leaves (Genesis 3:7) and then a garment of skin (Genesis 3: 21), is a significant feature of the first portent; a feature that highlights the unique nature of the birth that is about to occur which is also indicated by the echoes of Psalm 104:2 in which God is described as being *"wrapped in light as with a garment."* Its ties to the Genesis narrative are not, however, broken, with a link remaining as the woman cries out in the promised *"agony of giving birth"* (Genesis 3:16; Revelation 12:3). Koester notes that these birth pangs not only indicate that the child is about to be born but are also "a vivid metaphor for a community in distress,"[29] with the Revelation narrative foreshadowed in Jeremiah 4:31:

> *For I heard the cry of a woman in labour,*
>   *anguish as of one bringing forth her first child,*
> *the cry of daughter Zion gasping for breath,*
>   *stretching out her hands,*
> *"Woe is me! I am fainting before killers!"*[30]

The "killer" now appears as a voracious and destructive force of darkness in the form of *"a great red dragon, with seven heads and ten horns, and*

---

28. Boring, *Revelation*, 152.

29. Koester, *Revelation*, 544. See also Keller, who refers to the apocalyptic birth narrative as a "galactic metaforce" as "If apocalypse offers a dis/closure in and through collective crisis—this scene enfleshes the opening as the agony of giving birth" (Keller, *Facing Apocalypse*, 61).

30. See also Jeremiah 6:24; Micah 4:9–10; Koester, *Revelation*, 544.

seven diadems on his heads" and a tail which *"swept down a third of the stars of heaven and threw them to the earth"* (Revelation 12:3–4). It is image that appears to be rooted in, but not confined to, the ancient imagination as its presence as a fiery and destructive cosmic beast is revived in the response of the twenty-first-century imagination to a new image that has emerged within contemporary cosmology.

AN IMAGINATIVE ALTERNATIVE: RAVENOUS COSMIC BEASTS

The most ferocious storm in our galaxy rages right at its center. It is a maelstrom hotter than any star: a swirling disk of superheated gas firing two jets, one above and one below, that whirl and twist like tornadoes. In the middle sits an eye of perfect stillness—a sphere of total black, millions of kilometers across. This is the supermassive black hole at the center of the Milky Way.[31]

An example of Nagel's astonishing world that is currently extending the boundaries of the thinkable can be found in Sagittarius A-star, the black hole at the center of the Milky Way galaxy that lies about 26,000 light-years away from Earth and has a mass around four million times greater than the Sun.[32] Described as being amongst the most mysterious objects in the universe, this "ravenous cosmic beast" of twenty-first-century science that drags "passers-by" to certain doom[33] is an extremely dense entity from which no light can escape and with such strong gravitational pull that anything coming within its "event horizon," or "point of no return," will be "consumed" and never re-emerge.[34] It is an entity that astronomers have observed "awakening" about once a day and emitting "a brief burst of light before settling back into its slumber."[35] In 2017, a record-breaking "Black Hole Feeding Frenzy" was announced as another giant black hole

---

31. O'Connell, "Telescope," 101.
32. See "Supermassive Black Hole."
33. Marshall, "Blacks Holes."
34. See "Black Hole Image." Black holes are formed by stars that collapse when their hydrogen fuel source is burned up, with their compressed weight causing space to curve so intensely that it plunges into a black hole. Physicist Chris Impey refers to them as Einstein's Monsters which are "powerful and beyond anyone's control" and can only be understood by Einstein's theory of general relativity which says that space and time are distorted by matter (Impey, *Einstein's Monsters*, xvii–xviii).
35. Andrei, "Black Hole."

located in a small galaxy about two billion light-years from Earth was reported as having "ripped apart a nearby star and then continued to feed off its remains for close to a decade."[36] The report was based on data from three orbiting X-ray telescopes, the Chandra X-ray Observatory,[37] Swift Satellite,[38] and XMM-Newton space observatory[39] which had revealed evidence of a massive Tidal Disruption Event (TDE) in which the intense gravity from the black hole causes tidal forces that are able destroy an object such as a star that comes to close to it.[40]

By definition invisible, the first and closest possible image of a black hole was captured in April 2019 when the Event Horizon Telescope (EHT) collaboration,[41] revealed an image of the silhouette of a supermassive black hole fifty-five million light-years from Earth and about one thousand times as massive as Sagittarius A-star; an image described as "the behemoth at the heart of the galaxy M87"[42] and resembling an eye of fire, with the black hole outlined by the glowing hot gas surrounding its event horizon. The image was only possible because of the development

---

36. Durham, "UNH Researcher."

37. Detecting X-ray emission from exploded stars, clusters of galaxies, and matter around black holes, Chandra orbits above the Earth's atmosphere up to an altitude of 139,000 kilometers. See http://www.chandra.harvard.edu.

38. Designed to solve the mystery of the origin of gamma-ray bursts, which scientists believe to be "the birth cries of black holes" (Cook-Anderson and Neal-Jones, "Swift Mission").

39. The biggest scientific satellite built in Europe. See https://www.sci.esa.int/web/xmm-newton.

40. "During a TDE, some of the stellar debris is flung outward at high speeds, while the rest falls toward the black hole. As it travels inward, and is ingested by the black hole, the material heats up to millions of degrees and generates a distinct X-ray flare" (Mohon, "Black Hole Meal").

41. The EHT is an international network of eight ground-based radio telescopes that are linked together to create a giant virtual telescope with an aperture that almost equals the diameter of the Earth. Data from the telescopes were synchronized and combined to create a composite set of images. To complement the EHT findings, "The Chandra X-ray Observatory, Nuclear Spectroscopic Telescope Array (NuSTAR) and Neil Gehrels Swift Observatory space telescope missions, all attuned to different varieties of X-ray light, turned their gaze to the M87 black hole around the same time as the EHT in April 2017. NASA's Fermi Gamma-ray Space Telescope was also watching for changes in gamma-ray light from M87 during the EHT observations" (Landau, "Black Hole Image").

42. Wall, "One Year." At the center of Messier 87 (M87), an elliptical galaxy about 55 million light years from Earth, the supermassive black hole is 6.5 billion times the mass of the Sun (see "Black Hole Image").

of Very Long Baseline Interferometry (VLBI)[43] to detect radio waves or "light" in a region of the electromagnetic spectrum which is invisible to the naked human eye. Human sight is normally limited to the stars in our Milky Way Galaxy which, within a range of about 1,500 light years, are observable on a clear night.[44] On March 19, 2008, for a period of roughly forty seconds, it was, however, possible for the naked human eye to witness the most distant astronomical object ever directly seen, with a supernova or gigantic stellar explosion that happened so far away that its light took 7.5 billion years to reach Earth. Detected by NASA's Swift satellite, the luminous explosion in the form of a gamma ray burst,[45] occurred 3 billion years before our solar system formed.[46] It has consequently been called an echo from "the beginning of time,"[47] but in a news conference following the sighting, astrophysicist Jonathan Grindlay was reported as referring to the event as "the scream" or "birth pangs of a black hole."[48] It was a "birth" that heralded the dramatic formation of an entity that would require a radical departure from familiar forms of explanation, with the laws of physics appearing to break down as "space and time are broken apart"[49] in a region where, in the words of Rovelli, "space is so curved as to collapse in on itself and where time comes to a standstill."[50]

The cosmic region in Revelation 12, in which the cry of birth pangs resounds to herald a birth that will offer the possibility of transformative new life rather than destruction, is also one in which no physical laws can be applied. This is as the narrative makes its own radical departure from the familiar to an imaginative alternative at a point in time and space that

---

43. VLBI synchronizes the telescopes around the world to allow observation at a wavelength of 1.3mm within an angular resolution of 20 micro-arcseconds, which is "enough to read a newspaper in New York from a café in Paris." See "Astronomers Capture First Image."

44. On a clear night, in a location with a very dark sky, it is also possible to see the Andromeda Galaxy which appears as a "fuzzy patch of stars" (Tillman and Sohn, "Andromeda Galaxy").

45. An event which most often occurs when a massive star runs out of nuclear fuel and its core collapses to form a neutron star or black hole. This collapse releases an intense burst of high-energy gamma rays and ejects particle jets which, in moving through space at nearly the speed of light and ploughing into surrounding interstellar clouds, heat the gas and generate bright afterglows. See Naeye, "Stellar Explosion."

46. Grindlay, "Light," 177–78.

47. Crockett, "What Are Gamma."

48. Thompson, "Scream of Black Hole's Birth."

49. Brain, *Reality, Science*, 90.

50. Rovelli, *Reality Is Not*, 195.

is not identifiable within contemporary cosmology. The unfolding cosmic drama has begun with a vision which Koester describes as "emerging almost like a constellation coming to life in the evening sky,"[51] with the vision that follows presenting the modern reader with "something like a movie that thrills audiences with special effects, as heroes and villains traverse the galaxies in battles for control of the universe."[52] These are visions which, from the perspective of the audience, are, however, also invisible not only to the naked human eye but to any form of advanced technology and cannot, therefore, either respond to the questions directed to modern cosmology or be understood by the existing methods used to explain it. The imagery is instead addressed to the imagination of the hearer or reader,[53] with Gordon Fee suggesting that it reflects "narrative art at its finest" but warning that comments on it should be made "with a degree of trepidation lest the reader get involved too much in the explanation and thus lose the power of the narrative itself";[54] a power that emerges in the "sky-drama"[55] of a ferocious storm amidst which *"God's temple in heaven was opened"* (Revelation 11:19) and a great portent or sign indicating a momentous event[56] first appears in the form of the woman who is about to give birth. This is, however, immediately followed by a second portent in the form of a great red dragon; a ravenous and formidable cosmic beast that is powerful enough to cast constellations from the sky and seeking to *"devour her child as soon as it was born"* (Revelation 12:5).[57]

The imagery of the narrative, while perhaps familiar in some respects to its first audiences in its echo of ancient mythologies, is, however, a dramatic reformulation of and imaginative alternative to, the combat myths that were widespread in the ancient Near East and classical

---

51. Koester, *Revelation and the End*, 118.

52. Koester, *Revelation and the End*, 117.

53. Fee, *Revelation*, 165.

54. Fee, *Revelation*, 164. See also Carrington's description of the author as "an artist greater than Stevenson or Coleridge or Bach" (Carrington, *Meaning of the Revelation*, xvii).

55. Kendall Easley describes Revelation 12 as the beginning of a great sky-drama. See Easley, *Living with the End*, 50.

56. That may be calamitous or marvellous. See Thompson, *Concise Oxford Dictionary*, 1065.

57. Grant Osbourne notes that despite its power, the dragon is only "another portent" as opposed to the woman who is referred to as a "great portent" (Osbourne, *Revelation Verse*, 135).

world.[58] These were myths that involved a cosmic battle between two divine beings for universal kingship, with one often appearing as a monster or dragon representing the forces of chaos and "associated with disorder in society and sterility in nature, while the champion is linked with order and fertility."[59] As Ivan Benson points out, a violent and chaos-making draconic creature appears in Sumerian, Akkadian, Indian, Greek, Hittite, Egyptian, and Phoenician cultures, with the earliest known record found in a Mesopotamian seal cylinder depicting the destruction of a seven-headed dragon.[60] Babylonian mythology refers to "a serpentine monster with seven heads"[61] which has been identified with *Ti'âmat* and also to a "raging" or "red-gleaming" and potentially fiery or even bloody serpent in the Temple of *Marduk*.[62] The dragon *Typhon*, in Greek mythology was also powerful enough to cast the constellations from the sky while, in the late-Egyptian period, the dragon *Seth* was believed to be red and is depicted attacking *Isis* the mother of *Horus* in order to prevent *Horus* from controlling the land.[63] The closest account to the narrative of Revelation 12 is thought, however, to be Hyginus's version of the *Leto* myth about the birth of *Apollo*:

> Both depict the attack of a serpentine monster on a woman big with child. The flight of the woman in Revelation 12:14 with the two wings of the eagle is analogous to Leto's flight from Python with the help of the north wind. The aid of the personified earth in vs. 16 is analogous to that afforded Leto by Poseidon, god of the sea. The ultimate source of the woman's aid in Revelation is God himself, as the reference to "a place prepared for her by

---

58. Reddish describes John as "Christianizing" ancient pagan myths by stretching "the Christian story over the frame of pagan myth," with the mythical language being evocative rather than descriptive (Reddish, *Revelation*, 234).

59. "The conflict between the two thus has universal significance, and the order and fertility of the cosmos depends on its success" (Collins, *Combat Myth*, 2).

60. A cylinder dated in the Akkad dynasty of the twenty-fourth century. See Benson, "Revelation 12," 98.

61. Collins, *Combat Myth*, 77.

62. Benson, "Revelation 12," 98–99.

63. Benson, "Revelation 12," 99. Other draconic figures in ancient mythology include the Sumerian *Kur*, the Phoenician *Ophion*, the Egyptian *Apophis*, the Iranian *Azhi Dahaka*, and the Indian *Vritra*, which share the characteristics of a desire for kingship, an association with the forces of chaos and a "vicious and evil countenance" (Benson, "Revelation 12," 100).

God" shows (vs.6). This motif is analogous to Zeus's role in the Leto myth: she is rescued *Jouis iussu* (140.3).[64]

Despite its resonance with pagan mythology, it may, though, be argued that much of the imagery of the draconic creature and "story line" in the Revelation narrative can be explained on the basis of the allusions to the Old Testament and Christian tradition.[65] This is imagery which evolves primarily from the Old Testament, with a possible reworking of Canaanite mythology,[66] to show the power of God against the mighty serpent dragon *Leviathan* in Job 41:1–34; Psalm 74:14; and Isaiah 27:1; the powerful *Behemoth* in Job 40:15–24; the chaos monster *Rahab* in Job 9:13; 26:12; Psalm 89:10; and Isaiah 30:7 and 51:9; the Dragon in Job 7:12 and Ezekiel 29:3; and monsters of the land and sea that often represent kings and foreign nations as in Psalm 87:4; Isaiah 30:7; Jeremiah 51:34; and Ezekiel 29:3 and 32:2. There is also, however, a developmental trajectory from the serpent of the Eden narrative; a creature that originates as part of God's creation, then appears as a seemingly rational and convincing ally until it is exposed as the initiator of humanity's estrangement from God,[67] and evolves into an overtly aggressive and destructive adversary.[68]

---

64. Hyginus was a Roman collector of Greek stories (Collins, *Combat Myth*, 67). After researching the myth, W. K. Hedrick concludes, "The god Apollo was known through the cities to which the apocalypse was addressed and the myth of his birth to Leto and of his battle with Python was known throughout the world of the Roman Empire, but especially in Asia Minor" (Hedrick in Mazzaferri, *Genre*, 53). Mazzaferri suggests that Hedrick offers "one of the most cogent source-critical studies of Revelation 12 readily available" (39).

65. Fekkes lists the bibliographical surveys of the interpretation of Revelation 12 and states that "virtually no historical, mythological, structural, or linguistic stone has been left unturned in the attempt to illuminate the background and purpose of its symbols." While there has been and still is division over whether most of the chapter derives from a source in the form of "a popular pagan myth" that has been "taken over" or from predominantly the Old Testament and Christian tradition, he concludes that it "reflects a combination of pagan myth, OT prophecy and Christian tradition" (Fekkes, *Isaiah and Prophetic Traditions*, 177–78).

66. Benson argues that the background "for the Old Testament dragon is probably to be found in the Canaanite myths concerning Lotan, Tannin, and Shalyat" with description in Baal 1.1.1–4 having a striking resemblance to Isaiah 27:1 (Benson, "Revelation 12," 100). On the Old Testament use of the Leviathan and the close relationships with Ugaritic texts, see Bauckham, *Climax of Prophecy*, 186–89. He notes that Canaanite identification with the Dragon of Revelation 12, outside the Old Testament sources raises the issue of ascertaining to what extent its "myth of God's battle with the sea-monster was still a living myth in the world of the first century AD."

67. Bauckham, *Climax*, 198.

68. An evolution of the influence of evil that is creatively portrayed in C. S. Lewis's

The enmity between the woman and the serpent in Genesis 3:15 reappears with dramatic intensity as the life of her child is threatened and the "serpent dragon" is now portrayed as "the primeval and ultimate power of supernatural evil";[69] the "*ancient serpent*" who is finally named as "*the Devil and Satan, the deceiver of the whole world*" (Revelation 12:9). In this respect, as Reddish suggests:

> This dragon is Python from the Leto myth; he is also Tiamat, the seven-headed monster of the deep in Babylonian mythology; as well he is Leviathan, the serpent-like monster in Hebrew folklore . . . further, he is the deceitful serpent of the garden of Eden story; and he is also Satan, "the deceiver of the whole world" (12:9). He is each of these—and all of them combined—for he is the representation of all that is evil and chaotic and in opposition to God.[70]

There is a sense, therefore, in which the book of Revelation can be described as "a rebirth of images" in its flexible reworking of familiar imagery from not only multiple traditions but also "hundreds of Old Testament passages into new applications,"[71] with Leandro De Lima suggesting that in Revelation 12 there is a specific and creative echoing, broadening, and interpretation of the "old narrative" of Genesis 3.[72] This emerges through both a "rebirth of images" and the concept of a significant new birth that takes concrete form in a unique development of not only the narrative of Genesis 3 but also that of Luke 1:26–38 as, in the words of Fee "the essential story itself *begins* with the incarnation"[73] as the woman "*gave birth to a son, a male child, who is to rule all the nations with a rod of iron*" (Revelation 12:5). It is, however, a birth, that while offering the promise of transformative new life is immediately under threat from the forces of chaos that are represented by the imaginative alternative of a destructive and terrifying beast.

---

book *The Screwtape Letters*.

69. See Bauckham, *Climax*, 15, 193.
70. Reddish, *Revelation*, 234.
71. Gregg, *Revelation*, 20. See also Farrer, *Rebirth of Images*.
72. De Lima, "Power of Literary Art."
73. Fee, *Revelation*, 166.

EXTENDING THE BOUNDARIES OF THE THINKABLE: DEFEATING THE DRAGON

The bedrock nature of space and time and the structure of the universe exemplify intellectual domains where we are still groping for the truth—where we must still inscribe 'here be dragons.'[74]

In referring to apocalypse, Catherine Keller suggests that metaphor is too weak a notion and offers the term meta*force* as a substitute that better reflects the deeply entrenched patterns of destruction in Revelation's "core vision of evil."[75] In this respect, the biblical dragon is also perhaps better interpreted as a meta*force* representing the dark and destructive force of evil operating "across multiple temporal variations of spiritual and secular power."[76] The concept of mysterious and potentially dangerous beasts existing beyond the boundaries of the known world prevailed from the ancient Greek period into the Middle Ages and is evident in medieval cartography, with the distant edges of the earth illustrated as a realm of strange animals and monstrous beings;[77] beings that could potentially be a threat to humankind. As modern cosmology attempts to map the distant edges of the known universe revealing domains in which "we are still groping for the truth," the discovery of black holes indicates, as Astronomer Royal Sir Martin Rees suggests, that there are still "dragons" in the sense of mysterious and life-threatening entities existing at the boundaries of the thinkable. The language that is used to refer to black holes as ravenous cosmic beasts is not, however, intended to imply that they represent evil in the form of being "morally bad," "wicked" or intentionally "tending to harm."[78] Despite their use in popular culture as "metaphors for death and destruction,"[79] they appear to function as "gravitational engines" at the center of some galaxies, which use matter

---

74. Rees, *From Here*, 86.

75. Keller and Rivera, "Coloniality of Apocalypse."

76. A force that if dismissed or repressed becomes more dangerous when "acted out unconsciously" (Keller, *Facing Apocalypse*, 19).

77. Van Duzer, "*Hic sunt dracones*," 391. The uncharted territories on medieval maps were illustrated with mythical creatures, but as Van Duzer points out, there is actually only one map (a world map in a manuscript created ca. 1460–70) and one globe (the Lenox Globe ca. 1510) on which the legend *Hic sunt dracones* appears (389).

78. Thompson, *Concise Oxford Dictionary*, 467.

79. Impey, *Einstein's Monsters*, 23.

to create light in converting gravitational potential energy into radiant energy. Matter accelerating towards the event horizon of the black hole emits high-energy electromagnetic radiation that is able to "outshine the whole galaxy" leading to what Chris Impey suggests is "an irony of astrophysics [in] that something so dark can lead to so much light."[80]

The concept of light emerging from and overcoming darkness is, however, a key biblical theme but in contrast to the involuntary violence of the dark cosmic "beast" of astrophysics, the biblical dragon serves to represent the dark destructive power of an invisible but intentional source of evil that is a threat to the world in which "*God saw all He had done, and, look, it was very good*" (Genesis 1:31).[81] Its evolution from the Eden serpent leads to the suggestion that the Bible "tells the story of evil—its origin, its battle against good and its ultimate defeat at the hands of an eternally good God."[82] As a "perversion of good"[83] and "a violation of community," Grenz also suggests that the existence of evil is, consequently, a theme "that lies at the heart of the biblical drama"[84] and is manifest as a phenomenon that is first referenced in the second chapter of Genesis in connection to "*the tree of the knowledge, good and evil*" (Genesis 2:17).[85] Its initial presentation as an innocuous force in the form of the subtle and persuasive reasoning of a seemingly benevolent serpent gives little indication, however, of the terrifying creature that it will become. It is only the severity of the consequences for the human couple, after their capitulation to the lure of advancement promised by the acquisition of knowledge, that indicates the danger of this vulnerability to deception; a vulnerability arising from the seductive power of reason and the misuse of knowledge which does not appear to have diminished in a troubled twenty-first-century world within which what Reinhold Niebuhr described as "the powerful drift towards evil in us despite our conscious purposes"[86] does not appear to have abated.

In an address that was republished in 1986, a year after Nagel suggested that "we are still at a primitive stage of moral development,"[87]

---

80. Impey, *Einstein's Monsters*, 89, 119.
81. Alter, *Five Books*, 19.
82. Ryken et al., *Dictionary of Biblical Imagery*, 248.
83. Ryken et al., *Dictionary of Biblical Imagery*, 248.
84. Grenz, *Theology for the Community*, 227–28.
85. Alter, *Five Books*, 21.
86. Niebuhr, "Mystery and Meaning," 244.
87. Nagel, *View from Nowhere*, 186.

Niebuhr refers to the source of evil as a "deep mystery ... which has been simply resolved in modern culture." Writing in 1946 after the devastation of two world wars, he described this as a culture which "has interpreted man as an essentially virtuous creature who is betrayed into evil by ignorance, or by evil economic, political, or religious institutions" but suggested that:

> These simple theories of historical evil do not explain how virtuous men of another generation created the evil in these inherited institutions, or how mere ignorance could give the evil in man the positive thrust and demonic energy in which it frequently expresses itself. Modern culture's understanding of the evil in man fails to do justice to the tragic and perplexing aspect of the problem.[88]

An ongoing reluctance to address the problem of evil as a potentiality in the human condition can be found in a reflection on Niebuhr's work written in 2005 by historian and social critic, Arthur Schlesinger. Referring to Niebuhr's belief in the delusion of the myth of "national innocence," Schlesinger suggests that this "myth" was revived after the tragedy of the 9/11 terrorist attack in New York with lamentations about "the end of innocence" becoming favorite clichés substantiated by the ongoing belief that "human ignorance and unjust institutions remained the only obstacles to a more perfect world."[89] It is a belief that is also evident in the 2012 documentary *Four Horsemen* in which an international group of "thinkers" addressed what were considered to be "fundamental flaws" in the global economic systems that "condemn billions to poverty or chronic insecurity."[90] Using imagery from the book of Revelation's four seals of destruction (Revelation 6:1–8), four contemporary crises were described as galloping towards unprecedented disaster on a global scale. These were identified as burgeoning debt resulting from corrupt financial practices; the consequential iniquity and poverty, with a growing underclass condemned to a lifetime of deprivation; socially organized violence including

---

88. Niebuhr, "Mystery and Meaning," 244. See also Bracken, who refers to "the collective power of evil" emerging from the influence of the "prevailing mindset of the group" or community (Bracken, *Christianity and Process Thought*, 41–52).

89. Schlesinger makes the blunt but salutary comment that in the United States, "Whites coming to these shores were reared in the Calvinist doctrine of sinful humanity, and they killed red men, enslaved black men and later on imported yellow men for peon labor—not much of a background for national innocence" (Schlesinger Jr., "Forgetting Reinhold Niebuhr").

90. See Ashcroft, *Four Horsemen*.

not only terrorist groups but also military intervention operating under the command and often self-seeking agendas of foreign governments; and the growing environmental issues as the earth's resources are plundered to meet the rapacious consumer-driven demands of twenty-first-century life. The documentary concluded that the crises had arisen not simply from the moral failure of individuals as the issues were deeper than individual greed. They were also due to systemic failure and the manipulation of economic thinking, with power gained from "controlling the cognitive map or way that we think."[91] This highlighting of systematic failure and economic manipulation raised important issues but, in falling short of addressing Niebuhr's concerns about how the "evil" that they represent arose, it also appeared to substantiate his concern that:

> One school holds that men would be good if only political institutions would not corrupt them; another believes that they would be good if the prior evil of a faulty economic organization could be eliminated. Or another school thinks of this evil as no more than ignorance, and therefore waits for a more perfect educational process to redeem man from his partial and particular loyalties. But no school asks how it is that an essentially good man could have produced corrupting and tyrannical political organizations or exploiting economic organizations, or fanatical and superstitious religious organizations.[92]

If Niebuhr's concern is to be addressed it may, therefore, be necessary to retrace the biblical stages of the development of evil in which its appearance initially takes the form of a seemingly innocuous desire for self-improvement. This is to consider if it is a desire that may ignite what Ricoeur describes as an innate human fallibility[93] or inclination towards evil but, as Richard Kearney points out, this does not mean that "we are *intrinsically* evil; only that this potential exists within each one of us—and, as such, may be activated or not according to free choice."[94] It is, however, as biblical narrative reveals, an inclination that can evolve into a desire for power and control that is only attainable at the expense of and detriment to others. In this respect, it is perhaps unsurprising that the advances in astrophysics and cosmology have led Rees to echo Nagel in

---

91. Gillian Tett (Assistant Editor, *Financial Times*) in Ashcroft, *Four Horsemen*.
92. Niebuhr, "Children of Light," 169.
93. For Ricoeur, to be human is to be "fallible" as the possibility of moral evil is "inherent in man's constitution" (Ricoeur, *Fallible Man*, 133).
94. Kearney, "On the Hermeneutics of Evil," 71.

describing the human brain as "the most complicated thing that we know about in the universe"[95] as "some of the best-understood phenomena" are actually "far away in the cosmos" while the "everyday phenomena, especially those involving entities as complex as human beings, can be more intractable than anything in the inanimate world."[96] It is an intractability that is, however, chilling if he is correct in describing the twenty-first century as crucial in being the first era in forty-five million centuries in which the human species "can determine, for good or ill, the future of its entire biosphere" as the threats to our world come from ourselves rather than nature.[97]

How these threats can be addressed and whether confidence in the triumph of human altruism and technological endeavor against increasingly destructive but humanly driven forces of chaos can be sustained appears to be a key issue. In the 1990s, films such as *Deep Impact* and *Armageddon* offered responses of both human sacrifice and the use of nuclear weapons to the imminent destruction of the Earth by natural forces.[98] The more recent *Interstellar*, while also expressing confidence in human endeavor acknowledges, however, its failures, as humanity must now be saved from the consequences of its ecological devastation of the Earth.[99] Utilizing advances in quantum physics, salvation takes the form of an astronaut traveling in a spacecraft called *Endurance* through a wormhole[100] to another galaxy. In passing through an event horizon and

---

95. Rees, *From Here to Infinity*, 92.

96. Rees, *From Here to Infinity*, 30. An example of this intractability can be found in the suggestion that some of the biggest challenges that the EHT has had to deal have been and may remain social rather than technical, with Avi Loeb, the chair of Harvard's Department of Astronomy, stating that "the biggest achievement of this project is being able to coordinate different observatories in different countries around the world" as "astronomers are quite competitive, and convincing hundreds of them to work together and figure out who the leader is, why that person should be the leader and how they all should get credit is quite a challenge" (Choi, "How the Event").

97. Rees, *From Here to Infinity*, 13.

98. In *Deep Impact*, a spaceship called *Messiah* is used on a mission that would require the crew to sacrifice their lives in using nuclear warheads to destroy an eleven kilometer-wide comet on a collision course with Earth. In *Armageddon*, the threat of collision takes the form of a gigantic asteroid, with disaster also averted when an individual sacrifices his life to detonate a nuclear weapon.

99. Keller refers to the current narratives of cli-fi (climate fiction) and cli-sci (climate science) which unveil "entrenched civilizational patterns, with dire interhuman, interspecies, planetary consequences" (Keller, *Facing Apocalypse*, 5).

100. First theorized in 1916 and elaborated in 1935 when Einstein and Rosen used the theory of general relativity to propose the existence of "bridges" that connected two

descending into a black hole, he is somehow able to avoid the "spaghettification" caused by its stretching force of gravity[101] and collect data that will enable humankind to leave the dying Earth and find a new home in the universe.

The search to find what Nagel calls "our place in the world" appears destined to continue in both the human imagination and the stark reality of the growing number of refugees who, like the first biblical couple, are homeless in a hostile world. The fundamental question of whether human altruism and technological endeavor are sufficient to restore the broken relationships that exist both amidst humankind and between humanity, the environment, and other species, appears, however, to remain unanswered. Regardless of their origin, the forces of chaos remain rampant and continue to do harm,[102] exposing vulnerability and generating fear about the future; a future that appears to be equally chilling if salvation can only be found through the use of technology in the form of nuclear weapons, or the biomedical moral enhancement suggested by Savulescu and Persson. From a secular perspective, the biblical response to the forces of chaos presents the potentially unpalatable challenge that "human agency will never be enough to overcome the forces of evil."[103] It is a challenge that finds support in the events of history but, while it may appear possible to identify the biblical dragon in prevailing issues,[104] it is a beast that is being fed by a rapacious consumption of natural resources and avaricious consumerism that indicates a fallibility or inclination towards evil within the human condition. The biblical representation of evil

---

different points in space-time and theoretically created a "shortcut that could reduce travel time and distance." Such "shortcuts" came to be known as Einstein-Rosen bridges or wormholes (Tillman and Harvey, "What Are Wormholes?").

101. Impey, *Einstein's Monsters*, 117.

102. In writing about pandemic *pandemonium*, Keller refers to its original meaning of "all the demons," with *Pandæmonium* being the capital of Hell in Milton's *Paradise Lost*. She can therefore make the comment: "What a host of demons the pandemic has been revealing: not supernatural spooks but hellish systems of collective oppression, of normalized injustice—normally hidden, like all smart demons, in plain view" (Keller, "Pandemic Pandemonium").

103. Ryken et al., *Dictionary of Biblical Imagery*, 38.

104. Whether in institutions or in the current political and religious leaders who incite terrorism or endorse repressive and discriminatory behavior. Throughout history, the dragons' heads have been identified with political leaders opposing the church such as Roman kings (Victorinus); rulers of every age "who fell under the sway of evil" (Bede); Herod, Nero, Constantius, Muhammad, Mesemoth, and Saladin (Joachim of Fiore); as well as the papacy (Koester, *Revelation*, 526).

in the form of a mythical creature offers, however, hope in the possibility of resistance. In establishing evil as a separate but dependent entity that is reliant on being able to influence humankind in drawing out this inclination, it becomes an outer as well as an inner force.[105] It is, therefore, a force that must be faced but can also be resisted which, from a biblical perspective, is due to its ultimate defeat that lies at the heart of the Gospel narratives. This is through a process that is initiated by the incarnation account in the Lukan narrative and comes to a dramatic climax in the narratives of Revelation.

As Reddish points out, John is not, therefore, interested in explaining the origin of evil as, in taking its reality for granted and presenting it as a destructive force that threatens to overwhelm humankind, he is only concerned with the hope arising from the possibility of its defeat; a defeat that has in essence already occurred with the sacrificial death and resurrection of Jesus.[106] In this respect, the account of the birth of the male child who *"is to rule all the nations with a rod of iron"* but is immediately *"snatched away and taken to God and his throne"* (Revelation 12:5) can be interpreted as representing the birth, death, resurrection and ascension of Jesus, functioning, in the words of Ben Witherington as "a sort of merism circumscribing the whole earthly career of Jesus."[107] As Caird suggests, however, there is also of a sense in which the birth and death of Jesus are now brought together, with a focus on the Cross rather than the Nativity in order for John to continue the exposition of Psalm 2 and

---

105. In acknowledging this "extrahuman" dimension of evil in which it "seems to take on a life of its own," residing in the "systems that allow and foster the problems of society," Reddish warns that it can lead to "a failure to recognise our own responsibility for evil." It is, however, a failure that the Genesis narrative exposes as: "One of the most poignant aspects of the temptation story of Adam and Eve is when they both deny responsibility for their actions. 'The woman whom you gave to be with me, she gave me fruit from the tree,' said Adam, when God confronted him with his disobedience. 'The serpent tricked me,' said Eve, pointing the finger of blame elsewhere" (Reddish, *Revelation*, 242–45).

106. Reddish, *Revelation*, 235. See also Bauckham, who points out that "the biblical metanarrative does not explain evil, as though it were a problem it can solve and surmount . . . [it] engages evil not with explanation but with hope with God's redemption from and incalculable overcoming of evil" (Bauckham, *Bible*, 33).

107. Witherington III, *Revelation*, 169. As Sumney points out: "Many have noted that a great deal has been collapsed into a very few words here. The child is born, identified as the Messiah, and snatched away by God to the throne of God all in one verse. Thus John compresses the birth and ascension of Jesus to a single event" (Sumney, "Dragon Has Been Defeated," 105).

establish the Cross as the primary reference for the defeat of evil.[108] It is a defeat that the continuing forces of chaos indicate is not yet complete but, from a constructive perspective, the use of an imaginative alternative to represent the forces of darkness and chaos indicates the possibility of hope; hope that is not overwhelmed by seemingly insurmountable odds as it grounded in the messianic hope that in the words of Keller is able to face "into the dragon's mouth."[109] It is a possibility that, therefore, emerges through an interpretive approach of informed receptivity to the Revelation narrative that adopts what Keller refers to as an "apocalyptic mindfulness." In resisting what she describes as both optimistic denialism and pessimistic nihilism, and avoiding either literalizing or dismissing the supernatural creature, it is an approach that is expansive rather than reductionist in seeking to extend the boundaries of the thinkable. This is by "grasping at effectual language" and pressing "beyond flat factualities, secular or fundamentalist . . . and beyond despairing surrender" in order for the reader or hearer to understand that a text that is "charged with trauma" can also be charged with hope.[110]

It is, therefore, a mindfulness to the meta*force* of a supernatural dragon whose destructive presence is also a threat to the perceived boundaries of thinkable. This is as a presence that by "bothering" or "concerning" the hearer or reader of the narrative is able to draw them into "a heightened, even mediative attention" which, in minding or "facing" the danger that the creature represents, is able to activate what Keller names "response—ability."[111] In this respect, she can describe it as a mindfulness that calls for liberating and "activation attention" as this responsibility requires "both contemplative and activist activations"[112] from the hearer or reader. These are activations that become possible when the representation of evil and chaos in the form of a supernatural creature

---

108. Caird, *Revelation of St John*, 149–51. See also Brown, who sees the reference as being "not to Jesus' physical birth or to Jesus as an infant, but to Jesus' birth as the Messiah through his death" (Brown, *Introduction*, 293).

109. Keller, *Facing Apocalypse*, 72.

110. Keller, *Facing Apocalypse*, 17–18.

111. Keller, *Facing Apocalypse*, 18.

112. Keller, *Facing Apocalypse*, 18. In an earlier work, Keller refers to response that "invites the fullest sense of H. Richard Niebuhr's 'responsible self,' a self that is able to respond activates because of its receptivity to the other" (Keller, *God and Power*, 151). From a biblical perspective, this is a self that is always responsible to God and responsive to the divine call.

opens the way to the light of Christian hope as radiant light that is able to overcome darkness.

RADIANT LIGHT IN THE DARKNESS

Composite Image of Cassiopeia A Supernova Remnant[113]

The defeat of the forces of darkness by the light of Christian hope is a key feature of the Revelation narrative, but it is light that, if not extinguished in contemporary societies, appears for many to have grown increasingly dim. An interpretive approach that adopts Nagel's concepts of radical departure from the familiar to imaginative alternatives that extend the boundaries of the thinkable offers, however, a potential way forward to the discovery of the full-spectrum light of Christian hope that emerges from biblical narrative. This is discovery that is facilitated by conceptual similarities that can be found between the vision of the woman, dragon and child in Revelation 12:1–5 and the multiwavelength image of the Cassiopeia A Supernova remnant that was produced by the Fermi (Large Area Telescope) Collaboration in 2011; a composite image that reveals the light of the electromagnetic spectrum, with gamma rays from NASA's Fermi Gamma-Ray Space Telescope shown in magenta; X-rays from

---

113. NASA/DOE/Fermi LAT Collaboration, CXC/SAO/JPL-Caltech/Steward/O. Krause et al., and NRAO/AUI.

NASA's Chandra X-ray Observatory in blue and green; the visible light data captured by the Hubble Space Telescope shown in yellow; infrared data from NASA's Spitzer Space Telescope shown in red and radio data from the Very Large Array shown in orange.[114]

While contemporary cosmology does not explain John's cosmic visions, the image does potentially offer an insight into how biblical narrative uses imagery which traverses the full spectrum of theological light, in order to present aspects of reality that are invisible to the naked eye. "Seeing the light" from the perspective of the Revelation narrative is not, however, reliant on the visual and dependent on the development of advanced technology as "for all its apparent concreteness and vividness, the imagery of apocalyptic writing is essentially nonvisual and nonpictorial."[115] While such writing appears "to paint specific pictures," the images are often "almost impossible to put into composite pictorial form," with the "otherworldly" or "fantastic imagery" suggesting a world "that transcends ordinary reality."[116] The reality of a biblical perspective of the world is, therefore, portrayed in narrative that requires the hearer or reader to *listen* rather than *look* in order to learn about reality that seems to defy the human experience of time and space.[117] It is a requirement that has, however, also emerged in astrophysics with the announcement in February 2016 that a new window on the universe had been opened with the detection of gravitational waves.

Due to their complete darkness in the absence of any light, it was only in 2015 that the existence of astronomy's cosmic beast could be confirmed as the gravitational waves resulting from the collision and merger of two black holes about 1.3 billion years ago were detected when the Laser Interferometer Gravitational-Wave Observatory (LIGO) recorded the faint rising tone or "fleeting chirp" of the now tiny ripples that were once waves resulting from the collision. According to a LIGO press release, these are waves which "carry information about their dramatic origins and about the nature of gravity that cannot otherwise be obtained."[118] The

---

114. Reddy, "NASA's Fermi."

115. Ryken et al., *Dictionary of Biblical Imagery*, 37.

116. Ryken et al., *Dictionary of Biblical Imagery*, 37.

117. Elisabeth Schüssler Fiorenza suggests that "the Book of Revelation makes quite a different impression when it is heard than when it is analyzed. The hearer of the text is impressed by its rhythmic and archaic language, by the repetition of sounds and words, and by the wealth of colors, voices, symbols, and image associations" (Schüssler Fiorenza, *Book of Revelation*, 173).

118. Svitil et al., "Gravitational Waves."

Into the Realm of the Dragon

discovery of their existence has, therefore been described as an inflection point that will change the course of science as "areas that are off-limits to light" can now be examined.[119] In this respect, gravitational waves "tell an unseen story";[120] a story that we can hear but not see and must therefore listen to in order to better understand the reality of the vast cosmic landscape. The biblical story is also one that we can hear but not see, so must listen to in order to better understand the reality of the biblical landscape; a landscape that is first encountered as darkness covering the face of the deep until God said, *"'Let there be light.' And there was light"* (Genesis 1:2–3).[121]

According to Rees, speaking from the perspective of science,

> we are linked to the cosmos. All living things depend on the stars: they are energized by the heat and light from the Sun; they are made of atoms that were forged from pristine hydrogen, billions of years ago in faraway stars.[122]

The biblical perspective is similar in acknowledging the link to the cosmos through our creation from *"the dust of the ground"* (Genesis 2:7 NRSV). Its unique point of difference is, however, that humankind is also made in the image of God from whom the breath of life is given. It therefore gives humankind an additional dependency and source of energy that is manifest in the love of God as a life force. This is as a transcendent force that is not manifest as a performance of "condescending imperial mercy" but in a God who, in the words of Keller, "actually loves, is loved, is love."[123] The concept of love as a transcendent force is also raised in the film *Interstellar* in a discussion between an astronaut and a scientist about the meaning of love. For the astronaut, love's meaning arises from its function as a social utility but the scientist proposes that it may provide evidence of Nagel's "something more" as part of a "higher" dimension that cannot be consciously perceived or even understood. We are, however, able to perceive love despite its ability to transcend time

---

119. Green, "Detection of Gravitational Waves."
120. From the film *Einstein's Gravity Playlist*, Montana State University, eXtreme Gravity Institute, 2017.
121. Alter, *Five Books*, 17.
122. Rees, *From Here to Infinity*, 107.
123. Keller, *God and Power*, 110.

and space which leads her to suggest that we should "trust" it even if we cannot "understand" it.[124]

From a biblical perspective, understanding is, however, at least partially possible in narratives that reach a climax in the book of Revelation. While it was once thought to be written during a period of violent persecution, Jerry Sumney points out that many now contend that it addresses the isolation and oppression that early Christians experienced due to economic and social persecution and the consequent temptation to accommodate themselves to the economic, social and political pressures of the dominant culture.[125] Regardless of the situation, it offered a message of hope in troubled times; hope that was not solely reliant on human resources to defeat the forces of evil in whatever form they took. The current state of both our planet and human society indicates that Nagel is correct in suggesting that we have only reached a very primitive stage of moral development. He is also correct in stating that it has been arrived at "only by a long and difficult journey" as the history of humankind has revealed. His assumption that a much longer journey "lies ahead of us, if we survive"[126] is chilling and potentially accurate but his belief that it "would be foolish to try to lay down in advance the outlines for a correct method for ethical progress"[127] is challenged by the biblical narratives. In shedding biblical light in its varying forms, on the vulnerability and fallibility of the human condition, they offer the possibility of, and method for, ethical progress and the restoration of broken relationships through the transformative creativity of a loving God. This is a creativity which is, therefore, inherent in humankind, who are made in his image, and activated by his Spirit, thereby offering hope amidst the challenge of darkness; hope that resounds in the final chapter of the book of Revelation in which a radiant light has finally defeated the darkness and is explained in

---

124. Conversation between Brand and Cooper in Nolan, *Interstellar*.

125. Although this is a contested issue, Sumney takes the position that there is little evidence outside the text for a time of severe Christian persecution in the first century. See Sumney, "Dragon," 103–4. Schüssler Fiorenza argues, however, that the central purpose of the book is "to strengthen and to encourage the Christian communities of Asia Minor" and to give meaning to the present suffering of those experiencing harassment, persecution and possible execution (Schüssler Fiorenza, *Book of Revelation*, 59, 63, 200). See also Keller, who suggests: "Properly understood, the biblical apocalypse, whatever else it may be, is one long act of protest against the powers of the state" and "a work of profound solidarity with those suffering from persecution and injustice" (Keller, "Why Apocalypse, Now?," 187).

126. Nagel, *View from Nowhere*, 187.

127. Nagel, *View from Nowhere*, 187.

the words: "*It is I, Jesus, who . . . am the root and the descendent of David, the bright morning star*" (Revelation 22:16).

This constructive, interdisciplinary approach to the Revelation narrative has, together with its application to the narratives from Genesis and Luke, sought to demonstrate how they might contribute to a new vision of what Nagel refers to as the true extent of reality. This is a vision that is possible when a biblical mapping of the human condition and our relationship to the world, is not interpreted as challenging, or being opposition to, the mappings of science. It is instead interpreted as an overlay which, in being integrated with the discoveries of science can contribute to the creation of a better future for all living things that comprise our biosphere. This is by offering a complementary rather than competing perspective of the complex nature of reality; a perspective that anticipates Nagel's warning that the world "may contain not only what we don't know and can't yet conceive but also what we never could conceive"[128] as it confronts finite earthbound beings with the concept of the infinite. It is a perspective that also, however, anticipates the question that he subsequently raises, and is thereby able to challenge his conclusion that it may have no imaginable answer.

---

128. Nagel, *View from Nowhere*, 108.

12

An Indeterminate In/conclusion

We seem to be left with a question that has no imaginable answer: How is it possible for finite beings like us to think infinite thoughts.[1]

THE RELEVANCE OF NAGEL's question for biblical hermeneutics is perhaps found in its resonance with Marion Grau's declaration that:

> The divine and the experiences of God and the sacred are . . . a notorious hermeneutical problem. How to render, translate, interpret the unintelligible, the infinitely untranslatable without indeed admitting to its impossibility?[2]

In highlighting the danger of "jumping to hermeneutical conclusions,"[3] Grau is, therefore, led to what she describes as a position of "an indeterminate in/conclusion" as:

> Embracing the fragmentary nature of our knowledge and of the narratives we weave seems overall a more helpful strategy for resourcing the retelling and reimagining of ancient narratives newly experienced, more respectful for the fragility, beauty and

---

1. Nagel, *Last Word*, 74.
2. Grau, *Refiguring Theological Hermeneutics*, 189.
3. Grau, *Refiguring Theological Hermeneutics*, 190.

... sacredness of these narratives. The sacred and the holy thus receive a more fully captured respect for all its qualities, not just the domesticated ones, but indeed touching with respect as well as joy the *mysterium tremendum et fascinans*, its complexity, its indeterminacy.[4]

This is a position that is perhaps also inevitable for a book investigating the possibility of a hermeneutical approach which, in avoiding reductionism, is able to recapture a respect for biblical narrative that does not disclude its supernatural components. These are components that the book has suggested both refuse domestication and resist deportation, demanding instead recognition of mystery that both frightens and fascinates, threatens and attracts. It is mystery that therefore presents potentially significant interpretive challenges in exposing the epistemological complexity of concepts such as understanding, explanation, meaning, belief, and truth. These are, however, challenges that have also emerged in theoretical physics, with the ongoing mystery and paradox that appear to be part of quantum reality. They are also ongoing in the study of consciousness which Nagel describes as "the most conspicuous obstacle to a comprehensive naturalism that relies only on the resources of physical science."[5] Nagel's response to this obstacle and the possibility of questions that have no imaginable answers is to recommend the replacement of attempts at "decisive proof or refutation" with the careful development of rival, alternative conceptions to see how they "measure up."[6] This is a form of replacement that this book has explored in relation to a constructive and interdisciplinary approach to the interpretation of biblical narrative by proposing; firstly, that Nagel's thinking might offer critical insights for hermeneutical endeavor; secondly, that his thinking might suggest an interpretive paradigm from which to approach the challenge that the narratives' supernatural components appear to present to contemporary epistemology. This is a challenge that was succinctly expressed in 2012 by theoretical physicist Lawrence Krauss after the CERN announcement that the LHC had finally uncovered evidence for a particle consistent with the Higgs boson, the visible manifestation of the Higgs Field. In a subsequent *Newsweek* article, Krauss declared:

---

4. Grau, *Refiguring Theological Hermeneutics*, 189.
5. Nagel, *Mind and Cosmos*, 35.
6. Nagel, *Mind and Cosmos*, 127.

Assuming the particle in question is indeed the Higgs, it validates an unprecedented revolution in our understanding of fundamental physics and brings science closer to dispensing with the need for any supernatural shenanigans all the way back to the beginning of the universe—and perhaps even before the beginning, if there was a before... Humans, with their remarkable tools and their remarkable brains, may have just taken a giant step toward replacing metaphysical speculation with empirically verifiable knowledge. The Higgs particle is now arguably more relevant than God.[7]

It was, therefore, perhaps appropriate that the underground chamber beneath mountain foothills in which the LHC was constructed, was a laboratory described as a "cathedral of science."[8] Krauss admitted, however, that despite our remarkable tools and brains, the results could reinforce what he described as the "potentially uncomfortable possibility that our existence may be an accidental and purposeless consequence of conditions associated with the birth of the universe."[9] While this may be an acceptable premise for those believing it to be the inevitable consequence of scientific progress, it appears, however, that for increasing numbers the desire for what Nagel calls "something more" and the "insatiable hunger for belief" remains. At the same time as the construction of the LHC, another very different subterranean temple was under construction in the foothills of the Italian Alps driven by a vision that claimed to move beyond the realm of science to unite art, science, technology, and spirituality "in the research of new roads for the evolution of humanity." The *Damanhur* Temples of Humankind which now take up 8,500 cubic meters on five subterranean levels are described as arising at a point where four of the "Synchronic Lines" of the planet—as great rivers or pathways of energy that connect the Earth to the Universe—meet and are symbolized on the temple walls as four serpent-dragons. The temples were also designed to function as a laboratory, but this is a "Laboratory for the Future of Humanity" researching roads that are anticipated to both "challenge the boundaries of contemporary knowledge" by investigating the concept of the "impossible," and provide "a path of re-awakening to the Divine inside and outside of ourselves."[10]

---

7. Krauss, "How the Higgs Boson."
8. Anderson, "Genesis 2.0," 111.
9. Krauss, "How the Higgs Boson."
10. Described as a Federation of spiritual communities with its own Constitution

Enchantment, in the sense of awe and wonder in the search for the true extent of reality has, it seems, been rediscovered within two "near-magical" realms,[11] whether in the form of the mechanically generated power of high-energy particle beams traveling close to the speed of light, or river-pathways of energy depicted as mythical beasts. Regardless of the skepticism that the *Damanhur* project may generate, the driving force of its philosophy, with potentially wide-spread appeal, is the concept of an ecologically sound, multi-cultural community based on a vision of integration with, and respect for, the diversity of the environment and the animal and human world within it. There are echoes of this vision in the ground-breaking legislation passed in New Zealand in 2017 recognizing the Whanganui River as *Te Awa Tupua*,

> a spiritual and physical entity that supports and sustains both the life and natural resources within the Whanganui River and the health and well-being of the iwi, hapū, and other communities of the River.[12]

As an entity that has an "inalienable connection" with the *iwi* (tribe) and *hapū* (clans) of the Whanganui River as a source of spiritual and physical sustenance,[13] it is a river that can consequently be described as "a legal person" with all the corresponding "rights, powers, duties, and liabilities."[14] While new in legislative terms, the recognition of a physical and spiritual interconnection with the environment has roots that are deeply embedded in the indigenous culture of New Zealand. The renewed emphasis on the dimensions of this interconnection and the subsequent legislation indicate that Graham Ward may be correct in referring to the "implosion of secularism" which he believes has facilitated "a new return to the theological and a new emphasis on reenchantment."[15] The latter is an emphasis

---

and attracting thousands of visitors every year, *Damanhur* was officially recognized in 2005 as a model of a sustainable society by the Global Human Settlements Forum of the United Nations. See http://www.damanhur.org.

11. This term was used to describe the LHC laboratory at CERN. See Anderson, "Genesis 2.0," 113.

12. New Zealand Legislation, *Te Awa Tupua* 2.13.

13. "*Te Awa Tupua, Ko au te Awa, ko te Awa ko au*: I am the River and the River is me" (New Zealand Legislation, *Te Awa Tupua* 2.13.c).

14. New Zealand Legislation, *Te Awa Tupua* 2.14.

15. A return that Ward points out has not been "signaled" by theologians but rather by "filmmakers, novelists, poets, philosophers, political theorists, and cultural analysts" (Ward, "Introduction," xii).

that is also appearing in the field of consciousness studies with the re-emergence of Panpsychism,[16] which philosopher Philip Goff describes as "the view that consciousness is a fundamental and ubiquitous feature of physical reality"[17] and suggests

> offers a way of "re-enchanting" the universe . . . [as] the universe is *like us*; we *belong* in it. We need not live exclusively in the human realm, ever more diluted by globalization and consumerist capitalism. We can live in nature, in the universe . . . in the knowledge that there is a universe that welcomes us.[18]

There appears, therefore, to be increasing evidence to support Boeve's suggestion that societies are now not only post-Christian but also post-secular, with a renewed sensitivity to the spiritual and transcendent;[19] sensitivity that can be seen in the multidisciplinary *Institute of Noetic Sciences* (*IONS*), with the declared goal of establishing "a deeper understanding of the true nature of reality" which includes the problem of consciousness and its role in the physical world; an understanding achieved by bridging objective science and a subjective spirituality loosely defined as the "gaining of deep knowing through direct experience."[20] The intended outcome of this "deep knowing" appears

---

16. With ancient origins in the Presocratics and Plato, Panpsychism appears to be increasingly attracting the attention of both philosophers and neuroscientists as a way of integrating consciousness into a scientific picture of the world. It is integration that was, however, also suggested by some of the pioneers in quantum theory. In an interview published in *The Observer* on January 25, 1931, three winners of the Nobel prize for physics stated that: "the material universe and consciousness are made out of the same stuff" (Erwin Schrödinger); "I regard consciousness and matter as different aspects of one and the same thing" (Louis de Broglie); and "I regard consciousness as fundamental. I regard matter as derivative from consciousness. We cannot get behind consciousness" (Max Planck) (Strawson, "Galileo's Error").

17. Goff, *Galileo's Error*, 113.

18. Goff, *Galileo's Error*, 217. Goff cites an article by Nagel as his introduction to Panpsychism and subsequently builds upon the thinking of Strawson (see Strawson, "Realistic Materialism"). In the 1972 article that Goff references, Nagel concludes, however, that "panpsychism should be added to the current list of mutually incompatible and hopelessly unacceptable solutions to the mind-body problem" (Nagel, *Mortal Questions*, 193). Nearly fifty years later, Nagel continues to maintain that "panpsychism does not provide a new, more basic resting place in the search for intelligibility—a set of basic principles from which more complex results can be seen to follow. It offers only the form of an explanation without any content, and therefore doesn't seem to be much of an advance on the emergent alternative" (Nagel, *Mind and Cosmos*, 61).

19. Boeve, *Theology at the Crossroads*, 4, 41–42.

20. See "Interconnected Nature." See also the *Galileo Commission*, established by the *Scientific and Medical Network* to explore and expand "the frontiers of science,

to be a holistic and transformative understanding of ourselves and our world, with the founder of IONS suggesting that we need "a new story of who we are and what we are capable of becoming."[21]

The premise of this book is, however, that this renewed sensitivity and sense of reenchantment, together with the thinking of Thomas Nagel, offers the possibility of reclaiming an old story rather than creating something new. It is a possibility that is, somewhat ironically, opened up by the words of Richard Dawkins if his reference to the contribution of the scientist is replaced by that of the biblical theologian:[22]

> Rather than propose a new theory or unearth a new fact, often the most important contribution a . . . [biblical theologian] can make is to discover a new way of seeing old theories or facts . . . a change of vision can, at its best, achieve something loftier than a theory. It can usher in a whole new climate of thinking, in which many exciting and testable theories are born, and unimagined facts laid bare.[23]

It is a possibility that also emerges from theoretical physicist David Burman's suggestion that "in an increasingly fractured world, we need people who can bring together and combine divergent kinds of work";[24] a suggestion that finds support from Rovelli who sees the two diverse human activities of "inventing stories and following traces in order to find something" as activities that are not far removed from each other as "the border is porous" with myths nourishing science and science nourishing

---

medicine and spirituality" by working "at the interface between science, spirituality, and consciousness." The Network is described as being part of "the contemporary quest for a more spiritual mode of thinking and being that is compatible with science" and in 2019 published the Galileo Commission Report, entitled *Beyond a Materialist World-view—Towards an Expanded Science*.

21. As a member of the Apollo 14 space mission, engineer and astrophysicist Edgar Mitchell was the sixth person to walk on the moon, and the sense of universal connectivity that he experienced on the return to Earth led him to this suggestion. See Mitchell, "Birthed Amongst the Stars."

22. This is with reference to biblical theology that is focused on the narrative continuity in the Bible and balancing its literary, historical, and theological elements to "discern the theological world that flows out of this coherent 'story-shaped' reading of the Bible with varying degrees of reference to the historical events behind the text" (Klink and Lockett, *Comparison*, 94).

23. Dawkins, *Selfish Gene*, xi.

24. Burman, "One Culture, Not Two." There is a growing push across education sectors to adapt the integrated STEM (science, technology, engineering, and mathematics) focus to STEAM by the inclusion of the arts.

myths.[25] Peter Watson also argues that the sciences are converging and coalescing "to identify one extraordinary master narrative, one overwhelming interlocking coherent story: the history of the universe."[26] This is a history in which there are "intimate connections between physics and chemistry," links between quantum chemistry and molecular biology, alignments between particle physics and astronomy and a harmonization between genetics and linguistics, botany and archaeology, and climatology with myth.[27] In examining the ideas that he believes to be at the heart of science which includes the scientific order underlying myths,[28] Watson concludes that "ancient history is now an interlaced, interdisciplinary branch of science,"[29] with human behavior becoming "a point on which many sciences now converge."[30] This raises, however, the possibility that it is an interlacing in which myths may instead underly the scientific order as an integral part of understanding the complexities of the human condition. The book has, therefore, attempted to utilize these possibilities as inflection points[31] or a window of opportunity for biblical narrative to contribute to a holistic and transformative understanding of ourselves and our world. This is a contribution that it has suggested is enabled by extrapolating from Nagel's work, both hermeneutical insights and an interpretive paradigm that might offer a new way of "seeing" or approaching biblical narrative; a way in which seemingly unimaginable facts are laid bare by the use of the supernatural as a pragmatic tool to enable their disclosure.

The context of Part I concerned the impact of developments in science and technology on the use of the supernatural in biblical narrative and Christian tradition. This was in order to explore firstly, the

25. Rovelli, *Seven Brief Lessons*, 69.

26. Watson, *Convergence*, xxiv. Watson describes the discipline of psychology as both expanding in its association with economics but also disappearing at the margins where it is "dissolving" into chemistry, physics, genetics, ethnology, and sociology (387).

27. Watson, *Convergence*, xxv.

28. See chapter 14 in Watson, *Convergence*, 322–55.

29. Watson, *Convergence*, 371.

30. Which include physics, chemistry, genetics, evolutionary theory, ethnology, and socio-biology (Watson, *Convergence*, 389).

31. For Wallach, these are turning points in history that provide a window of opportunity "to assert a degree of control" over the type of future that we are potentially creating for humanity and the opportunity for new initiatives or "adjustments in the rate of progress or shifts in the trajectory of unfolding research" (Wallach, *Dangerous*, 10–11).

hermeneutical significance of Nagel's critique of "scientist" assumptions arising from perceptions of the epistemological dominance of scientific naturalism and materialist reductionism, and his suggestion that there is a need to move away from reductionist or eliminative revisions of current concepts. His subsequent advocacy for expansionist revision that is open to new discoveries while still preserving features of the old, was highlighted as inadvertently having particular relevance for the interpretation of biblical narrative and understanding of Christian doctrine. This is if the narratives are approached through the lens of his acknowledgment of; firstly, the limits of both human language and our conceptual and cognitive abilities; secondly, the need for a better understanding of the relation between facts and conceptual schemes; and thirdly, the potential dangers of reductive approaches that deny the reality of what may lie beyond our ability to describe or understand. It was concluded that moving beyond reductionism to expansionist revision that Nagel describes as "imagining possibility," could enhance the potential of biblical narratives to offer an enlarged conception of reality and thereby respond to his call for the need for "something more"; a something more which he suggests might emerge from other forms of understanding.

The detrimental consequences that Nagel suggests result from a "defensive world-flattening reductionism" that he links to a "fear of religion," were then explored in relation to their impact on biblical hermeneutics. This was specifically in relation to the interpretation of supernatural components in biblical narrative and their reduction to labels such as myth and story, useful fiction or historically factual phenomena. Nagel's explanation of what he calls the "God hypothesis" was used to highlight underlying assumptions that might drive interpretive methods and then to raise the question of the potentially unique nature of biblical language and its referential function. This is as a nature that, by inextricably combining literal and figurative language, appears to resist the reductive categorization of grammatical terminology and hold in tension the mystery of the transcendent and radically unfamiliar, with the known and familiar. It is a nature that, therefore, might also resist dismissal of the narratives' supernatural content which contributes to an understanding of not only ceaseless creativity in the universe but also the capacity for ceaseless destruction. The ongoing recognition in the developing sciences of what Nagel refers to as an astonishing world, was then considered in relation to the requirement for a nonreductive conceptual framework within which understanding and orientation can emerge. This is a framework that may, however, have an ancient precedent in a biblical conception of reality; a conception emerging in narratives that also acknowledge the wonder and mystery of an astonishing world and may, therefore, offer a unique response to Nagel's search for an understanding of humankind as a specific expression of what he believes to be the physical and mental character of the universe.[32]

The next insight for hermeneutical endeavor emerged from the scientific search for what Nagel refers to as the "true extent of reality" in a world that extends beyond the limits of language and the reach of our minds. This is reality unfolding from scientific mapping that, in operating at the boundaries of the thinkable, challenges both our intuitive conception of the world and our ability to articulate it. Rovelli's suggestion that this is, consequently, reality that demands both "in-depth" revision of our conceptions and a rethinking of "the grammar of our understanding of the world"[33] was subsequently highlighted. This was in order to consider; firstly, how biblical narrative might offer a unique in-depth conceptual revision that is able to supplement and expand our ideas about the nature of reality and in particular the human condition; secondly, how this might be seen as a relevant collaborative, rather than combative, expansion in which some unexpected conceptual similarities can be found in the challenge to interpret both biblical perspectives of reality and perspectives emerging in the study of consciousness and cosmology. These similarities were then considered through an exploration of the findings of contemporary cosmology and astrophysics, with a focus on the observation of what is now known to be ancient light and the seemingly paradoxical concept of its wave-particle duality.

As challenges to what Nagel describes as "our intuitive conception of the world,"[34] these scientific concepts were used to consider a response to the challenges presented to our intuition and understanding by the invisible realities that exist within a biblical perspective of the world; realities that also expose what Heisenberg, in reference to developments in quantum theory, called the "really serious" problem of the limitations of ordinary language based on old concepts which could not be applied everywhere.[35] The recognition within science of the need to not only "use

---

32. Nagel, *Mind and Cosmos*, 69.
33. Rovelli, *Reality*, 127.
34. Nagel, *Concealment and Exposure*, 172.
35. Heisenberg, *Physics and Philosophy*, 151.

An Indeterminate In/conclusion

existing language to reach beyond its existing limits"[36] but also to expand it, with new terms introduced and "the old ones . . . applied in a wider field or differently from ordinary language,"[37] was highlighted in order to suggest that this might already apply to the biblical writers' use of language. Human consciousness was then considered as an area which Nagel believes to be "one of the most astonishing things about the world"[38] due to the mystery that still surrounds what he describes as the "affliction" of "the pervasive self-consciousness that makes us human."[39] The potential resonance of his thinking with a biblical portrayal of the emergence of self-consciousness was then explored in order to demonstrate how this account might subsequently contribute to the ongoing search to find what he refers to as our place in the world; a search to uncover answers to what he calls the "mortal questions" about human life, "about its end, its meaning, its value, and about the metaphysics of consciousness."[40]

Nagel's emphasis on the need to understand the problems that this search might encounter, to recognize what can and cannot be understood by certain existing methods and avoid what he describes as "the hazards of combining perspectives that are radically distinct"[41] was then explored. This was to highlight his belief that "the methods needed to understand ourselves do not yet exist"[42] and its potential implications for biblical hermeneutics; implications that concern both *what* and *how* a biblical perspective of the human condition might contribute to this understanding when the intelligibility and relevance of biblical narrative are increasingly questioned. Nagel's emphasis on establishing a deeper understanding of the epistemological issues at the heart of perceived problems in order to be able to ask the right questions was examined with reference to scientific endeavor. This was to identify its relevance for biblical interpretation and to argue that the "right" questions to address to biblical narrative may not be those emerging from either science or modern historical criticism; questions that concern objective factual content and relate to the perceived issue of whether and where the labels of history or fiction can be applied. The need for different non-reductive

---

36. Nagel, *Secular Philosophy*, 31.
37. Heisenberg, *Physics and Philosophy*, 149.
38. Nagel, *Mind and Cosmos*, 53.
39. Nagel, "Analytic Philosophy."
40. Nagel, *Mortal Questions*, ix.
41. Nagel, *View from Nowhere*, 209.
42. Nagel, *View from Nowhere*, 10.

categories and criteria, within an investigative rather than presumptive approach was subsequently raised. This was as an approach that might begin with the willingness of the hearer or reader to enter into the spirit of biblical narrative by seeking to discover, and then allowing it to set, its own terms for interpretation. These terms were considered with reference to the potentially unique nature of biblical language which, therefore, makes unique demands on the hearer or reader.

An approach to understanding this nature was then explored by moving from Nagel's description of the acquisition of what he calls "ordinary natural" language as a path to understanding and articulating reality, to the purpose of the acquisition and development of language that can be traced in biblical narrative. The adequacy and limits of the "language of daily life"[43] were considered in relation to the challenges of articulating reality that is epistemologically confronting, challenging, and confounding; reality that is not confined to a biblical perspective of the world but is now also a significant feature of the quantum world. The issue was then raised about the significance of what Alter identifies as the literal force of biblical language in which narrative details are crucial in providing meaning to the hearer or reader.[44] This led to an exploration of the *sensus literalis* which, in an expanded rather than reductive form that does not disclude but is also not dependent on historical veracity, might function as a potentially integral part of biblical language; language in which words may be literal but not literalistic and mean what they say in the context of the narratives. In this respect, they cannot be reduced to competing options of either allegory, myth, symbol or history but are rather what Frei calls, "the right description," with the narratives describing and depicting "precisely what they mean to describe and depict."[45] Literal meaning from this perspective, therefore becomes "literate meaning," with historical reference, storied referent and canonical sense being partial dimensions of the literal sense.[46] The possibility of a historical kernel within the narratives is not, therefore, either removed or given center stage but allowed instead to function as a seed from which meaning emerges as a continually unfolding process. This is, however, a process which in looking forward as well as back may require the use of specific and even new tools with which to discover meaning.

43. Heisenberg, *Across the Frontiers*, 226.
44. Alter, *World*, 87–88.
45. Frei, *Writings from the Archives*, 75.
46. Vanhoozer, *Is There a Meaning*, 307–9.

An Indeterminate In/conclusion

The final insight emerged from Nagel's advocacy of the need to not only select the right tools but also to develop new intellectual tools to assist the potentially radical conceptual shift that might be necessary to enable new forms of understanding. For Nagel, this is understanding of an integrated theory of reality in which mind can be accommodated in a theory that is not solely dependent on physical reductionism. His call for "entirely new intellectual tools, and . . . reflection on what appears impossible"[47] appears however, to have hermeneutical significance for the challenge that the biblical writers also faced in introducing radically different concepts; concepts that, while appearing impossible in a secular and scientifically orientated culture, might also have appeared impossible in the context of both ANE and Classical epistemology. The issue of selecting the right tools for biblical interpretation was approached by reference to Hooker's critique of critical methods that may be used inappropriately. This is without recognition of either their limitations or potential for misuse if there is an underlying interpretive agenda that might be acknowledged but also might be unrecognized.

The possibility of the need for entirely new tools was explored with reference to the radical conceptual challenges that Nagel highlights as arising in attempts to understand the underlying reality of special relativity and quantum theory. Nagel's reference to these challenges in theoretical physics, in his approach to the mind-body problem, was used to consider how they might also provide insights for the interpretation of a biblical perspective of reality. This is as a perspective in which concepts of space and time might also "diverge radically from the intuitive concepts that we all use in thinking about our surroundings."[48] A prerequisite to this consideration was, however, acknowledgment of the warning Nagel gives about the potential issues arising from the use of concepts and terminology developed to account for very different kinds of things, and the hazards of combining perspectives that are radically distinct. Criteria for a legitimate use of scientific concepts were then established which included having a genuine and relevant intellectual goal in mind, a good understanding of the science being applied and justification of its relevance. This was in order to extrapolate some of the concepts and terminology that reflect what Polkinghorne describes as an unexpected kinship between quantum physics and theology; kinship that emerges

---

47. Nagel, *View from Nowhere*, 52.
48. Nagel, *Concealment and Exposure*, 171.

in the challenge to articulate and understand the presence of paradox, ontological flexibility, and seemingly irreducible mystery that appear to exist in both the quantum and biblical perspectives of reality.

The goal of this extrapolation was to enable the construction of a contemporary hermeneutical approach to the interpretation of a biblical perspective of the world. This is as a perspective that might, as the book of Job indicates, set an ancient precedent for Nagel's description of a world that science increasingly confirms as extending beyond the reach of our minds, with our understanding not only limited to what we can know but also in relation to what we can conceive.[49] It was suggested that a contemporary hermeneutic would, therefore, require both understanding of the unique terms under which biblical narrative might operate and anticipation of its silent response to questions concerning its relationship with either history or science. It should, therefore, be open to the potential of what Barr refers to as a tangential relationship but Barth describes as involving "wrappings" in which the properties of history and story are mixed and resist reductive disentanglement. It was argued that this is, subsequently, a relationship that has conceptual similarities to the wave and particle properties of light which provide contradictory pictures of reality and utilize different languages in their expression but are both needed to explain the phenomena of light.

The concept of shedding light was then used to contrast the focus of looking *back* in time within contemporary cosmology to that of looking *forward* as a feature of the biblical text. This was with reference to both Ricoeur's suggestion of how an interweaving of history and story allows new worlds to open up in *front* of a narrative text, and Nagel's concluding comment in *Mind and Cosmos* that decisive proof or refutation are not always the most credible form of progress.[50] It was suggested that Nagel's subsequent call for radical departure from familiar forms of naturalistic explanation to explore imaginative alternatives that extend the boundaries of the thinkable, might offer the possibility of a contemporary approach to biblical narrative; an approach that is able to function with integrity within the current epistemological climate. This possibility was explored in conjunction with four aspects of Ricoeur's thinking which were considered as significant complementary components of this approach. The first concerned his understanding of the complexity

---

49. Nagel, *View from Nowhere*, 90.
50. Nagel, *Mind and Cosmos*, 127.

of the human condition and the limitations of science as we "struggle with the believable and the unbelievable of our time in order to make a place for intelligent discourse."[51] The second emerged from his reference to dimensions of reality which, in being part of an initial state of pre-critical "naïve" awareness, are more original than the scientific object.[52] His suggestion of differing states of critical awareness was adopted after an adaptation of his potentially pejorative terminology which contrasts a "primitive naïveté" to a mature, sophisticated critically informed naïveté that might subsequently claim epistemological superiority. This terminology was replaced by "original receptivity" and "informed receptivity," with the latter representing a receptivity that is enhanced by interdisciplinary engagement. This led to the third aspect which concerns the need for a long route of multiple detours investigating other disciplines to break new paths. It was argued that there is a biblical precedent for the action of often radical departure into new and unknown territory. This is departure from the familiar that is both epistemological and physical, beginning with the creation narratives and the departure of the biblical couple from Eden and continuing in the narratives that follow.

Ricoeur's advocacy of a methodology involving investigation into possibilities emerging from other disciplines was considered as opening the way to a constructive interpretive approach. The fourth aspect subsequently concerned the role of the productive imagination in providing what Nagel refers to as imaginative alternatives; alternatives that offer an expanded vision of reality in which new worlds can shape our understanding of ourselves.[53] The role of the imagination in the construction of new ideas about reality was considered in relation to the discovery of aspects of the "slippery ground" of the quantum world that continue to present conceptual and imaginative challenges. This was in order to reinforce the possibility of a hermeneutical convergence between the ongoing struggle to articulate the unique perspective of quantum reality and the challenge that the biblical writers faced in presenting their unique perspective of reality within the limitations of language. The acknowledgment of the need for "story" as well as mathematics in the realm of physics was used to explore the significance of both imagination and story as fundamental to human cognition and the relevance that this might have for the interpretation of biblical narrative.

51. Ricoeur, *Philosophy of Paul Ricoeur*, 224.
52. Ricoeur, *Philosophy of Paul Ricoeur*, 70.
53. Ricoeur, *Hermeneutics and the Human Sciences*, 181.

The process of story-telling was then considered as the combination of multiple narrative forms in a unified product that demands a hermeneutical approach with a broader concept of truth than one within which "true" history with a direct referential claim and "fictional" story with an indirect referential claim are opposed.[54] It is a product that, therefore, appears to resist reductive approaches that diminish its potential and this was illustrated by reference to the wave function in quantum theory. This was to consider the possibility that in being both *history-like* and *fiction-like* in nature, biblical narrative has an inherent duality, holding in superposition the two forms of discourse which, in being complementary and entangled, enable multiple possibilities of transformational story; possibilities that emerge when interpretation moves beyond what Ricoeur describes as the "narrow boundaries" of the ostensive or "first order reference" of language to productive reference that enlarges our concept of the world.

Part I concluded by laying out a framework for a hermeneutic that might enable this move; a hermeneutic that incorporates Nagel's three concepts of firstly, *radical departure from familiar ways of thinking* to secondly, *imaginative alternatives* that thirdly, *extend the boundaries of the thinkable*. This is a framework that emerges from a position of informed receptivity and an awareness of the need to ask the right questions and use or develop the right tools. It is a position that also acknowledges the role of the productive imagination and allows the biblical narratives to function on their own potentially unique and often genre-defying terms. It therefore enables a hermeneutical approach that seeks to replace a reductive vision of reality with an expanded vision; a vision that is able to challenge conceptual boundaries in order to better understand the human condition and particularly the role of the human imagination in facilitating this understanding.

Part II used the theme of moving "Into the Light" to focus on the application of the hermeneutic to three biblical narratives. It began with a second "stepping back" into the mythical world of the ancient imagination as the world from which the narratives emerged. This was in order to trace what Nagel refers to as the human will to believe and attempts to make sense of the challenges of being human in an often hostile world, through what Midgely describes as the vital human function of myth-making in providing a sense of meaning to human life and death. The

---

54. Ricoeur, *Ricoeur Reader*, 116.

purpose of mythological expression as a way forward amidst the chaos and confusion of human life was then explored. In comparison to the creation stories of the ANE, the biblical creation narratives were considered as the presentation of a radically new vision for humanity. The concept of how this might be a revelatory and inspired vision was then explored in relation to the role of the imagination. This was with reference to Ricoeur's notion of an expanded concept of biblical revelation which emerges as the creative imagination breaks through the closed world of ordinary experience to project and open up a new world.

The focus then returned to the twenty-first century to explore potential links between the ancient and contemporary world and identify the task of a contemporary biblical hermeneutic. These are links emerging from attempts by the language of both myth and contemporary science to articulate what is beyond known and tangible reality. The potential points of resonance between theoretical physics and theology were then considered as the former increasingly appears to face seemingly unresolvable mystery as an integral part of reality. This is in the sense of an order of existence that is both beyond the visible and the usual or normal, in appearing to transcend the laws of nature. It was subsequently suggested that a foundational task of a contemporary biblical hermeneutic may involve identifying and exploring connections between the mythic expression of the ancient world and contemporary epistemology in order to enable biblical narrative to contribute to the increasingly vital quest to repair the fractured relationships in an increasingly fragile world.

The hermeneutic developed from Nagel's work was then applied to three biblical narratives as a constructive interpretive approach that, in avoiding a reductionism that may be antithetical to biblical narrative, is able to heed Hans Iwand's warning that if you

> break it apart and separate it into many, many small pieces like a clock, you will study and examine these pieces in detail, but you will not be able to put it back together. The clock-work—its particular way of chiming the hours—will be destroyed. It is not important that we study the individual pieces in isolation, but rather understand how the pieces interact with each other, producing movement that keeps everything going.[55]

The narratives, from Genesis, Luke and Revelation, were selected to indicate this interaction and movement, with the supernatural cherubim,

---

55. Iwand in Oeming, *Contemporary Biblical Hermeneutics*, 41.

angel, and serpent-dragon interpreted as tools that open the way to the transcendent by radically departing from the familiar in order to present a unique vision of reality. This is a vision which is not a *revision* of traditional interpretation that is subordinated to the discoveries of cosmology, physics, geology, paleoanthropology, genetics, and evolutionary biology; a revision that is called for by Daniel Harlow:

> For Christianity to remain intellectually credible and culturally relevant, it must be willing to revise—and thereby enrich—its formulation of classic doctrines if the secure findings of science call for revision.[56]

It is rather an adjustment to an expanded and constructive vision that does not seek security in the "secure findings" that are obtained from scientific endeavor which, as Gleiser points out, can only be partial and of limited validity as there is always more to explain beyond the reach of a theory.[57] This is, therefore, a vision which, in acknowledging but operating independently from, although in some respects collaboratively with, the findings of science, will facilitate a new way of thinking which will be informed by, rather than reform, classic doctrines. From this perspective, the supernatural components in the narratives become essential elements of narrative kernels which are described by literary critic Seymour Chatman as

> narrative moments that give rise to cruxes in the direction taken by events . . . nodes or hinges in the structure, branching points which force a movement into one or two (or more) possible paths.[58]

These are kernels which he suggests "cannot be deleted without destroying the narrative logic" and emphasizes that in "the classical narrative text, proper interpretation of events at any given point is a function of the ability to follow these ongoing sections, to see later kernels as consequences of earlier."[59] In this respect, the supernatural components

---

56. Harlow, "After Adam," 192.

57. As cited in chapter 1, see footnote 11.

58. Chapman, *Story and Discourse*, 53. Chapman develops the thinking of Roland Barthes in translating his narrative concepts of *noyau* and *catalyse* as "kernel" and "satellite" (53–54).

59. Chapman, *Story and Discourse*, 53. In computer technology, a "kernel" is the small central module or core of an operating system that loads first and remains in the main memory providing all the essential services required by the other parts of the system. In a similar sense, Ricoeur refers to narrative kernels occupying a central place and playing an exceptional role within the biblical text, with imaginative, poetic

of the Genesis, Lukan and Revelation narratives are, therefore, integral to the narrative logic in a developmental and consequential sequence of events. This is as components that challenge perceived boundaries of the thinkable and offer access to a new way of thinking that Nagel suggests is needed in any search to understand the human condition within a climate of "dominant scientific naturalism, heavily dependent on speculative Darwinian explanations of practically everything."[60]

Nagel's critique of reductive Darwinian materialism is not intended to open the door to theism as he explicitly states that "I do not find theism any more credible than materialism as a comprehensive worldview."[61] As a self-declared atheist who not only does not believe in God but also admits that he does not "want there to be a God" he, therefore, appears to be an unlikely and uncomfortable bedfellow for biblical hermeneutics. This book has, however, suggested that this may not be the case by inviting him, not into the bedchamber, but as a guest at a theological table. This is a table that Abraham believes will benefit from the inclusion of philosophers so that rather than being confined to the "crumbs that fall from each other's tables," philosophers and theologians can both bring "a full plate of food and their recipes to the feast" and thus a wider range of epistemological resources.[62] It is a table that Nagel's work suggests might also benefit from the inclusion of other guests to bring a wider and perhaps even exotic range of food to the "feast." This is an inclusion that may consequently allow theology to return to other tables from which it is currently excluded and contribute to the formulation of a new vision of integrated reality; a contribution that is facilitated by the evaporating boundaries between seemingly diverse disciplines and the subsequent opportunity for hermeneutical endeavor to respond to the observation of Manfred Oeming:

> Biblical research is called to continually face new cultural and intellectual trends, even if these may seem confusingly complex at first. The goal must always be to develop adequate approaches to the Bible. The complexity of the material requires a type of

---

language in unique stories centered upon kernel events allowing thought to develop beyond the perceived or expected limits of reason (Ricoeur, *Figuring the Sacred*, 40).

60. Nagel, *Mind and Cosmos*, 127.
61. Nagel, *Mind and Cosmos*, 22.
62. Abraham, "Systematic Theology," 68.

exegete who is also willing and able to see beyond the boundaries of his or her exegetical discipline.[63]

The book has, however, proposed that this is an exegetical response that the "material" both anticipates and can accommodate due to its acknowledgment in the third chapter of Genesis that *"the eyes of the two were opened"* (Genesis 3:7),[64] and subsequent portrayal of the implications of this action in the narratives that follow.

A BITE OF THE APPLE: GENESIS, EVE, ENVY, PINK LADY . . . ?[65]

We have . . . bitten of the apple, and our eyes have been opened and our memories are indelibly stamped with the new vision of reality.[66]

In his essay "Adam's Apple," within a section entitled *A Newer Testament* in his book *Mythomania*, Peter Conrad describes the glowing into life of the Mac computer screen in which the back-lit icon of a white apple appears; a logo which has been described as "one of the most ubiquitous logos in the history of branding."[67] It is an apple from which "the first fatal bite has already been taken"[68] and this symbolic fruit, with its commonly assumed association with the third chapter of Genesis, has, for Conrad, become representative of the consumerism that he suggests has replaced religion in contemporary culture. This is a consumerism which, in the words of Bauckham,

> by offering endlessly new objects of consumption . . . postpones indefinitely the realization that human life is oriented to more than such things; it harnesses the desire for God to material objects of consumption so that, satisfied by none of these, it goes on seeking its goal in object after object offered it by advertising. The insatiability of the desire for God is distracted

---

63. Oeming, *Contemporary Biblical Hermeneutics*, 145.
64. Alter, *Five Books*, 25.
65. Some of the varieties of apple available in New Zealand.
66. Harvey, *Historian and Believer*, 115.
67. Watson, "Meet Rob Janoff."
68. Conrad, *Mythomania*, 23.

into insatiability for the products of the market . . . marked with promises much greater than they can fulfil.[69]

As Conrad points out, the biblical text does not, however, mention an apple. It refers only to the fruit of a tree that *"was good for eating," "lust for the eyes,"* and *"lovely to look at"* (Genesis 3:6).[70] Alter translates *ta'awah* as lust in terms of "that which is intensely desired"[71] and it is a state of being that Conrad suggests is now generated, nurtured and facilitated by the Internet which provides often immediate access to a plethora of manipulated perspectives of reality; perspectives that are enabled by communication platforms with unprecedented access to information as pod casts, blogs, tweets and TED talks produce "byte"[72] size pieces of information that can be easily digested.

In 2015, using "traceroute" technology which goes over every sequence of the Internet creating a visual trace, the *Opte Project* released its latest "visual representation of the metaphysical space of the Internet," mapping the paths along which information travels across the world.[73] It is a mapping that highlights the achievement of technology in the growth and extent of global connectivity, a consequence of which is claimed to be a significant reduction of social isolation and the enabling of a higher level of engagement in society for individuals and communities that were previously disenfranchised.[74] According to a Deloitte report in 2014, the expansion of Internet access to the 4.3 billion people who were currently unconnected could potentially be a panacea in promoting "public services, social cohesion and digital inclusion"; enabling health improvements; unlocking universal education and the knowledge-based economy; offering "unprecedented opportunities for economic growth in developing countries"; supporting enterprise and innovation to "increase employment and reduce extreme poverty"; and enabling "significant improvements in quality of life and skills contributing to social inclusion."[75] The

---

69. Bauckham, *Bible*, 41.
70. Alter, *Five Books*, 24.
71. Alter, *Genesis*, 12.
72. A unit of data that is eight bits (binary digits) long, the byte was originally designed to store character data but has now become "the fundamental unit of measurement for data storage" (Christensson, "Byte Definition").
73. The images produced use different colors to indicate the locations of web addresses and the connectivity between users (Linshi, "See What").
74. Ross, "Networking."
75. See *Value of Connectivity*.

report was commissioned by Facebook which perhaps raises questions about its economic motivation, but another question that arises concerns whether technology, that enables and encourages connectivity within a consumer driven culture, counters or contributes to what Goff highlights as the alienation of a scientific worldview. This is a worldview that

> seems to present us with an immense universe entirely devoid of meaning, in which human beings are a tiny and painfully temporary accident.... We seem to have nothing in common with the universe, no real home within it. The "big picture" story of the universe is one of insentient and meaningless physical processes, from which we are a senseless aberration. In the absence of a place in the universe, we have only consumerism and the endless quest for economic growth to make sense of our lives.[76]

As recognition of the consequences of this quest grows, the issue of how the "big picture" story of the Bible might offer a way forward has underpinned this book. This is as a response to Nagel's suggestion that "the methods needed to understand ourselves do not yet exist"[77] and that something more than the fundamental laws of physics is needed to understand the human condition. The book has proposed that a biblical perspective of reality might offer an important supplement to developing scientific perspectives of reality,[78] and considered how confidence in the value of a biblical perspective of the human condition can be restored within the context of twenty-first-century epistemology. This is in order to establish a way back to a biblical perspective of the world as a precursor to moving forward. It is a way back that must, however, avoid what Nagel refers to as the solutionism of "large, wet answers" to "large relevant questions"[79] and Keller describes as "the delusions of a simple answer, a simple self, a simple God."[80] This is because

> the more we ask, search and test our answers, the deeper the questions take us.... This deepening process is not just about voiding, emptying, and deconstructing. Rather the emptying out, the kenosis of prior meanings, lets precisely the immense, sparkling dimensionality of life into our awareness. We might say

---

76. Goff, *Galileo's Error*, 216.
77. Nagel, *View from Nowhere*, 10.
78. Or it could perhaps be argued that the perspectives of contemporary science are a supplement to the biblical perspectives of reality.
79. Nagel, *Mortal Questions*, ix.
80. Keller, *God and Power*, 151.

that it lets us share a hint, a facet, of the divine perspective on the universe. We cannot then occupy a God's-eye view, but we can glimpse, imagine, and remember its unfathomable expanse.[81]

Fifty years ago, sociologist Thomas O'Dea suggested that diminishing "old Enlightenment bigotry" offered the possibility that Christianity would once again be listened to but raised the issue of what, if anything, it might have to say as, when "real questions" were asked, they too often received "regrettable, superficial and short-circuited answers."[82] He also suggested that while many young people did not understand religion, they still suspected that there might be a realm somewhere that transcends the "sphere of everydayness." They, therefore, sought contact with such a realm secretly wishing for a utopian society but distrusting all ideologies and utopias.[83] Fifty years later, it is a search that appears to be ongoing, with many questions still unanswered for those both outside but also within Christian communities. Serene Jones cites a young Roman Catholic and recently graduated Yale Divinity School student:

> I feel like our generation is standing in the rubble of demolished houses hoping someone shows up to help us figure out how to build something beautiful and safe. We don't have much theological know-how; we aren't immersed in a faith tradition that needs to be undone because we have not been religiously traditioned. We need someone to share with us the wisdom, the know-how, the basic rules of community—because we don't know those anymore. It seems to me that the basic stories, practices, and beliefs of the Christian faith can be that for our generation. The trick is that the church needs to show up on the site of the previous, demolished house and not spend all its time bemoaning the demolition but instead put its energy into helping us creatively build a new house (knowing all along that many of the rules that built the previous house will still apply).[84]

It is perhaps ironic that confidence in this rebuild might emerge from the speculation of an atheist philosopher on the limitations of a reductionist neo-Darwinian account of the origin and evolution of life.[85] This book has suggested, however, that Nagel inadvertently offers both

---

81. Keller, *God and Power*, 150.
82. O'Dea, *Alienation*, 173.
83. O'Dea, *Alienation*, 173.
84. Jones, "Bounded Openness," 50–51.
85. Nagel, *Mind and Cosmos*, 6.

critical hermeneutical insights and the framework for a hermeneutic that allows biblical narratives to offer an important perspective on the human condition. In making an often radical departure from the familiar, that may be ontological or epistemological, these are narratives that utilize supernatural entities and concepts in order to extend the boundaries of the thinkable. The book has, therefore, proposed a constructive, theologically traditional, but also intellectually critical and interdisciplinary, hermeneutical approach that enables the narratives to remain connected to the present-day world and its pressing concerns. This is to allow them to contribute to what Nagel calls the search for systematic understanding of how we and other things fit into the world; a world that he warns, with unintended theological resonance, may have dimensions that in extending beyond the reach of our minds[86] will surpass all understanding. In this respect, while acknowledging the danger of premature hermeneutical conclusions in the presence of infinity, the book does, however, conclude that it may be important to consider whether it is not only, as Haught suggests in the subtitle of his review of *Mind and Cosmos*,[87] "What Nagel Could Learn From Theology," but also, what theology and biblical hermeneutics might learn from Thomas Nagel.

---

86. Nagel, *View from Nowhere*, 90.
87. Haught, "Darwin's Nagging Doubt," 9.

Epilogue

The title *From Eden to Interstellar Space* refers to the theme of journeying into the unknown, both physically and conceptually. The book has also been a journey into the unknown from a personal perspective as, when I began, I had no idea where it would take me and whether a biblically based Christian faith that has been a part of my life for as long as I can remember would remain intact. The challenges to this faith have often been considerable, when personal experience has seemed incompatible with the approach to Christian belief manifest in the church communities that I have been part of. I have also witnessed the struggle of others to adhere to perceptions of biblical testimony, subsequent doctrine and creedal expressions of belief that appear to be at odds with both their own experiences and contemporary epistemology, particularly in relation to the supernatural components of the biblical text.

This hermeneutical journey has, therefore, been undertaken to discover whether there is still a possibility that the Bible might have an important contribution to make toward both an understanding of the human condition and the restoration of broken relationships in an increasingly fragile world. In selecting an atheist philosopher as a starting point, I deliberately chose a predominantly secular route to confront the issues raised by those for whom traditional "religion" does not, or no longer appears to, make sense and have meaning. I did not anticipate how lonely and challenging this route would become in leading away from my church community and into territory of doubt and uncertainty. There may be no way back, but I hope that there is a way forward. I have been continually surprised and encouraged by the ongoing discovery that this is territory that can be accommodated by a biblical perspective of reality;

a perspective emerging from narratives in which Nagel's proposition that both mind and cosmos are more complex and extensive than we may ever be able to conceive is already identified and addressed. I am, therefore, hopeful that, as Nagel suggests, the right questions are precursors to imaginable answers, and that moving from a reductionist to an expansionist interpretive approach to biblical narrative, it may be possible to discover, in the words of Annie Dillard, that "God has not absconded but spread, as our vision and understanding of the universe have spread, to a fabric of spirit and sense" that is grand, subtle, and "powerful in a new way."[1]

---

1. Dillard, *Pilgrim*, 20.

Bibliography

Abbas, Niran, ed. *Mapping Michel Serres*. Ann Arbor: University of Michigan Press, 2005.
Abbott, Derek. "The Reasonable Ineffectiveness of Mathematics." *Proceedings of the IEEE* 101.10 (2013) 2147–53.
Abraham, William J. "Canonical Theism and the Future of Systematic Theology." In *Canonical Theism: A Proposal for Theology & the Church*, edited by William J. Abraham et al., 287–302. Grand Rapids: Eerdmans, 2008.
———. "Systematic Theology as Analytic Theology." In *Analytic Theology: New Essays in the Philosophy of Theology*, edited by Oliver D. Crisp and Michael C. Rea, 54–69. Oxford: Oxford University Press, 2009.
Aczel, Amir D. *Entanglement: The Greatest Mystery in Physics*. Chichester, UK: Wiley, 2003.
Allison, Dale C. *Constructing Jesus: Memory, Imagination and History*. Grand Rapids: Baker Academic, 2010.
Alter, Robert. *The Five Books of Moses: A Translation with Commentary*. New York: Norton, 2004.
———. *Genesis: Translation and Commentary*. New York: Norton, 1996.
———. *The World of Biblical Literature*. New York: Basic Books, 1992.
Amos, Jonathan. "Planck Telescope: A Map of All the 'Stuff' in the Cosmos." *BBC News*, March 27, 2013. https://www.bbc.com/news/science-environment-21940434.
Ananthaswamy, Anil. *The Edge of Physics: The Journey to Earth's Extremes to Unlock the Secrets of the Universe*. Boston: Houghton Mifflin Harcourt, 2010.
Anderson, Kurt. "The Genesis 2.0 Project." *Vanity Fair*, January 2010, 112–23.
Andrei, Mihai. "Black Hole at the Centre of Our Galaxy Bursts Out." *ZME Science*, November 7, 2012. https://www.zmescience.com/space/supermassive-black-hole-sagittarius-a-bursts-07112012.
Anglican Church in Aortearoa, New Zealand, and Polynesia (ACANZP). *A New Zealand Prayer Book/He Karakia Mihinare o Aotearoa*. Christchurch: Genesis, 1989.
Arbib, Michael A., and Mary B. Hesse. *The Construction of Reality*. Cambridge: Cambridge: University Press, 1986.
Aristotle. *Metaphysics*. Translated by W. D. Ross. http://classics.mit.edu/Aristotle/metaphysics.html.

Arkoun, Mohammed. *The Unthought in Contemporary Islamic Thought*. London: Saqi, 2002.

Armstrong, Karen. *The Case for God: What Religion Really Means*. London: Bodley Head, 2009.

———. *The Lost Art of Scripture: Rescuing the Sacred Texts*. London: Bodley Head, 2019.

Artigas, Mariano. *The Mind of the Universe: Understanding Science and Religion*. Philadelphia: Templeton Foundation, 2000.

Ashcroft, Ross, dir. *Four Horsemen*. Motherlode, March 14, 2012. https://www.imdb.com/title/tt1671513.

"Astronomers Capture First Image of a Black Hole." *Event Horizon Telescope*, April 10, 2019. Online. https://eventhorizontelescope.org/press-release-april-10-2019-astronomers-capture-first-image-black-hole.

Atkins, Peter. *Creation Revisited*. Harmondsworth, UK: Penguin, 1994.

———. "The Limitless Power of Science." In *Nature's Imagination: The Frontiers of Scientific Vision*, edited by John Cornwell, 122–32. Oxford: Oxford University Press, 1995.

———. *On Being: A Scientist's Exploration of the Great Questions of Existence*. Oxford: Oxford University Press, 2011.

Auerbach, Erich. *Mimesis: The Representation of Reality in Western Literature*. Translated by William R. Trask. Princeton: Princeton University Press, 2003.

Austin, J. L. *How to Do Things with Words*. The William James Lectures. Oxford: Clarendon, 1962.

"Babylonian Map." *Digital Maps of the Ancient World*. https://digitalmapsoftheancientworld.com/ancient-maps/babylonian-map-of-the-world.

Bacon, Greg, et al. "Evaporating Peaks: Pillars in the Monkey Head Nebula." *NASA.gov*, May 23, 2018. https://svs.gsfc.nasa.gov/30953.

Baggett, David. "On Thomas Nagel's Rejection of Theism." *Harvard Theological Review* 106 (2013) 227–38.

Baggott, Jim. *Farewell to Reality: How Modern Physics Has Betrayed the Search for Scientific Truth*. London: Constable & Robinson, 2013.

Baker, John Austin. "Carried about by Every Wind?: The Development of Doctrine." In *Believing in the Church: The Corporate Nature of Faith*, edited by J. Taylor, 262–85. London: SPCK, 1981.

Ball, Philip. *Beyond Weird: Why Everything You Thought You Knew about Quantum Physics Is . . . Different*. London: Vintage, 2019.

Barbour, Ian G. *Myths, Models, and Paradigms*. London: SCM, 1974.

———. *Religion and Science: Historical and Contemporary Issues*. San Francisco: Harper, 1997.

Barr, James. "Some Thoughts on Narrative, Myth, and Incarnation." In *Interpretation and Theory*, edited by John Barton, 65–73. Vol. 1 of *Bible and Interpretation: The Collected Essays of James Barr*. Oxford: Oxford University Press, 2013.

Barrow, John, and Frank Tipler. *The Anthropic Cosmological Principle*. Oxford: Clarendon, 1986.

Barth, Karl. *Church Dogmatics* III/3. Translated by G. W. Bromiley and R. J. Ehrlich. Edinburgh: T&T Clark, 1960.

———. *Dogmatics in Outline*. Translated by G. T. Thompson. London: SCM, 1949.

———. *Nein! Antwort an Emil Brunner*. Theologische Existenz Heute 14. Munich: Kaiser, 1934.

---. "The Strange New World within the Bible." In *The Word of God and the Word of Man*, edited by Douglas Horton, 28–51. Translated by Douglas Horton. Boston: Pilgrim, 1928.

---. *The Word of God and the Word of Man*. Edited by Douglas Horton. Translated by Douglas Horton. Boston: Pilgrim, 1928.

Barton, John. *Reading the Old Testament: Method in Bible Study*. London: Darton, Longman & Todd, 1984.

Bauckham, Richard. *The Bible in the Contemporary World*. London: SPCK, 2016.

---. *The Climax of Prophecy: Studies on the Book of Revelation*. Edinburgh: T&T Clark, 1993.

Beavis, Mary Ann. "Jezebel Speaks: Naming the Goddesses in the Book of Revelation." In *A Feminist Companion to The Apocalypse of John*, edited by Amy-Jill Levine with Maria Mayo Robbins, 131–46. London: T&T Clark, 2009.

Beller, Mara. *Quantum Dialogue: The Making of a Revolution*. Chicago: University of Chicago Press, 1999.

Benson, Ivan M. "Revelation 12 and the Dragon of Antiquity." *Restoration Quarterly* 29.2 (1987) 97–102.

Berger, Peter L. *A Rumor of Angels: Modern Society and the Rediscovery of the Supernatural*. London: Penguin, 1969.

---. "Secular Theology and the Rejection of the Supernatural: Reflections on Recent Trends." *Theological Studies* 38.1 (1977) 39–56.

Berry, Roger J. "The Virgin Birth of Christ." *Science and Christian Belief* 8.2 (1996) 101–10.

Berry, Thomas. "The New Story: Comments on the Origin, Identification, and Transmission of Values." *CrossCurrents* 37.2/3 (1987) 187–99.

"Black Hole Image Makes History." *Jet Propulsion Laboratory*, April 10, 2019. Online. https://www.jpl.nasa.gov/news/black-hole-image-makes-history.

Bock, Darrell L., and Mikel Del Rosario. "The Table Briefing: Was the Virgin Birth Copied from Myths?" *Bibliotheca Sacra* 175.700 (2018) 460–69.

Boeve, Lieven. *Theology at the Crossroads of University, Church, and Society: Dialogue, Difference, and Catholic Identity*. London: Bloomsbury, 2016.

Borg, Marcus J. "The Meaning of the Birth Stories." In *The Meaning of Jesus: Two Versions*, by Marcus J. Borg and N. T. Wright, 179–86. New York: HarperCollins, 1999.

Boring, M. Eugene. *Revelation*. Louisville: Westminster John Knox, 2011.

Bouteneff, Peter C. *Beginnings: Ancient Christian Readings of the Biblical Creation Narratives*. Grand Rapids: Baker Academic, 2008.

Bracken, Joseph A., SJ. *Christianity and Process Thought: Spirituality for a Changing World*. Philadelphia: Templeton Foundation, 2006.

---. *Subjectivity, Objectivity, and Intersubjectivity: A New Paradigm for Religion and Science*. Philadelphia: Templeton Foundation, 2009.

Brain, John. *Reality, Science, and the Supernatural: Can Science Support Belief in a Creator God?* N.p.: CreateSpace Independent, 2016.

Bray, Gerald. *Biblical Interpretation: Past & Present*. Downers Grove, IL: InterVarsity, 1996.

Bregman, Rutger. *Humankind: A Hopeful History*. Translated by Elizabeth Manton and Erica Moore. London: Bloomsbury, 2020.

Bremer, Józef. "*Mind and Cosmos: Why the Materialist Neo-Darwinian Conception of Nature Is Almost Certainly False* by Thomas Nagel." *Forum Philosophicum* 17.2 (2012) 269–73.

Brotton, Jerry. *A History of the World in Twelve Maps*. New York: Penguin, 2014.

Brown, Raymond E. *The Birth of the Messiah: A Commentary on the Infancy Narratives in the Gospels of Matthew and Luke*. New York: Doubleday, 1993.

———. "The Book of Revelation (The Apocalypse)." In *An Introduction to the New Testament: The Abridged Edition*, edited by Marion L. Soards, 284–98. New Haven: Yale University Press, 2016.

———. *An Introduction to the New Testament*. London: Doubleday, 1997.

———. "Luke's Description of the Virginal Conception." *Theological Studies* 35 (1974) 360–62.

———. "The Problem of the Virginal Conception of Jesus." *Theological Studies* 33 (1972) 3–34.

Brueggemann, Walter. *Texts under Negotiation: The Bible and Postmodern Interpretation*. Minneapolis: Fortress, 1993.

Brunner, Emil. "Die Frage nach dem 'Anknüpfungspunkt' als Problem der Theologie." *Zwischen den Zeiten* 10 (1932) 505–32.

Bryant, David J. *Faith and the Play of Imagination: On the Role of Imagination in Religion*. Macon, GA: Mercer University Press, 1989.

Buber, Martin. *On the Bible: Eighteen Studies*. Edited by Nahum N. Glatzer. New York: Schocken, 1982.

Buechner, Frederick. *Beyond Words*. New York: HarperCollins, 2004.

Buffagni, Silvia. *Damanhur: Temples of Humankind*. New York: COSM, 2006.

"Building Blocks." *NASA.gov*. Online. https://science.nasa.gov/universe/overview/building-blocks.

Bultmann, Rudolf. "New Testament and Mythology: The Mythological Element in the Message of the New Testament and the Problem of Its Re-Interpretation." In *Kerygma and Myth*, edited by Hans Werner Bartsch, 1–44. Translated by Reginald H. Fuller. New York: Harper & Row, 1961.

———. "On the Problem of Demythologizing." In *New Testament & Mythology and Other Basic Writings*, edited by Schubert M. Ogden, 155–63. Translated by Schubert M. Ogden. Philadelphia: Fortress, 1984.

Burman, David. "One Culture, Not Two." In *A New STEAM Age: Challenging the STEM Agenda in Research*, edited by Suzie Leighton and Peter Mitchell, 30–32. London: Culture Capital Exchange, 2016. Online. https://tcce.co.uk/wp-content/uploads/2016/06/Challenging-the-STEM-agenda-in-research.pdf.

Bussey, Peter. *Signposts to God: How Modern Physics & Astronomy Point the Way to God*. Downers Grove, IL: IVP Academic, 2016.

Caird, G. B. *The Language and Imagery of the Bible*. London: Duckworth, 1980.

———. *The Revelation of St John the Divine*. London: Black, 1996.

Canale, Fernando L. *Back to Revelation-Inspiration: Searching for the Cognitive Foundation of Christian Theology in a Postmodern World*. Lanham, MD: University Press of America, 2001.

Carlyle, Thomas. "Signs of the Times." In *Selected Writings*, edited by Alan Shelston, 59–84. Harmondsworth, UK: Penguin, 1971.

Carrington, Philip. *The Meaning Of The Revelation*. London: SPCK, 1931.

Carroll, Lewis. *Alice's Adventures in Wonderland and Through the Looking-Glass*. London: Tiger, 1993.

Carroll, Sean. *The Particle at the End of the Universe: How the Hunt for the Higgs Boson Leads Us to the Edge of the World*. New York: Penguin, 2012.

———. *Something Deeply Hidden: Quantum Worlds and the Emergence of Spacetime*. London: Oneworld, 2019.

Cassuto, Umberto. *From Adam to Noah*. Part 1 of *A Commentary on the Book of Genesis*. Jerusalem: Magnes, 1964.

Chalmers, David J. "Facing Up to the Problem of Consciousness." *Journal of Consciousness Studies* 2 (1995) 200–219.

———. "The Virtual and the Real." *Disputatio* 9.46 (2017) 309–52.

Chalmers, David J., and Kelvin J. McQueen. "Consciousness and the Collapse of the Wave Function." In *Consciousness and Quantum Mechanics*, edited by Shan Gao, 11–64. New York: Oxford University Press, 2022.

Changeux, Jean-Pierre, and Paul Ricoeur. *What Makes Us Think? A Neuroscientist and a Philosopher Argue about Ethics, Human Nature, and the Brain*. Translated by M. B. DeBevoise. Princeton: Princeton University Press, 2000.

Chapman, Seymour. *Story and Discourse: Narrative Structure in Fiction and Film*. Ithaca: Cornell University Press, 1978.

Childs, Brevard. "The Sensus Literalis of Scripture: An Ancient and Modern Problem." In *Beiträge zur alttestamentlichen Theologie*, edited by H. Donner et al., 80–93. Göttingen: Vandenhoeck & Ruprecht, 1997.

Choi, Charles Q. "How the Event Horizon Telescope Hunts for Black Hole Silhouettes." *Space.com*, April 10, 2019. Online. https://www.space.com/how-event-horizon-telescope-photographs-black-holes.html.

Chopra, Deepak, and Leonard Mlodinow. *War of the Worldviews: Science vs Spirituality*. London: Rider, 2011.

Chorost, Michael. "Where Thomas Nagel Went Wrong." *Chronicle of Higher Education*, May 13, 2013. Online. http://chronicle.com/article/Where-Thomas-Nagel-Went-Wrong/139129.

Christenson, Tom. "The Oddest Word: Paradoxes of Theological Discourse." In *The Boundaries of Knowledge in Buddhism, Christianity, and Science*, edited by Paul D. Numrich, 164–83. Göttingen: Vandenhoeck & Ruprecht, 2008.

Christensson, Per. "Byte Definition." *TechTerms.com*, May 2, 2019. https://techterms.com/definition/byte.

Clark, Stephen R. L. "Supernatural Explanations and Inspirations." *European Journal for Philosophy of Religion* 9.3 (2017) 49–64.

Clayton, Philip. *Mind and Emergence: From Quantum to Consciousness*. Oxford: Oxford University Press, 2004.

Clayton, Philip, and Paul Davies, eds. *The Re-Emergence of Emergence: The Emergent Hypothesis from Science to Religion*. Oxford: Oxford University Press, 2008.

Clayton, Philip, and Steven Knapp. *The Predicament of Belief: Science, Philosophy, and Faith*. Oxford: Oxford University Press, 2011.

Collins, Adela Yarbro. *The Combat Myth in the Book of Revelation*. Missoula, MT: Scholars, 1976.

Collins, Francis. *The Language of God: A Scientist Presents Evidence for Belief*. New York: Simon & Schuster, 2006.

Conrad, Peter. *Mythomania: Tales of Our Times from Apple to Isis*. London: Thames & Hudson, 2017.

Coogan, Michael D., ed. *The New Oxford Annotated Bible*. 3rd ed. Oxford: Oxford University Press, 2001.

Cook-Anderson, Gretchen, and Nancy Neal-Jones. "Swift Mission Images the Birth of a Black Hole." *NASA.gov*, January 21, 2005. https://swift.gsfc.nasa.gov/news/2005/05-019.html.

Cornwell, John, ed. *Nature's Imagination: The Frontiers of Scientific Vision*. Oxford: Oxford University Press, 1995.

Cosgrove, Denis, ed. *Mappings*. London: Reaktion, 1999.

Cottingham, John. *How to Believe*. London: Bloomsbury, 2015.

Couprie, Dirk L. *Heaven and Earth in Ancient Greek Cosmology: From Thales to Heraclides Ponticus*. New York: Springer, 2011.

Cranfield, Charles E. B. "Some Reflections on the Subject of the Virgin Birth." *Scottish Journal of Theology* 41 (1988) 177–89.

Crick, Francis. *The Astonishing Hypothesis: The Scientific Search for the Soul*. New York: Scribner, 1994.

Crisp, Oliver D. *God Incarnate: Explorations in Christology*. London: T&T Clark, 2009.

———. "The Virgin Birth: Where Dogma and History Meet?" Paper presented at the Logos Institute for Analytic and Exegetical Theology Conference, University of St Andrews, St Andrews, Scotland, June 1–3, 2017.

Crockett, Christopher. "What Are Gamma Ray Bursts?" *EarthSky.org*, October 14, 2013. https://earthsky.org/space/gamma-ray-bursts-are-the-most-powerful-explosions-in-the-universe.

Crossan, John Dominic. *Jesus: A Revolutionary Biography*. San Francisco: HarperCollins, 1994.

Cutting, Gary, et al. "Nagel's Untimely Idea: Is There More to Nature than Matter?" *Commonweal* 140.9 (2013) 14–19.

Dalley, Stephanie. *Myths from Mesopotamia: Creation, the Flood, Gilgamesh, and Others*. Oxford: Oxford University Press, 1989.

Davidson, Donald. "Empirical Content." In *Truth and Interpretation: Perspectives on the Philosophy of Donald Davidson*, edited by Ernest LePore, 320–32. Oxford: Blackwell, 1986.

Davies, Paul. *The Cosmic Blueprint: New Discoveries in Nature's Creative Ability to Order the Universe*. Philadelphia: Templeton Foundation, 2004.

———. *God and the New Physics*. New York: Simon & Schuster, 1983.

———. *The Goldilocks Enigma: Why Is the Universe Just Right for Human Life?* London: Penguin, 2007.

Dawes, Gregory W. "Why Historicity Still Matters: Raymond Brown and the Infancy Narratives." *Pacifica* 19.2 (2006) 156–76.

Dawkins, Richard. *The Blind Watchmaker: Why the Evidence of Evolution Reveals a Universe without Design*. New York: Norton, 1996.

———. *The God Delusion*. London: Bantam, 2006.

———. *The Selfish Gene*. 2nd ed. Oxford: Oxford University Press, 1989.

De La Torre, Miguel A. *Genesis*. Louisville: Westminster John Knox, 2011.

Dennett, Daniel C. *From Bacteria to Bach and Back: The Evolution of Minds*. New York: Norton, 2017.

"Depressive Disorder (Depression)." *World Health Organization*, March 31, 2023. Online. https://www.who.int/en/news-room/fact-sheets/detail/depression.

Descartes, René. "Rules for the Direction of the Mind." In vol. 1 of *The Philosophical Writings of Descartes*, edited by John Cottingham et al., 9–76. Translated by Dugald Murdoch. Cambridge: Cambridge University Press, 1985.

d'Espagnat, Bernard. *On Physics and Philosophy*. Princeton: Princeton University Press, 2006.

Dillard, Annie. *Pilgrim at Tinker Creek*. New York: HarperCollins, 1974.

"Do You Believe in the Virgin Birth?" *Spectator*, December 15, 2007. Online. https://www.spectator.co.uk/article/do-you-believe-in-the-virgin-birth.

"Eagle Nebula 'Pillars of Creation.'" *HubbleSite.org*, January 5, 2015. Online. https://hubblesite.org/contents/media/images/3862-Image.

Easley, Kendall. *Living with the End in Sight: Meditations on the Book of Revelation*. Nashville: Holman, 2000.

Education, Communications, and Outreach Group (ECOG). *LHC: The Guide*. February 2017. http://cds.cern.ch/record/2255762/files/CERN-Brochure-2017-002-Eng.pdf.

Edwards, James R. *The Gospel According to Luke*. Grand Rapids: Eerdmans, 2015.

Einstein, Albert. *On Cosmic Religion and Other Opinions & Aphorisms*. Mineola, NY: Dover, 2009.

Einstein, Albert, and Leopold Infeld. *The Evolution of Physics: From Early Concepts to Relativity and Quanta*. 2nd ed. New York: Simon & Schuster, 1966.

Eiseley, Loren. *The Immense Journey: An Imaginative Naturalist Explores the Mysteries of Man and Nature*. New York: Random House, 1957.

Eisenberg, Evan. *The Ecology of Eden: Humans, Nature, and Human Nature*. New York: Knopf, 1998.

Ekstrand, Thomas. *Max Weber in a Theological Perspective*. Leuven: Peeters, 2000.

Eliade, Mircea. *Tales of the Sacred and the Supernatural*. Philadelphia: Westminster, 1981.

Evely, Louis. *The Gospels without Myth: A Dramatic New Interpretation of the Gospels and Christian Dogma*. Translated by J. F. Bernard. Garden City, NY: Doubleday, 1971.

Fabiny, Tibor. "The Literal Senses and the 'Sensus Plenior' Revisited." *Hermathena* 151 (1991) 9–23.

Farrer, Austin. *A Rebirth of Images: The Making of St. John's Apocalypse*. 1963. Reprint, Eugene: Wipf & Stock, 2007.

Fee, Gordon. *Revelation*. Eugene, OR: Cascade Books, 2013.

Fekkes, Jan. *Isaiah and Prophetic Tradition in the Book of Revelation: Visionary Antecedents and Their Developments*. Sheffield: JSOT, 1994.

Fennell, Jon. "Plausibility and Common Sense: *Mind and Cosmos* by Thomas Nagel." *The Polanyi Society Periodical* 40.1 (2013–14) 45–52.

Ferguson, Andrew. "The Heretic." *The Weekly Standard* 18.27 (2013). Online. http://www.weeklystandard.com/articles/heretic_707692.html.

Festinger, Leon. *A Theory of Cognitive Dissonance*. Stanford: Stanford University Press, 1957.

Feynman, Richard P. *QED: The Strange Theory of Light and Matter*. Rev. ed. Princeton: Princeton University Press, 2006.

———. "Quantum Behavior." In *Quantum Mechanics*, edited by Robert B. Leighton and Matthew Sands. Vol. 3 of *The Feynman Lectures on Physics*. New Millennium ed. New York: Basic, 2011. http://www.feynmanlectures.caltech.edu/III_01.html#Ch1-S7 1/3/19.

Fitzmyer, Joseph A. "The Virginal Conception of Jesus in the New Testament." *Theological Studies* 34.4 (1973) 541–75.

Floridi, Luciano. *The Ethics of Information*. Oxford: Oxford University Press, 2013.

———. *The Fourth Revolution: How the Infosphere Is Reshaping Human Reality*. Oxford: Oxford University Press, 2014.

Foster, Benjamin R. *Before the Muses: An Anthology of Akkadian Literature*. 3rd ed. Bethesda, MD: CDL, 2005.

"Fourteen Mind-Bending Facts about Ancient Standing Stones." *The Human Origin Project*. Online. https://humanoriginproject.com/facts-standing-stones.

Frank, Adam, et al. "The Blind Spot." *Aeon*, January 8, 2019. Online. https://aeon.co/essays/the-blind-spot-of-science-is-the-neglect-of-lived-experience.

Frei, Hans W. "Conflicts in Interpretations." *Theology Today* 49.3 (1992) 344–56.

———. *The Eclipse of Biblical Narrative: A Study in Eighteenth and Nineteenth Century Hermeneutics*. New Haven: Yale University Press, 1974.

———. *The Identity of Jesus Christ: The Hermeneutical Bases of Dogmatic Theology*. Rev. ed. Eugene, OR: Cascade Books, 2013.

———. *Theology and Narrative: Selected Essays*. Edited by George Hunsinger and William Placher. New York: Oxford University Press, 1993.

———. *Types of Christian Theology*. New Haven: Yale University Press, 1992.

———. *Writings from the Archives: Theology and Hermeneutics*. Vol. 1 of *Reading Faithfully*. Edited by Mike Higton and Mark Alan Bowald. Eugene, OR: Cascade Books, 2015.

Fromm, Erich. *You Shall Be as Gods*. Greenwich: Fawcett, 1966.

Frye, Northrop. *The Great Code: The Bible and Literature*. New York: Harcourt Brace Jovanovich, 1982.

Fuller, Reginald H. "The Virgin Birth: Historical Fact or Kerygmatic Truth?" *Biblical Research* 1 (1956) 1–8.

Funk, Robert W., and Roy W. Hoover. *The Five Gospels: What Did Jesus Say? The Search for the Authentic Words of Jesus*. New York: HarperCollins, 1993.

Gabbatt, Adam. "Big Bang Goes Phut as Bird Drops Baguette into CERN Machinery." *Guardian*, November 6, 2009. https://www.theguardian.com/science/2009/nov/06/cern-big-bang-goes-phut.

Gavrilyuk, Paul L. "Scripture and the *Regula Fidei*: Two Interlocking Components of the Canonical Heritage." In *Canonical Theism: A Proposal for Theology & the Church*, edited by William J. Abraham et al., 27–42. Grand Rapids: Eerdmans, 2008.

Geary, James. *I Is an Other: The Secret Life of Metaphor and How It Shapes the Way We See the World*. New York: HarperCollins, 2011.

Gebhardt, Chris. "Pioneer 10: First Probe to Leave the Inner Solar System and Precursor to Juno." *NSF*, July 15, 2017. Online. https://www.nasaspaceflight.com/2017/07/pioneer-10-first-probe-inner-precursor-juno.

Gell-Mann, Murray. *The Quark and the Jaguar: Adventures in the Simple and the Complex*. New York: Holt, 1994.

George, Arthur, and Elena George. *The Mythology of Eden*. Lanham, MD: Hamilton, 2014.

Gieser, Suzanne. *The Innermost Kernel: Depth Psychology and Quantum Physics. Wolfgang Pauli's Dialogue with C. G. Jung*. Berlin: Springer, 2005.

Gilbert, Jérémie. "Custodians of the Land: Indigenous Peoples, Human Rights and Cultural Integrity." In *Cultural Diversity, Heritage and Human Rights: Intersections in Theory and Practice*, edited by Michele Langfield et al., 31–44. London: Routledge, 2010.

Gilkey, Langdon. *Shantung Compound: The Story of Men and Women Under Pressure*. New York: HarperCollins, 1966.

———. *Society and the Sacred: Towards a Theology of Culture in Decline*. New York: Crossroad, 1981.

Gleiser, Marcelo. *The Island of Knowledge: The Limits of Science and the Search for Meaning*. New York: Basic, 2014.

———. *A Tear at the Edge of Creation: A Radical New Vision for Life in an Imperfect Universe*. Hanover, NH: Dartmouth, 2010.

Glouberman, Mark. "The Being of Mind: Thomas Nagel's *Mind and Cosmos* and the Book of Genesis." *Iyyun* 66 (2017) 3–26.

Goff, Philip. *Galileo's Error: Foundations for a New Science of Consciousness*. New York: Pantheon, 2019.

The Good News Bible: Today's English Version. New York: American Bible Society, 1976.

Goodenough, Ursula. *The Sacred Depths of Nature*. New York: Oxford University Press, 1998.

Grau, Marion. "Methodological Themes and Patterns in Constructive Theologies." In *What is Constructive Theology? Histories, Methodologies, and Perspectives*, edited by Marion Grau and Jason Wyman, 53–74. London: T&T Clark, 2020.

———. *Refiguring Theological Hermeneutics: Hermes, Trickster, Fool*. New York: Palgrave Macmillan, 2014.

Graves, Mark. *Mind, Brain, and the Elusive Soul: Human Systems of Cognitive Science and Religion*. Aldershot, UK: Ashgate, 2008.

Gray, Heather, and Bruno Mansoulié. "The Higgs Boson: The Hunt, the Discovery, the Study, and Some Future Perspectives." *ATLAS Experiment*, July 4, 2018. Online. https://atlas.cern/updates/feature/higgs-boson.

Green, Brian. "The Detection of Gravitational Waves Was a Scientific Breakthrough, but What's Next?" *Smithsonian Magazine*, April 2016. Online. https://www.smithsonianmag.com/science-nature/detection-gravitational-waves-breakthrough-whats-next-180958511.

Green, Garrett. "'The Bible As . . .': Fictional Narrative and Scriptural Truth." In *Scriptural Authority and Narrative Interpretation*, edited by Garrett Green, 79–96. Philadelphia: Fortress, 1987.

———. *Imagining God: Theology and the Religious Imagination*. Grand Rapids: Eerdmans, 1989.

———. *Theology, Hermeneutics, and Imagination: The Crisis of Interpretation at the End of Modernity*. Cambridge: Cambridge University Press, 2000.

Gregg, Steve. *Revelation: Four Views. A Parallel Commentary*. Nashville: Nelson, 1997.

Gregoire, Carolyn. "How Yoga Became A $27 Billion Industry—And Reinvented American Spirituality." *HuffPost*, December 16, 2013. Online. http://www.huffingtonpost.com/2013/12/16/how-the-yoga-industry-los_n_4441767.html.

Grenz, Stanley J. *Theology for the Community of God*. Grand Rapids: Eerdmans, 1994.

Grenz, Stanley J., and Roger E. Olson. *Twentieth-Century Theology: God & the Word in a Transitional Age*. Downers Grove, IL: InterVarsity, 1992.

Gribbon, John. *Schrödinger's Kittens and the Search for Reality*. London: Weidenfeld & Nicolson, 1995.

Grindlay, Jonathan. "Light on the Distant Universe." *Nature* 455 (2008) 177–78.

Gunkel, Hermann. *Genesis: Translated and Interpreted*. Translated by Mark E. Biddle. Macon, GA: Mercer University Press, 1997.

Gunton, C. E. "Transcendence, Metaphor, and the Knowability of God." *Journal of Theological Studies* 31 (1980) 501–16.

Guth, Alan H. "Eternal Inflation and Its Implications." *Journal of Physics. A, Mathematical and Theoretical* 40.25 (2007) 6811–26. Online. https://physics.princeton.edu/~cosmo/sciam/assets/pdfs/guth-2007.pdf.

Haidt, Jonathan. *The Righteous Mind: Why Good People Are Divided by Politics and Religion*. London: Penguin, 2012.

Hall, H. R. *Ancient History of the Near East*. London: Methuen, 1916.

Hamilton, Victor P. *The Book of Genesis, Chapters 1–17*. New International Commentary on the Old Testament 1. Grand Rapids: Eerdmans, 1990.

Harlow, Daniel. "After Adam: Reading Genesis in an Age of Evolutionary Science." *Perspective on Science and the Christian Faith* 62.3 (2010) 179–95.

Harris, Sam. *The End of Faith: Religion, Terror, and the Future of Reason*. New York: Norton, 2004.

———. *The Moral Landscape: How Science Can Determine Moral Values*. London: Bantam, 2011.

Harvey, Van A. *The Historian and the Believer: The Morality of Historical Knowledge and Christian Belief*. London: SCM, 1967.

Haught, John F. "Darwin's Nagging Doubt: What Thomas Nagel Could Learn From Theology." *Commonweal*, October 11, 2013. 9–11.

———. *Deeper than Darwin: The Prospect for Religion in the Age of Evolution*. Boulder, CO: Westview, 2003.

———. *Is Nature Enough? Meaning and Truth in the Age of Science*. Cambridge: Cambridge University Press, 2006.

Hauser, Marc D. *Moral Minds: How Nature Designed Our Universal Sense of Right and Wrong*. London: Abacus, 2008.

Hawking, Stephen. *A Brief History of Time: From the Big Bang to Black Holes*. London: Bantam Dell, 1988.

Heaney, Robert S. *Post-Colonial Theology: Finding God and Each Other Amidst the Hate*. Eugene, OR: Cascade Books, 2019.

Heidel, Alexander. *The Babylonian Genesis*. Chicago: University of Chicago Press, 1951.

Heisenberg, Werner. *Across the Frontiers*. Translated by Peter Heath. New York: Harper & Row, 1974.

———. *Physics and Beyond: Encounters and Conversations*. Translated by Arnold J. Pomerans. London: Harper & Row, 1971.

———. *Physics and Philosophy: The Revolution in Modern Science*. London: Allen & Unwin, 1959.

Hendel, Ronald S. "The Flame of the Whirling Sword: A Note on Genesis 3:24." *Journal of Biblical Literature* 104.4 (1985) 671–74.

Henderson, Mark. "Two Tiny Dots Flicker: The Great CERN Adventure Is On." *The Times*, September 11, 2008. Online. https://www.thetimes.com/article/two-tiny-dots-flicker-the-great-cern-adventure-is-on-cv8h0gbvpwr.

Hewlett, Martinez. "What Does It Mean to Be Human? Genetics and Human Identity." In *Human Identity at the Intersection of Science, Technology, and Religion*, edited by Nancey Murphy and Christopher C. Knight, 147–63. Surrey: Ashgate, 2010.

Hick, John. *The Myth of God Incarnate*. Edited by Paul Badham. London: SCM, 1997.

Higginbottom, Gail, and Roger Clay. "Origins of Standing Stone Astronomy in Britain: New Quantitative Techniques for the Study of Archaeoastronomy." *Journal of Archaeological Science: Reports* 9 (2016) 249–58.

Hippolytus. *Fragments of Writings Third Century*. Vol. 2 of *The Writings of Hippolytus, Bishop of Portus*. Translated by S. D. F. Salmond. Edinburgh: T&T Clark, 1869.
Hooker, Morna D. "On Using the Right Tool." *Theology* 75.629 (1972) 570–81.
Horowitz, Wayne. "The Babylonian Map of the World." *Iraq* 50 (1988) 147–65.
Hosinski, Thomas E. *The Image of the Unseen God: Catholicity, Science, and Our Evolving Understanding of God*. New York: Orbis, 2017.
Howard, Thomas. "Myth: Flight to Reality." In *The Christian Imagination*, edited by Leland Ryken, 335–42. Colorado: WaterBrook, 2002.
Howell, Elizabeth. "How Many Galaxies Are There?" *Space.com*, March 19, 2022. Online. https://www.space.com/25303-how-many-galaxies-are-in-the-universe.html.
———. "Pioneer 10: Greetings from Earth." *Space.com*, September 18, 2012. Online. http://www.space.com/17651-pioneer-10.html.
"Hubble Team Breaks Cosmic Distance Record." *HubbleSite.org*, March 3, 2016. Online. https://hubblesite.org/contents/news-releases/2016/news-2016-07.html.
"The Human Genome Project." *National Human Genome Research Institute*. Online. https://www.genome.gov/human-genome-project.
Humphrey, Edith M. "Infancy Narratives." In *Dictionary for Theological Interpretation of the Bible*, edited by Kevin J. Vanhoozer, 325–27. Grand Rapids: Baker Academic, 2005.
Huyssteen, J. Wentzel van. *Alone in the World? Human Uniqueness in Science and Theology*. Grand Rapids: Eerdmans, 2006.
Hyers, Conrad. "Biblical Literalism: Constricting the Cosmic Dance." *The Christian Century* 99.25 (1982) 823–27.
———. *The Meaning of Creation: Genesis and Modern Science*. Atlanta: John Knox, 1984.
Ihde, Don. *Hermeneutic Phenomenology: The Philosophy of Paul Ricoeur*. Evanston, IL: Northwestern University Press, 1971.
Impey, Chris. *Einstein's Monsters: The Life and Times of Black Holes*. New York: Norton, 2019.
"Information Age." *Dictionary.com*. Online. https://www.dictionary.com/browse/information-age.
Ingram, Paul O. *Theological Reflections at the Boundaries*. Eugene, OR: Cascade Books, 2012.
"The Interconnected Nature of Reality." *IONS*. Online. https://noetic.org/about/noetic-sciences.
Jackelén, Antje. "'Knowing Too Much Is Knowing Too Little': A Theological Appraisal of the Boundaries of Knowledge." In *The Boundaries of Knowledge in Buddhism, Christianity, and Science*, edited by Paul D. Numrich, 149–63. Göttingen: Vandenhoeck & Ruprecht, 2008.
Jacobsen, Thorkild. *The Treasures of Darkness: A History of Mesopotamian Religion*. New Haven: Yale University Press, 1976.
Jenson, Robert W. *On Thinking the Human: Resolutions of Difficult Notions*. Grand Rapids: Eerdmans, 2003.
Johnson, Dru. *Epistemology and Biblical Theology: From the Pentateuch to Mark's Gospel*. London: Routledge, 2018.
Johnson, Elizabeth A. *Naming God She: The Theological Implications*. Edited by Sandy Russell. Boardman Lecture 37. Philadelphia: University of Pennsylvania, 2000.

———. *Quest for the Living God: Mapping Frontiers in the Theology of God*. New York: Continuum, 2008.

Johnson, Todd M. "Christianity Is Fragmented—Why?" *Gordon-Conwell Theological Seminary*, November 6, 2019. Online. https://www.gordonconwell.edu/blog/christianity-is-fragmented-why.

Jones, Jeffrey M. "US Church Membership Falls Below Majority for First Time." *Gallup*, March 29, 2021. Online. https://news.gallup.com/poll/341963/church-membership-falls-below-majority-first-time.aspx.

Jones, Richard H. *Analysis and the Fullness of Reality: An Introduction to Reductionism and Emergence*. New York: Jackson Square, 2013.

Jones, Serene. "Bounded Openness: Postmodernism, Feminism, and the Church Today." *Interpretation* 55.1 (2001) 49–59.

Jones, Serene, and Paul Lakeland. *Constructive Theology: A Contemporary Approach to Classical Themes*. Minneapolis: Fortress, 2005.

Jung, Carl G. "Two Kinds of Thinking." In *Symbols of Transformation*, edited by Gerhard Adler and R. F. C. Hull, 4–46. Vol. 5 of *Collected Works of C. G. Jung*. Princeton: Princeton University Press, 1956.

Justin Martyr. *The Dialogue with Trypho*. Translated by A. Lukyn Williams. Translations of Christian Literature 1—Greek Texts. London: Macmillan, 1930. Online. https://earlychurch.org.uk/pdf/e-books/williams_a-lukyn/dialogue-with-trypho_williams.pdf.

Kane, Gordon. *The Particle Garden: Our Universe as Understood by Particle Physicists*. New York: Helix, 1995.

———. *Supersymmetry and Beyond: From the Higgs Boson to the New Physics*. New York: Basic, 2013.

Kant, Immanuel. *An Answer to the Question: "What is Enlightenment?"* Translated by H. B. Nisbet. Rev. ed. London: Penguin, 2009.

———. *Critique of Pure Reason*. Translated by F. Max Müller. Rev. ed. London: MacMillian, 1981.

Kass, Leon R. *The Beginning of Wisdom: Reading Genesis*. Chicago: University of Chicago Press, 2003.

———. "On Bioethics, the Bible, and 'Athens and Jerusalem.'" Interview with Bill Kristol. YouTube. December 20, 2015. https://www.youtube.com/watch?v=dfVnNJOQJkU.

Kauffman, Stuart A. *At Home in the Universe: The Search for Laws of Self-Organization and Complexity*. New York: Oxford University Press, 1995.

———. *Investigations*. New York: Oxford University Press, 2000.

———. *Reinventing the Sacred: A New View of Science, Reason, and Religion*. New York: Basic, 2008.

Kaufman, Gordon D. *In the Beginning . . . Creativity*. Minneapolis: Fortress, 2004.

———. *In the Face of Mystery: A Constructive Theology*. Cambridge: Harvard University Press, 1993.

———. "Mystery and God: Living within the Boundaries of Human Knowledge." In *The Boundaries of Knowledge in Buddhism, Christianity, and Science*, edited by Paul D. Numrich, 129–48. Göttingen: Vandenhoeck & Ruprecht, 2008.

———. *The Theological Imagination: Constructing the Concept of God*. Philadelphia: Westminster, 1981.

Kearney, Richard. "On the Hermeneutics of Evil." In *Reading Ricoeur*, edited by David M. Kaplan, 71–88. Albany, NY: State University of New York Press, 2008.

———. *The Wake of Imagination*. London: Routledge, 1998.
Keel, Othmar. *The Symbolism of the Biblical World*. Translated by T. Hallett. Winona Lake, IN: Eisenbrauns, 1997.
Keller, Catherine. *Cloud of the Impossible: Negative Theology and Planetary Entanglement*. New York: Columbia University Press, 2015.
———. *Facing Apocalypse: Climate, Democracy, and Other Last Chances*. Maryknoll, NY: Orbis 2021.
———. *God and Power: Counter-Apocalyptic Journeys*. Minneapolis: Fortress, 2005.
———. "Pandemic Pandemonium." *Australian Broadcasting Corporation*, May 24, 2020. Online. https://www.abc.net.au/religion/pandemic-pandemonium-catherine-keller/12281594.
———. "Why Apocalypse, Now?" *Theology Today* 49.2 (1992) 183–95.
Keller, Catherine, et al., eds. *Postcolonial Theologies: Divinity and Empire*. St. Louis: Chalice, 2004.
Keller, Catherine, and Mayra Rivera. "The Coloniality of Apocalypse." *The Immanent Frame: Secularism, Religion, and the Public Sphere*, March 31, 2021. Online. https://tif.ssrc.org/2021/03/31/the-coloniality-of-apocalypse.
Kitchen, Philip. *Life after Faith: The Case for Secular Humanism*. New Haven: Yale University Press, 2014.
Kliever, Lonnie D. *The Shattered Spectrum: A Survey of Contemporary Theology*. Atlanta: John Knox, 1981.
Klink, Edward W., III, and Darian R. Lockett. *A Comparison of Theory and Practice: Understanding Biblical Theology*. Grand Rapids: Zondervan, 2012.
Knight, George T. "The Definition of the Supernatural." *Harvard Theological Review* 3.3 (1910) 310–24.
Koch, Christof. *Consciousness: Confessions of a Romantic Reductionist*. Cambridge: MIT Press, 2012.
Koester, Craig R. *Revelation: A New Translation with Introduction and Commentary*. New Haven: Yale University Press, 2014.
———. *Revelation and the End of All Things*. Grand Rapids: Eerdmans, 2001.
Krauss, Lawrence M. "How the Higgs Boson Posits a New Story of Our Creation." *Newsweek*, July 9, 2012. Online. https://www.newsweek.com/how-higgs-boson-posits-new-story-our-creation-65567.
Krentz, Edgar. *The Historical-Critical Method*. Eugene, OR: Wipf & Stock, 2002.
Kugel, James. "On the Bible and Literary Criticism." *Prooftexts* 1.3 (1981) 217–36.
Küng, Hans. *The Beginning of All Things: Science and Religion*. Translated by John Bowden. Grand Rapids: Eerdmans, 2007.
———. *Christianity: Essence, History, and Future*. Translated by John Bowden. New York: Continuum, 2006.
———. *The Church*. Translated by Ray Ockenden and Rosaleen Ockenden. London: Burn and Oates, 1967.
Kunnuthary, Varghese A. *Schleiermacher on Christian Consciousness of God's Work in History*. Eugene, OR: Pickwick, 2008.
Kwok, Pui-Lan. *Postcolonial Imagination and Feminist Theology*. Louisville: Westminster John Knox, 2005.
"L2, the Second Lagrangian Point." *European Space Agency*. Online. https://www.esa.int/Science_Exploration/Space_Science/L2_the_second_Lagrangian_Point.
LaCocque, André. *The Trial of Innocence: Adam, Eve, and the Yahwist*. Eugene, OR: Cascade Books, 2006.

LaCocque, André, and Paul Ricoeur. *Thinking Biblically: Exegetical and Hermeneutical Studies*. Translated by David Pellauer. Chicago: University of Chicago Press, 1998.

Lamont, Mike, and Stefano Bertolasi. "LHC Report: Stoat-Ally Back on Track!" *CERN*, May 17, 2016. Online. https://home.cern/news/news/accelerators/lhc-report-stoat-ally-back-track.

Landau, Elizabeth. "Black Hole Image Makes History; NASA Telescopes Coordinated Observations." *NASA.gov*, April 10, 2019. Online. https://www.nasa.gov/mission_pages/chandra/news/black-hole-image-makes-history.

LaRosa, John. "$1.8 Billion US Meditation Market Grows with New Apps and the Growth of Yoga." *MarketResearch.com* (blog), October 17, 2022. Online. https://blog.marketresearch.com/1.8-billion-u.s.-meditation-market-grows-with-new-apps-and-the-growth-of-yoga.

Lash, Nicholas. "The Question of God Today." In *Transcending the Boundaries in Philosophy and Theology: Reason, Meaning, and Experience*, edited by Kevin Vanhoozer and Martin Warner, 130–43. Hampshire, UK: Ashgate, 2007.

Laszlo, Ervin. *The Connectivity Hypothesis: Foundations of an Integral Science of Quantum, Cosmos, Life, and Consciousness*. Albany, NY: State University of New York Press, 2003.

———. "Interview with Ervin Laszlo by Guido Ferrari." Interview by Guido Ferrari, January 15, 2014. YouTube. https://www.youtube.com/watch?v=Wm1t9HeJN1E.

———. *Science and the Reenchantment of the Cosmos: The Rise of the Integral Vision of Reality*. Rochester, VT: Inner Traditions, 2006.

"Latest Step toward World's Largest Telescope That Will Observe 'First Stars and Galaxies Ever Formed.'" *Phys.org*, December 21, 2018. Online. https://phys.org/news/2018-12-latest-world-largest-telescope-stars.html.

Le Guin, Ursula. "Speech at National Book Awards: 'Books Aren't Just Commodities.'" *Guardian*, November 20, 2014. Online. http://www.theguardian.com/books/2014/nov/20/ursula-k-le-guin-national-book-awards-speech.

Leeuw, Marc de. "The Anthropological Presupposition: Paul Ricoeur's Search for the Just." In *Paul Ricoeur in the Age of Hermeneutical Reason: Poetics, Praxis and Culture*, edited by Roger W. H. Savage, 35–47. London: Lexington, 2015.

Leiter, Brian, and Michael Weisberg. "Do You Only Have a Brain? On Thomas Nagel." *Nation*, October 3, 2012. Online. https://www.thenation.com/article/archive/do-you-only-have-brain-thomas-nagel.

Lennox, John C. *God's Undertaker: Has Science Buried God?* Oxford: Lion Hudson, 2009.

Levertov, Denise. "Contraband." In *A Book of Luminous Things: An International Anthology of Poetry*, edited by Czeslaw Milosz, 278. New York: Harcourt Brace, 1996.

Lewis, C. S. "Bluspels and Flalansferes: A Semantic Nightmare." In *Selected Literary Essays*, edited by W. Hooper, 251–65. Cambridge: Cambridge University Press, 1969.

Lichtenstein, Murray H. "The Fearsome Sword of Genesis 3:24." *Journal of Biblical Literature* 134.1 (2015) 53–57.

Lichtheim, Miriam. *Ancient Egyptian Literature*. Vol 2. Berkeley: University of California Press, 1976.

Lightman, Alan. *The Accidental Universe: The World You Thought You Knew*. New York: Pantheon, 2013.

———. *Ancient Light: Our Changing View of the Universe*. Cambridge: Harvard University Press, 1991.

———. *The Discoveries: Great Breakthroughs in Twentieth-Century Science*. New York: Vintage, 2005.

Lima, Leandro de. "The Power of Literary Art in Revelation 12:1–6." *Unio Cum Christo* 2.2 (2016) 209–23.

Lincoln, Andrew T. *Born of a Virgin? Reconceiving Jesus in the Bible, Tradition, and Theology*. Grand Rapids: Eerdmans, 2013.

———. "How Babies Were Made in Jesus' Time." *Biblical Archaeology Review* 40.6 (2014) 42–49.

Lindbeck, George A. "The Church's Mission to a Postmodern Culture." In *Postmodern Theology: Christian Faith in a Pluralist World*, edited by Frederic B. Burnham, 37–55. New York: Harper & Row, 1989.

———. *The Nature of Doctrine: Religion and Theology in a Postliberal Age*. Louisville: Westminster John Knox, 1984.

———. "Review of *The Myth of God Incarnate*, John Hick." *Journal of Religion* 59.2 (1979) 248–50.

Lindsay, Mark R. "The Heavenly Witness to God: Karl Barth's Doctrine of Angels." *Scottish Journal of Theology* 70.1 (2017) 1–18.

Linneman, Eta. *Historical Criticism of the Bible: Methodology or Ideology*. Translated by Robert Yarbrough. Grand Rapids: Kregel, 1990.

Linshi, Jack. "See What the Internet Actually Looks Like." *Time*, July 13, 2015. Online. https://time.com/3952373/internet-opte-project.

Livingston, James C., et al. *The Twentieth Century*. Vol. 2 of *Modern Christian Thought*. 2nd ed. Minneapolis: Fortress, 2006.

Lucretius. *On the Nature of Things*. Translated by William Ellery Leonard. Online. http://classics.mit.edu/Carus/nature_things.1.i.html.

Lüdemann, Gerd. *Virgin Birth?: The Real Story of Mary and Her Son Jesus*. New York: Trinity, 1998.

Machen, J. Gresham. *The Virgin Birth of Christ: A Classic Defense of the Supernatural Birth of Our Lord*. New York: Harper, 1932.

Mackay, Hugh. *Beyond Belief: How We Find Meaning, with or without Religion*. Sydney: Macmillan Australia, 2016.

Magli, Giulio. *Archaeoastronomy: Introduction to the Science of Stars and Stones*. Cham, Switzerland: Springer, 2016.

Mankiller, Wilma. "Being Indigenous in the Twenty-First Century." *Cultural Survival*, June 9, 2010. Online. https://www.culturalsurvival.org/publications/cultural-survival-quarterly/being-indigenous-21st-century.

Marshall, Michael. "Introduction: Blacks Holes." *New Scientist*, January 6, 2010. Online. http://www.newscientist.com/article/dn18348-introduction-black-holes.html.

Mazzaferri, Frederick David. *The Genre of the Book of Revelation from a Source-Critical Perspective*. New York: de Gruyter, 1989.

McCall, Thomas H. *An Invitation to Analytic Christian Theology*. Downers Grove, IL: InterVarsity, 2015.

McFadden, Johnjoe, and Jim Al-Khalili. "The Origins of Quantum Biology." *Proceedings of the Royal Society A: Mathematical, Physical, and Engineering Sciences* 474.2220 (2018). Online. https://royalsocietypublishing.org/doi/10.1098/rspa.2018.0674.

McFague, Sallie. *Metaphorical Theology: Models of God in Religious Language.* Philadelphia: Fortress, 1982.

McGinn, Colin. *The Problem of Consciousness.* Oxford: Blackwell, 1993.

McGrath, Alister E. *A Fine-Tuned Universe: The Quest for God in Science and Theology.* Louisville: Westminster John Knox, 2009.

McGrath, Alister E., and Joanna Collicutt McGrath. *The Dawkins Delusion? Atheist Fundamentalism and the Denial of the Divine.* Downers Grove, IL: InterVarsity, 2007.

McKenzie, Ross H. "Emergence, Reductionism and the Stratification of Reality in Science and Theology." *Scottish Journal of Theology* 64.2 (2011) 211–35.

McLeish, Tom. *Faith & Wisdom in Science.* Oxford: Oxford University Press, 2014.

Mellor, Philip A. "The Virgin Birth and the Theology of Beauty." *Irish Theological Quarterly* 57.3 (1991) 196–208.

Mettinger, Tryggve N. D. *The Eden Narrative: A Literary and Religio-Historical Study of Genesis 2—3.* Winona Lake, IN: Eisenbrauns, 2007.

Midgley, Mary. "Atomistic Visions: The Quest for Permanence." In *The Essential Mary Midgley*, edited by David Midgley, 319–29. London: Routledge, 2005.

———. "Reductive Megalomania." In *Nature's Imagination: The Frontiers of Scientific Vision*, edited by John Cornwall, 133–47. Oxford: Oxford University Press, 1995.

———. *Science as Salvation: A Modern Myth and its Meaning.* London: Routledge, 1992.

———. *Wisdom, Information, and Wonder: What Is Knowledge For?* London: Routledge, 1991.

Millard, Alan R. "A New Babylonian 'Genesis' Story." *Tyndale Bulletin* 18 (1967) 3–18.

Mitchell, Edgar. "Birthed Amongst the Stars." *IONS.* Online. https://noetic.org/about/origins.

Mitchell, Stephen, trans. *Gilgamesh.* New English Version. London: Profile, 2004.

Moberly, R. W. L. *The Theology of the Book of Genesis.* Old Testament Theology. Cambridge: Cambridge University Press, 2009.

Mohon, Lee. "Black Hole Meal Sets Record for Duration and Size." *NASA.gov*, February 6, 2017. Online. https://www.nasa.gov/mission_pages/chandra/news/black-hole-meal-sets-record-for-length-and-size.html.

Morozov, Evgeny. *To Save Everything, Click Here: Technology, Solutionism, and the Urge to Fix Problems that Don't Exist.* London: Penguin, 2013.

Murphy, Nancey. *Beyond Liberalism & Fundamentalism: How Modern and Postmodern Philosophy Set the Theological Agenda.* Harrisburg, PA: Trinity, 2007.

———. "Reductionism and Emergence: A Critical Perspective." In *Human Identity at the Intersection of Science, Technology, and Religion*, edited by Nancey Murphy and Christopher C. Knight, 79–96. Surrey, UK: Ashgate, 2010.

Naeye, Robert. "A Stellar Explosion You Could See on Earth!" *NASA.gov*, March 21, 2008. Online. https://www.nasa.gov/mission_pages/swift/bursts/brightest_grb.html.

Nagel, Thomas. "Analytic Philosophy and Human Life." *Economia Politica* 26.1 (2009). Online. https://as.nyu.edu/content/dam/nyu-as/philosophy/documents/faculty-documents/nagel/Analytic%20Philosophy%20and%20Human%20Life.doc.

———. "Books of the Year 2009: Beckett, Tóibín, Mantel and Bolaño Feature in This Year's List." *Times Literary Supplement*, November 25, 2009. Online. http://entertainment.timesonline.co.uk/tol/arts_and_entertainment/the_tls/article6931364.ece.

———. *Concealment and Exposure & Other Essays*. Oxford: Oxford University Press, 2002.
———. "Conceiving the Impossible and the Mind-Body Problem." *Philosophy* 73.285 (1998) 337–52.
———. "The Core of 'Mind and Cosmos' (The Stone)." *New York Times*, August 18, 2013. Online. https://archive.nytimes.com/opinionator.blogs.nytimes.com/2013/08/18/the-core-of-mind-and-cosmos.
———. *Equality and Partiality*. Oxford: Oxford University Press, 1991.
———. "The Facts Fetish." *New Republic*, October 19, 2010. Online. https://newrepublic.com/article/78546/the-facts-fetish.
———. *The Last Word*. Oxford: Oxford University Press, 1997.
———. "Letter to the Editor." *Times Literary Supplement*, December 9, 2009. Online. http://www.the-tls.co.uk/tls/public/article706905.ece.
———. "Letter to the Editor." *Times Literary Supplement*, January 1, 2010. Online. http://www.the-tls.co.uk/tls/public/article706905.ece.
———. "The Limits of Objectivity." Lecture delivered at Brasenose College, Oxford University, Oxford, UK, May 4, 11, 18, 1979. Tanner Lecture on Human Values. Online. https://tannerlectures.utah.edu/_resources/documents/a-to-z/n/nagel80.pdf.
———. *Mind and Cosmos: Why the Materialist Neo-Darwinian Conception of Nature Is Almost Certainly False*. Oxford: Oxford University Press, 2012.
———. *Mortal Questions*. Cambridge: Cambridge University Press, 1979.
———. *Other Minds: Critical Essays 1969–1994*. Oxford: Oxford University Press, 1995.
———. "A Philosopher Defends Religion." *New York Review of Books*, September 27, 2012. Online. https://www.nybooks.com/articles/2012/09/27/philosopher-defends-religion.
———. *The Possibility of Altruism*. Princeton: Princeton University Press, 1970.
———. "Reason, Almost." *New Republic*, January 24, 2012. Online. https://newrepublic.com/article/100050/reason-thinking-fast-slow-kahneman.
———. "Reductionism and Antireductionism." In *The Limits of Reductionism in Biology*, edited by Gregory R. Bock and Jamie A. Goode, 3–14. Novartis Foundation Symposium 213. Chichester, UK: Wiley, 2008.
———. *Secular Philosophy and the Religious Temperament: Essays 2002–2008*. Oxford: Oxford University Press, 2010.
———. *The View From Nowhere*. Oxford: Oxford University Press, 1986.
———. *What Does It All Mean?: A Very Short Introduction to Philosophy*. Oxford: Oxford University Press, 1987.
———. "Why So Cross?" *London Review of Books* 21.7 (1999) 22–23. Online. http://www.lrb.co.uk/v21/n07/thomas-nagel/why-so-cross.
"NASA Spacecraft Embarks on Historic Journey into Interstellar Space." *Jet Propulsion Laboratory*, September 12, 2013. Online. https://www.jpl.nasa.gov/news/nasa-spacecraft-embarks-on-historic-journey-into-interstellar-space.
Need, Stephen W. *Truly Divine and Truly Human: The Story of Christ and the Seven Ecumenical Councils*. London: SPCK, 2008.
Nelson, Kevin. *The Spiritual Doorway in the Brain: A Neurologist's Search for the God Experience*. New York: Penguin, 2011.

New Zealand Legislation, Parliamentary Counsel Office. *Te Awa Tupua (Whanganui River Claims Settlement) Bill (129–1)*. Online. https://www.legislation.govt.nz/bill/government/2016/0129/6.0/whole.html.

Niebuhr, Reinhold. "The Children of Light and the Children of Darkness." In *The Essential Reinhold Niebuhr: Selected Essays and Addresses*, edited by Robert McAfee Brown, 160–81. New Haven: Yale University Press, 1986.

———. *Man's Nature and His Communities: Essays on the Dynamics and Enigmas of Man's Personal and Social Existence*. 1965. Reprint, Eugene, OR: Wipf & Stock, 2012.

———. "Mystery and Meaning." In *The Essential Reinhold Niebuhr: Selected Essays and Addresses*, edited by Robert McAfee Brown, 237–49. New Haven: Yale University Press, 1986.

Nissiotis, Nikos. "Mary in Orthodox Theology." In *Concilium: Mary in the Churches*, edited by Hans Küng and Jurgen Moltmann, 25–39. Edinburgh: T&T Clark, 1983.

Nolan, Christopher, dir. *Interstellar*. Paramount Pictures, 2014. https://www.imdb.com/title/tt0816692/characters/nm0004266.

Nozick, Robert. *Philosophical Explanations*. Cambridge, MA: Harvard University Press, 1981.

Numrich, Paul D. "Reality and Knowledge." In *The Boundaries of Knowledge in Buddhism, Christianity, and Science*, edited by Paul D. Numrich, 9–21. Göttingen: Vandenhoeck & Ruprecht, 2008.

O'Callaghan, Paul. "Is the Christian Believer Conservative or Liberal?" *Church, Communication and Culture* 4.2 (2019) 137–51.

O'Connell, Cathal. "A Telescope the Size of the Earth." *Cosmos* 79 (2018) 100–103.

O'Dea, Thomas F. *Alienation, Atheism, and the Religious Crisis*. New York: Sheed & Ward, 1969.

Oeming, Manfred. *Contemporary Biblical Hermeneutics: An Introduction*. Translated by Joachim Vette. Aldershot, UK: Ashgate, 2006.

Osbourne, Grant R. *Revelation Verse by Verse*. Bellingham: Lexham, 2016.

Paige, Jonathan. "Pop Goes the Hadron Collider as Weasel Chews through Wire." *Times*, April 30, 2016. Online. http://www.thetimes.co.uk/article/pop-goes-the-hadron-collider-as-weasel-chews-through-wiring-tvgmp25b7.

Pannenberg, Wolfhart. *Jesus—God and Man*. Translated by Lewis L. Wilkins and Duane A. Priebe. 2nd ed. Philadelphia: Westminster, 1977.

———. *What Is Man? Contemporary Anthropology in Theological Perspective*. Translated by Duane A. Priebe. Philadelphia: Fortress, 1970.

Parris, David Paul. *Reception Theory and Biblical Hermeneutics*. Eugene, OR: Pickwick, 2009.

Parsons, Mikeal C. *Luke*. Grand Rapids: Baker Academic, 2015.

Peacocke, Arthur. "DNA of Our DNA." In *The Birth of Jesus: Biblical and Theological Reflections*, edited by George J. Brooke, 59–67. Edinburgh: T&T Clark, 2000.

Pepper, Miriam, and Ruth Powell. *Religion, Spirituality, and Connections with Churches: Results from the 2018 Australian Community Survey*. NCLS Occasional Paper 36. Sydney: NCLS Research, 2018.

Perrenod, Stephen. *Dark Matter, Dark Energy, Dark Gravity: Enabling a Universe That Supports Intelligent Life*. 2nd ed. N.p.: CreateSpace Independent, 2011.

Petrie, W. M. Flinders. *A History of Egypt*. Vol 2. London: Methuen, 1896.

Pinker, Steven. "What Has Gotten Into Thomas Nagel? Two Philosophers Expose the Shoddy Reasoning of a Once-Great Thinker." *Twitter* (@sapinker), October 16, 2012. Online. https://twitter.com/sapinker/status/258350644979695616.

"Pioneer 10 at Jupiter." *NASA.gov*, February 13, 2018. Online. https://science.nasa.gov/resource/pioneer-10-at-jupiter.

"Pioneer 10 Sends Last Signal." *NASA.gov*, March 23, 2003. Online. https://science.nasa.gov/missions/pioneer/pioneer-10-sends-last-signal.

Placher, William C. *The Domestication of Transcendence: How Modern Thinking About God Went Wrong*. Louisville: Westminster John Knox, 1996.

———. *Unapologetic Theology: A Christian Voice in a Pluralistic Conversation*. Louisville: Westminster John Knox, 1989.

"Planck Reveals an Almost Perfect Universe." *European Space Agency*, March 21, 2013. Online. https://www.esa.int/Science_Exploration/Space_Science/Planck/Planck_reveals_an_almost_perfect_Universe.

Plantinga, Alvin. "Coherentism and the Evidentialist Objection to Belief in God." In *Rationality, Religious Belief, and Moral Commitment: New Essays in the Philosophy of Religion*, edited by Robert Audi and William J. Wainwright, 109–38. Ithaca: Cornell University Press, 1986.

———. "A Secular Heresy." *New Republic*, November 15, 2012. Online. https://newrepublic.com/article/110189/why-darwinist-materialism-wrong.

Polanyi, Michael. *Personal Knowledge: Towards a Post-Critical Philosophy*. London: Routledge & Kegan Paul, 1958.

Polkinghorne, John. *Beyond Science: The Wider Human Context*. Cambridge: Cambridge University Press, 1996.

———. *Faith, Science, and Understanding*. New Haven: Yale University Press, 2000.

———. *One World: The Interaction of Science and Theology*. London: Templeton Foundation, 2007.

———. *Quantum Physics & Theology: An Unexpected Kinship*. London: SPCK, 2007.

———. *Reason and Reality: The Relationship Between Science and Theology*. London: SPCK, 1991.

———. *Theology in the Context of Science*. London: SPCK, 2008.

———. *Warrant and Proper Function*. New York: Oxford University Press, 1993.

———. *Where the Conflict Really Lies: Science, Religion, and Naturalism*. Oxford: Oxford University Press, 2011.

Porter, Stanley E., and Beth M. Stovell. "Trajectories in Biblical Hermeneutics." In *Biblical Hermeneutics: Five Views*, edited by Stanley E. Porter and Beth M. Stovell, 9–24. Downers Grove, IL: IVP Academic, 2012.

Prickett, Stephen. *Words and The Word: Language, Poetics, and Biblical interpretation*. Cambridge: Cambridge University Press, 1986.

Prothero, Stephen. *God Is Not One: The Eight Rival Religions That Run the World*. New York: Harper Collins, 2010.

Pryke, Louise M. *Gilgamesh*. Gods and Heroes of the Ancient World. London: Routledge, 2019.

Raner, Guy H. "Einstein on His Personal Religious Views." *Freethought Today* 21.9 (2004). Online. https://ffrf.org/publications/item/13319-einstein-on-his-personal-religious-views.

Raymo, Chet. *Honey from Stone: A Naturalist's Search for God*. Cambridge: Cowley, 1987.

Reagan, Charles E., and David Stewart. *The Philosophy of Paul Ricoeur: An Anthology of His Work*. Boston: Beacon, 1978.

Reddish, Mitchell G. *Revelation*. Macon, GA: Smyth & Helwys, 2001.

Reddy, Francis. "NASA's Fermi Closes on Source of Cosmic Rays." *NASA.gov*, February 16, 2010. Online. https://www.nasa.gov/universe/nasas-fermi-closes-on-source-of-cosmic-rays.

Rees, Martin. *From Here to Infinity: Scientific Horizons*. London: Profile, 2011.

Reynhout, Kenneth. *Interdisciplinary Interpretation: Paul Ricoeur and the Hermeneutics of Theology and Science*. Lanham, MD: Lexington, 2013.

Ricoeur, Paul. *The Conflict of Interpretations: Essays in Hermeneutics*. Edited by Don Ihde. Evanston, IL: Northwestern University Press, 1974.

———. *Fallible Man*. Translated by Charles A. Kelbley. New York: Fordham University Press, 1986.

———. *Figuring the Sacred: Religion, Narrative, and Imagination*. Edited by Mark I. Wallace. Translated by David Pellauer. Minneapolis: Fortress, 1995.

———. *Freud and Philosophy: An Essay on Interpretation*. Translated by Denis Savage. New Haven: Yale University Press, 1970.

———. *Hermeneutics & the Human Sciences*. Edited and translated by John B. Thompson. Cambridge: Cambridge University Press, 1981.

———. *Interpretation Theory: Discourse and the Surplus of Meaning*. Fort Worth, TX: Texas Christian University Press, 1976.

———. "On Interpretation." In *Philosophy in France Today*, edited by Alan Montefiore, 175–97. Translated by Kathleen Mclaughlin. Cambridge: Cambridge University Press, 1983.

———. *The Philosophy of Paul Ricoeur: An Anthology of His Work*. Edited by Charles E. Reagan and David Stewart. Boston: Beacon, 1978.

———. *Reflections on the Just*. Translated by David Pellauer. Chicago: University of Chicago Press, 2007.

———. *A Ricoeur Reader: Reflection and Imagination*. Edited by Mario J. Valdés. Toronto: University of Toronto Press, 1991.

———. *The Rule of Metaphor: Multi-Disciplinary Studies of the Creation of Meaning in Language*. Translated by Robert Czerny et al. Toronto: University of Toronto Press, 1977.

———. *The Symbolism of Evil*. Translated by Emerson Buchanan. Boston: Beacon, 1967.

———. "Toward a Hermeneutic of the Idea of Revelation." Translated by David Pellauer. *Harvard Theological Review* 70.1–2 (1977) 1–38.

Rieger, Joerg. "Constructive Theology." In *Encyclopaedia of Sciences and Religions*, edited by Anne L. C. Runehov and Luis Oviedo, 483–86. New York: Springer, 2013.

Riley, William. "Who Is the Woman of Revelation 12?" *Proceedings of the Irish Biblical Association* 18 (1995) 15–39.

Robbins, Vernon K. *Exploring the Texture of Texts: A Guide to Socio-Rhetorical Interpretation*. Valley Forge, PA: Trinity, 1996.

Robinson, Neal. "Mohammed Arkoun." In *The Qur'an: An Encyclopaedia*, edited by Oliver Leaman, 66–67. London: Routledge, 2006.

Robinson, Robert B. "Narrative Theology and Biblical Theology." In *The Practice and Promise of Biblical Theology*, edited by John Reumann, 129–42. Minneapolis: Fortress, 1991.

Ross, Alec. "Networking the World for Global Opportunity." *Brookings Blum Roundtable*, August 3, 2015. Online. https://www.brookings.edu/wp-content/uploads/2016/07/RossNetworkingtheWorld.pdf.

Rouch, Abigail Frymann. "Hark! The Herald Angels Sing Version Incurs Ire of Bishops as It Removes Reference to Mary's Virginity." *Telegraph*, December 23, 2018. Online. https://www.telegraph.co.uk/news/2018/12/23/hark-herald-angels-sing-version-incurs-ire-bishops-removes-reference.

Rovelli, Carlo. *Reality Is Not What It Seems: The Journey to Quantum Gravity*. Translated by Simon Carnell and Erica Segre. London: Penguin, 2016.

———. *Seven Brief Lessons of Physics*. Translated by Simon Carnell and Erica Segre. New York: Riverhead, 2016.

Ruse, Michael. "Dawkins et al Bring Us into Disrepute." *Guardian*, November 2, 2009. Online. https://www.theguardian.com/commentisfree/belief/2009/nov/02/atheism-dawkins-ruse.

Ryken, Leland. *The Christian Imagination*. Colorado Springs, CO: WaterBrook, 2002.

Ryken, Leland, et al., eds. *Dictionary of Biblical Imagery*. Downers Grove, IL: InterVarsity, 1998.

Saemz, Aaron. "NIH Awards $40 Million to Map the Wiring of the Brain." *SingularityHub*, October 14, 2010. Online. https://singularityhub.com/2010/10/14/nih-awards-40-million-to-map-the-wiring-of-the-brain.

Sagan, Carl. *Cosmos*. New York: Random House, 1980.

Sahtouris, Elisabet. "From a Mechanistic and Competitive to a Reenchanted and Co-Evolving Cosmos." In *Science and the Reenchantment of the Cosmos: The Rise of the Integral Vision of Reality*, edited by Ervin Laszlo, 101–8. Rochester, VT: Inner Traditions, 2006.

Salecl, Renata. *Choice*. Big Ideas. London: Profile, 2012.

Saler, Benson. "Supernatural as a Western Category." *Ethos* 5.1 (1977) 31–53.

Sample, Ian. *Massive: The Hunt for the God Particle*. London: Virgin, 2010.

Samson, Alain. "An Introduction to Behavioral Economics." *BehavioralEconomics*, 2014. Online. https://www.behavioraleconomics.com/resources/introduction-behavioral-economics.

Santmire, Paul H. "The Genesis Creation Narratives Revisited: Themes for a Global Age." *Interpretation* 45.4 (1991) 366–79.

Savulescu, Julian, and Ingmar Persson. "Moral Enhancement." *Philosophy Now* 91 (2012). Online. https://philosophynow.org/issues/91/Moral_Enhancement.

———. *Unfit for the Future: The Need for Moral Enhancement*. Oxford: Oxford University Press, 2012.

Schaeffer, Anaïs. "The Standard Model, Set in Stone." *CERN*, March 11, 2013. Online. http://home.web.cern.ch/cern-people/updates/2013/03/standard-model-set-stone.

Schleiermacher, Friedrich. *The Christian Faith*. 3rd ed. London: Bloomsbury, 2016.

Schlesinger, Arthur, Jr. "Forgetting Reinhold Niebuhr." *New York Times*, September 18, 2005. Online. https://www.nytimes.com/2005/09/18/books/review/forgetting-reinhold-niebuhr.html.

Schüssler Fiorenza, Elisabeth. *The Book of Revelation: Justice and Judgment*. Minneapolis, MN: Fortress, 1998.

———. *Jesus: Miriam's Child, Sophia's Prophet*. London: Bloomsbury, 2015.

Schwartz, Regina, ed. *The Book and the Text: The Bible and Literary Theory*. Oxford: Blackwell, 1990.

Scott, Nora E. "The Metternich Stela." *Metropolitan Museum of Art Bulletin* NS 9.8 (1951) 201–17. Online. https://doi.org/10.2307/3258024.

Sheldrake, Rupert. *The Science Delusion: Freeing the Spirit of Enquiry*. London: Coronet, 2012.

Sheriffs, Deryck. *The Friendship of the Lord: An Old Testament Spirituality*. Eugene, OR: Wipf & Stock, 2004.

Sherrington, Charles. *Man on His Nature*. Cambridge: Cambridge University Press, 1941.

Shinn, Roger. "The Shattering of the Theological Spectrum." *Christianity and Crisis* 23 (1963) 168–71.

———. "Whatever Happened to Theology?" *Christianity and Crisis* 35.8 (1975) 106–20.

Simms, Karl. *Paul Ricoeur*. London: Routledge, 2003.

Smith, Barbara Herrnstein. *Belief & Resistance: Dynamics of Contemporary Intellectual Controversy*. Cambridge: Harvard University Press, 1997.

Smith, Timothy P. *How Big Is Big and How Small Is Small: The Sizes of Everything and Why*. Oxford: Oxford University Press, 2013.

Smith, Walter. *Hymns of Christ and the Christian Life*. London: Macmillan, 1867.

Sokal, Alan, and Jean Bricmont. *Fashionable Nonsense: Postmodern Intellectuals' Abuse of Science*. New York: Picador, 1998.

Spencer, Scott F. "The Literary/Postmodern View." In *Biblical Hermeneutics: Five Views*, edited by Stanley E. Porter and Beth M. Stovell, 48–69. Downers Grove, IL: IVP Academic, 2012.

Stephens, John, and Robyn McCallum. *Retelling Stories, Framing Culture: Traditional Story and Metanarratives in Children's Literature*. New York: Garland, 1998.

Sternberg, Meir. *The Poetics of Biblical Narrative: Ideological Literature and the Drama of Reading*. Bloomington: Indiana University Press, 1987.

Stiver, Dan R. *The Philosophy of Religious Language*. Cambridge, MA: Blackwell, 1996.

———. *Ricoeur and Theology*. London: Bloomsbury T&T Clark, 2012.

Strawson, Galen. "Galileo's Error by Philip Goff Review—A New Science of Consciousness." *Guardian*, December 27, 2019. Online. https://www.theguardian.com/books/2019/dec/27/galileos-error-by-philip-goff-review.

———. "Realistic Materialism: Why Physicalism Entails Panpsychism." *Journal of Consciousness Studies* 12.10–11 (2006) 3–31.

Street, Sharon. "A Darwinian Dilemma for Realist Thinkers of Value." *Philosophical Studies* 127.1 (2006) 109–66.

Strittmatter, Peter. "Large Binocular Telescope Achieves First Binocular Light." *Large Binocular Telescope Organization*, February 28, 2008. Online. http://www.lbto.org/firstbinocularlight_press_release.htm.

"A Subatomic Venture." *European Organization for Nuclear Research*, 2008. Online. https://public-archive.web.cern.ch/en/Science/Science-en.html.

Sumney, Jerry L. "The Dragon Has Been Defeated—Revelation 12." *Review & Expositor* 98.1 (2001) 103–15.

"Supermassive Black Hole Sagittarius A*." *NASA.gov*, August 29, 2013. Online. https://www.nasa.gov/image-article/supermassive-black-hole-sagittarius.

Svitil, Kathy, et al. "Gravitational Waves Detected 100 Years After Einstein's Prediction." *LIGO*, February 11, 2016. Online. https://www.ligo.caltech.edu/news/ligo20160211.

Sweeney, James P. "Modern and Ancient Controversies over the Virgin Birth of Jesus." *Bibliotheca Sacra* 160 (2003) 142–58.

Swimme, Brian, and Thomas Berry. *The Universe Story: From the Primordial Flaring Forth to the Ecozoic Era—A Celebration of the Unfolding of the Cosmos*. San Francisco: HarperSanFrancisco, 1992.

Tacey, David. *Religion as Metaphor: Beyond Literal Belief*. New Brunswick, NJ: Transaction, 2015.

Taçon, Paul S. C., et al. "Birth of the Rainbow Serpent in Arnhem Land Rock Art and Oral History." *Archaeology in Oceania* 31 (1996) 103–24.

Tarnas, Richard. *Cosmos and Psyche: Intimations of a New World View*. London: Viking Penguin, 2006.

———. *The Passion of the Western Mind: Understanding the Ideas That Have Shaped Our World View*. New York: Ballantine, 1991.

Taylor, Charles. *A Secular Age*. Cambridge, MA: Harvard University Press, 2007.

———. "Western Secularity." In *Rethinking Secularism*, edited by Craig Calhoun et al., 31–53. Oxford: Oxford University Press, 2011.

———. "What Is Secularity?" In *Transcending Boundaries in Philosophy and Theology: Reason, Meaning, and Experience*, edited by Kevin Vanhoozer and Martin Warner, 57–76. Aldershot: Ashgate, 2007.

Taylor, Mark C. *After God*. Chicago: University of Chicago Press, 2007.

"Te Urewera Act." *New Zealand Environment Guide*, November 17, 2017. Online. https://www.environmentguide.org.nz/regional/te-urewera-act.

Teilhard de Chardin, Pierre. *The Phenomenon of Man*. Rev. English ed. New York: Harper & Row, 1965.

Thiemann, Ronald F. *Revelation and Theology: The Gospel as Narrated Promise*. Eugene, OR: Wipf & Stock, 1985.

Thiselton, Anthony C. *The Thiselton Companion to Christian Theology*. Grand Rapids: Eerdmans, 2015.

Thompson, Angela. "Scream of Black Hole's Birth Detected Halfway across the Universe." *Space.com*, September 10, 2008. Online. https://www.space.com/5826-scream-black-hole-birth-detected-halfway-universe.html.

Thompson, Della, ed. *The Concise Oxford Dictionary*. 9th ed. Oxford: Clarendon, 1995.

Thompson, Mark. *A Down to Earth Guide to the Cosmos*. London: Bantam, 2013.

Thornhill-Miller, Branden, and Peter Millican. "The Common-Core/Diversity Dilemma: Revisions of Humean Thought, New Empirical Research, and the Limits of Rational Religious Belief." *European Journal for Philosophy of Religion* 7.1 (2015) 1–49.

Tillman, Nola Taylor, and Ailsa Harvey. "What Are Wormholes?" *Space.com*, October 21, 2017. Updated March 5, 2024. Online. https://www.space.com/20881-wormholes.html.

Tillman, Nola Taylor, and Rebecca Sohn. "Andromeda Galaxy: Facts about Our Closest Galactic Neighbor." *Space.com*, October 26, 2023. Online. https://www.space.com/15590-andromeda-galaxy-m31.html.

Tomlinson, Dave. *Re-Enchanting Christianity: Faith in an Emerging Culture*. London: Canterbury, 2008.

Tononi, Giulio. *Phi: A Voyage from the Brain to the Soul.* New York: Pantheon, 2012.

Torrance, Thomas F. *Christian Theology and Scientific Culture.* New York: Oxford University Press, 1980.

———. "The Doctrine of the Virgin Birth." *Scottish Bulletin of Evangelical Theology* 12 (1994) 8–25.

———. *God and Rationality.* London: Oxford University Press, 1971.

———. *Theology in Reconciliation: Essays Towards Evangelical and Catholic Unity in East and West.* London: Chapman, 1975.

Tucker, Mary Evelyn, and John Brim. "The Evolutionary and Ecological Perspectives of Pierre Teilhard de Chardin and Thomas Berry." In *The Wiley-Blackwell Companion to Religion and Ecology*, edited by John Hart, 394–409. Hoboken, NJ: Wiley, 2017.

Turner, Mark. *The Literary Mind: The Origins of Thought and Language.* Oxford: Oxford University Press, 1996.

Unger, Roberto. *The Religion of the Future.* Cambridge: Harvard University Press, 2014.

"UNH Researcher Discovers a Black Hole Feeding Frenzy that Breaks Records." *UNH Today*, February 6, 2017. Online. https://www.unh.edu/unhtoday/news/release/2017/02/06/unh-researcher-discovers-black-hole-feeding-frenzy-breaks-records-0.

Value of Connectivity: Economic and Social Benefits of Expanding Internet Access. London: Deloitte, 2014. Online. https://www2.deloitte.com/content/dam/Deloitte/uk/Documents/technology-media-telecommunications/deloitte-uk-tmt-value-of-connectivity-tmt.pdf.

Van Duzer, Chet. "*Hic sunt dracones*: The Geography and Cartography of Monsters." In *The Ashgate Research Companion to Monsters and the Monstrous*, edited by Asa Simon Mittman and Peter J. Dendle, 387–436. Burlington, VT: Ashgate, 2013.

Vanhoozer, Kevin J. *The Drama of Doctrine: A Canonical Linguistic Approach to Christian Theology.* Louisville: Westminster John Knox, 2005.

———. *Is There a Meaning in This Text?: The Bible, the Reader, and the Morality of Literary Knowledge.* Grand Rapids: Zondervan, 1998.

———. "Once More into the Borderlands: The Way of Wisdom in Philosophy and Theology after the 'Turn to Drama.'" In *Transcending the Boundaries in Philosophy and Theology: Reason, Meaning, and Experience*, edited by Kevin Vanhoozer and Martin Warner, 31–54. Hampshire, UK: Ashgate, 2007.

———. "What Is Theological Interpretation of the Bible?" In *Dictionary for Theological Interpretation of the Bible*, edited by Kevin J. Vanhoozer et al., 19–25. Grand Rapids: Baker Academic, 2005.

Vernon, Mark. "The Most Despised Science Book of 2012 Is . . . Worth Reading." *Guardian*, January 4, 2013. Online. http://www.theguardian.com/commentisfree/belief/2013/jan/04/most-despised-science-book-2012.

Viladesau, Richard. *Theological Aesthetics: God in Imagination, Beauty, and Art.* New York: Oxford University Press, 1999.

Vosper, Gretta. "A Little Bit about Me." *Gretta Vosper: Minister, Author, Atheist.* Online. https://www.grettavosper.ca/about/little-bit.

———. "What's God Got to Do with It?" *Toronto Star*, February 9, 2009. Online. https://www.thestar.com/opinion/2009/02/09/whats_god_got_to_do_with_it.html.

———. *With or without God: Why the Way We Live Is More Important than What We Believe.* Toronto: Harper Collins, 2009.

"Voyager 2 Illuminates Boundary of Interstellar Space." *Jet Propulsion Laboratory*, November 4, 2019. Online. https://www.jpl.nasa.gov/news/voyager-2-illuminates-boundary-of-interstellar-space.

Waal, Frans B. M. de. "Morality and the Social Instincts: Continuity with the Other Primates." Lecture delivered at Princeton University, Princeton, NJ, November 19–20, 2003. Tanner Lecture on Human Values. Online. https://tannerlectures.utah.edu/_resources/documents/a-to-z/d/deWaal_2005.pdf.

Walach, Harald. *Beyond a Materialist Worldview: Towards an Expanded Science*. London: Scientific and Medical Network, 2019.

Wall, Mike. "One Year after Epic Black Hole Photo, Event Horizon Telescope Team Is Dreaming Very Big." *Space.com*, April 20, 2020. Online. https://www.space.com/event-horizon-telescope-black-hole-photos-future.html.

Wallace, Mark I. *The Second Naiveté: Barth, Ricoeur, and the New Yale Theology*. Macon, GA: Mercer University Press, 1990.

Wallach, Wendell. *A Dangerous Master: How to Keep Technology from Slipping Beyond Our Control*. New York: Basic Books, 2015.

Ward, Graham. "Introduction: Where We Stand." In *The Blackwell Companion to Postmodern Theology*, edited by Graham Ward, xii–xxvii. Oxford: Blackwell, 2001.

———. *Unbelievable: Why We Believe and Why We Don't*. London: Tauris, 2014.

Ward, Keith. *More Than Matter?: Is There More to Life Than Molecules?* Grand Rapids: Eerdmans, 2010.

Warnock, Mary. "Imagination: Aesthetic and Religious." *Theology* 83.696 (1980) 403–9.

Watson, Imogen. "Meet Rob Janoff: The Man Who Put the Byte in the Apple Logo." *Drum*, July 30, 2019. Online. https://www.thedrum.com/news/2019/07/30/meet-rob-janoff-the-man-who-put-the-byte-the-apple-logo.

Watson, Peter. *Convergence: The Idea at the Heart of Science*. London: Simon & Schuster, 2016.

Watson, Simon. "Transversal Rationality: The Challenge of Assigning 'Cognitive Parity' to the Sciences and Theology." *Toronto Journal of Theology* 27 (2011) 37–50.

"Webb vs Hubble Telescope." *James Webb Space Telescope*. Online. https://jwst.nasa.gov/comparison_about.html.

Weber, Max. "Science as a Vocation." In *Essays in Sociology*, edited by Hans Heinrich Gerth and C. Wright Mills, 129–56. London: Routledge & Kegan Paul, 1967.

Wedberg, Anders. *Filosofins historia. Antiken och medeltiden*. 2nd ed. Stockhom: Bonniers, 1968.

Weinberg, Steven. *The First Three Minutes*. New York: Basic, 1977.

Wenham, Gordon J. *Genesis 1—15*. Word Biblical Commentary 1. Waco, TX: Word, 1987.

Westermann, Claus. *Genesis*. Translated by David E. Green. Grand Rapids: Eerdmans, 1987.

———. *Genesis 1—11*. Translated by John J. Scullion. Continental Commentaries. Minneapolis: Augsburg, 1974.

"What Is Cyberpsychology and Why Is It Important?" *New Jersey Institute of Technology*, February 7, 2023. Online. https://www.njit.edu/admissions/blog-posts/what-cyberpsychology-and-why-it-important.

Whitehouse, W. A. "God's Heavenly Kingdom and His Servants, the Angels: An Account of Kirchliche Dogmatik III/3 §51 by Karl Barth." *Scottish Journal of Theology* 4 (1951) 376–82.

Wick, David. *The Infamous Boundary: Seven Decades of Heresy in Quantum Physics.* New York: Copernicus, 1996.

Wiles, Maurice. "'Myth' in Theology." *Bulletin of the John Rylands Library* 59 (1976) 226–46.

Wilkinson, David. *The Message of Creation.* Nottingham: InterVarsity, 2002.

Wilkinson, John. "Apologetic Aspects of the Virgin Birth of Jesus Christ." *Scottish Journal of Theology* 17.2 (1964) 159–81.

Williams, Rowan. "The Literal Sense of Scripture." *Modern Theology* 7.2 (1991) 121–34.

Wimsatt, W. K., Jr., and Monroe C. Beardsley. "The Intentional Fallacy." *Sewanee Review* 54.3 (1946) 468–88.

Witherington, Ben, III. *Revelation.* New Cambridge Bible Commentary. Cambridge: Cambridge University Press, 2003.

Wittgenstein, Ludwig. "A Lecture on Ethics." *Philosophical Review* 74.1 (1965) 3–12.

Wolterstorff, Nicholas. "The Migration of the Theistic Arguments: From Natural Theology to Evidentialist Apologetics." In *Rationality, Religious Belief, and Moral Commitment,* edited by Robert Audi and William J. Wainwright, 38–81. Ithaca: Cornell University Press, 1986.

Wood, Alice. *Of Wings and Wheels: A Synthetic Study of the Biblical Cherubim.* Beihefte zur Zeitschrift für die alttestamentliche Wissenschaft 385. Berlin: de Gruyter, 2008.

Wood, Donald. "'An Extraordinary Acute Embarrassment:' The Doctrine of Angels in Barth's Göttingen Dogmatics." *Scottish Journal of Theology* 66.3 (2013) 319–37.

Wyman, Jason, Jr. *Constructing Constructive Theology: An Introductory Sketch.* Minneapolis: Fortress, 2017.

Yates, David. "Mind and Cosmos." *Analysis* 73.4 (2013) 801–6.

Zimmermann, Nigel. *Levinas and Theology.* London: Bloomsbury, 2013.

Zornberg, Avivah Gottlieb. *The Murmuring Deep: Reflections on the Biblical Unconsciousness.* New York: Schocken, 2009.

www.ingramcontent.com/pod-product-compliance
Lightning Source LLC
Chambersburg PA
CBHW052216300426
44115CB00011B/1705